Tourism Distribution Channels

Practices, issues and
transformations

Dimitrios Buhalis and Eric Laws

continuum
LONDON • NEW YORK

Continuum

The Tower Building   370 Lexington Avenue
11 York Road   New York
London SE1 7NX   NY 10017-6503

First published 2001

British Library Cataloguing-in-Publication Data
A catalogue record for this book is available from the British Library.

ISBN: 0-8264-5469-0 (hardback)
      0-8264-5470-4 (paperback)

Designed and typeset by Ben Cracknell Studios
Printed and bound in Great Britain by Bookcraft, Bath

Contents

Part 1: Tourism distribution: theory, practice and issues

Part 4: Transformation in tourism distribution

List of figures

List of tables

Contributor profiles

ABOUT THE EDITORS

Dimitrios Buhalis is Senior Lecturer and Course Leader in *e*Tourism at the School of Management Studies for the Service Sector, University of Surrey. Dimitrios is also Adjunct Professor at MBA in Hospitality Management at the Institut de Management Hôtelier International (Cornell University ESSEC) in Paris. He serves as Vice Chairman of the International Federation of Information Technology and Tourism (IFITT) and the Chair of the Meetings of the Tourism Society. Dimitrios earned his BSc in Business Administration (BBA) from the University of the Aegean Islands in Greece. He gained his MSc and PhD in Tourism Management and Marketing from the University of Surrey. His doctorate and post-doctorate research concentrated on the impacts of technology on the distribution channels of tourism and the implications for the strategic management and marketing of small and medium-sized tourism enterprises in the European periphery. Dimitrios regularly works as an adviser for the World Tourism Organization and the European Commission.

Eric Laws is Professor of Hospitality and Tourism Management at The Robert Gordon University, Aberdeen, Scotland. He is also Visiting Professor at the University of Limerick, Ireland. He has written three books on tourism management: *Tourism Marketing: Service and Quality Management Perspectives* (Stanley Thornes, 1991), *Tourist Destination Management: Issues, Analysis and Policies* (Routledge, 1995) and *Managing Packaged Tourism, Relationships: Responsibilities and Service Quality in the Inclusive Holiday Industry* (TIPB, 1997). He co-edited four, including this title, and has published many academic papers on service quality, destination impacts and the structure of the tourism industry. He has presented short courses in tourism management in various European, Asian and Australian Universities.

ABOUT THE CONTRIBUTORS

Jaco Appelman is a PhD candidate at the Erasmus Institute of Management, where research by the Economics and Management Department of the Erasmus University Rotterdam is carried out. From 1992 through 1998 he was affiliated with the University of Nijmegen at the Department of Development Studies and held positions as lecturer, study-co-ordinator and student-counsellor. He researched different aspects of tourism development in Thailand and Albania, with an emphasis on economic behaviour and institutionalization. His current topic is the dynamic interplay between action and structure in a tourism setting. His case study focuses on the relationship between agencies and airlines.

Marion Bywater is a business writer and consultant. She is author of *European Tour Operator Industry* published by the Economist Intelligent Unit in 1995 and of *European Retail Travel* published by Travel and Tourism Intelligence in 1998.

Francesco Casarin is Associate Professor at the University of Padova, Italy, and a member of the Department of Economics. He has written widely on the tourism product concept, market segmentation and the communication mix. He is the author of three books on tourism. His current research interests include marketing for tourism, the marketing/information technology interface and relationship marketing. He has connections with the CISET International Centre for Tourism Studies, Venice.

Chris Cooper is Foundation Professor of Tourism Management and head of the School of Tourism and Leisure Management, UQ Business School, University of Queensland. He has an honours degree and a PhD from University College London and before beginning an academic career worked in market planning for the tourism and retail sectors in the UK. Chris Cooper has authored a number of leading textbooks in tourism and has worked closely with the World Tourism Organization in developing the status of tourism education on the international stage. He is co-editor of *Current Issues in Tourism*, the author of many academic papers in tourism and has worked as a consultant and researcher in every region of the world.

Rob Davidson is Senior Lecturer in Tourism at the University of Westminster, specializing in conference and business travel. After six years as Education and Training Manager with the British Tourist Authority, Rob Davidson moved, in 1989, to France where he worked as a tourism consultant and lecturer at the University of Montpellier and the University of Lyon. He is the author of several textbooks, including *Tourism, Travel and Tourism in Europe, Business Travel*, and *Tourism Destinations*, as well as a number of articles in the professional and academic press. He returned to the UK in 1998 to take up his current position.

Daniel R. Fesenmaier is a Professor in the Department of Leisure Studies and Director of the National Laboratory for Tourism and Commerce, University of Illinois. He received a PhD in Geography from the University of Western Ontario, Canada. Dr Fesenmaier is author of a number of articles focusing on the use of information in travel decisions, the use of information technology for tourism marketing and the development of knowledge-based systems for tourism marketing organizations. He has co-authored a monograph on community tourism development entitled *Assessing and Developing Tourism Resources*, is co-editor of *Recreation Planning and Management, Communication Systems in Tourism Marketing* and *Recent Advances in Tourism Research Methodology* and is co-founding editor of an international journal, *Tourism Analysis*, and a monograph series, *Advances in Tourism Applications*.

Andrew J. Frew is Head of Department of Hospitality and Tourism Management at Queen Margaret University College, Edinburgh. Since 1979 he has specialized in hospitality and tourism information technology with research covering international reservations networks, destination systems, intelligent software agents and global electronic distribution. He is currently chair of HITA Europe and a board member of IFITT. He is also a regular contributor to international journals, conferences and forums. He has been active in many consultancy and contract research projects in the last ten years, embracing diverse aspects of information systems, and is currently engaged in a number of European-wide tourism ICT projects in research and education.

Frank Go currently holds the Bewetour Chair at the Rotterdam School of Management, Erasmus University, the Netherlands. Formerly he was affiliated with universities in Canada and Hong Kong. His present academic interests are in relationship marketing management. He is particularly interested in promoting cultural identity in the context of regional development, including the tourism, hospitality and retail sectors.

Denis Harrington is Lecturer in Management Studies at Waterford Institute of Technology, Ireland. He has a specialist interest in change and new developments within the international tourism sector and is currently directing research in the area. Denis is co-author of *Managing Service Quality*.

Atsuko Hashimoto is Assistant Professor in the Department of Recreation and Leisure Studies and teaches on the Tourism Studies Degree Programme at Brock University. She worked for the Canadian Tourism Commission in Japan prior to completing her postgraduate degrees at the University of Surrey, UK. She taught at the University of Luton, UK, before moving to Canada. Her main areas of research include environmental perceptions and tourism, Japanese female travellers and social issues in tourism planning and development.

Simon Hudson is Associate Professor in the Tourism Management Group at the University of Calgary. He has held previous teaching positions at Buckinghamshire College and the University of Brighton. Prior to working in academia, he spent several years working for UK tour operators, and also ran his own successful business for eight years. Dr Hudson has lectured and consulted in many aspects of tourism, but specializes in the marketing of tourism. His research is focused on sports tourism, and he has published several articles and book chapters from his work on the ski industry. His first book called *Snow Business* has just been published by Continuum.

Paul Hudson is Operations Manager Specialist Products, JMC Holidays.

John Jenkins is Senior Lecturer in Leisure and Tourism Studies at the University of Newcastle, Australia. John has a PhD from the University of New England, Australia. He has co-authored and co-edited several books, including *Tourism and Public Policy*, *Tourism Planning and Policy*, *Tourism and Recreation in Rural Areas* and *Outdoor Recreation Management*. He has also published articles on related topics in many journals. His current research interests include the political economy of tourism, the political and administrative histories of national parks in Australia, and the geography of 'Biggles'.

Øystein Jensen is Associate Professor in Tourism and Service Marketing at the Norwegian School of Hotel Management in Stavanger. He obtained his Masters' degree in Business Economy from the University of Fribourg in Switzerland and a PhD from the Aarhus School of Business in Denmark. He has been teaching marketing in business schools in Norway for twenty years, and regularly undertakes research at tourism research institutes in Switzerland and Italy. His main research fields are within relationship marketing, marketing channels, service quality and destination marketing.

Brian King is Head of the School of Hospitality, Tourism and Marketing at Victoria University. He has authored three books: *Creating Island Resorts*, *Developing Products* and *Sales Supervision* and co-authored *Tourism Marketing in Australia*. He is Joint Editor-in-Chief of the international journal *Tourism, Culture and Communication*, Asia Pacific Editor for the *International Journal of Tourism Research* and a member of the Executive Advisory Committee for the *Journal of Vacation Marketing*. He has broad-ranging research interests, including planning for tourism in developing countries and island microstates, hospitality and tourism operations, resort and destination marketing, hospitality and tourism education and the tourism behaviour of migrant communities.

Jan Lewis is Associate Lecturer in the School of Tourism and Leisure Management, UQ Business School, at the University of Queensland's Ipswich Campus. She has a Graduate Diploma in Business (Tourism) from Edith Cowan University in Perth, Western Australia, and is completing her Masters' degree in Tourism Management.

Graham Miller is Senior Lecturer in Tourism at the University of Westminster, UK. His main research interests are in the role of the consumer in promoting change within the tourism industry. Previous research developed indicators that the consumer can use in their choice of holiday and explored how these measures can be used to promote a more sustainable tourism industry. He has also conducted research into the accessibility of tourism establishments in the UK for the disabled consumer and the adherence of the industry with the recent Disability Discrimination Act.

Peter O'Connor is Assistant Professor at the Institut de Management Hôtelier International (IMHI), an MBA programme specializing in international hospitality management jointly administered by the Cornell School of Hotel Administration and the ESSEC Business School. He received his PhD in Hospitality and Technology from the Queen Margaret University College and his MSc in Management Information Systems from Trinity College, Dublin and earned his BSc in Hotel and Catering Management from the Dublin Institute of Technology. His primary research, teaching and consulting interests focus on the use of technology in the hospitality and tourism sectors. He has developed expertise on the use of electronic channels of distribution in tourism, and on how information technology can be used to enhance both the management and operational effectiveness of hospitality organizations. He has authored two leading textbooks on technology in the hospitality business: *Using Computers in Hospitality* (Cassell, UK, 2000 – now in its second edition) and *Electronic Information Distribution in Hospitality and Tourism Industries* (CABI, UK, 1999), as well as numerous articles in both the trade and academic presses.

Linda Osti studied Tourism Management at the University of Plymouth before taking a post as postgraduate researcher at the University of Trento, Italy, in the field of information technologies and market research. She is also a researcher at the Department of Tourism Management of the European Academy Bolzano/Bozen, Italy. In 2000 she contributed to the Autonomous Province of Trento in the development of a Tourism Development Plan. Her research interests include tourism destination management, cultural and heritage tourism and information technologies applied to market research methodologies.

Grace Wen Pan is currently studying for a PhD in tourism at the School of Tourism and Hotel Management, Griffith University, Australia. She completed her Master of Business (Research) at Queensland University of Technology, Australia, in 2000. Her areas of research interest are services marketing, business networks, international business, female issues in international business, cross-cultural studies, tourism marketing and the Chinese and Australian tourism markets. Her work experience, prior to coming to study in Australia, included an executive position with one of the biggest Chinese travel agencies. She completed a Bachelor of Economics degree at Shanghai International Studies University, China.

Harald Pechlaner is Assistant Professor at the Department of Management of the University of Innsbruck. In 1999 he was Visiting Professor at the Department of Hospitality and Tourism of the University of Wisconsin Stout. He studied Management at the University of Verona (Italy) and Innsbruck (Austria) before undertaking his PhD studies at the Department of Management at the University of Innsbruck in Austria. Between 1993 and 1998 he was Managing Director of the Governmental Tourism Administration of the Autonomous Province of Bolzano, South-Tyrol, Italy and director of the South-Tyrolean Tourism Board. His research interests include tourism destination management and cultural tourism management.

John Power is Managing Director of Tactix, a UK management consultancy company, and an active consultant on strategic issues for tourism organizations. Previously he was Training & Development Manager with Allied Breweries in the UK and Senior Training Adviser at the Hotel Industry Training Board, UK. He is also an associate consultant with Roffey Park Management Centre, UK, and the Institute of Public Administration, Ireland. His research work is primarily concerned with processes of change and learning in service organizations and he has presented his work at training workshops in the UK and overseas.

Bruce Prideaux is Lecturer in tourism at the University of Queensland, Australia. His teaching centres on tourism transport, tourism policy and Asian tourism issues and his research interests are issues pertaining to resort development, tourism transport, issues in Asian tourism, particularly in Korea, East Timor and Indonesia, and regional tourism developement. He is editor of the *Asia Pacific Journal of Transport*, Book Review Editor of the *Australian Journal of Hospitality Management* and treasurer of the Queensland Chapter of PATA. He is also a Fellow of the Chartered Institute of Transport in Australia, a member of the Queensland Korea Chamber of Commerce and a member of the Ecotourism Society of Australia. Prior to his current role, he worked in various capacities in the Queensland Department of Transport.

Noel Scott has spent five years at Tourism Queensland as Research and Strategic Services Manager. He has represented the State of Queensland on National Research Committees and is a past State Chairman of the Market Research Society of Australia. He is the inaugural 'Martin Oppermann Memorial Scholarship' holder and is currently studying for a PhD in Tourism; his thesis is entitled 'Consumer Trends in Tourism'. He holds a Masters of Business Administration and a Masters in Marketing as well as an honours' degree in Chemistry.

Carina Slavik is General Manager of Travel Ys International based in Melbourne, Australia. She was instrumental in the initial research and development of this new commercial business venture for the YWCA of Australia. Carina holds Bachelors' and Masters' degrees in Business (Tourism). Prior to joining the YWCA in 1994, Carina worked in a management capacity in the hotel and tour operations sectors and in management consulting (marketing) with KPMG Peat Marwick and Deloitte Touche Tohmatsu.

Tim Snaith is founder and CEO of Global Consultancy. He has carried out a wide range of consultancy and research projects for both the public and private sectors. The integration of theoretical knowledge and professional experience has been welcomed by businesses across a variety of sectors (IT, Government, Education, Tourism and Leisure), where he has established a reputation for delivering innovative commercial solutions that contribute significantly to profitability.

John Swarbrooke is Principal Lecturer in Tourism and Postgraduate Programme Director at Sheffield Hallam University. He has written several books in recent years, including *Consumer Behaviour in Tourism, Sustainable Tourism Management, Marketing Tourism, Hospitality and Leisure in Europe* and *The Development and Management of Visitor Attractions*. John is Professeur Visitant at the Institut Management Hôtelier International, Paris. He has worked on consultancy projects in Greece, Italy, Indonesia, Palestine, Russia and the UK. John has been an invited keynote speaker at major international conferences in Athens, Bandung, Benidorm, Funchal, Innsbruck, Istanbul, Jakarta, Kasimierz Dolny, London, Palma de Mallorca and Thessaloniki. He is also secretary of ATLAS, the European network of universities teaching tourism and leisure.

David J. Telfer is Assistant Professor in the Department of Recreation and Leisure Studies and the co-ordinator of the Tourism Studies Degree Programme at Brock University. Previously he taught tourism at the University of Luton, UK, in the Department of Tourism and Leisure. He completed his postgraduate degrees at the University of Waterloo, Canada, and conducted field research in Indonesia. His main areas of research include tourism and development theory, links between tourism and agriculture, wine tourism and the backward economic linkages of tourism.

Dorota Ujma is a lecturer in the Department of Tourism and Leisure at the University of Luton, Luton Business School. Her current research interests are focused upon tourism marketing; specifically distribution in tourism, health resorts and tourism organizations and associations and their role in the travel trade. She has been involved in a number of projects incorporating an exchange of ideas with staff / students from universities in Eastern Europe, especially Poland.

Yong-Hyun Cho is a PhD candidate in the Department of Leisure Studies at the University of Illinois. He has undergraduate and Masters' degrees from Seoul National University in Landscape Architecture. Yong-Hyun has extensive experience in recreation resource planning and development. His current research interests focus on the relationships between the use of information technology and destination image formation with a special focus on the use of virtual experience for tourism marketing and development.

PART 1

Tourism distribution: theory, practice and issues

CHAPTER 1

Introduction: tourism distribution channels: practices, issues and transformations

Eric Laws and Dimitrios Buhalis

There are several reasons for editing a book with tourism distribution as its focus. Increasingly distribution is regarded as one of the most critical managerial decisions, which can actually determine the competitiveness and profitability of organizations. Surprisingly, however, there is little research on the topic and the limited literature available is inadequate to provide guidance for tourism and hospitality managers. This book aims to examine several aspects of the tourism distribution channel and more importantly to stimulate research and discussion on the topic by providing the underlying theory as well as several practical aspects from a wide range of sectors and regions around the world.

At an operational level, a key decision for managers is how to make their products available to consumers. In the 4P's marketing typology, this function is referred to as 'place', a rather misleading term when analysing tourism! 'Distribution' is less confusing, because it implies the selection of outlets from which holidaymakers can purchase their tours. However, despite the significance of distribution, this term somewhat obscures the central distinguishing feature of tourism as an industry: tourism shifts consumers to the places where their holiday products are created, the destinations. Importantly, in other industries, manufacturers bring components together centrally, then reach out to the wider marketplace through supplier networks which consumers approach to make their purchases. For tourism, the destination and its range of attractions and activities is likely to remain the core product, the focus of tourists' motivations and experiences for the foreseeable future. More fundamentally, the significance of destination consequences of tourist activity are increasingly seen as the basis for sustainability of the industry, and the nature of those consequences is being recognized as partly dependent on the way tourism is organized locally. To a large extent, that is an outcome of the tourism distribution solutions adopted, particularly the organization of holiday packages and the infrastructure needed to support tourism.

Tourism then, differs from most industries because its clients travel to the points where their tourism experience is produced. In contrast, other industries face the logistical challenges inherent in moving goods or services from distant production sites to their consumers, and to this end they depend on complex chains of distribution involving specialized activities such as wholesaling, warehousing, transportation, retailing and other associated activities. The management of distribution channels has long been an important area of study for many sectors of industry, but this book is one of a few to focus attention on the distinctive challenges of distribution in the tourism industry.

The distinguishing features of tourism distribution are the various ways in which tourism products such as transport, accommodation and activities are packaged, promoted and made available for tourist consumption, the relative strengths of organizations performing the various distribution functions, and the importance of information to influence consumer choice. Although it is a relatively new industry (mass international tourism dates from the same era as jet air travel), distribution systems based mainly on destination marketers, principals, tour operators and travel agents (travel retailers) were established rapidly to cope with the complexities of international bookings for spatially distant markets. From the start these have been subject to change under market pressures arising from entrepreneurial innovation in an industry noted for its intense competition, but recently it has become apparent that external influences are becoming pre-eminent in shaping new solutions to traditional distribution problems, and in providing new opportunities for product development, interfirm collaboration and market development.

STRUCTURE OF THE BOOK

Porter (1980) has argued that every industry has an underlying structure that gives rise to its operational and competitive characteristics. The objective of the first three parts of this book is to describe and examine the types of distribution system currently used in the tourism industry, and to provide critical commentary on their strengths and weaknesses. The fourth section of the book focuses attention on developments in tourism distribution. In a book of this scale it is not possible to provide a comprehensive treatment of all known forms of distribution, and it is hoped that the varying situations catalogued here, and the different analytical approaches adopted, will encourage further research into tourism distribution.

Many of the authors of chapters in Parts 1, 2 and 3 have discussed factors tending to change tourism distribution, notably aspects of information technology, but readers should be aware of three caveats. In the first place, the editorial philosophy guiding the selection of these contributions was that they should document and analyse functional current aspects of tourism distribution, and IT is but one feature. Contributors in the first three sections were asked not to place undue emphasis on this, partly because there is an increasing literature on the topic published in specialized books and journals. Secondly, other factors have the potential to transform relationships between tourism industry members and the distribution of tourism services. These include:

- the emergence of partnership forms of management,
- alliance channel management modes rather than adversarial approaches to distribution,
- network- and systems-based quality control methods,
- longer term perspectives underpinning sustainable visions of tourism, and
- recognition of the significance of the local destination communities.

These themes are part of the discussion in every chapter of this book. The third point is that authors were writing to quite tight length constraints, and so have been restricted from fully developing the rich content of the particular situation they chose to analyse. It is hoped that the gain is in terms of clarity and specificity, even though this is at the expense of detail and breadth.

The chapters in Part 1 deal with the theory of distribution as applied to the tourism industry (Buhalis, Chapter 2; Ujma, Chapter 3) and in particular in the leisure and business sectors (Laws, Chapter 4; Davidson, Chapter 5). Ethical issues in the management of tourism distribution are addressed also (Swarbrooke, Chapter 6) as well as service quality aspects of tourism distribution (Harrington and Power, Chapter 7; Jensen, Chapter 8).

Part 2 provides detailed discussions of industry practices in tourism distribution. Casarin (Chapter 9) contrasts distribution systems in various European countries and identifies differences between Northern and Southern Europe. Bywater (Chapter 10) provides an authoritative analysis of the complex ownership patterns of the European travel industry. This is particularly important as the strategic alliances and mergers of European tour operators in the last five years have revolutionized the distribution arena for all players involved. The structure of the industry and some of the competitive practices are analysed by Hudson *et al.* (Chapter 11) who examine the switch selling practices in the UK travel agencies as part of the vertical integration of the industry. King and Slavik (Chapter 12) examine the problems of distribution in the accommodation sector with a case study on the YWCA. The legislative framework of airline distribution is the subject of Appelman and Go's chapter (Chapter 13), whilst Prideaux (Chapter 14) illustrates how technology has evolved the distribution mechanisms of airlines.

The common topic for chapters in Part 3 is destination and regional perspectives on distribution issues. Osti and Pechlaner (Chapter 15) provide a review of communication issues in NTO distribution strategies, Hashimoto and Telfer (Chapter 16) profile tourism distribution channels in Canadian tourism. The remaining three chapters in this section are concerned with Australian destination distribution. Jenkins (Chapter 17) discusses distribution strategies for regional and national tourism organizations, Wen Pan and Laws (Chapter 18) examine the challenges of reaching and serving a new market, Chinese outbound tourists to Australia, and Scott and Laws present a model of destination channels for destination marketing based on a Queensland case study (Chapter 19).

Part 4 focuses on change in tourism distribution. Cooper and Lewis (Chapter 20) have provided a wide-ranging review of the trends leading to transformation in the tourism industry. O'Connor, Buhalis and Frew (Chapter 21) examine the significance of information technology in transforming tourism distribution channels and in developing great opportunities and challenges for most actors in the industry. Cho and Fesenmaier (Chapter 22) open a new dimension in their discussion of experience marketing using the virtual tour. In the brief concluding chapter of the book (Chapter 23) the editors provide a brief commentary on the potential for further research into tourism distribution issues and practices and hope to initiate further discussion and research in the area.

Inevitably contributions vary in content and style as they explore a wide range of issues from a several perspectives. However, they all provide useful insights to the tourism distribution channel and raise more questions than answers, probing further research and exploration on this increasingly significant issue. Although inevitably a wide range of issues need further discussion and research, this volume provides the basis for starting to explore critical aspects of distribution and offers a foundation for investigating the area and for encouraging further discussion and debate.

REFERENCE

Porter, M. (1980) *Competitive Strategy: Techniques for analysing industries and competitors.* Free Press, New York.

CHAPTER 2

Tourism distribution channels: practices and processes

Dimitrios Buhalis

Distribution is becoming one of the most critical factors for the competitiveness of tourism organizations and destinations. Setting appropriate distribution channels effectively determines whether they can be included in the set of decision-making models of prospective consumers. The globalization of the industry intensifies the information required for all tourism transactions, and thus more effective communication and distribution channels are required in order to provide sufficient information and to undertake a transaction. To the degree that distribution channels provide this information and facilitate the transaction, they extensively influence the prosperity of both tourism enterprises and tourism destinations all over the world. Distribution channels often both influence consumer behaviour, and determine the ability of the industry to respond to consumers' requests efficiently. Hence they determine the competitiveness of suppliers and destinations.

Increasingly tourism distribution channels have profound effects on the competitiveness and profitability of tourism organizations. As a result, tourism distribution channels attract more attention by contemporary researchers and strategists. The following paragraphs attempt to illustrate the role, performance and implications of tourism intermediaries, as presented in the relatively limited literature, and in particular to illustrate their role in the tourism industry operation and profitability. As tourism distribution channels vary according to the type of products and countries, this chapter concentrates on the European leisure market. Although similar principles normally apply in global and business tourism, several differences are evident, preventing generalizations. The most challenging element of the tourism distribution channel is its dynamic structure, which enables participants to keep changing partners in order to maximize their profitability and competitiveness. The fluidity that characterizes the distribution channel of tourism makes it extremely difficult to analyse its structure and interrelations as the only constant is change. It is critical therefore to appreciate the factors that generate change in order to be able to analyse any given distribution channel and to be able to improve it for the benefit of the organizations involved.

DISTRIBUTION CHANNELS IN THE TOURISM INDUSTRY

The primary distribution functions for tourism are information, combination and travel arrangement services. Most distribution channels therefore provide *information* for prospective tourists; bundle tourism products together; and also establish mechanisms that enable consumers to make, confirm and pay for *reservations*. In tourism the position of the distribution sector is much stronger than that of other trade intermediaries. Travel agents and tour operators as well as charter brokers, reservation systems and other travel distribution specialists have a far greater power to influence and to direct demand than their counterparts in other industries do. Since they do, in fact, control demand, they also have increased bargaining power in their relations with suppliers of tourist services and are in a position to influence their pricing, their product policies and their promotional activities. Thus, distribution is starting to assume a much more central position in the strategy of most tourism organizations and destinations (World Tourism Organization,1975; Morrison,1994a).

Several scholars attempt to define the tourism distribution channel concept. Wanhill (1993) suggests that 'the principal role of intermediaries is to bring buyers and sellers together, either to create markets where they previously did not exist or to make existing markets work more efficiently and thereby to expand market size'. Moreover, Middleton (1988) proposes that 'a distribution channel is any organised and serviced system, created or utilised to provide convenient points of sale and/or access to consumers, away from the location of production and consumption, and paid for out of marketing budgets'. However, this definition ignores the promotional and marketing research activities undertaken by tourism distribution channels, while it underestimates their information provision function. In addition, it excludes local distribution channels, such as box offices or incoming travel agencies at destinations. Furthermore, McIntosh defines tourism distribution channels, as 'an operating structure, system or linkages of various combinations of travel organization, through which a producer of travel products describes and confirms travel arrangements to the buyer' (Mill and Morrison, eds, 1985). The promotional element of the channels is still ignored but the information provision function is highlighted in this definition. Moreover, the World Tourism Organization (1975) suggests that 'a distribution channel can be described as a given combination of intermediaries who co-operate in the sale of a product. It follows that a distribution system can be and in most instances is composed of more than one distribution channel, each of which operates parallel to

- Facilitation of access to often remote tourism products, for both bookings and purchasing
- Provision of information by using discussions, leaflets, maps, brochures, video, CDs
- Consumers' guidance/consultation for particular packages or products
- Undertake pre and post experience marketing research on consumers' needs and experiences
- Assemble tourism products from different providers according to tourists' expectations
- Facilitate selling process of tourism products, by reserving and issuing travel documents
- Ameliorate inventory management by managing demand and supply
- Issue of travel documentation, i.e. ticketing, vouchers, etc.
- Utilize a clearing system where each channel member receives payments for their services
- Spreading the commercial risk involved between tourism distribution channel members
- Arranging details and ancillary services, such as insurance, visa, currency
- Promotion of particular products or packages, in co-operation with principals
- Complaint handling for both customers and industry

Figure 2.1 Functions and benefits emerging through the tourism distribution channel

and in competition with other channels.' Figure 2.1 summarizes all functions and benefits attributed to the distribution channel of tourism.

Three different types of intermediaries are normally used in order to access and purchase products, i.e. outgoing travel agencies (retailers), tour operators (wholesalers) and incoming (handling) travel agencies based at destinations. The tourism distribution channel is illustrated in Figure 2.2, where it is demonstrated that consumers may purchase various components directly from producers, while numerous distribution and sales intermediaries are involved in promoting the tourism product. Prospective tourists may also use more than one category or tourism distribution channel for one trip. For example, they can use an outgoing travel agent for a 'seat only' charter product and book directly accommodation and catering. Hitherto the vast majority of tourists in Northern Europe have been purchasing leisure packages using all three intermediaries. They visit an outgoing travel agency and purchase a package put together by a tour operator which is handled by an incoming agency.

National or regional tourist organizations are used by both tourists and travel trade for additional information, support documentation, classification and inspection of tourism products, co-operation in promotion, and special arrangements. In this sense they facilitate the tourism distribution channel function. A number of organizations offering ancillary services (such as banks, news agencies attractions, credit card companies, special privileged user cards, societies, religious groups and organizations) seem to promote and organize travelling. Therefore they may also be considered as part of the tourism distribution channel. The *length, level or stage* of a tourism distribution channel is determined by the number of intermediaries involved between final consumers and principals. Moreover, distribution channel strategies can be characterized as *intensive*, which involves maximizing the travel product's exposure by distributing through all available intermediaries; *exclusive*, when a limited amount of channels and outlets are utilized; or *selective*, which is a mixture of the intensive and exclusive strategies (Kotler, 1988, p. 537; Gee, Makens and Choy, 1989; Mill and Morrison, eds, 1985).

A general trend for *horizontal and/or vertical integration* can be observed in the tourism industry. *Horizontal integration* takes place at the same level of any tourism distribution channel and essentially enables homogeneous enterprises to distribute their products more efficiently and effectively. Franchising, consortia and 'code-sharing' airlines are typical examples of horizontally integrated organizations. *Vertical integration* emerges when organizations at one level in the tourism distribution channel merge with members from other levels to achieve economies of scale, better cost control, co-ordinated brand management, more channel control and increased bargaining power. Mergers between tour operators and outgoing travel agencies, airlines and accommodation establishments are typical examples of vertical integration. A detailed analysis of each member of the tourism distribution channel, namely accommodation establishments, incoming travel agencies, tour operators, outgoing travel agencies and public tourism offices, is undertaken below.

The technological revolution has demonstrated that several additional players, such as Computer Reservations Systems (CRSs), Global Distribution Channels (GDSs) and Destination Management Systems (DMSs), emerged to facilitate the distribution of tourism products. The proliferation of the Internet strengthened the role of electronic intermediaries and developed their position to a strategic one for tourism suppliers and to a potential threatening one for traditional distributors. Electronic intermediaries not only facilitate distribution but also affect the other marketing mix 'P's', as they increasingly determine the price by assessing real time demand and available supply; manipulate and formulate tourism industry products by combining and specializing products according to customers' needs and wishes; and finally facilitate promotion by targeting specific markets and establishing communication. They also transform the business model for several organizations by introducing new distribution strategies such as creating or co-branding Internet portals, auctions, name-your-price and other innovative distribution strategies. To a certain extent electronic tourism distribution channels dictate the choice of

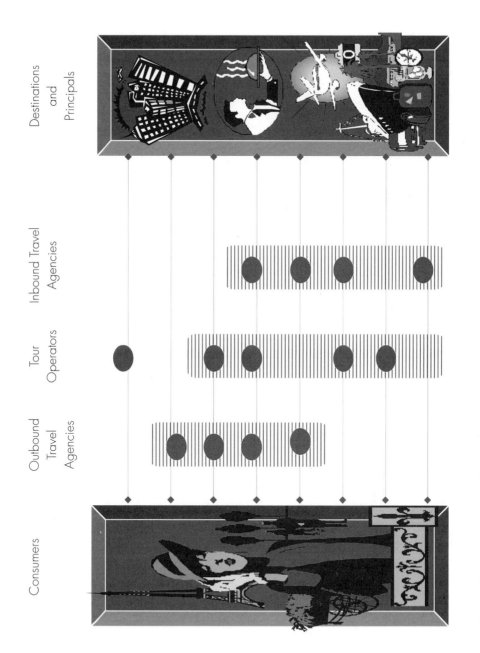

Figure 2.2 Tourism distribution mechanism

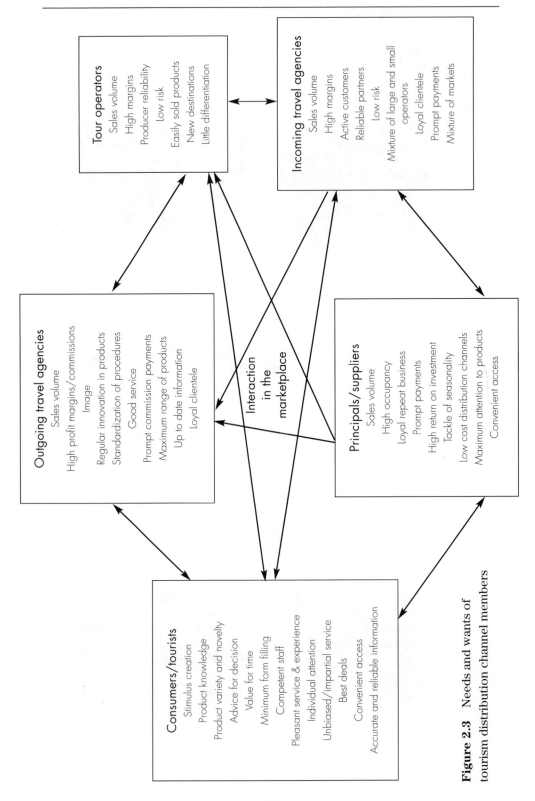

Figure 2.3 Needs and wants of tourism distribution channel members

product as the difference between products becomes secondary to the easiness of getting an entire transaction completed (Buhalis, 1998, 2000a, 2000c).

Understandably, each tourism distribution channel member has different *needs and wants*, as illustrated in Figure 2.3. Unfortunately, some of these needs are conflicting and antagonistic, and therefore a degree of *channel conflict* is inevitable. This is mainly due to the natural tendency of each player to maximize their profit margin at the expense of their partners, as consumers are prepared to pay a fairly fixed amount for their products. Power distribution within the tourism distribution channel affects channel control and leadership, while organizations often need to redesign their channels in order to resolve these conflicts.

Tourism distribution decisions should therefore be regarded as pivotal to the marketing mix, and their interdependency with the other elements should be emphasized. As intermediaries influence both branding and image of tourism products, suitable intermediaries should be utilized by tourism suppliers for their distribution. Middleton (1994, p. 201) highlights that 'paradoxically, the inability in travel and tourism to create physical stocks of products, adds to rather than reduces the importance of the distribution process. In marketing practice, creating and manipulating access for consumers is one of the principal ways to *manage demand* for highly perishable products.'

OUTGOING TRAVEL AGENCIES

Outgoing travel agencies are one of the most important elements of the tourism distribution channel, as they act as an interface between the tourism industry and outbound consumers. A clear distinction between inbound and outbound agencies is made here, although agencies in several countries are likely to undertake both activities. A comprehensive approach on outgoing travel agencies' operations within the tourism distribution channel is provided below, based on Beaver (1993) and Renshaw (1992). Holloway (1989) suggests that 'the main role of agents is to provide a convenient location for the purchase of travel. At the locations they act as booking agents for holidays and travel, as well as a source of information and advice on travel services. Their customers look to them for expert product knowledge and objectivity in the advice offered.' In addition, outgoing travel agencies provide ancillary travel services such as travellers' cheques, foreign currency, provision of passports and visas, as well as travel insurance. This research concentrates on leisure outgoing travel agencies, in contrast with business outgoing travel agencies and consolidators, as the Aegean Islands are predominantly a leisure destination.

A retail travel agent is essentially a commissioned intermediary who serves as sales outlet for tourism principals and wholesalers and as such the travel agent usually does not own the services he or she sells to travellers. Unlike other retailers, outgoing travel agencies cannot stock travel products. Instead, they only stock travel information in the form of brochures, leaflets and data as well as use the personal expertise of travel consultants. Consequently, agencies carry limited financial risk, as they never purchase tourism products in advance. They only reserve/confirm/ purchase/issue travel documents, i.e. tickets, vouchers, only upon request from customers.

As demonstrated in Figure 2.2, outgoing travel agencies take part in several channel configurations. They are approached by prospective tourists (individual or group) who normally inquire about a very wide range of information: rates, schedules, location, facilities and services, availability, booking procedures, issuing of tickets/vouchers, travel insurance, currency, transfers, travel formalities. In addition, consumers might ask for recommendation for a forthcoming travel opportunity. Consequently, outgoing travel agencies need to search through their files/brochures/directories/databases/CRSs/GDSs/Internet in order to identify suitable tourism products, which satisfy consumers' needs and requirements. Outgoing travel agencies can sell individual tourism products or packages, while they can design a customized product for customers' special needs, by contacting directly principals or incoming travel agencies at destinations.

In the UK and other Northern European countries, outgoing travel agencies tend to focus exclusively on outbound tourism, unlike travel agencies in Southern Europe where both inbound and outbound tourism services are regularly on offer. In addition, business outgoing travel agencies can be involved in organizing *special arrangements for corporate clients, groups, conferences and incentives*. Outgoing travel agencies, especially in Northern European countries, tend to specialize in some elements of the tourism product, depending on their market, orientation, location and business partners. Thus, there is a clear distinction between *leisure and business travel agencies*. Several outgoing travel agencies specialize in air transportation ticketing and some of them go further by becoming 'consolidators' or 'bucket shops', buying tickets in bulk from scheduled airlines and selling them at discounted rates. Renshaw (1992) suggests that outgoing travel agencies contribute to the tourism value chain by offering numerous benefits for consumers: personal service, expert advice, unbiased advice on a wide range of products, ancillary services, convenience and location, and a greater choice of products. These values enable them to influence consumers' choice.

Classification and types of outgoing travel agencies

Outgoing travel agencies can be classified in numerous categories depending on several variables such as the geographical spread, size, type of business and type of appointment. A great degree of differentiation can be observed between outgoing travel agencies in various countries. In Southern Europe, for example, agencies often undertake the role of tour operators, and inbound travel agencies as well. First, their *geographical coverage of activity* is a variable for classification to multinational, national or regional outgoing travel agencies. Only a few outgoing travel agencies operate globally, mainly due to consumer needs and differences in consumption pattern differences. However, globalization increasingly provides both the scope and opportunity for geographical expansion. Secondly, they can be characterized as multiples, mintiples, miniples and independents, according to their *size and the number of outlets*. Multiples are normally nationwide agencies, which operate more than perhaps 100 outlets, and are often owned by a large travel corporation. They tend to be located on most city high street locations. Multiples can achieve economies of scale and have advantages of large-scale purchasing power, investment in new technology and national promotional campaigns. Multiples often are parts of diagonally integrated tour operators (e.g. Lunn Poly belongs to Thomson) and hence they concentrate on package holidays and have almost withdrawn from most service-intensive products. Mintiples focus on a particular region where they enjoy a high profile. They are located centrally and offer some business travel services. In contrast, independent outgoing travel agencies can be a single to six outlet agency, normally managed by their proprietor or partners and serving their local community. Independent or small outgoing travel agencies tend to specialize in niche markets, and thus, accommodate their clients' needs adequately.

Thirdly, a distinction between *leisure and business outgoing travel agencies* is essential in most countries, as they often serve totally different products and markets. Business outgoing travel agencies tend to arrange travel for business travellers and corporations. In return for customers' high loyalty, outgoing travel agencies offer a number of special arrangements such as discounted rates; extended credit; commission free accommodation booking; extra services; implants, i.e. personnel located within a corporation; or fixed annual fee for all travel arrangements. In contrast, general/leisure outgoing travel agencies are located in high streets and primarily serve holidaymakers. They usually display tour operators' brochures and sell inclusive packages, although a very wide range of travel requests can be satisfied. Smaller, independent outgoing travel agencies tend to specialize in some types of leisure activity and/or a destination, or even may design tailor-made holidays for independent travellers. Finally, holiday shops/outgoing travel agencies specialize almost exclusively in the inclusive tour market and to a large extent exclude other types of business. Often they belong to multiples or to very small independents.

Fourthly, British outgoing travel agencies can be characterized according to the *organization which has appointed them*. The majority of travel agencies in the UK are Association of British Travel Agent members. IATA (International Air Transport Association) members are also assessed and need to certify not only their financial standing but also their staff's ability to sell air transportation. In contrast, non-IATA concentrate on inclusive tours. Similar associations operate in most countries, and thus, outgoing travel agencies' designation would rate their ability and reliability.

It is estimated that about 40,000 outgoing travel agencies operate in Europe, while another 32,400 outgoing travel agencies function in the USA. The magnitude of this sub-sector is demonstrated by Smith and Jenner (1994) who suggest that over 200,000 people are employed in outgoing travel agencies, an average of six persons per outlet, while a $50 billion combined annual turnover is estimated.

Outgoing travel agencies' needs, wants and profitability

Outgoing travel agencies are profit-making organizations aiming to maximize their earnings by optimizing both the volume of customers served and their profit margin. This is achieved by selling higher commission/profit margin products, as well as selecting partners with high reliability and a strong image, who can sell their products relatively easily. Hitherto, outgoing travel agencies have been paid a commission for all products they manage to reserve and sell. Roughly a range of 8 to 12 per cent covers the commission for the majority of products sold through incoming travel agencies internationally (Renshaw, 1992; Beaver, 1993). As far as the profitability and cost-benefit analysis of the British outgoing travel agencies is concerned, Keynote (1994, p. 24) suggests that, in 1993, they had an average turnover of around £1 million per outlet. Table 2.1 illustrates a typical British agency cost and revenue breakdown, indicating their profitability.

Table 2.1 Outgoing travel agencies' cost and benefit breakdown. *Source*: Adapted from Wanhill, 1993, p. 194

Sales	Percentage	Costs and expenses	Percentage
Inclusive tours	53.0	Payroll expenses	46.5
Air tickets	33.0	Advertising	3.0
Other tickets	4.9	Energy	1.5
Insurance	1.0	Administration	6.5
Car hire	0.3	Repairs and maintenance	0.5
Miscellaneous	7.8	Accommodation expenses	12.5
Revenue		Depreciation	2.5
Commissions	9.5	Total cost	85
Other income	0.5		
Total	10.1	**Net income**	16.0

Moreover, *override or incentive commissions* are additional incentives paid by principals or wholesalers to stimulate extra bookings and increase outgoing travel agencies' loyalty. In most cases, override commissions (up to 17 to 18 per cent) are a form of performance bonus, based on a graduated rate schedule according to volume of business generated. Principals and tour operators who offer override commissions often achieve 'preferred supplier' status and enjoy preferential racking of their brochures and merchandising. Outgoing travel agencies are often accused of directional or switch selling towards those suppliers. Other incentives may be offered either to outgoing travel agencies' organization or personnel, such as educational or familiarization trips, free flights or holidays, free shopping vouchers, or goods such as colour televisions or compact discs. Often cash incentives apply for preferred partners or parent tour operator bookings. An analysis of the contribution of holidays to European outgoing travel agencies' turnover is demonstrated in Table 2.2. It can be observed that Northern European outgoing travel agencies make more than half of their income by selling holidays, while their Southern European counterparts have ticketing and individual travel arrangements as their main source of earnings. Following a number of American airlines, several suppliers applied a commission capping policy or ceased to pay commissions in the late 1990s. They took advantage of the Internet developments and direct communication opportunities and argued that if customers felt that travel agencies offered a valuable service they should be prepared to pay for it as an extra. This is transforming the business model for most travel agencies and forces them to rethink their strategy. Most agencies specializing in business travel have already introduced fee-based accounts as their commission-based work declines rapidly.

Critical issues in outgoing travel agencies' position in the tourism distribution channels

Numerous structural issues affect the prosperity of outgoing travel agencies as well as their contribution to the tourism industry. Perhaps the most critical one is the horizontal and vertical integration observed in the market, which effectively restructures the distribution of power and enhances conflict opportunities within the tourism distribution channel. As Bywater demonstrates in Chapter 10, both horizontal and vertical integration can be observed in the tourism distribution channel, affecting the position of outgoing travel agencies. *Horizontal integration or 'the march of multiples'* occurs when outgoing travel agencies amalgamate through mergers or takeovers. *Vertical integration* in the tourism industry essentially means that several outgoing travel agencies are linked with other tourism distribution channel members. Ownership and strategic alliances between outgoing travel agencies, tour operators and major principals such as airlines and hotels are evident throughout the tourism industry. As a consequence, leisure travel retailing becomes enormously concentrated, which essentially increases tour operators' power within the tourism distribution channel.

TOUR OPERATORS

The most significant contribution of tour operators in the distribution channel is the package tour. A combination of different products is assembled together

Table 2.2 Operational figures for European outgoing travel agencies. *Source*: Adapted from Smith and Jenner, 1994; (+) Hotelline, 1990a, p. 1

Country	Number of agencies	Number of outlets	Number of outlets (+)	Average turnover per outlet (£m)	Employment per outlet	Packages sold per outlet	Package as % of holiday	Holidays as % of turnover	Ticketing and other as % of turnover	CRS penetration (%)
Austria			1,152							
Sweden			640							
Denmark			400			2,600	25.0	50	50	75
Netherlands	1,639		2,595			2,200	28.2	75	25	100
Germany	9,500		8,000	1.37	5.5	2,100	31.5	57	43	60
UK	2,572	6,997	n/a	1.36	4–5	2,000	26.5	50	50	40
Belgium			1,700			1,900	37.6	70	30	
Switzerland			1,500			1,700	21.9			
France	2,602	3,805	4,000	2.08	7	1,400	8.1	30	70	99
Spain	2,280	4,831	5,000	1.41	10	450	5.0	27	73	80
Italy		5,150	4,222	1.17	5–6	350	4.0			60
Luxembourg			n/a				32.0	70	30	
Ireland			370				12.9	50	50	
Portugal			650				7.3	40	60	
Greece			3,582				1.8	15	85	
EU average	34,175	40,105		1.46	6	1,500	17.5			

into 'tourism packages' or 'inclusive tours'. Packages are defined as 'a selected travel and tourism product, marketed under a particular product or brand label, and sold at an inclusive price' (Middleton, 1988). The EU 'package directive' defines *tour operators* as 'organizers', which 'means the person who, other than occasionally, organizes packages and sells or offers them for sale, whether directly or through a retailer'. The directive also defines *package* as 'the pre-arranged combination of not fewer than two of the following when sold or offered for sale at an inclusive price and when the service covers a period of more than twenty-four hours or includes overnight accommodation: a) transport, b) accommodation c) other tourist services not ancillary to transport or accommodation and accounting for a significant proportion of the package' (EC, 1990). As tour operators make bulk reservations on various tourism products, before distributing them through outgoing travel agencies, they are often regarded as wholesalers. A great variation between tour operators' practices and strategies can be observed in various countries. However, Northern European operators have to a certain extent standardized packages towards sun-sand-sea-sex destinations due to the horizontal integration experienced. In contrast, Southern European tour operators predominately concentrate on short breaks-sightseeing-shopping-shows in European capitals, as most of their clients are residents or neighbours to sunny destinations.

Tour operators as distributors and producers/principals

Tour operators undertake a wide range of activities in order to negotiate with suppliers as well as prepare and sell their packages to consumers. They normally pre-reserve and sometimes pre-purchase a number of travel services such as aircraft seats, accommodation and transfers at destinations, and set up a package at a single price. Packages are standardized and repetitive and they are normally comprised by two or more elements of transport, accommodation, catering, entertainment, attractions, and other facilities and services (such as travel insurance). Product packages are marketed to the general public, described in print or other media, and offered for sale to prospective customers at a published, inclusive price, in which the costs of the product components cannot be separately identified. Buying in bulk generates immense discounts and economies of scale. Tour operating is a process of combining aircraft seats and beds in hotels (or other forms of accommodation) in a manner which will make the purchase price attractive to potential holidaymakers. By doing so several main benefits emerge for consumers, principals and destinations as demonstrated in Table 2.3.

Table 2.3 Benefits for and power over other distribution channel members. *Source*: Adapted from Buhalis, 1995

Consumers/tourists

- lower priced holidays due to their negotiation ability, bargaining power, economies of scale
- information about a destination
- ensure familiarity and safety for destination-naïve travellers and speak customers' language
- reduce some of tourism products' intangibility
- 'protection plans', 'customer promises', insurances, guarantees, 'commitments', comforts tourists in respect of the strange, foreign and unknown
- reduce risks through bonding organizations (e.g. ABTA, Tour Operators' Study Group, AITO, ATOL)

Tourism enterprises/principals

- increase the occupancy of principals, especially during the low season and thus
- reduce seasonality
- promote the product in distant markets and undertake a comprehensive marketing function and increase product visibility
- undertake a degree of principals' risk

Destinations

- improve the accessibility of destinations by operating charter flights or coaches
- support the marketing efforts of destinations by promoting them through brochures and by increasing their visibility in the marketplace
- stimulate demand through promotions, advertisement and educational trips for the clerks of outgoing travel agencies
- brand and project the images of destinations
- expand the tourism season and increase seasonality
- may promote several environmental initiatives and improvements

---

In essence, tour operators offer the branding and distribution mechanisms to an amalgam of tourism products provided by different principals. By contracting and combining individual suppliers and products, tour operators are to a certain degree producers or manufacturers of tourism products rather than simply distributors. In addition, tour operators tend to oversee the entire holiday experience by providing representatives, who are capable of solving most problems during their holiday. They also assess the satisfaction of their clients after their trip. In this sense, tour operators monitor the performance of the entire tourism industry. Hence, tour operators arrange and supervise the delivery of tourism packages, which they formulate by combining several tourism products. Larger tour operators play a fundamental role in passenger transportation and thus, they either own their carriers and/or they co-operate closely with several transportation providers. Consequently, they determine consumers' accessibility to destinations, especially for remote and insular regions. Charter airlines are established to enable direct, reliable and inexpensive transportation for prospective tourists, while a mechanism involving all convenient transportation media is used to transfer consumers whilst at a destination. However, in most destinations, tour operators are often unable to control the production and delivery of these products and services, with the exception of some charter airlines, which are owned by large/mass tour operators. Increasingly, tour operators appreciate tourists' special interests and specific activity requirements, and attempt to provide themed and activity holidays built around a central theme or activity, such as ski, bird-watching, history, etc. This is a response to the evident inadequacy of the traditional '4S's' tourism product to satisfy the emerging sophisticated tourism demand. In this case tour operators are more evidently producers of tourism services and thus can be characterized as principals.

Preparing inclusive tours and contacting

Tour operators have to undertake marketing research during the preparation and inclusive tour design phase. They explore the overall market size and the demand trends, as well as the attractiveness of their products and destinations. They also analyse their profit margins in each destination and calculate the accumulative benefit based on all the activities undertaken on the short and longer term. A period of negotiation follows, when tour operators contact tourism principals or incoming travel agencies and inquire about accommodation as well as numerous facilities and services for their clientele. Two major types of contracts are normally used by tour operators for suppliers and accommodation establishments in particular. Either block reservations (allotment or allocation) or block pre-purchases (commitment or guarantee). *Allotments* are contracts based on the expected volume and time of business. Tour operators do not pre-purchase facilities, they simply pre-book them and have the right to use them up until a release period which may be few days before customers arrive. This effectively reduces tour operators' financial risk, as they are under no financial obligation if they do not use facilities. *Commitment* contracts are used when tour operators pre-purchase products, regardless of whether they will manage to use them or not. This type of contract is used extensively for transportation (charter flights) and often for small self-catering accommodation properties or in well-established hotels in traditional destinations which enjoy high demand. As the majority of the risk passes from the principal to tour operators, they normally purchase the products for much lower prices. A combination between the two types of contracts is also used extensively, especially for accommodation establishments with strong demand or within destinations with limited capacity to spread the risk and at the same time to ensure a number of available facilities. Similarly, tour operators contract airline seats or entire aircrafts. Tour operator may contract an aircraft for the whole season (a 'time charter') or for specified flights (a 'whole-plane charter') or may purchase blocks of seats on a scheduled service or a chartered airline (a 'part charter') (Wanhill,1993). Tour operators need to achieve a higher than 90 per cent utilization factor in order to break even, and this is perhaps their greatest risk (Fitch, 1987; Josephides, 1993, 1994a and b).

Price is probably the most important element of the package marketing mix as holidays have a high elasticity of demand and the high competition levels at their markets mean that often price wars emerge. Thus, price of service is central to negotiations, as tour operators attempt to minimize their costs by reducing supplier charges. By offering cheaper holidays to the market they hope to increase their market share and profitability. Should tour operators fail to achieve adequate capacity in a fashionable destination at the desired prices, they turn to less attractive areas, where they can find cheaper products (Allen, 1985).

Sheldon (1994) suggests that volume, past performance and the financial standing of the company determine the amount of discounts on rack rates achieved. Discounts can vary between 10 per cent (minimum travel agent discount) and over 50 per cent, depending on the demand for a particular year, attractiveness of the area, facilities offered, uniqueness of destination, period of year, and volume of business. Tour operators as wholesalers are able to negotiate discounts of up to 70 per cent off the normal tariff, especially in resorts dealing with large numbers of visitors (Buhalis, 1995, 2000b).

Packaging, marketing, promoting and executing inclusive tours

As soon as contracts are completed, the second phase, i.e. *tour marketing*, commences. The main marketing tool for tour operators is brochures, which include information for both tourism products and destinations. Brochure design is a very complicated and expensive process. The production costs are 2 to 5 per cent of the total tour price and a conversion rate of one booking to ten brochures is accepted as the industry norm. The cost of each brochure copy varies according to its size, quality of printing, number of printouts, etc., but an average of £1 per brochure is often quoted. A large percentage of brochures is wasted, even without having been looked at by any consumers as they get dated before reaching consumers (Gilbert and Houghton, 1991; Gilbert and Soni, 1991; Hodgson,1993).

The last phase is the *tour administration at a destination* and the post-experience service. Under the 1992 EU Package Directive, tour operators bear responsibility for the implementation of their programme and the services offered by the entire range of contributors to their product. Although specialized tour operators are more likely to offer escorted tours, whereby a tour manager accompanies holidaymakers throughout their journey, volume package tour operators employ a number of representatives to accompany tourists during their transfers and are available for certain periods for additional services. Representatives also promote excursions and social events organized by incoming travel agencies and/or tour operators, as well as supervise the appropriateness of the several products involved. In small destinations, tour operators representation is undertaken by local incoming travel agencies. *Post-experience services* include responses to compliments and complaints, as well as analysis of consumers' questionnaires (Wanhill, 1993). This feedback is instrumental in both the planning and marketing of package holidays, while it often determines whether a collaboration with a partner will continue for the following seasons.

Classification and types of tour operators

There are several ways to describe the type of tour operator, but there is a clear distinction between *large/mass* operators, covering a very wide range of destinations and tourism products, and *small/specialists* who normally provide holidays for few destinations and/or specialize in themed or activity holidays. In the UK, the former ones normally belong to the Federation of Tour Operators (FTO) and the Tour Operators' Study Group (TOSG), while the latter ones are often members of the Association of Independent Tour Operators (AITO). Tour operators can be categorized from very small to very large as demonstrated in Table 2.4. Smaller tour operators tend to concentrate on differentiation and value-added strategies, while the majority of large tour operators attempt to achieve cost advantage and thus, to increase their market share and turnover rather than their profit margin. Consequently, larger tour operators exercise their purchasing power to negotiate prices with tourism suppliers and pay less attention to service quality, while smaller ones are often more demanding on quality and the elements of the tourism product provided to the customer and are less persistent on prices (Sheldon,1986).

Table 2.4 Volume of tourists and tour operators' size

Size of tour operator	Volume of holidaymakers served yearly
Very small	0–999
Small	1,000–9,999
Medium	10,000–99,999
Large	100,000–999,999
Very large	More than 1,000,000

Moreover, the *geographical spread* of tour operators varies according to the country of origin and their size. Increasingly there is high horizontal integration in Europe and thus most of the larger British and German organizations operate throughout Europe (see Chapter 10).

Other criteria can be used to categorize tour operators in meaningful sizes, such as the ownership and strategic alliances, the decision-making processes, the number of destinations served, the financial performance and stability, as well as the professionalism of the enterprise.

TOUR OPERATORS' NEEDS, WANTS AND PROFITABILITY

Traditionally large/mass tour operators have concentrated their effort on increasing their sales volume, often at the expense of their profit margins. Attempting to be competitive in tour operating usually means to offer the minimum possible price and thus, their profitability is consistently marginal. Smaller operators tend to address niche markets and normally charge premium prices for specialized services. In addition, as tour operators' responsibilities for the delivery of the tourism product increase, due to new regulations and specifically the EU travel package directive (Atherton, 1994), they need more reliable producers to offer quality services consistently and fulfil their promises to consumers, while they attempt to minimize the risk on their operations emerging from exogenous factors, such as currency fluctuations or local conflicts.

Attempting to split down the *cost of a week package holiday* is a very difficult exercise, as different tour operators, from different countries, charge different prices and operate on a dissimilar cost structure (Monopolies and Mergers Commission, 1989). Both tour operators' characteristics and orientation, as well as operational practices in their market, determine the profit margins and mark-ups charged, while quality of holiday, distance from destination, demand and supply at a destination, efficiency and availability of fleet determine the associated costs. These factors are illustrated as holidays are often cheaper in certain countries of origin, such as the UK and the Scandinavian countries, where large/mass tour operators have accumulated strong bargaining power and therefore provide cheaper holidays for tourists. Josephides (1993) suggests that British holidaymakers are more price, rather than quality, conscious and thus enjoy lower prices than other Europeans. He claims that 'a recent TUI survey put the British, Finns and Danish at the bottom of a table illustrating per capita expenditure on package holidays – the Italians, Swiss and Austrians spending twice as much'. Moreover, Wanhill (1993) aggregates the price structure for a 14-night inclusive tour, by assessing each element in Table 2.5. As it can be observed, almost one-third of the cost of a holiday is spent on each of accommodation and transportation, while overheads are kept to a minimum. A minimal profit margin is achieved, mainly due to fierce competition in the marketplace.

Table 2.5   Tour operators' price structure for a typical two-week holiday. *Source*: Wanhill, 1993

Direct cost	%	Indirect costs	%	Net income	%
Accommodation	41	Payroll expenses	4	Trading profit	3
Air seats	35	Marketing	3	Interest on deposits	1
Transfers, excursions	2	Office expenses	2		
Travel agents' commission	10	*Total*	9		
Total	88				

Tour operators' financial performance and profitability

Acquiring financial information on the profitability of tour operators is enormously difficult, not only because few people can provide accurate numbers, but also because fierce competition in the marketplace makes this information strictly confidential. However, in the case of some large tour operators, published annual reports provide insights into their financial situation. Relatively low *profit margins* have been achieved by the 50 largest European and 30 top British tour operators. Fitch (1987) suggests that 'package tour operators in the UK, taken as a whole, tend to operate on a level of net profit which would be deemed unacceptable in most other industries'. Bywater (1992) claims for European tour operators that 'a net profit of 4–5% is regarded as excellent, 1–2% fairly widely regarded as normal'.

Interestingly, one of the vital contributors to tour operators' profit margin is the *interest received*. That represents one-fourth of the net income emerging from package holidays, or 1 per cent of a 14-night inclusive tour price. Analysis in Thomson's and Airtours' annual reports suggests that the latter figures may be an understatement. 'Net interest income' contributed the 8.6 per cent of Thomson's 'operating profit from continuing operations', while in 1992 it had a contribution of 19.17% (Thomson annual report in 1993). Similarly, Airtours' 'bank interest receivable' contributed the 26.6 per cent and 28.1 per cent of 'operating profit before abortive bid costs' in 1993 and 1992 respectively (Airtours annual report of 1993). However, assessing tour operators' *return on investment (ROI) or pre-tax return on net assets* demonstrates that the two tour operators achieve quite high ROI, in comparison with other industries. As little capital is required for tour operators' start-up and operation, they enjoy much higher returns than manufacturers, although this is to a certain extent justified by the higher risk involved in tour operations. Hence, it seems that the 'pile up and sell cheap' strategy provides excellent results for tour operators, and offers higher profitability than other economic activities, which require higher fixed financial commitments. In conclusion, despite fierce competition in the marketplace and the enormous discounting on consumer prices large tour operators manage to achieve good returns on their investments or capital employed. This is probably a result of offering very cheap holidays subsidised by great discounts from principals, as a result exercising their bargaining power. Thus, tour operators' shareholders are normally pleased with the financial results of their company and consumers are satisfied by the prices they pay. Smaller tour operators are not expected to be as profitable, due to their inability to exercise power within the tourism distribution channel and attract similarly high discounts. Consequently profitability differs significantly between different types of tour operators. Smaller tour operators find it increasingly more difficult to compete with their vertically integrated counterparts, who can offer much cheaper tourism packages and still be profitable. They claim that the three major tour operators in the UK formulate a monopolistic environment, jeopardizing the prosperity of the smaller ones (Allen, 1985; Monopolies and Mergers Commission, 1986 and 1989; Kirker, 1994).

Finally, although consumers enjoy the cheap prices they achieve, they start to realize that the quality of the services they receive suffers. Consequently, they complain about the inadequate and 'less than promised' service they have received during their holiday experience. Perhaps one of the biggest paradoxes currently in the tourism industry is that the UK's fastest growing holiday company, the profit-thriving Airtours, consistently achieves the worst satisfaction record and recommendation factor by its customers, in comparison with all other tour operators, and is described as the company achieving among the poorest ratings for accommodation, brochures, representatives and travel arrangements (*Holiday Which*, 1995).

Critical issues in tour operators' position in tourism distribution channels

Over the last 40 years, European tour operators achieved a dominant position in the European holiday tourism distribution channel. Their domination arose through their understanding of the market and perhaps even more importantly, through vertical integration, which enables them to achieve bargaining power, economies of scale and synergies, and therefore empowers them to offer reliable and cheap holidays for customers. The vertical integration and concentration of European tour operators restructures the tourism industry and affects the competitiveness of the entire industry. Tour operators often incorporate transportation, hospitality and entertainment organizations, which enables them to offer consistent services and reduce the profit margin of each sub-organization in order to maximize market share and to maximize the corporation's profitability. As Bywater analyses in Chapter 10, this concentration enables European tour operators to expand geographically to other countries, in order to increase their market share and their bargaining power on a European level. They increasingly become the nucleus of tourism distribution channels and therefore increase their bargaining power over their channel partners.

INCOMING TRAVEL AGENCIES (OR HANDLING AGENCIES OR INCOMING TOUR OPERATORS)

Incoming travel agencies (often referred to as incoming tour operators, 'ground operators', handling, receiving or inbound agents) are the least well-known members of the distribution channel. They are often omitted in the tourism distribution channel study and there is very little research undertaken in this area. Their major activities usually involve the planning and execution of tour packages on a destination level. They often act as intermediaries between tour operator and principals, while they represent tour operators for both tourists and local authorities. They normally cover hotel transfers, overnight accommodation, sightseeing and special arrangements and supervise the product delivery by the local suppliers (Gee *et al*, 1989). In contrast with Northern Europe, there is a vague distinction between incoming and outgoing travel agencies in the majority of the Southern European countries. Thus, it is very usual for travel agencies to serve both inbound and outbound travellers.

Incoming travel agencies' major function and role in the tourism distribution channel

It is quite difficult to describe precisely incoming travel agencies' operations, as there is great differentiation and flexibility between their activities. However, their functions can be divided into individual and travel trade services, according to the receiver of their services. Figure 2.4 displays several activities undertaken by incoming travel agencies. Perhaps the most accurate description for their operation is that they undertake all commissionable jobs at a destination. First, they bridge tour operators with destinations, by undertaking various responsibilities for their local representation. Normally, tour operators meet incoming travel agencies at international tourist exhibitions or in their first visit to a destination and commence a co-operation. An incoming travel agency is appointed as a tour operator's representative and assumes responsibilities in identification, negotiation, contract, reservation of appropriate tourism products at destinations. In addition local travel agencies are often required for the legal representation of tour operators at the destination. Nevertheless, when tour operators have a strong interest in a destination, they normally undertake the contracting function directly.

Tour operator
oriented
activities

- Bridge between tour operators and destinations
- Contact between tour operators and principals
- Negotiation of prices and contracts with principals and tour operators
- Dissemination of information material for destination
- Inspection of accommodation, catering, transportation and entertainment
- Arrange payment of local principles on behalf of tour operators
- Reservation of accommodation and services for tour operators
- Local handling and looking after tour operators' clients
- Transfers for tour operators' clients to and from accommodation
- Welcome meeting and presentation of destination
- Coach rental
- Provision of office facilities for tour operator's representatives
- Local complaint handling
- Legal representation of tour operator to local authorities
- Participation in international exhibitions

- Pre-purchase of accommodation and distribution
- Organization of entertainment, folklore nights
- Organization of special interests and activity holidays
- Sightseeing and excursion organizations

- Arrange Frequent Individual Travellers (FITs) packages
- Conference and meeting organization
- Individual reservation for accommodation
- Vehicle rental, e.g. cars, bike, boats
- Sightseeing/excursion/local performances ticketing
- Currency exchange
- Ancillary services
- Destination general information

- Outbound tourism services (mainly in Southern Europe)

Individual
tourist
oriented
activities

Figure 2.4   Major functions for incoming travel agencies

Classification and types of incoming travel agencies

There is no classification and typology of incoming travel agencies offered in the literature. However, several criteria can be utilized in order to classify them. The geographical coverage of a destination can classify incoming travel agencies into organizations covering from a small resort to an entire destination country. Closely related is the number of branches an agency operates at a destination, as they offer operational bases in several resorts. Naturally, the more branches, the larger the incoming travel agencies and vice versa. In addition, the number of employees, as well as the number of tour operators' representatives accommodated in an incoming travel agency's office can provide meaningful inferences for its size. Finally, the size and types of assets, such as coaches and accommodation establishments, would indicate the economic substance of a company. As far as the typology of incoming travel agencies is concerned, a vague distinction can be made between those operating exclusively with tour operators and those offering their services directly to the public. However, in most cases a combination of services and clientele is served. Number and firms of associated tour operators also demonstrate the size of operation an incoming travel agency is capable of handling, as well as its operational orientation. Finally, the associations where incoming travel agencies belong can also provide some insight into their operation. British incoming travel agencies are normally members of BITOA (British Incoming Tour Operators' Association). Typically, incoming travel agencies are very small enterprises, run by their proprietor on a local level. Instead of having a great geographical coverage themselves, they often formulate strategic partnerships with counterparts in other destinations in order to offer a comprehensive service to their clients.

Incoming travel agencies' needs and wants

Volume of business and higher margins are the major goals attempted for services provided directly to consumers. Moreover, as illustrated in Figure 2.3, incoming travel agencies' needs and wants are often closely related with their major customers' desires. Apart from reliable, loyal and economically stable partners, agencies which operate primarily with tour operators tend to have similar aims, i.e. high volume and low profit margins. Moreover, incoming travel agencies would prefer active tourists, who would join their excursions and rent vehicles, as they make the majority of their profit from these services. A combination of large and small tour operators, as well as a mixture of partners from different countries, would spread their risk, and enable a reaction to fluctuations in a particular market. Even more importantly, incoming travel agencies need prompt payments in order to pay back their suppliers and avoid conflicts.

As far as the *remuneration* and cost-benefit analysis of incoming travel agencies are concerned, there is no data on their breakdown, as cost and benefits vary greatly depending on their type and orientation. However, incoming travel agencies' major remuneration for services provided to tour operators includes *handling fees*, which are essentially a fixed fee per tourist arriving at a destination, and *transfer fees*, depending on the distance between port/airport and accommodation establishments, and the method of transportation. In addition, they often have the *exclusive right to organize excursions* at a destination for tour operators' customers, while they gain commission for other services required, such as ticketing and accommodation contracting. Similarly, with other intermediaries, there is a small barrier to entry for incoming travel agencies, while minor capital investment is required.

Critical issues in incoming travel agencies' position in the tourism distribution channel

Incoming travel agencies play a very crucial role in the tourism distribution channel, as they act as intermediaries between their local tourism industry and tour operators. They provide feedback to tour operators and enable them to comprehend the local business environment. Incoming travel agencies provide their in-depth knowledge and contacts at the destination level, and through their ability to identify suitable suppliers efficiently and quickly. In addition, they organize the logistics of travellers' local transfers and arrange entertainment and sightseeing based on tour operators' requirements. Speaking the same language with suppliers and understanding their culture better, they facilitate tour operators' contracting and operating functions. Incoming travel agencies *represent their destination* internationally, as they attend exhibitions and visit other tourism distribution channel members, attempting to persuade them to include a destination in their programme or increase the contribution of that destination.

CONCLUSIONS: THE TOURISM DISTRIBUTION CHANNEL IN A CONSTANT TRANSFORMATION

This chapter attempts an analysis of the nature, role, typologies, functions and major benefits for the main intermediaries in the tourism distribution channel, namely outgoing travel agencies, tour operators and incoming travel agencies. The great complexity of the travel trade and the dissimilarity of operational practices in different countries of origin and destinations makes it difficult to define and establish strategies, tactics, operation features, practices and functions that are used worldwide. As a consequence, this analysis illustrates that distribution channel members are fairly fluid in terms of their roles, interests, operations and perspectives. Each member of the tourism distribution channel aims at maximizing their profitability and is doing so by either identifying niche product and charging premium prices or by selling commodity/undifferentiated tourism product at a high volume but low profit margin. The strategic objectives of the channel members as well as the concentration in the marketplace and the challenges of information technology (Buhalis, 2000a and 2000c) will ensure that members of the tourism distribution channel will constantly seek opportunities for achieving their strategies.

REFERENCES

Allen, T. (1985) 'Marketing by a small tour operator in a market dominated by big operators'. *European Journal of Marketing*, **19**(5), 83–90.

Atherton, T. (1994) 'Package holidays: legal aspects'. *Tourism Management*, **15**(3), 193–9.

Beaver, A. (1993) *Mind Your Own Travel Business: A manual of retail travel practice.* Beaver Travel Publishers, UK.

Buhalis, D. (1995) 'The impact of information telecommunication technologies on tourism distribution channels: implications for the small and medium sized tourism enterprises' strategic management and marketing'. Guildford: University of Surrey PhD thesis, Department of Management Studies.

Buhalis, D. (1998) 'Strategic use of information technologies in the tourism industry'. *Tourism Management*, **19**(3), 409–23.

Buhalis, D. (2000a) 'Information technology in tourism: the state of the art'. *Tourism Recreation Research*, **25**(1), 41–58.

Buhalis, D. (2000b) 'Relationships in the distribution channel of tourism: conflicts between hoteliers and tour operators in the Mediterranean region'. *Journal of International Hospitality, Leisure and Tourism Administration*, **1**(1), 113–39.

Buhalis, D. (2000c) 'Information technology and tourism'. In W. Gartner and D. W. Lime (eds) *Trends in Outdoor Recreation, Leisure and Tourism.* CAB International, UK, pp. 47–63.

Bywater, M. (1992) *The European Tour Operator Industry.* Special report No. 2141. Economist Intelligence Unit, London.

Bywater, M. (1994) 'Who owns whom in the European travel trade'. *Travel and Tourism Analyst*, No. 3, pp. 73–92.

EC (1990) 'Council Directive of 13 June 1990 on package travel, package holidays and package tours (90/314/EEC)'. *Official Journal of the European Communities*, L 158/59, 23.6.90, pp. 59–64.

Fitch, A. (1987) 'Tour operators in the UK'. *Travel and Tourism Analyst*, No. 1, pp. 29–43.

Gee, C., Makens, J. and Choy, D. (1989) *The Travel Industry* (2nd edn). Van Nostrand Reinhold, New York.

Gilbert, D. and Houghton, P. (1991) 'An exploratory investigation of format, design and use of the UK tour operator brochures'. *Journal of Travel Research*, **30**(2), 20–5.

Gilbert, D. and Soni, S. (1991) 'UK tour operators and consumer perspectives'. *The Service Industries Journal*, **11**(4), 413–24.

Hodgson, P. (1993) 'Tour operator brochures design-research revisited'. *Journal of Travel Research*, **22**(1), 50–2.

Holiday Which (1995) *Which Tour Operator.* Consumers' Association, January, pp. 6–9.

Holloway, C. (1989) *The Business of Tourism* (3rd edn). Pitman, Plymouth.

Hoteline (1990a) 'A look at the European travel market'. *Hoteline*, Sept./Oct., **4**(5), Hotel and Travel Index, Red Travel Group, p. 1.

Josephides, N. (1993) *Environmental Concern – What's in it for the tourism industry.* Proceedings of the conference: Tourism and the environment: challenges and choices for the 1990s. 16–17 November 1992, Queen Elizabeth II Conference Centre, London, European Union, Brussels, pp. 51–6.

Josephides, N. (1994a) 'The real extent of trade naivety'. *Travel Weekly*, No. 1242, 16 November, p. 11.

Josephides, N. (1994b) 'Tour operators and the myth of self regulation'. *Tourism in Focus, Tourism Concern*, No. 14, Winter, pp. 10–11.

Keynote (1994) *Travel Agents and Overseas Tour Operators: A market sector overview* (10th edn). London.

Kirker, C. (1994) 'Independents will go on fighting despite OFT ruling'. *Travel Trade Gazette UK*, 17 August, No. 2123, p. 66.

Kotler, P. (1988) *Marketing Management: Analysis, planning and control* (6th edn). Prentice Hall International Editions, New Jersey.

Middleton, V. (1988) *Marketing in Travel and Tourism*. Heinemann, London.

Middleton, V. (1991) 'Whiter the package tour?' *Tourism Management*, **12**(3), 185–92.

Middleton, V. (1994) *Marketing in Travel and Tourism* (2nd edn). Butterworth-Heinemann, London.

Mill, P. and Morrison, A. (eds) (1985) *The Tourism System: An introductory text*. Prentice Hall International Editions, New Jersey.

Monopolies and Mergers Commission (1986) *Foreign Package Holidays*. Presented to Parliament by the Secretary of State for Trade and Industry, HMSO, London.

Monopolies and Mergers Commission (1989) *Thomson Travel Group and Horizon Travel Ltd: A report on the merger situation*. Presented to Parliament by the Secretary of State for Trade and Industry by Command of her Majesty, Cm554, HMSO, London.

Morrison, A. (1994a) *Small Tourism Business: Product distribution systems*. Proceedings of the conference of hospitality management education, Napier University, April, Edinburgh.

Renshaw, M. (1992) *The Travel Agent: Centre for travel and tourism*. Business Education Publishers, Sunderland.

Renshaw, M. (1994) 'Consequences of integration in UK tour operating'. *Tourism Management*, **15**(4), 243–5.

Sheldon, P. (1986) 'The tour operator industry: An analysis'. *Annals of Tourism Research*, **13**(3), 349–57.

Sheldon, P. (1994) 'Tour operators'. In S. Witt and L. Moutinho (eds) *Tourism Marketing and Management Handbook* (2nd edn). Prentice Hall International Editions, London, pp. 399–403.

Smith, C. and Jenner, P. (1994) 'Travel agents in Europe'. *Travel and Tourism Analyst*, No. 3, pp. 56–71.

Wanhill, S. (1993) 'Intermediaries'. In C. Cooper, J. Fletcher, D. Gilbert and S. Wanhill (eds) *Tourism: principles and practice*. Pitman, London, pp. 189–203.

World Tourism Organization (1975) *Distribution Channels*. World Tourism Organization, Madrid.

CHAPTER 3

Distribution channels for tourism: theory and issues

Dorota Ujma

INTRODUCTION

This chapter looks at distribution theories and synthesizes them with tourism industry practices. It consists of two main parts: the first deals with general theories applicable to the concept of distribution, and in the second theories are applied to tourism and illustrated by examples from the industry.

Distribution started to take over at the end of the twentieth century as one of the most important strategic dimensions for the competitiveness of tourism companies. Distribution was to some extent the underlying reason for the development of specific organizational forms in the tourism industry. The large corporate companies tend to use all possible ways of selling tourism products and services to ultimate customers. They sell their own packaged holidays via vertically integrated and independent travel agents; they sell their products directly on the telephone to the ultimate customers; and they are expanding the volume of sales made on the Internet. Each of those methods is catering for a different market segment and is managed under a different brand name. Different ways of distributing products through different channels, at the same time avoiding unnecessary conflicts and tensions, have been investigated for at least 30 years in various industries. It has been recognized as an important issue in the study of tourism.

DEFINITIONS OF MARKETING CHANNELS

Understanding consumer needs is particularly important in service industries' channels of distribution. Stern *et al.* (1996, p. 31) state that 'channels should be

Figure 3.1 Distribution channel structure

viewed as an orchestrated network that creates value for end-users by generating form, possession, time and place utilities'. This system consists of agencies which 'in combination, perform all the activities required to link producers with users to accomplish the marketing task' (Berman, 1996, p. 5). Christopher (1992, p. 129) states that the distribution channel can be characterized as 'a number of intermediaries acting independently of each other and often with conflicting objectives and requirements'. Fill (1995) notes that products flow through a variety of organizations, which co-ordinate their activities to make the offering available to end-users. Various organizations perform different roles in a chain of activity; they act as manufacturers, agents, distributors, etc. As demonstrated in Figure 3.1, each organization is a customer to the previous one and a supplier to a next one in an industry's value chain.

For these reasons it is not possible to have one definition of the marketing channel that can be acceptable to all viewpoints. In the context of managerial decision-making, Rosenbloom (1995, p. 5) defines the marketing channel as 'the external contractual organisation that management operates to achieve its distribution objectives'. It is external, because it exists outside the specific company – and it is more inter-organizational than intra-organizational. Contractual organizations are all those firms and parties engaged in the flows within the channel and responsible for negotiatory functions, consisting of buying, selling and transferring title to products or services. Usually these organizations are referred to as wholesalers and retailers, but various examples of definitions of channel players can be found in the literature.

Channel players have a number of tasks to perform. In order to do so they need to co-operate in an integrated and co-ordinated manner. The co-operation between different members can be defined, after Skinner *et al.* (1992, p. 176), as 'joint striving toward individual and mutual goals'. Stern (1969) suggests that the co-operating channel members become interdependent, because each member of a distribution channel is dependent upon the behaviour of other channel members. If any member changes its behaviour at any point, change will be caused throughout the whole channel. The fact that channel members are external to each other does not help to achieve co-ordination and co-operation. At the same time a distribution channel is an open system. It exists in and adapts to a changing external environment. It is not an easy task to co-ordinate 'a super-organisation comprised of interdependent institutions and agents' (Stern *et al.*, 1996, p. 281). Internal and external factors considerably influence the process of managing the channels of distribution.

ECONOMIC AND BEHAVIOURAL ASPECTS
IN CHANNELS RESEARCH

Stern and Reve (1980) state that channel theories were fragmented into two seemingly disparate disciplinary orientations: an economic and a behavioural approach. According to them these two orientations should be viewed as complementary, because the former deals with outputs obtained in some behavioural processes.

Economic aspects – understanding of channel emergence

Economic reasons are the foremost determinants of channel structures (Stern *et al.*, 1989). The emergence of the wide variety of intermediaries can be explained in terms of four logically related steps in an economic process:

1. intermediaries can increase the efficiency of the process of exchange,
2. they align the quantities and assortments produced with the quantities and assortments consumed,
3. they make transactions routine, and
4. they facilitate the searching process.

Table 3.1 Benefits and cost for using an intermediary in a product/service distribution. *Source*: Based on Christopher, 1992

Benefits for suppliers

- Wider coverage of the market
- Convenient points of sale for customers
- Lower selling/operating costs
- Wider product range
- Knowledge of the market
- Consideration of customer finance

Costs for suppliers

- Loss of margin (paid to intermediary)
- Loss of marketing control/power over the process
- Ultimate customer service beyond a supplier's control
- High priority given to intermediaries rather than customers

According to Christopher (1992), intermediaries bridge five gaps: the time, space, quantity, variety and communications-information gaps; in effect they reduce the transactional links between a manufacturer and clients. Potential benefits and costs for a manufacturer using intermediaries are shown in Table 3.1. Factors constraining effective communication between suppliers, for example destination managers, and their customers are: distance, time and information.

Coulson-Thomas (1992) notes that the selection of the most appropriate channel will depend on a number of factors, like the company strategy regarding marketing and distribution, customers, products and costs involved. The market is the major constraint – the type, number and distribution of customers, their purchasing power and patterns and the absolute level of sales will impact upon the choice of intermediaries.

Behavioural dimension of channels research

A marketing channel as a system requires purpose and direction, co-operation, conflict resolution and leadership. Research undertaken during the past three decades has enhanced our understanding of how companies can optimally organize and manage their channels of distribution. Gaining and exercising influence by channel partners and the behavioural reactions to it have been thoroughly examined. Some of the behavioural concepts like dependence, co-operation, power and conflict have an impact on channels of distribution and therefore will be introduced in the following paragraphs.

DEPENDENCE AND CO-OPERATION

Each member of a distribution channel is dependent upon the behaviour of other channel members. Four different approaches have been used to assess dependence levels in channel relationships:

1. The 'sales and profit' approach (El-Ansary and Stern, 1972), which postulates that the larger the percentage of sales and profit contributed by the source firm to the target firm, the greater the target's dependence on the source.
2. The 'role performance' approach (Frazier, 1983), which assesses a firm's role performance in carrying out its role in relation to another company down or up the channel.
3. The 'specific assets – offsetting investment' approach (Heide and John, 1988), which maintains that offsetting investments help to safeguard the target company against opportunism by the source.
4. The 'trust' approach (Moorman et al., 1993; Ganesan, 1994), in which a long-term relationship is built on the extent to which companies trust one another.

According to Emerson (1962, cited in Stern et al., 1996) the dependence of an agent B on the principal A is:

1. directly proportional to B's motivational investment in goals mediated and controlled by A, and
2. inversely proportional to the availability of those goals to B outside the A–B relationship (see Figure 3.2).

The more time and effort the agent B invests in training on a tour operator A's products, the more it becomes dependent upon A. When more tour operators offer similar training for their products and the agent B sees the possibility of selling their products along with A's products, the dependence of the agent on the first tour operator will be reduced. Channel members do not incline naturally toward co-ordinated behaviour, but if the network is to function effectively, co-operation between members is very important. Interdependence, specialization and expertise should be encouraged. Interdependence, however, is rarely distributed in a uniform and equitable way and this inequality is a major source of power (Fill, 1995).

Frazier (1999) advocates that it is better for the relationship if each firm in a channel possesses a high level of dependence. In such cases, each firm enjoys a high level of power and the bonds between the firms tend to be strong, promoting trust and commitment because of the common interests, attention and support. The symmetry in dependence does not necessarily mean that the relationship will be functional. Channel power is a factor in altering actions by channel members to induce a more co-ordinated outcome.

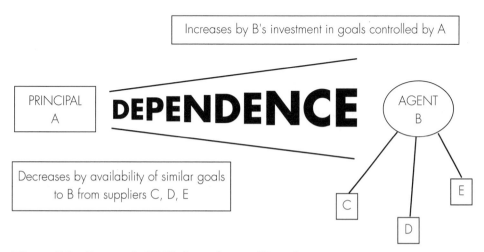

Figure 3.2   Emerson's (1962) dependence of B on A

POWER AND LEADERSHIP

There is a connection between the concept of control, influence and power. Stern *et al.* (1996) define power as 'the ability of one channel member to get another channel member to do what it otherwise would not have done', while Rosenbloom (1995) defines power as 'the capacity of a particular channel member to control or influence the behaviour of another channel member'. However, according to Frazier (1999), confusion still exists among the power, communication and control constructs in both a conceptual and an operational sense. Power is often said to have negative effects on channel relationships, especially by those researchers who concentrate on relationship marketing. In fact, the current trend is to avoid using the term 'power' altogether and focus instead on replaceability, dependence or interdependence.

Marketing channel management deals with the choice and control of channel players. Control of them may be gained by implementing and exercising power within the channel. French and Raven (1958) introduce a concept of 'bases' of power. Although they originally dealt with leadership issues in organizations, their typology was extended to distribution channels. Those 'bases' are sources of gaining power over channel players. They name them as rewards, coercion, expertness, reference and legitimacy. A firm may possess power because of the rewards it can bestow and the punishment it is capable of dealing out, owing to its special knowledge in a given area or the desire of others to identify with it or its position in a hierarchy. The types of power are sometimes divided into two groups: a coercive power source, and non-coercive power sources. The second group contains all the rest of the categories but coercion, because all involve a willingness to yield to the power of another organization due to the rewards offered.

The power of channel members is determined by a number of factors. Certain factors, when possessed by a channel member, *indicate* that this channel member has a potential basis for modifying the behaviour of another channel member. However, these factors do not *guarantee* that a channel member can exert influence (Wilemon, 1972). The factors are:

- brand ownership and the demand characteristics of a channel member's products and services
- a channel member's role within its channel
- ownership control over other channel members
- contractual agreements between the members of a channel (franchising, alliances and agreements)
- the financial strength of a channel member.

Power exists in many forms. Its form may contain the important descriptive characteristic of a channel member at a point in time. By investing in power sources the channel member increases its ability to affect channel behaviour and outcomes (Stern *et al.*, 1996). A channel leader is the institution which formulates marketing policies for other channel members and therefore controls their marketing decisions (Stern *et al.*, 1989). In the absence of a channel leader the administration of a channel becomes dependent on the price mechanism of intermediary markets through which co-operation of the different channel members is secured. The channel leader may gain access to power sources because of the specific characteristics, experience or history of its firm and its management (Etgar, 1977). The leader, however, must exercise its power carefully to avoid producing a degree of conflict, which could disrupt channel performance. From the channel members' point of view, it is much more productive and efficient if there is a channel leader and channel management is not left to market-led economic forces.

CONFLICT

Conflict is built into the channels because of a network of interdependence with conflicting interests and benefits. Conflict can be defined as a situation in which one channel member perceives another channel member to be engaged in behaviour that prevents or impedes it from achieving its goals (Stern *et al.*, 1996). As conflict quite often represents a deterioration in the levels of co-operation between partners, communication is an important co-ordinating mechanism for all members of the network. Lucas and Gresham (1985) list the causes of conflict and cluster them under the following groupings: goal incongruity, questions regarding domain, differences in perceptions and problems in communication. Conflict can have positive or negative effects on productivity; both too much and too little conflict can make an organization dysfunctional. However, conflict can have positive effects as well, as it is often the main motivation for change. Communication absence or failure will inevitably lead to unco-ordinated behaviour and to actions which are not in the best interests of the network. Fill (1995) proposes that by recognizing and understanding the bases of power and the levels of co-operation and form of the relationships between members, the communication pattern, frequency and style can be adjusted to complement the prevailing conditions.

Tourism distribution issues

Tourism consists of a relatively small number of large suppliers and a relatively large number of small suppliers (Go, 1993). As recognized by Wilson and Crotts (1995) buyer–seller relationships in the travel trade are complex, given the nature of the tourism product (specifically package tours). A tourism distribution channel is defined as 'an operating structure, system or linkage of various combinations of travel organizations through which a producer of travel products describes and confirms travel arrangements to the buyer' (Mill and Morrison, 1992). It is so much easier for a customer to contact a travel agent and purchase a holiday than to contact all the potential suppliers of the sub-components of the package. Travel retailers help bridge distance, time and information gaps by outlets located in the customer's vicinity, providing facilities for advanced reservations and providing comprehensive information (Laws, 1997).

Differences between channels in manufacturing industries and in tourism

Distribution concepts were initially established in order to optimize the physical movement of commodities, which should reach the customer at the right time, in the right place and on the right terms. The intangible tourism service cannot be physically displayed or inspected at the point of sale. It is bought before the time of its use and away from the destination, because the destination is simply a place of consumption. This makes tourism dependent upon representations and descriptions in printed or audio-visual forms, and therefore information is the cement that holds together producers within the travel industry (Poon, 1994). The links between and among tourism producers and consumers are provided by the flow of information.

The main differences between marketing channels in the travel and tourism industry and other industries concern the directions of different flows apparent in the channels. A flow is defined by Stern *et al.* (1996, p. 10) as 'a set of functions performed in sequence by channel members'. There are eight universal flows which include physical possession, ownership, promotion (usually forward flows) negotiations, financing, risking (both directions), ordering and payment (usually backward flows) (Figure 3.3). The ideas of product flow, ownership flow and title transfer are not always obvious or applicable to services marketing, where there is often little tangible evidence of ownership or title removing much of the conventional concept of 'a channel of distribution'. In a service industry the flows are movements of information and clients rather than the items sold.

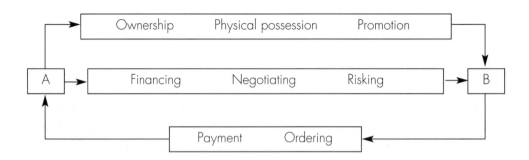

Figure 3.3   Eight flows in the channels of distribution

Distribution channels in tourism

Tourism marketing channels are defined in a simplified way, when compared to general definitions of channels, but they can be, in fact, even more complicated than in manufacturing industries. Medlik (1996, p. 84) describes the ways in which channels might be organized: 'in travel and tourism providers of tourism attractions, facilities and services may sell direct to consumers or use one or more intermediaries (such as tour operators and travel agents). Most large producers use a combination of distribution channels for their products and this combination is described as the distribution mix.' Middleton (1995) emphasizes that channels are 'organized and serviced systems created to provide convenient access to consumers, away from the location of production and consumption and paid for out of marketing budgets'. Woodruffe (1995) refers to the concept of the 'place' element of the marketing mix, which in tourism is concerned chiefly with two main issues: accessibility and availability. 'Place' does not mean only the location of a tourist attraction or facility. As illustrated in Figure 3.4, it is the location of all points of sale that provide customers with access to tourist products.

The travel distribution system consists of tourists, suppliers and three main types of intermediaries: tour operators, retail travel agents and so called 'speciality channellers'. The last group is sometimes referred to as a support network and includes incentive travel firms, meeting and convention planners, hotel representatives, association executives, corporate travel offices, etc. (Bitner and Booms, 1982; Fill, 1995). The division for travel agents, tour operators and principals/suppliers is a general one, because the number of tourism channel players is much larger. The examples of some of the channel players quoted in the literature are shown in Table 3.2.

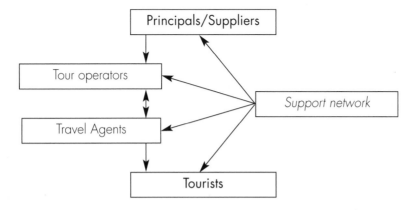

Figure 3.4   Tourism distribution channel

The EC Directive on Package Travel (1990) uses the terms 'organizers' and 'retailers' instead of travel agents and tour operators, which acknowledges the lack of EU-wide agreement on the meaning of these two latter terms. The term 'organizer' is defined as a person who organizes packages, and offers them for sale, whether directly or through a retailer. The 'retailer', an equivalent to a travel agent, is defined as a person who sells or offers for sale the package put together by the organizer (Downes, 1996, pp. 69–87). There is no agreement about the difference between the range of services provided by the supplier, tour operator and travel agent, and the extent to which a tour operator is a wholesaler for the tourism product or a supplier. The terminology confusion can be also found in the USA and Australia where these terms have different usage and meanings.

The traditional tourism distribution channel consisted of small, independent retailers whose objectives were to maximize their own profits. In time these retailers started to specialize and a group of tour operators emerged as well. Further specialization changed the pattern of tourism channels and induced both vertical and horizontal integration. 'Some of the most familiar travel retailers are . . . owned by large tour operators, with the result that the organisation is in effect an integrated business system' (Laws, 1997, p. 120). These processes are connected with the organizational and ownership patterns in the channels.

A tourism distribution chain begins with a principal. The principal is a supplier of a service in the tourism industry and provides the basic travel products, the 'core' product (Renshaw, 1992, pp. 2–3). Destinations are often omitted from the description of a distribution chain, although they represent principals, tourism and local authorities and create a vital element on the supply side. Medlik (1996, p. 201) narrows the group of 'principals' down only to those companies which sell their products through retail travel agents. He adds tour operators to the group of principals, arguing that a tour operator gives authority to an agent who may then act and represent him and sell his product. Medlik argues that a tour operator creates a new product and thus is, in fact, a manufacturer of travel products with a role in some ways similar to that of a bulk-breaker in wholesale goods distribution. Renshaw (1992) drew attention to another difference between tour operators and wholesalers: tour operators sell individual units to individual members of the public, not in bulk, and they take the risk. A travel agency is usually described as an organization selling travel and ancillary services on behalf of principals for a commission. The main functions of travel agents are those of a retailer – to provide access to the market for a principal and to provide a location for the customer to buy travel services – but there are also differences between a travel agent and a 'regular' retailer. Travel agents carry no stock, except brochures, and never actually purchase the product and therefore bear limited financial risk. So far agents receive commission on sales and are therefore compared to insurance brokers or estate agents. However, it is generally accepted in the industry that the travel agent is a retailer.

Table 3.2   Channel players in tourism

Principals

Suppliers of a service in travel and tourism industry, provide the basic travel products, the 'core' product, such as transport, accommodation and amenities. 'Principal' means first in rank of importance: without them there would be no further organizations down the chain of distribution (Renshaw, 1992, pp. 2–3)

They give authority to an agent who may then act for or represent the principal. In travel and tourism hotels, transport operators and tour operators are principals when they sell their products through retail travel agents (Medlik, 1996, p. 201)

Tour operators

Organizations which buy individual travel services (such as transport and accommodation) from their providers (such as carriers and hotels) and combine them into a package of travel, the tour, which is sold with a mark-up to the public directly, or through intermediaries (Medlik, 1996, p. 250)

Assemblers of brought-in parts who produce the holiday package. They plan, organize, finance and sell the complete holiday package, which includes transport, accommodation and food (Renshaw, 1992, p. 4)

Travel agent

Organization selling travel services on behalf of principals for a commission. Most travel agents also normally provide ancillary services, such as obtaining passports and visas, travellers' cheques, currencies and travel insurance. The main functions of the travel agent are those of a retailer – to provide access for a principal to the market and to provide a location for the customer to buy travel services (Medlik, 1996, p. 259)

Full-service travel agents

Traditional agents who sell all travel, accommodation and related services such as travel insurance, enabling clients to create independent 'packages'

Holiday shops

Catalogue sales outlets for the tour operators who have already pre-selected and packaged a range of holidays (Laws, 1997, p. 116)

ORGANIZERS

RETAILERS

Organizational patterns in the tourism channels

Recent rapid economic, social and political change providing powerful incentives for tourism interests to recognize their interdependencies and to engage in joint decision-making generated inter-organizational alliances. Collaboration is essential for multinational firms, tourism coalitions or co-operative marketing strategies. Hankeland (1995) draws attention to the fact that although collaboration among participants is essential, such collaboration networks may be affected by opposing interests among the participants. One conspicuous feature of the travel industry is that the network structure is highly changeable. In addition, the industry is fiercely competitive on price and therefore all members of the channel compete to increase their share from the distribution cost. The cost needs to remain minimal to ensure the competitiveness of the product (Buhalis, 1995).

The importance of stable personal ties is considered to be decisive in maintaining well-functioning collaborative relationships. The basis for confidence in the relationship is gained by personal contact with collaborating partners in the first place, then educationals (trips organized for travel agencies' staff at destinations), good reputation among customers and good quality brochures (Hankeland, 1995). The tour wholesaler builds a network of relationships among functionally specialized firms to produce a synergistic product. It is not sufficient to simply contract inputs from facilities and services at prearranged times to create a satisfactory experience for consumers. The attitude and style in which each organization renders its services is also important (Smith, 1994).

Some vertically integrated travel organizations act as one unit. Although different parts of them are located at different levels of distribution and, in theory, following the Monopolies and Mergers Commission investigation, they should act independently, they still belong to one entity. Thomson probably is the most obvious tourism example. In terms of forward integration the most important link for selling its product is via an intra-organizational distribution line, i.e. its own retail outlets (Lunn Poly) and through a direct-sell tour operator (Portland). However, Thomson uses independent travel agents as well, thus employing inter-organizational links. In terms of backward integration, Thomson is notable for integration on the supply side too.

In the 1990s direct channels became more and more popular, as information technology facilitated the process of 'streamlining of the distribution chain' (Hoffman, 1994). In those channels consumers tend to contact the suppliers of tourism products directly. There are also tour operators selling their products directly to the public, omitting travel agents. Tourists use direct channels more as they become more knowledgeable. Agents are increasingly being left behind the skilled consumers who are able to invest more heavily in specialized product-knowledge acquisition (Richards, 1995). Such consumers increasingly turn to direct product suppliers and package their own travel product, bypassing the travel agent. Usually there is no charge to the customer for using travel agent's services. This

Table 3.3 Approaches to assess dependence levels in tourism distribution channel relationships

The 'sales and profit' approach

The more holidays of a specific tour operator sold by a travel agent, the more reliant the agent will be on the tour operator. To a lesser extent the converse applies to a tour operator. If it has one agent, who sells most of its products – the operator will rely on that channel partner. If a tour operator relies mainly on a travel agencies network, especially if there is one big chain selling most of that tour operator's products, it makes him reliant on this specific network. The agency, knowing that, can put pressure on the tour operator and demand better terms of payment, etc.

El-Ansary and Stern, 1972

The 'role performance' approach

The agent will start selling more products of the tour operator that co-operates and communicates more often and more efficiently, as well as being helpful and supportive.

Frazier, 1983

The 'specific assets – offsetting investment' approach

If an agent invests in an IT system which helps to sell not only a specific tour operator's products, but also other tour operators', then the tour operator knows that the agent may switch to other suppliers easily, if the relationship is not beneficial. Therefore it will, in theory, try to maintain the relationship on a healthy level.

Heide and John, 1988

The 'trust' approach

When a relationship of trust is established between a retailer and a tour operator, deposits paid by a travel agent to a tour operator may be reduced or cancelled. Sometimes credit services can be offered by partners too.

Moorman et al., 1993; Ganesan, 1994

situation could change in the future, which could further increase the numbers of independent tourists 'going direct' rather than through a retailer. Some of the tourism associations have suggested of late that agents should introduce fees for customers, because relying only on commission provided by tour operators makes travel agents vulnerable and leaves them in a weak negotiating position.

Dependence and co-operation, power and leadership and conflict in tourism channels

Tourism is a combination of service industries including transportation services, accommodation, attractions, food service, travel distributors and tourism promoters. There is no physical movement of commodities, but rather a movement of tourists, who go to the destinations (Gartner and Bachri, 1994). Each segment of the tourism industry is dependent on the others for success, therefore dependence is 'written into' tourism. The concepts of dependence, co-operation, power and conflict are thus highly relevant in tourism. In the context of tourism the intermediaries react violently when airlines or larger tour operators decide to decrease the level of average commission for travel agents for sale of airline tickets or package holidays. They try to fight back – and *conflict* occurs whenever the interests of a channel member are challenged. Table 3.3 illustrates how the generic approaches to assess *dependence* levels in channel relationships apply to tourism.

Power and leadership in the tourism distribution channel

In most industries the supplier or producer has decisive control over the product, pricing, quality and distribution. Travel and tourism principals are the exception: travel intermediaries have far greater power to influence and direct consumer demand compared to other industries. 'Unlike other products which flow from producer to consumer, tourists flow to the product. This inverted distribution system relies on intermediaries to perform much more than simple delivery services' (Gartner and Bachri, 1994). The balance of power in tourism distribution channels is sometimes perceived as the relationship between demand and supply (Mill and Morrison, 1992). It changes while the balance between those two variables changes. The tour operator might have had the power, for example, in the early stages of destination development. At this point destinations and other suppliers may be more willing to make concessions to a wholesaler who will actively promote a new destination to a mass market. Once the destination gains in popularity, the tour operators' influence is reduced and they may even be excluded. Similarly Konieczna-Domanska (1994) argues that the relationship of power and dependency between principals and travel agents gives the latter group the opportunity of demanding special terms, conditions and standards connected with the quality of tourism products. However, sometimes when competition between intermediaries in the market is high, tour operators and travel agents are dependent upon suppliers.

When demand is larger than supply, principals are more powerful than anybody else in the tourism chain, while in the opposite case travel agents and tour operators are more powerful in the chain.

The location of power in tourism channels of distribution changes over time. From the supply perspective it is possible to forecast which principals are going to be more powerful by looking at the tourist area life cycle. The evolution of tourism is closely linked to the evolution of destinations (Cooper *et al.*, 1993). Buhalis (1995, 2000) has demonstrated the role of tour operators in packaging and managing tourism products often at the expense of destinations and suppliers. His research undertaken in Greece demonstrates that Mediterranean hoteliers find the power of tour operators from Northern European countries very challenging, as tour operators increasingly reduce their profit margins and force them to reduce quality standards in order to fuel their price-driven competition in the markets.

Gartner and Bachri (1994) noted the connection between the importance of different groups of channel players in terms of their power in developed and developing countries. On the basis of an Indonesian case study, they concluded that a tour operator will have more influence in the travel decision the greater the distance of visitor origin to destination, because tour operators are often the first and most influential link in the tourist flow chain. The dependence of developing countries on foreign tour operators derives fundamentally from the expertise of these operators as producers and wholesalers of tourism-related services, their knowledge of the market – particularly international – and their access to the relevant complimentary services. Tourists depend on tour operators as sources of presumably expert information about product quality and consumption expectations. Tour operators are accepted as specialists in the areas of marketing, public relations and management because of their skill in linking a country's destinations to the traveller and their awareness of the power of information. It is clear that this gives them a future negotiating advantage.

Nowadays tour operators are generally perceived as the most influential group within the channel of tourism distribution. Their position between the supply side, represented by principals, and the demand side, represented by travel retailers and consumers, gives them the advantage over these two groups. Some of their key techniques, giving them advantage over other channel players, are (Buhalis, 2000):

- Timing contract negotiations to coincide with periods of low occupancy
- Using customer satisfaction surveys to their advantage
- Directing tourists to particular properties
- Making the sale of unused rooms difficult for hoteliers
- Altering the image of destinations and properties
- Playing hotels against each other
- Oligopsony (few buyers).

The aforementioned examples give the tour operators enhanced power over hoteliers and other groups of suppliers. According to Wilemon (1972), channel members' power can also be gained due to the following characteristics:

- *Brand ownership*
  Orient Express will have power over channel intermediaries owing to its uniqueness. Even the big tour operators are aware of this factor.
- *A channel member's role within its channel*
  Some tour operators manage their channels, directing their agencies towards potential, profitable markets. They create the list of agents' customers on the basis of data obtained from agents and then direct their retailers towards the most beneficial market segments. Unfortunately this is a rather unusual practice, suggesting a very good relationship in the channel.
- *Ownership control over other channel members*
  The best example for ownership control is a hard vertical integration, where businesses from different levels of distribution unite to control various stages of production (supply side) and sales (demand side). Large operators not only buy hotels and other accommodation establishments in holiday destinations and resorts, and airlines to control transport and accommodation, but also establish or buy travel agencies or direct-sell operators to stay in touch with tourists as well.
- *Contractual agreements between the members of a channel* (franchising, alliances and agreements between travel companies from different sectors of tourism create a form of soft vertical integration, giving them advantages of ownership, but with much lower costs).
- *The greater the financial strength of a channel member the more likely is the possibility of becoming a channel leader.*

The covert nature of some aspects of the travel trade makes it difficult to find out how the tourism system is operating, where most influence is being exerted, and what likely outcomes may result. Insider knowledge would be required, depending on a wide network of relationships and sources of information (Doswell, 1997, p. 76). However, there is no substitute for the analysis of the dynamics of power and its structure in an industry to reach plausible conclusions about who controls the marketing channel. The ultimate answer as to who should lead a channel must be left to an empirical analysis of power and the relevant payoffs from its use on a case-by-case basis (Stern *et al.*, 1989; Bywater, 1992).

THE FUTURE OF CHANNEL INTERMEDIARIES

New trends emerging in the tourism environment are changing the process of value creation in the tourism industry. This change influences the relative position of different players in the industry. Laws (1997) argues that a factor distorting the operation of channels is that a dominant member, usually a major tour operator, can offer extra inducements beyond what is a normal business practice, to entice retailers (or their staff) to sell particular holiday brands. These inducements may be extra incentives and volume performance targets. The key information-exchange role of the retailer has been a primary factor in shifting the balance of power in the chain of distribution away from the manufacturer to the retailer in most European markets. The role of experiential information, provided in 'educationals' or 'familiarization trips' for agency staff, is important in making product choices and that role makes them essential for the consumer. Some commentators say that players closer to consumers will gain, others pinpoint the companies that can most efficiently control the production and distribution of the industry's information.

Back in 1982 Bittner and Booms saw travel agents as being endangered. They predicted that travel agents' roles would change because more competition would be prevalent in the industry. This new competition would be coming from new technology, new banking systems, diversification and strong consolidation in the tourist market. They suggested that travel agents should have invested in their use of marketing techniques, knowing their clients, product line analysis, use of information systems, knowledge of travel destination and suppliers, and how to interact and negotiate successfully with them.

In the mid-1990s the concept of diagonal integration was introduced as 'a process by which firms use information technology to logically combine services (e.g. financial and travel services) for best productivity and most profits' (Poon, 1994, p. 216). As a result travel agents, airlines and suppliers on site were all expected to increase their influence within the industry, while the role of tour operators was expected to decline (Bennett, 1995). Owing to the information technology development the three aforementioned groups of channel players would be able to replace the tour operators by user-friendly computer systems, linking together principals and retailers and thus performing the tour operators' role.

There is an increasing concentration of power in the hands of fewer large tour operators. However, as tourism diversifies, there are large numbers of agencies dealing with the more specialized types of tourism. Vertical integration is increasingly common, with the same companies controlling tour operators, retail agencies, airlines and hotels. Larger tour operators have acquired their own chains of retail agencies, securing their distribution system and, naturally, the sale of their own 'in-house' packages. Travel agents are being encouraged and offered incentives to give loyalty to one of the major players. Thomson introduced a 'preferred agent' scheme, Airtours – a 'partners in profit' scheme (Reynolds, 1999). Smaller agencies, gathered in associations like Advantage Travel Centres and ARTAC Worldchoice, decided to align with Airtours and Thomas Cook respectively. First Choice, the only big tour operator without its own retail chain, started to invest in retail chains. Some of their retailers differ from the high street travel outlets, as they offer entertainment while the process of travel product selection is taking place. Consolidation processes have speeded up. From a British perspective the four major players (Thomson, Airtours, Thomas Cook and First Choice) have entered the 'acquisition trail' (Reynolds, 1999) and are now responsible for 80 per cent of package holidays, 66 per cent of flying and over 50 per cent of retail distribution. The industry is highly dependent on technological change and therefore as volatile as ever, particularly as it enters more regional and global concentration stages.

However, specialized tour operators and travel agents are likely to survive in the market. Anderson and Weitz (1989) argue that balanced power relationships imply greater stability and in order to avoid conflict, channel members should regularly monitor the performance and satisfaction levels of all channel members. Here communication is a critical element in maintaining a healthy relationship. The development of a stable and harmonious relationship between travel agent and tour operator can cement the links between both parties and secure their future by delivering best possible products and services on the basis of mutual efforts. It does not solve the problem for destinations and principals in them, although thanks to information technology they may be able to get in touch with their ultimate customers. Atherton (1994) implied that there will be more and more use of audio-visual and computerized marketing tools which present more accurate and timely information on which to build expectation of enjoyment. Some think that 'virtual reality' technology may replace not only travel agents and tour operators, but also the tourist and entertainment industry, in which case the whole discussion on who is going to lead the channels or survive becomes pointless.

REFERENCES

Anderson, E. and Weitz, B. (1989) 'Determinants of continuity in conventional industrial channel dyads'. *Marketing Science*, **8**(4), 310–23.
Atherton, T. (1994) 'Package holidays: legal aspects'. *Tourism Management*, **15**(3), 193–9.
Bennett, M. (1995) 'The consumer marketing revolution: the impact of IT on tourism'. *Journal of Vacation Marketing*, **1**(4), 376–82.
Berman, B. (1996) *Marketing Channels*. John Wiley & Sons, Cheltenham.
Bitner, M. and Booms, B. (1982) 'Trends in travel and tourism marketing: the changing structure of distribution channels'. *Journal of Travel Research*, **20**(4), 39–44.
Buhalis, D. (1995) 'The impact of information telecommunications technologies on tourism distribution channels: implications for the small and medium-sized tourism enterprises' strategic management and marketing'. Guilford: University of Surrey, PhD thesis, Department of Management Studies.
Buhalis, D. (2000) 'Relationships in the distribution channel of tourism: conflicts between hoteliers and tour operators in the Mediterranean Region'. *International Journal of Hospitality and Tourism Administration*, **1**(1), 113–39.
Buhalis, D. and Cooper, C. (1998) 'Competition or co-operation? Small and medium sized tourism enterprises at the destination'. In E. Laws, B. Faulkner and G. Moscardo (eds) *Embracing and Managing Change in Tourism: International case studies*. Routledge, London, pp. 324–46.

Buhalis, D. (1999) 'Limits of tourism development in peripheral destinations: problems and challenges'. *Tourism Management*, **20**(1), 183–5.

Bywater, M. (1992) *The European Tour Operator Industry*. Economist Intelligence Unit, London.

Christopher, M. (1992) *The Strategy of Distribution Management*. Butterworth-Heinemann, Oxford.

Cooper, C., Fletcher, J., Gilbert, D. and Wanhill, S. (1993) *Tourism Principles and Practice*. Pitman, London.

Coulson-Thomas, C. J. (1992) *Marketing Communications*. Butterworth-Heinemann, Oxford.

EC Directive on Package Travel, Package Holidays and Package Tours (1990) Council Directive (90/314/EEC): *Official Journal of the European Communities*, L 158/59, 23/6/90, pp. 59–64.

Doswell, R. (1997) *Tourism: How Effective Management Makes the Difference*. Butterworth-Heinemann, Oxford.

Downes, J. (1996) 'The package travel directive: implications for organisers and suppliers'. *Travel & Tourism Analyst*, **1**, 78–92.

El-Ansary, A. and Stern, L. (1972) 'Power measurement in the distribution channel'. *Journal of Marketing Research*, **9**(1), 47–52.

Emerson, R. (1962) 'Power-dependence relations'. *American Sociological Review*, 27 February, pp. 32–3.

Etgar, M. (1977) 'Channel environment and channel leadership'. *Journal of Marketing Research*, **14**(2), 69–76.

Fill, C. (1995) *Marketing Communications: Frameworks, Theories And Applications*. Prentice Hall, London.

Frazier, G. (1983) 'On the measurement of interfirm power in channels of distribution'. *Journal of Marketing Research*, **20** (May), 158–66.

Frazier, G. (1999) 'Organizing and managing channels of distribution'. *Academy of Marketing Science Journal*, **27**(2), 226–40.

Frazier, G. and Summers, J. (1984) 'Interfirm influence strategies and their application within distribution channels'. *Journal of Marketing*, **48** (Summer), 43–55.

French, J. and Raven, B. (1958) 'The bases of social power'. In D. Cartwright (ed.) *Studies in Social Power*. Institute for Social Research, Ann Arbour, University of Michigan.

Ganesan, S. (1994) 'Determinants of long-term orientation in buyer–seller relationships'. *Journal of Marketing*, **58** (April), 1–19.

Gartner, W. and Bachri, T. (1994) 'Tour operators' role in the tourism distribution system: an Indonesian case study'. *Journal of International Consumer Marketing*, **6**(3/4), 161–79.

Go, F. (1993) 'Competing & co-operating in the changing tourism channel system'. *Journal of Travel & Tourism*, **2**(23), 229–43.

Hankeland, J. (1995) 'Tourism marketing through the distribution channel'. *The Tourism Review*, **2**, 18–24.

Heide, J. and John, G. (1988) 'The role of dependence balancing in safeguarding transaction-specific assets in conventional channels'. *Journal of Marketing*, **52** (January), 20–35.

Hoffman, J. D. (1994) 'Emerging technologies and their impact on travel distribution'. *Journal of Vacation Marketing*, **1**(1), 95–103.

Konieczna-Domanska, A. (1994) Uslugi posrednictwa i organizacji w rozwoju rynku turystycznego. Monografie i Opracowania, Oficyna Wydawnicza Szkoly Glownej Handlowej, Warszawa (The Intermediary and Organization Services in the Development of Travel and Tourism Market).

Laws, E. (1997) *Managing Packaged Tourism: relationships, responsibilities and service quality in the inclusive holiday industry*. International Thomson Business Press, London.

Lucas, G. and Gresham, L. (1985) 'Power, conflict, control, and the application of contingency theory in marketing channels'. *Journal of the Academy of Marketing Science*, **13**(3), 25–38.

Medlik, S. (1996) *Dictionary of Travel, Tourism and Hospitality* (2nd edn). Butterworth-Heinemann, Oxford.

Middleton, V. (1995) *Marketing in Travel and Tourism* (2nd edn). Butterworth-Heinemann, Oxford.

Mill, R. and Morrison, A. (1992) *The Tourism System – An Introductory Text*. Prentice Hall International Editions, Englewood Cliffs, New Jersey.

Moorman, C., Zaltman, G. and Deshpande, R. (1993) 'Factors affecting trust in marketing research relationships'. *Journal of Marketing*, **57** (January), 81–101.

Poon, A. (1994) *Tourism, Technology and Competitive Strategies*. CAB, UK.

Renshaw, B. (1992) *The Travel Agent*. Centre for Travel and Tourism Business Education Publishers, Sunderland.

Reynolds, I. (1999) 'The changing face of the UK travel industry'. *Journal of Vacation Marketing*, **6**(1), 5–7.

Richards, G. (1995) 'Retailing travel products: bridging the information gap'. *Progress in Tourism and Hospitality Research*, **1**(1), 17–30.

Rosenbloom, B. (1995) *Marketing Channels: a management view* (5th edn). Dryden, New York.

Skinner, S. J., Gassenheimer, J. B. and Kelley, S. W. (1992) 'Co-operation in supplier–dealer relations'. *Journal of Retailing*, **68**(2), 174–93.

Smith, S. (1994) *Tourism Analysis: a handbook*. Longman Scientific and Technical, Harlow.

Stern, L. (1969) *Distribution Channels: behavioral dimensions*. Houghton Mifflin Company, Boston.

Stern, L. and Reve, T. (1980) 'Distribution channels as political economies: a framework for comparative analysis'. *Journal of Marketing*, **44** (Summer), 52–64.

Stern, L., El-Ansary, A. and Brown, J. (1989) *Management in Marketing Channels*. Prentice Hall International Editions, Englewood Cliffs, New Jersey.

Stern, L., El-Ansary, A. and Coughlan, A. (1996) *Marketing Channels* (5th edn). Prentice Hall International Editions, Upper Saddle River, New Jersey.

Wilemon, D. (1972) 'Power and negotiation strategies in marketing channels'. *Southern Journal of Business*, **2** (February), 71–82.

Wilson, D. and Crotts, J. (1995) 'An integrated model of buyer–seller relationship in the international travel trade'. *Progress in Tourism and Hospitality Research*, **1**(2), 125–40.

Woodruffe, H. (1995) *Services Marketing*. Pitman Publishing, London.

CHAPTER 4

Distribution channel analysis for leisure travel

Eric Laws

INTRODUCTION

The purposes of this chapter are to provide some contexts for the analysis of tourism distribution and to highlight some of the key issues presented elsewhere in this book, drawing on a range of theoretical literature. The chapter focuses on the different conceptual approaches to tourism distribution, the significance of consumer decision-making for the roles of distribution channel members, particularly in respect of packaged holidays, and distribution channel members' varying contributions to holidaymaker satisfaction through the functioning of the overall tourism system.

TRAVEL DISTRIBUTION CHANNELS

The term 'distribution channel' is generally used to connote the route by which manufactured products are moved from the producer to the consumer: another view emphasizes the concomitant changes in ownership of title to the goods as they pass from one organization to another. In a service industry such as tourism, ownership is not a factor, since the flows are movements of information and finance rather than the items sold.

The distribution channels for tourism include sales direct to consumers by principals such as transport companies, hotels and tour operators, and indirect distribution systems which utilize specialized intermediaries who service clients with information to assist in closing a sale on behalf of any of their principals. Two points can be made immediately. First from the perspective of any channel member,

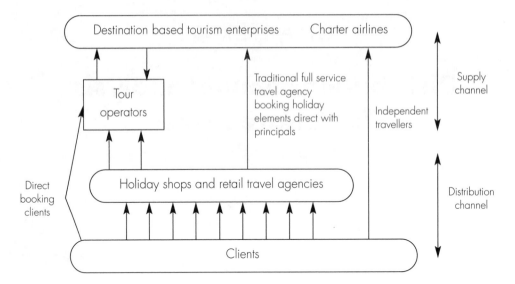

Figure 4.1 Layered distribution for the holiday industry. *Source*: Laws, 1997

some channel partners are 'upstream' (for example, hotels) and provide the tourism product to trade, while others are 'downstream' (notably retail travel agents) and deal with the ultimate customer of travel products. Secondly, while all the distribution channel members influence consumer expectations, relatively few of them directly affect the client's holiday experiences and satisfaction. The vacation itself is the experience of the resort, cruise or tour, as Duke and Persia (1993) point out. As Figure 4.1 indicates, there is a multiplicity of specialist organizations through which tourism products are distributed from principals to consumers.

Taking the packaged holiday sector as an example, distribution channel management tasks for a tour operator include: the selection of retailer travel agents, setting up discount structures to reward and motivate distribution channel members and their staff, organizing the logistical services required to distribute brochures and other sales support through the system so that it is available to potential clients. In tourism retailing, brochures are one of the main basis on which clients base their decisions, and they also include the booking forms that function as a contract between clients and travel organizations. These tasks are continuous, the need to work with their retail partners beginning again for tour operators about the time when the coming season's brochures are finalized. The need arises from the specialized nature of the contributions to tourism distribution of tour operators in creating the packaged holiday product, and the travel retailers who stimulate customers' interest, deal with their queries and process their bookings. Table 4.1 lists some of the factors constraining effective communication between tour operators and their customers, indicating the ways in which travel retailers help bridge these gaps. Tour operators and travel retailers are therefore in a synergistic business relationship.

Table 4.1 Factors constraining tour operators' dealings with consumers, and the roles of travel retailers

Factors	Travel agents' functions
Distance	Outlets located in customers' vicinity
Time	Provide facilities for advanced reservations
Information	Provide comprehensive information

RETAIL TRAVEL AGENTS

Through their high profile presence in major shopping centres, retail travel agents provide consumers with readily available information about a wide range of destinations spanning the globe, while principals can gain a detailed and rapid understanding of consumers' fast changing holiday preferences through analysis of the information requests and bookings which travel agents undertake on behalf of these principals for their clients. Retail travel agents therefore play crucial roles in the tourism distribution system, and are the predominant point of contact between travellers and travel suppliers (Snepenger *et al.* 1990; Holloway and Robinson, 1995). Two main types of travel retailer can be distinguished. These are holiday shops which concentrate on the sale of packaged holidays and directly associated products such as insurance, and the full service agencies providing advice and sales on the full range of tourism services. Traditionally, retail travel agents provided the local area with access to the full range of services. During the last quarter of the twentieth century, various forms of selective or exclusive distribution were adopted.

It is no accident that the sector of tourism which operates high street shops is generally called 'travel agencies'. Their origin is as agents dealing with the services of travel and accommodation companies, and it was customary until the late 1980s for every agency to offer a full service including the sale of coach, rail and air tickets, travel insurance and hotel bookings as well as to sell package holidays. Many of these services required very specialized and detailed product knowledge as well as agency licences issued by the suppliers. However, the value of sales for many of their principals was quite small, with the result that margins were not sufficient to sustain the agency business. In addition, these services often required quite intense sales support to clients, and it became apparent to the managers of travel agency chains that it would be more profitable to concentrate on the sale of package holidays. Their average selling price was quite high, one sales transaction generally results in multiple sales since families (or couples) travel together, and commission rates tended to be higher than for some travel services. Thus, many travel agencies evolved into more specialized 'holiday shops' and a further development saw them becoming selective about which tour operators' products to offer. This can be understood at two levels: in the first place they choose which brochures to display on their racks or to feature in window displays, and secondly, many agencies keep additional brochures in their files, from which they sell on request. Three reasons can be advanced for the associated decisions to rack, file or not deal with particular tour operators. Bad experiences with a particular company fall into several categories, and if persistent or extreme can result in the agency's decision not to deal with it any longer. Relevant factors include low (or relatively low) commission rates, difficulties in collecting commissions, and consumers' complaints about their holiday experiences. On the other hand, an agency may promote one tour operator in the hope that it can create a high level of sales which will result in better support in terms of staff training, brochure suppliers and higher levels of commission or overrides. This arrangement is sometimes linked to an exclusive local deal whereby only one agency racks a particular brochure in the town, or where competing brochures are not racked in the same agency. Holiday shops are often members of a nationwide or international chain, which is itself likely to be part of an integrated tourism group including tour operating, aircharter and other travel products, although many of these retailers are small, independent operations.

During the last two decades of the twentieth century, vertical and horizontal integration has occurred in travel distribution to rationalize the ownership of retail travel outlets so that they are more effective in selling the services of the major tour operators. Some of the most familiar travel retailers are in fact owned by large tour operators (even though they often operate under separate trading names), with the result that they are in effect an integrated distribution system. This provides several advantages, including the maximum retention of profits within the group, enhanced selling strength for the holiday brands which results from inhouse retailing, reduced outlets available for competitors' brands, and opportunities for improvements in retail staff training in the tour operator's own brands, products and business systems. One further advantage is significant: the integrated tour operator and travel retailer has greater command of and more rapid access to information on constantly changing market conditions, and is therefore in a stronger position to make informed decisions about when, and how much, to adjust prices or which resorts or departures to promote at particular times. Against this, concerns have been expressed by consumer groups and regulatory bodies that the overall effect is to reduce the choice available to consumers, while trade bodies are concerned about the future prospects for smaller companies, both retailers and tour operators, in a market dominated by the continuing growth of integrated, and increasingly multinational, organizations.

DISTRIBUTION CHANNEL MANAGEMENT ISSUES

A distribution system can be described by the extent to which it is integrated, by the way in which this is achieved, and by the extent to which distribution channel members cover the market (Frazier *et al.*, 1989; Gattanora, 1990). From an organization's perspective, the distribution channel comprises the external organizations that are contracted to achieve its management distribution objectives. Rosenbloom (1978) and Mallen (1978) have focused attention on the relative ability of members in a distribution chain to influence other members' actions. This can be understood in more than one way: it is partly a matter of the dependency of one organization on its partners in the chain of distribution, but analysis is also concerned with matters such as their goal congruency, and methods of limiting conflicts between them. The way in which such matters are made explicit and then managed has implications for the likelihood of long lasting co-operation between distribution channel partners. One strategic response to the problems for managers resulting from the need to share profit or the relative lack of control implied by channel distribution systems is to merge with (or acquire) a company at a different level in the chain.

INTEGRATION IN HOLIDAY DISTRIBUTION

The major tour operators are in effect Vertically Integrated Marketing Channels (VIMS) in which one organization (the tour operator) dominates other members including the upstream tourism product suppliers such as hotels and charter airlines, and the downstream travel retailers. Overall this results in improved effectiveness and economy for the channel members. Variations include Corporate VIMS in which all stages of the marketing channel are combined under one organization, while Administered VIMS have independent members, the co-ordination being achieved by informal means. Although individual channel members retain their autonomy, one dominates, usually because of its power and size. In another variation, Contractual VIMS, contracts set out the terms of relationships between members. Another dynamic factor in tourism distribution is horizontal integration, enabling a retailer or a tour operator to become more dominant in its sector by combining with similar organizations. This has advantages over intrinsic growth since a takeover can be accomplished in a few days and brings with it most of the other organization's clients, staff and premises. An important result is that competition within the sector is reduced, and made less potent because of the increased size of the new operation. At the higher levels of corporate size, takeovers and mergers raise the possibility of monopoly control in the market, and proposals for mergers between the largest companies may have to be approved by a government regulator such as the Monopolies and Mergers Commission.

TOURISM DISTRIBUTION CHANNELS
AND DESTINATION OUTCOMES

These integrated tourism companies benefit from significant scale advantages which are often used to reduce the price at which holiday packages are retailed, but as Buhalis (2000) has pointed out, there are many ways in which conflict can arise between channel members. The pressure is often felt most acutely by destination-based suppliers who are not (usually) incorporated into these integrated organizations. The consequences are evident in declining quality of infrastructure in many mass-market resorts because there is insufficient revenue to provide an adequate tax base for development or maintenance. Many models of tourism distribution neglect to pay sufficient attention to destinations, yet they are the key to understanding tourism, because by definition the industry is based on providing services away from the clients' home. In spending time, undertaking activities and spending their money in destinations, tourists influence the way these places develop. When their arrival and activities are organized industrially by major tour operators, visitor numbers to destinations which are equivalent in scale only to quite small towns can easily reach several million annually. The effects are spectacular and rapid, and often unwelcome to residents. The dynamics outlined here have been analysed in a number of articles (e.g. Morgan, 1994; Laws and Cooper, 1998), which discuss policies adopted in destinations such as Majorca to form alliances with their major tour operator partners to overcome some of these problems.

Britton (1987, pp. 132–4) drew on dependency theory to examine the 'influence that metropolitan based corporations exert over the nature of tourism development in small Pacific island nations'. He documented how they are

> emeshed in a global tourism system over which they have little or no influence . . . advertising strategies shape tourist expectations – leading visitors to seek the types of experiences and facilities associated with mass tourism . . . [the governments of micro states] turn to companies to provide the necessary capital to finance large scale hotels and train staff. The ability of these to offer large commissions to overseas tour operators also enables them to gain control over various sectors of tourist industries. Profits often flow to overseas corporations and local elites. Small scale, locally owned enterprises are either relegated to activities which lie beyond the immediate interests of larger corporations, or find roles as subcontractors. The final outcome is a form of tourism that primarily satisfies the commercial interests of overseas concerns and only partially meets local development needs.

Laws and Cooper (1998) have expressed their concern that traditional mass-market resorts are often inadequately served by distribution channels. Their reliance on inclusive tour operators clientele has led to the commodification of the resort product by intermediaries. In recognition of these issues and the changing tourism marketplace, many resorts are currently setting new objectives for their marketing, and revising their strategies to take into account the wish to seek new ways to target and serve their preferred clienteles (Cooper, 1990). However, inclusive holidays are a key element of business for these resorts, and the inclusive holiday industry is characterized by a high degree of differential power, where the initiative is often vested in the major tour operators. This suggests that many mass-market resorts are unable to put into effect the strategic marketing and planning approaches which theory often suggests as solutions to the problems faced by resorts in this stage of development. There is a need for a wide range of research into the nature of these problems, and of how improvement processes are being implemented.

TOURISM SYSTEMS

In part, the issues outlined above stem from a parochial management approach to tourism, in which component businesses concentrate on maximizing their short-term profit or growth objectives rather than considering the overall functioning of the tourism system and the needs of the network of organizations of which it is comprised. Three stages can be identified in general models of system processes. Inputs are required in the form of equipment, skills, resources and clients' demands for the industry's products. But, a system's outputs also include the profit and work which it creates, and the effects of its operations on other interests. For tourism, the most important of these is arguably those of the destination's residents. The intermediate stage of systems analysis connecting inputs with outputs is concerned with the internal processes whereby organizations transform those inputs into outputs, and distribution is one of these processes. The various components or elements of the system are interlinked, and the efficiency of the system operating within its boundary will be affected by changes to any of the elements of which it is composed: the entire system is affected if one component changes. Taking a view of a system is to recognize particular systems boundaries; setting a clear boundary around the system under investigation emphasizes the inputs and outputs for investigation. Outside the boundary of any system are a range of other entities which influence its activities, and which are affected by them: the system is itself part of the environment for other systems. Proponents of systems analysis also recognize the need for an organization to monitor the external environment within which it operates.

Taking a view of tourism distribution channels as a system (Figure 4.2) invites examination of the allocation between members of the functions it entails, and of the ability of any of its members to increase their profit by shifting costs elsewhere in the

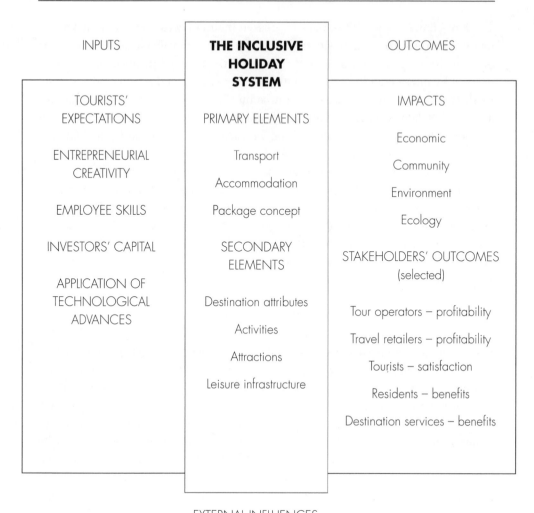

INPUTS   **THE INCLUSIVE HOLIDAY SYSTEM**   OUTCOMES

INPUTS	PRIMARY ELEMENTS	IMPACTS
TOURISTS' EXPECTATIONS	Transport	Economic
ENTREPRENEURIAL CREATIVITY	Accommodation	Community
EMPLOYEE SKILLS	Package concept	Environment / Ecology
INVESTORS' CAPITAL	SECONDARY ELEMENTS	STAKEHOLDERS' OUTCOMES (selected)
APPLICATION OF TECHNOLOGICAL ADVANCES	Destination attributes / Activities / Attractions / Leisure infrastructure	Tour operators – profitability / Travel retailers – profitability / Tourists – satisfaction / Residents – benefits / Destination services – benefits

EXTERNAL INFLUENCES

Tastes   Competition   Technology   Legislation   Demographics   Politics

Figure 4.2 General model of the inclusive holiday industry system. *Source*: Laws, 1997

channel. For example, a national tourist organization might benefit from tour operator or airline advertising which features it as a destination. Similarly, a tour operator often requires the travel retailers with which it trades to have staff trained in its systems and products so that the majority of client inquiries can be handled at the agency level, rather than by the tour operator's staff; this also encourages agency staff to sell a particular operator's products as they are more familiar with both its holidays and its reservations procedures. Table 4.2 outlines another aspect, analysing tourism from systems perspectives by demonstrating the network of mutual dependencies which link tourism industry distribution channel members.

CONSUMER CHOICE AND THE TOURISM DISTRIBUTION CHANNEL

Since one of the key roles for travel agencies is that of advising customers about the suitability and quality of various travel products (Gee and Fayos-Sola, 1997), it is important to understand the ways in which consumers make their choices. A key function of tourism distribution is to provide consumers with information and to influence their choice of holiday product. Understanding consumers' information search behaviour is crucial to strategic decision-making (Uysal and Fesenmaier, 1993; Moorthy, *et al.*, 1997). Raaij (1986) has shown that consumer preferences are partly a reflection of what is available in the market, but also reflect what consumers consider to be 'ideal' products, a concept which combines image and expectation. Therefore, there is a potential risk that the holiday experience may not match what the consumer had anticipated. The general marketing services literature indicates that more search for decision-making information occurs when risk rises (Murray, 1991, p. 40).

Travel decision-making processes have been the subject of considerable research, but there is little consensus beyond the broad elements which influence most holidaymakers. The field of literature has been well summarized in several recent papers including Moorthy *et al.* (1997), Fodness and Murray (1998) and Klenosky and Gitelson (1998). Of particular relevance to the issues discussed in the present book, there is still debate over the ordering of the choice of elements in a holiday (the accommodation, the resort, the mode of transport); the decision-makers (in a family or a group of friends, what relative influence do the various members have, what forms of bargaining or consensus management take place?), and the trade-off between the effort invested in searching for information compared to the relief that a decision has been made, often followed by searches for more specific information regarding what to do during the destination stay.

Information search can be deliberate or casual. A large proportion of holiday purchasers use one or more travel agents to obtain information, but only use one agent to book their package travel. Woodside and Ronkainen (1980) also find that the longer the distance is to be travelled, the more reliance there is on travel agents, especially when travelling to foreign countries. Information search may begin with no clear focus, or it may be concerned with only several possible destinations. Stabler (1990) notes that this opportunity set is the holiday opportunities which exist at any point in time. It may exclude particular destinations through prejudice, boredom or other causes or it may be very general in nature. Increasingly, a wide range of information sources are consulted (Snepenger *et al.*, 1990). The sources of tourist information include advertising through all kinds of media, such as TV

Table 4.2 Interdependencies in the inclusive holiday system. *Source*: Laws, 1997

System member	Destination	Tour operator	Principals	Travel agent
Destination		Tour operator provides regular batches of visitors	Quality of visitors' experiences depends on standards of hotels, etc.	Staff knowledge and enthusiasm of destination can be critical factor in clients choice
Tour operator	Depends on primary features (climate, scenery, culture, ski infrastructure). Ability to exploit these commercially depends on the range and quality of tourism services offered		Major expense for tour operator, also critical in ensuring customer expectations met	Sales agent directing high street clients to specific tour operators' products
Principals – hotels and airlines	Depend on destinations for primary appeals and for social or technical infrastructure, such as sewers, roads, educational standards of staff and airport facilities	Tour operators provide flows of customers throughout season to specific destinations at agreed prices		Generally minimal for holiday products as their services are embodied in tour operators' products
Travel agent	Depends on destinations for briefings, staff familiarization tours and point of sales materials	Dependent on tour operators for creating a market through advertising, for staff training, brochures and CRS for sales	Depends on hotels and airlines for sales support and staff training	

Table 4.3 A holiday choice model with information search implications

Aspect of choice	Destination issue	Role of information	Most salient sources
Complexity	WHERE?	Answers specific queries; raises other issues; compounds the difficulty of choice	Travel agent; VICs (etc.); media advertising; Internet
Risk	Will it be: fun? safe? too costly?	Reassurance	Experience; friends; travel writers; travel agent
Choice	Would an alternative have been better?	Information streams coming from competing destinations	Friends' holiday anecdotes; travel writers
Experience	Quality and style	n.a.	Destination services
Evaluation	Future bookings by this client and friends	n.a.	Experience; friends' anecdotes

and print, with travel agents as the other main source (Sheldon, 1993). The distinctive feature of advertising is the consistently positive tone of its claims (Raitz and Dakhil, 1989), although this may detract from its credibility.

Awareness of travel destinations is created and enhanced by travel reporting in the media, guide books and other documentaries such as nature films (Laws, 1995). Electronic online systems are regarded as increasingly important information sources (and booking avenues) for the future. Muller (1998, p.200) predicts the following order of importance of most major information sources by the year 2005:

1. Online information via Internet, teletext, etc.
2. Radio, TV features, videos
3. Reports from recommendations of acquaintances and family
4. Other books, magazines
5. Travel guides
6. Information, travel agency advice
7. Travel destination decision reached without using these information sources
8. Travel operators' catalogues, brochures

Many researchers agree that personal sources of information, including previous experience and word-of-mouth recommendations from friends and acquaintances is the most important factor in risk reduction strategies when trip planning (Raitz and Dakhil, 1989; Murray, 1991; Sheldon, 1993; Fodness and Murray, 1997). Dellaert *et al.* (1998) argue that tourists' decisions are complex with multi-faceted elements, which are interrelated and evolve over time. The key factors in holiday choice are varied, and can include cost, availability, or various psychic benefits such as the exclusivity or relative newness of a particular type of holiday component including specific hotels, modes of transport or available activities. Thus, tourist information search is a lengthy process involving a sequence of steps (Raaij, 1986). Table 4.3 attempts to synthesize the points outlined above, highlighting the information implications of the various aspects of choice including complexity and risk in making a choice, and the role of experience in subsequent evaluation of satisfaction with it.

INVOLVEMENT IN HOLIDAY CHOICE

Tourism is a deliberate purchase, in which limited financial resources are invested in buying time to visit a chosen resort, implying both that the tourist cannot visit alternative resorts during that vacation, and that he or she has chosen not to spend money and time on alternative products. Consumers' degrees of interest and 'involvement' in purchasing particular products or services range from low to high. Involvement is likely to be high when the purchase has functional and symbolic significance, and entails some financial risk (Asseal, 1987).

Four aspects of holidays suggest that many tourists experience a high degree of involvement in choosing their holiday destination:

- Holidays are expensive.
- Holidays are complex both to purchase and experience.
- There is a risk that the resort may not prove satisfying.
- The resort reflects the holidaymaker's personality.

In the case of journeys by air, low involvement passengers are satisfied if an airline provides an on-time flight with reasonable standards of comfort and catering. Any service enhancements such as a sophisticated entertainment system or fine meals are received with pleasure. In contrast, a high involvement passenger expects that enhanced service as a minimum requirement and looks for additional evidence of superior service such as the latest style of seating or enhanced facilities at the airport. The basic service is insufficient to please a high involvement passenger.

Table 4.3   A holiday choice model with information search implications

Aspect of choice	Destination issue	Role of information	Most salient sources
Complexity	WHERE?	Answers specific queries; raises other issues; compounds the difficulty of choice	Travel agent; VICs (etc.); media advertising; Internet
Risk	Will it be: fun? safe? too costly?	Reassurance Information streams coming from competing destinations	Experience; friends; travel writers; travel agent
Choice	Would an alternative have been better?	n.a.	Friends' holiday anecdotes; travel writers
Experience	Quality and style	n.a.	Destination services
Evaluation	Future bookings by this client and friends		Experience; friends' anecdotes

THE QUALITY OF TOURISTS' EXPERIENCES

It is important to note that the various members of the tourism distribution system have different abilities to influence clients' satisfaction. Despite their significance in influencing travel product choice, travel agents have very little influence over their clients' actual experiences whilst on holiday, despite recent legislation which renders them liable for unsatisfactory services (Grant and Mason, 1993; ABTA, 1994). However, it is quite possible for any of the many companies providing services during the journey or while in the destination to affect customer satisfaction, either by pleasing them or by not meeting their expectations.

Service quality is the outcome of the various travel suppliers' activities and the judgement of their experiences by tourists themselves (Laws, 2000). Gronross (1990) argues that service quality comprises two fundamental components, technical quality ('what' is delivered) and functional quality ('how' the service is delivered), with an important third component, the organization's image. If the quality of tourism services could be determined by managerial decisions, then all clients participating in one service episode should experience it in similar ways. The fact that this often does not happen can be illustrated from analysis of customer correspondence, through focus group methods and from our individual experiences. Assuming that all clients were in fact offered identical service, any remaining differences they report in the satisfaction which they experienced could be ascribed to any or all of three major variables. These are their individual attitude at the time, their involvement (enthusiasm) with the holiday, and differences in their prior experience of similar services. The degree of quality experienced in a service transaction can be considered to give rise to a level of satisfaction which may vary between customers. Lewis and Booms (1983) identified the following factors as significant in understanding this variability in the enjoyment of services:

- Service quality is more difficult for the consumer to evaluate than the quality of goods.
- Service quality perceptions result from a comparison of consumer expectations with actual service performance.
- Quality evaluations are not made solely on the outcome of a service; they also involve evaluations of the process of service delivery.

Wilkie (1986) argued that two key factors determine how something is perceived: its stimulus characteristics and the characteristics of the consumer. He continues by indicating that: 'The issue of which stimuli consumers choose to perceive becomes a key question.' The question of individually perceived service standards underlines the problem for managers seeking to design and deliver services satisfying the expectations of many clients. 'Customer perceived quality is rather a blend of objective facts and subjective judgements, of knowledge as well as ignorance. . . . Nor can manufacturers consider themselves experts . . . Quality has become an integrating concept between production orientation and marketing orientation' (Gummesson, 1988). Harington and Akehurst (1996) undertook a detailed review of 21 leading articles on the topic of service quality, and from this identified some 60 terms used by various authors to define the dimensions of quality. The most frequently discussed general factors were service delivery and interactions (14), standards of performance (12), technical factors (10) and image (7).

Consumer satisfaction modelling is based on the gaps which may be perceived by customers between what they had anticipated and their experiences as the various events in a service unfold (Parasuraman et al., 1985; Laws, 1986). Zeithmal et al. (1988) argued that the customer reaches a judgement about the quality of service actually experienced when measured against the perceived service. Debate still continues on the appropriateness of the gap approach, including its core constructs of consumer satisfaction, expectations and quality (Chadee and Mattsson, 1996; Laws, 2000 and 2002).

CHANGE FACTORS IN TOURISM DISTRIBUTION SYSTEMS

Distribution management implies a long-term business relationship between members, but like other forms of human relationship it may be based on dislike and distrust or the recognition and nurturing of mutual advantages. Scanning a few months' editions of the travel trade press, and particularly the letters pages, will provide ample evidence of the divergent views of distribution channel members of their partners' policies.

Many of the chapters in this book emphasize the significance of the network of relationships between companies which underpins the tourism system, and the various ways in which this is organized in different sectors and countries. Insights into the complexity and the dynamics of these relationships can be obtained by adopting the theoretical perspectives of network and alliance theory or relationship marketing (McKenna, 1991; Gummesson, 1994), and by viewing the holiday industry systemically. 'Relationship marketing strategies are concerned with a broader scope of external "market" relationships which include suppliers, business referral and "influence" sources. It also focuses on the staff relationships critical to the success of marketing plans and a resolution of the competing interests of customers, staff and shareholders by changing the way managers "manage" the activities of the business' (Payne and Ballantyne, 1991). Gummesson points out that even the most powerful companies such as IBM cannot develop, manufacture and market their products and services on their own. They enter into alliances with customers, competitors and suppliers to gain operational and cost advantages and for access to markets. He contrasts this perspective on management philosophies with the more familiar idea of competition. Whereas competition means winning over somebody, or even destroying them to become the biggest in the field, this short-term, greedy way of doing business may prejudice long-term survival.

New forms of tourism may result from understanding the contribution which various types of business can make to the tourism value chain.

> Distribution is the most important activity along the tourism chain. Without adequate air access and product distribution channels in the marketplace, the best destinations in the world would find it difficult to survive. Two key aspects of distribution are important for tourism destinations, air transportation and the role of tourist boards and promotion agencies in the marketplace. (Poon , 1993, p. 326)

Until the 1980s, making a holiday reservation for a client usually entailed at least one (and usually several) lengthy telephone calls between agency and tour operator. They were lengthy because telephone lines were expensive and in scarce supply, resulting in frequently engaged lines, and secondly because the reservations

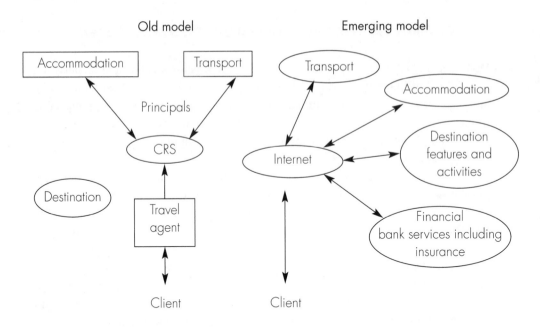

Figure 4.3 Patterns of information-technology-based tourism distribution

information was held manually by most principals, with the need for reservations staff to check availability on a number of charts relating to departure and return journeys, and for rooms in each hotel. Under these conditions many travel agencies used counter-top telephone amplifiers, so that staff could do other tasks while waiting for a tour operator to pick up their call, or to service it. On answering, the tour operator's staff had to physically enter booking information on reservations charts which showed visually how many seats were available on each flight. Confirmation of hotel bed space often meant the further delay and expense of an international phone call or telex message. Most of the delay and uncertainty outlined above was obviated by tour operators' investment in computerized reservations systems accessible to agents.

The introduction by Thomson of the first UK videotext computerized reservations system (TOPS, in 1982) was followed four years later by the closing of the company's telephone reservations facility (Laws, 1997). TOPS, although it has now been superseded by more sophisticated systems, tripled the productivity of the company's reservations staff. It also increased the ability of travel agents to sell effectively since the availability of specific holidays could be confirmed to clients while they were in the shop, and the more customer oriented retailers realized that sales could be gained by encouraging clients to observe the information on the screen as an agent sought alternatives for them. It has been argued by some tourism experts that many of these functions can now be carried out by individuals, in their own homes, thus reducing the future need for travel agents or tour operators

(Buhalis, 1998). As Figure 4.3 shows, the way tourism distribution use information technology is changing, with much wider public access to both information and bookings which modern technology is bringing, and the advent of new organizations designed around these technologies.

Channel relationships are generally considered to be under increasing pressure from technologically based information systems, likely to bring changes in the operation of traditional channels in the medium term rather than to cause their imminent demise (Sheldon, 1993; Jones, 1995; Cano and Prentice, 1998). This effect is common to many industries, and the combination of technology and information is reshaping business across the globe (Kale and McIntyre, 1991; Tiwana, 1998).

Over the coming decades, the distribution systems described in this book are likely to continue to be subject to significant change. However, traditional travel retailers have the key advantage of significant high street or shopping centre presence, inviting inquiries which skilled agents can easily convert into sales. In contrast, some expertise and patience is required to navigate the Internet, and investment in the equipment is also needed. At present, only a minority of homes have Internet access, although the proportion is forecast to rise rapidly. Importantly, studies of Internet users indicate that they share many characteristics with frequent travellers, and the proportion of commercial Internet sites specializing in travel services is increasing.

The Internet now offers potential travel purchasers a new pattern of direct, home-based access to current information on the availability of travel services linked to rapid and simple booking facilities. This has the potential to alter existing channel structures by providing much more convenient and direct links to a very wide range of distant providers in contrast to the current pattern in which clients visit (or phone) retailers who then contact CRS systems on their behalf. It is also likely that the new pattern of information and booking illustrated in Figure 4.3 will provide additional benefits to the consumer in terms of special offers and other cost savings, while enhancing the possibility of making bookings for immediate travel, and offer the consumer a wide range of tourism and related products including local information not immediately available through conventional travel retailers. Against this, there are convincing arguments that traditional, old model information and booking services utilizing travel retailers and CRS systems are robust, and are likely to persist for the foreseeable future. They offer a familiar mode of conducting business, and provide the benefit of direct human contact and a perceived level of travel expertise. In Europe, at least, there is also the advantage of the legal responsibility to consumers for quality and performance imposed on all travel sellers.

REFERENCES

ABTA (1994) *Members' Handbook*. Columbus Press, London.

Asseal, H. (1987) *Consumer Behaviour and Marketing Action*. Kent Publication Co., Boston, Mass.

Britton, S. (1987) 'Tourism in Pacific Island States: constraints and opportunities'. In S. Britton and W. Clarke, (eds) *Ambiguous Alternatives: Tourism in Small Developing Countries*. University of South Pacific, Suva, Fiji, pp. 113–39.

Buhalis, D. (1998) 'Strategic use of information technologies in the tourism industry'. *Tourism Management*, **19**(3), 409–23.

Buhalis, D. (2000) 'Relationships in the distribution channel of tourism: conflicts between hoteliers and tour operators in the Mediterranean region'. *International Journal of Hospitality and Tourism Administration*, **1**(1), 113–39.

Cano, V. and Prentice, R. (1998) 'Opportunities for endearment to place through electronic "visiting": WWW homepages and the tourism promotion of Scotland'. *Tourism Management*, **19**(1), 67–73.

Chadee, D. and Mattson, J. (1996) 'An empirical assessment of customer satisfaction in tourism'. *Service Industries Journal*, **16**(3), 305–20.

Cooper, C. P. (1990) 'Resorts in decline: the management response'. *Tourism Management*, **11**(1), 63–7.

Duke, C. R. and Persia, M. A. (1993) 'The effects of distribution channel level on tour purchasing attributes and information sources'. In M. Uysal and D. R. Fesenmaier (eds) *Communication and Channel Systems in Tourism Marketing*. Haworth Press, Binghampton, N.Y.

Dellaert, B., Ettema, D. and Lindh, C. (1998) 'Multi-faceted tourist travel decisions: a constraint-based conceptual framework to describe tourists' sequential choices of travel components'. *Tourism Management*, **19**(4), 313–20.

Fodness, D. and Murray, B. (1997) 'Tourist information search'. *Annals of Tourism Research*, **24**(3), 503–23.

Fodness, D. and Murray, B. (1998) 'A typology of tourist information search strategies'. *Journal of Travel Research*, **37**(2), 109–19.

Frazier, G., Gill, J. and Sudhir, K. (1989) 'Dealer dependency levels and reciprocal actions in a channel of distribution in a developing country'. *Journal of Marketing*, **53** (January) 50–69.

Gattorna, J. (1990) 'Developing a channel strategy'. In J. Gattorna (ed.) *The Gower Handbook of Logistics and Distribution* (4th edn). Gower, Aldershot, pp. 99–101.

Gee, C. and Fayos-Sola, E. (1997) 'Travel distribution systems'. In *International Tourism: A Global Perspective*. World Tourism Organization, Madrid, pp. 95–116.

Grant, D. and Mason, S. (1993) *The Package Travel, Package Holidays and Package Tours Regulations*. University of Northumbria Travel Law Centre.

Gronross, C. (1990) *Service Management and Marketing, Managing: The Moments of Truth in Service Competition*. Lexinton Books, Mass.

Gummesson, E. (1988) 'Service quality and product quality combined'. *Review of Business*, **9**(3), 1–11.

Gummesson, E. (1994) 'Making relationship marketing operational'. *International Journal of Service Industry Management*, **5**(5), 5–20.

Harington, D and Akehurst, G. (1996) 'An exploratory investigation into managerial perceptions of service quality in UK hotels'. *Progress in Tourism and Hospitality Research*, **2**(2), 135–50.

Holloway, J. C. and Robinson, C. (1995) *Marketing For Tourism* (3rd edn). Longman, Harlow.

Jones, C. (1995) *Technology for Today and the Future*. 44th PATA Annual Conference, pp. 205–19.

Kale, S. and McIntyre, R. (1991) 'Distribution channel relationships in diverse cultures'. *International Marketing Review*, **8**(3), 31–45.

Kotler, P., Haider, D. H. and Rein, I. (1993) *Marketing Places*. The Free Press, New York.

Klenosky, D. and Gitelson, R. (1998) 'Travel agents destination recommendations'. *Annals of Tourism Research*, **25**(3), 661–74.

Laws, E. (1986) 'Identifying and managing the consumerist gap'. *Service Industries Journal*, **6**(2), 131–43.

Laws, E. (1995) *Tourist Destination Management: Issues, Analysis and Policies*. Thomson International Business Press, London.

Laws, E. (1996) 'Perspectives on pricing decisions in the inclusive holiday industry'. In I. Yoeman and T. Ingold (eds) *Yield Management – A Strategy for Service*. Cassells, London.

Laws, E. (1997) *The Inclusive Holiday Industry: Relationships, Responsibility and Customer Satisfaction*. Thomson International Business Press, London.

Laws, E. (2000) 'Service quality in tourism research: are we walking tall (yet)?' *Journal of Quality Assurance in Hospitality and Tourism*, **1**(1), 31–56.

Laws, E. (2002) *Tourism Service Quality*. Butterworth-Heinemann, Oxford.

Laws, E. and Cooper, C. (1998) 'Inclusive tours and commodification: the marketing constraints for mass market resorts'. *Journal of Vacation Marketing*, **4**(4), 337–52.

Lewis, R. C. and Booms, B. H. (1983) 'The marketing aspects of service quality'. In L. Berry, G. Shostack and G. Upah (eds) *Emerging Perspectives on Services Marketing*. American Marketing Association, Chicago.

McKenna, R. (1991) *Relationship Marketing: Successful Strategies for the Age of the Customer*. Addison Wesley, Reading, Mass.

Mallen, B. (1978) 'Channel power: a form of economic exploitation'. *European Journal of Marketing*, **12**(2).

Moorthy, S., Ratchford, B. and Talukdar, D. (1997) 'Consumer information search revisited: theory and empirical analysis'. *Journal of Consumer Research*, **23**, March, 263–77.

Morgan, M. (1994) 'Homogenous products, the future of established resorts'. In W. Theobald (ed.) *Global Tourism, The Next Decade*. Butterworth-Heinemann, Oxford.

Muller, H. (1998) 'Long-haul tourism 2005 – Delphi study'. *Journal of Vacation Marketing*, **4**(2), 193–201.

Murray, K. (1991) 'A test of services marketing theory: consumer information acquisition activities'. *Journal of Marketing*, **55**, January, 10–25.

Parasuraman, A., Zeithmal, V. A. and Berry, L. L. (1985) 'A conceptual model of service quality and its implications for future research'. *Journal of Marketing*, **49**, 41–50.

Payne, A. and Ballantyne, D. (1991) *Relationship Marketing: bringing quality, customer service and marketing together*. Butterworth-Heinemann, Oxford.

Poon, A. (1993) *Tourism, Technology and Competitive Strategies*. CAB International, UK.

Rosenbloom, B. (1978) *Marketing Channels: A Management View* (6th edn). Dryden Press, Fort Worth.

Raaij, W. (1986) 'Consumer research on tourism mental and behavioural constructs'. *Annals of Tourism Research*, **13**, 1–9.

Raitz, K. and Dakhil, M. (1989) 'A note about information sources for preferred recreational environments'. *Journal of Travel Research*, Spring, pp. 45–9.

Sheldon, P. (1993) 'Destination information systems'. *Annals of Tourism Research*, **20**, 633–49.

Snepenger, D., Meged, K., Snelling, M. and Worrall, K. (1990) 'Information search strategies by destination-naïve tourists'. *Journal of Travel Research*, Summer, pp. 13–17.

Stabler, M. (1990) 'The concept of opportunity sets as a methodology for selling tourism places'. In G. Ashworth and B. Goodall (eds) *Marketing Tourism Places*. Routledge, London.

Tiwana, A. (1998) 'Interdependency factors influencing the World Wide Web as a channel of interactive marketing'. *Journal of Retailing and Consumer Services*, **5**(4), 245–53.

Uysal, M. and Fesenmaier, D. R. (eds) (1993) *Communication and Channel Systems in Tourism Marketing*. Haworth Press, Binghampton, N.Y.

Wilkie, W. L. (1986) *Consumer Behaviour*. Wiley, New York.

Woodside, A. and Ronkainen, I. (1980) 'Vacation travel planning segments self- planning vs. users of motor club and travel agents'. *Annals of Tourism Research*, **7**(3), 385–94.

Zeithmal, V. A., Berry, L. A. and Parasuraman, L. A. (1988) 'Communication and control processes in the delivery of service quality'. *Journal of Marketing*, **52**, April, 35–48.

CHAPTER 5

Distribution channel analysis for business travel

Rob Davidson

INTRODUCTION

The market for business travel and tourism may be loosely defined as being composed of 'people travelling for purposes which are related to their work' (Davidson, 1994a). Business travel and tourism activities can be classified in several ways, but the distinction most commonly made is between individual business (or corporate) travel – composed of trips made to carry out duties which are a regular, normal and necessary part of the traveller's employment – and participation in occasional work-related group events such as conferences, seminars, product launches, exhibitions and incentive programmes. Regarding the supply of business travel and tourism products and services, Table 5.1 shows that there are a number of suppliers common to all sectors: transport providers, accommodation and catering operators, and suppliers of leisure and recreation facilities. Most business travel and tourism activities – with the possible exception of one-day events – depend on these basic services. As a minimum, those travelling for work-related purposes need transport, food and accommodation, as well as something to do to help them relax at the end of the working day. In addition to these basic needs, each sector has its particular specialist suppliers of the products and services it requires in order to function effectively.

Linking all of these suppliers with the appropriate buyers is the role of the various specialist intermediaries involved in the distribution of business travel and tourism services and products. All of these intermediaries have undergone – and continue to undergo – significant changes in the context of a fast-changing business travel and tourism market environment. However, as it is in the distribution of individual, or corporate, business travel that the greatest upheavals have been

Table 5.1 Business travel distribution channel: structure, players and requirements

Sector	Main buyers	Possible intermediaries	Main suppliers
Individual business travel	Companies and other organizations (governmental, professional, etc.), possibly through: – inhouse travel managers – secretaries/PAs	Business/corporate travel agencies Travel management companies, possibly through: – implants – dedicated online booking services	Transport providers Accommodation and catering operators Leisure and recreation suppliers
Conferences and other meetings	Corporate sector Governmental sector Associations – academic – professional – trade – fraternal – religious, etc., possibly through: – inhouse travel managers – inhouse conference organizers – secretaries/PAs	Professional conference organizers Venue-finding agencies Convention bureaux Destination management companies/ground handlers Specialist marketing consortia	Transport providers Accommodation and catering operators Leisure and recreation suppliers Conference centres Management training centres Hotels meetings facilities Universities 'Unusual venues' Audio-visual contractors Telecommunications companies (video/satellite conferencing facilities) Interpreters
Incentive travel	Corporate sector, possibly through: – inhouse travel managers – inhouse conference organizers	Incentive travel houses Business travel agencies Destination management companies/ground handlers	Transport providers Accommodation and catering operators Leisure and recreation suppliers
Exhibitions/ trade fairs	Corporate sector	Exhibition organizers	Transport providers Accommodation and catering operators Leisure and recreation suppliers Exhibition centres Stand contractors

experienced, this chapter will focus exclusively on that sector. . Between them, these activities comprise the principal sectors of the business travel and tourism market. Table 5.1 shows the structure of this market, including the main intermediaries responsible for the distribution of business travel and tourism products and services. Private companies, large and small, are clearly the main buyers, although they are by no means the only types of organization purchasing in this market. Representatives and employees of government bodies and agencies – international, national and local – also need to travel and meet regularly, in order to function effectively; and members of associations of all types are also important consumers, particularly in the conferences sector.

BUSINESS TRAVEL AGENCIES

While travel for leisure purposes dominates the work of most high street travel agencies, some such agencies have a business travel specialist, or a business travel department, catering exclusively for the needs of corporate clients. There are also travel agencies, known as business travel agencies, or occasionally, business house agencies, which deal solely with business travel. These business travel agencies are key intermediaries in the business travel services distribution chain, and their changing role in that chain will be examined in the following pages. Owing to the intermediary nature of their function, business travel agencies rarely find themselves in face-to-face contact with the business travellers they serve. They mainly follow their instructions, transmitted by telephone, fax or e-mail, and send the travel documents by courier to the traveller's place of work. Occasionally, for large companies with extensive travel needs, the business travel agency may operate through an 'implant'. An implant is 'a division of a travel agency that is located within the corporate offices of an organisation. The equipment and employees belong to the travel agency, but their utilisation is dedicated to the one company's needs' (Lewis *et al.*, 1995).

Before examining the precise role of business travel agencies, it is important to note that travel arrangements, especially for small companies, may be made directly with suppliers, without recourse to any intermediary. Secretaries and Personal Assistants still have this function in some companies, and also commonly found is the use of inhouse specialist business travel managers, employed by companies to negotiate and manage travel arrangements for employees, either directly, or through one or more business travel agencies. As will be discussed, it is also becoming increasingly possible for the actual business travellers themselves to make their own bookings.

DISTINCTIONS BETWEEN THE BUSINESS TRAVEL MARKET AND THE LEISURE TRAVEL MARKET

Business travellers and leisure travellers are different breeds with different needs. Some of those differences account for certain key characteristics of the business travel market. Crucially, whereas in the leisure tourism market the client is also the end-consumer of the service purchased (the holiday, short-break, or visit to a theme park, for example), this is not usually the case for the purchase of business travel services. With the notable exception of the self-employed, those who pay the bills arising from business travel are not usually the same people who actually make the trips. The fact that payment for the services used by business travellers does not normally come out of their own pockets partly explains their higher daily spend, compared with the amounts spent by those travelling for leisure.

Consequently, for business travel agents and suppliers, business travellers are generally considered to be a highly sought-after client group, because of their higher spend, higher yield qualities. They also represent the most important type of traveller in terms of volume in many cases: 51 per cent of all travellers on Virgin Trains' West coast service travel on business, a figure which rises to 64 per cent on the London–West Midlands part of the route. On that section, 35 per cent of passengers travel first class, and almost all of them are business travellers (BTF/BTAC, 1999). Although fewer in number than their leisure counterparts, business travellers are far more important to travel suppliers than their total numbers would indicate. They use airlines, rental cars, hotels, and travel agents to a greater extent than pleasure travellers do and pay premium prices for enhancements to the basic service (Mill, 1992). Furthermore, because business trips are taken throughout the year, with very little seasonal variation, in most developed countries business travel is the 'bread and butter' market for the tourism industry for much of the year.

The aforementioned characteristics make business travel an extremely attractive sector. But although the rewards for suppliers and intermediaries can be considerable, this is a sector which also provides a number of specific challenges. Business travellers are, generally speaking, highly demanding and experienced travellers. Service quality is more important to them than price. One of their expectations in terms of service quality is that their time will not be wasted while travelling. In this respect, they tend to be more time-sensitive than leisure travellers, and punctuality is essential.

> People travelling on business tend to get frustrated with the many demands of travel which are beyond their control. Principal among these are the time required to travel, the long waits, and the delays of arrivals and departures. They also have more personal frustrations – being away from home and families, being alone, and living out of suitcases. (Mill, 1992)

Just as important as time-efficiency is the element of flexibility, the ability to easily change their tickets for other times and even other destinations, according to the dictates of the work to be done. Leisure travellers do not generally change their plans in this way. This flexibility is a major constituent in the higher prices which are paid for business travellers' fares. The need for speed and ingenuity on the part of business travel agents is another essential characteristic of this sector. In the case of an unexpected, emergency business trip, the booking of the necessary travel tickets and accommodation must be done immediately and quickly in what can be very difficult circumstances. Getting two executives from the UK to New York before the end of the US working day when all transatlantic flights that day appear to be full is the type of challenge which business travel agents must take in their stride.

Business travel agencies also can get closely involved in the financial aspect of their clients' purchases, particularly when they handle all of a client's travel requirements. This involvement may include negotiating rates on the client's behalf, managing their travel budget, and keeping managers informed of their company's spending on business travel and accommodation, for example. Part of the challenge for the business travel agency is to balance the employer's wish to control travel costs (by, for example, insisting on employees using the most economic class of travel) with employees' need to arrive at their destination fit for work.

THE CHANGING MARKET ENVIRONMENT

Familiarity with the main features of the contemporary market environment within which business travel services are bought and sold is essential to an understanding of the changing role of business travel agents. Clearly, the volume of business travel undertaken is linked to the amount of economic activity going on at the origin and destination of the business traveller. However, Rowe (1994) points out that although macroeconomic influences have a major demand on the demand for business travel, other factors, such as the role of trading blocs, also influence the rate of growth. The relatively favourable economic conditions enjoyed by much of the developed world at the beginning of the twenty-first century, have created an expectation of reasonably strong growth in the short to medium term. The World Travel and Tourism Council has forecast an average annual growth in business travel and tourism across Europe, the largest business travel generating region in the world, of 3.7 per cent in real terms between 1998 and 2010 (O'Brien, 1998a). However, this growth in spending has not come from a return to the extravagance which characterized much business travel until the late 1980s.

One reason why company expenditure on business travel continues to rise in real terms is that business travel air fares have risen rapidly over the past few years. But the main factor contributing to the growth is the sheer volume of people travelling on business, which has never been so great. Increasing globalization means that few companies can afford to stay at home, but with the prevailing cost-conscious attitude towards spending on business travel, the challenge for the corporate sector is on to find creative solutions that cut costs without jeopardizing growth or damaging staff morale. Fortunately for most companies, the lessons have already been learned and put into practice.

During the recession of the early 1990s, many finance directors examined their costs and for the first time discovered how much they were spending on business travel. As a consequence of these revelations, most companies took a number of initiatives to control their spending on business travel and to manage their travel budgets more skilfully. The techniques included introducing and enforcing corporate travel policies, trading down in class of travel and accommodation, and centralized travel purchasing, either through the company's own travel manager or through one or more appointed business travel agency (Davidson, 1994b). Despite a return to a healthier economic climate for much of the world, these techniques have continued to be used by companies, who are only too aware of how much business travel is costing them. Accounting for 7 per cent of total operating costs, travel for business-related purposes is now the corporate sector's third-largest category of controllable expense, behind salaries and data-processing, but ahead of advertising (American Express, 1999). In business as a whole, there is now a search by organizations for accountability and control, focusing on cost and profit. As far as travel is concerned, corporations are now seeking more travel at less cost. These, in more detail, are the cost-cutting techniques used:

Corporate travel policies are used by companies to exercise some degree of control over their employees' transport and accommodation arrangements. Generally, these specify the class of travel permitted, the grade of hotels to be used, and, where special rates have been negotiated, stipulate the actual hotels or hotel chains to be used. In the 1999 Carlson Wagonlit Travel Business Travel survey (1999), 80 per cent of companies with over 500 employees claimed to have a formal policy. Two-thirds of these were said to cover air travel, hotels, car-hire and rail travel.

Trading down in terms of travel and accommodation services has also become widely institutionalized. For example, Air Canada reports that 70 to 80 per cent of passengers booked on its SuperComfort economy class are business travellers, while at BA, business travellers make up 25 per cent of its 10 million economy class passengers (*Time*, 1999).

Consolidation of travel agents by corporate clients is a further example of a technique widely employed during the early 1990s and which has continued even into the post-recessionary times which followed. Instead of having a number of business travel agencies handling different elements of their travel needs, companies are increasingly putting their whole travel account out to tender with a view to appointing one travel agent to handle the whole account. Fifty-two per cent of all companies surveyed in 1999 by Carlson Wagonlit Travel claimed to have consolidated their global travel arrangements into a single travel management company. Of the rest, 33 per cent reported that they would consider consolidating their global travel arrangements in the future (Carlson Wagonlit Travel, 1999).

This trend directly impacts upon business travel agencies themselves, favouring some – those who win the coveted corporate accounts – and penalizing those who lose them. O'Brien believes that consolidation works to the advantage of the large business travel agency chains: 'This move tends to favour the appointment of the larger corporate specialists . . . The smaller independent travel agents recognise that their survival is likely to become precarious in the future if they are reliant on maintaining individual corporate accounts worth more than £0.3m per annum, since they are likely to lose them to the big multiples' (O'Brien, 1998b).

COMMISSION CAPPING AND REDUCED COMMISSION PAYMENTS

As well as coming under growing pressure from corporate clients determined to reduce their overheads, business travel agents are also operating in a context characterized by radical changes on the part of suppliers, in particular the airlines. Worldwide airlines are actively examining the way they do business. After the recession, deregulation in Europe led to greater competition on many routes. Rise of European low-cost carriers meant that the airlines found their profit margins under pressure (*Financial Times*, 1999a). Now, in common with most commercial businesses, the airline sector is actively seeking to reduce its operating costs, using a range of measures designed to maximize their own profit margins. And this is increasingly happening at the business travel agent's expense. Business travel agents rely heavily on the income they receive from procuring air travel for their clients. Estimates suggest that 75 per cent of their total income arises from air travel sales (O'Brien, 1998b). Consequently, when airlines introduce new operating techniques, business travel agents selling their flights are radically affected. Two of those techniques, commission capping and the use of new technology, will now be examined.

Distribution costs worldwide are estimated to account for 25 per cent of airlines' sales and marketing budgets and close to two-thirds of this is the commission paid to travel agents. (O'Brien, 1998a). Therefore, it is not surprising that, at the beginning of the twenty-first century most airlines are seeking to reduce their distribution costs. One obvious way to achieve this objective is to cut the commission paid to business travel agents who sell their flights. In choosing this solution, the airlines were rebelling against what they regard as too many parallel distribution costs – airlines pay a fee to Global Distribution Systems, commission to travel agents, and provide free travel in the form of frequent flyer schemes to travellers. Commission capping, a technique used in the USA for some time, was first employed by the budget airline Ryanair in the 1990s, when they reduced their commission rate from 9 per cent to 7.5 per cent. Other airlines followed, with the result that considerable savings were made – at business travel agencies' expense. United Airlines, for example, has been reported as saying that it will save $150m a year through its latest commission reduction (*Financial Times*, 2000a). British Airways has announced that as from Spring 2001 it will demolish the commission payments to travel agencies and instead they will be paying reduced service charges.

But business travel agents have not always been passive in their acceptance of this technique which has so radically altered their way of operating. Travel agents in the Caribbean stopped selling tickets for American Airlines in protest, when the airline cut commission payments from 9 per cent to 6 per cent. Agents in Argentina, Peru, South Africa and Australia have all protested against commission-cutting airlines. Nevertheless, despite such protestations, it is clear to most in the air travel industry that the trend towards commission cutting is unstoppable. Many believe that the solution for travel agents is to protest less and get on with the task of redefining themselves. The redefinition process is under way, as business travel agencies are finding new ways to adapt to the changing market environment within which they operate. With the firm prospect of further commission capping on the horizon, part of the response by business travel agents has been to move towards a remuneration system based on fee-based travel management and travel agency consultancy services. With fee-based travel management, in order to cover its operating costs, the business travel agency is paid a management fee by the client whose travel and accommodation it arranges. In return, as well as receiving these services, the client receives a share of the revenue the business travel agent earns from the suppliers, including override commission. In levying fees to cover lost commission earnings, European business travel agencies are simply following in the steps of their transatlantic counterparts. In the USA, where commission capping has been in existence for some time, the American Society of Travel Agents (ASTA) estimates that two-thirds of US travel agents now levy fees for services provided (O'Brien, 1998a).

The largest business travel agents have been the quickest to respond to the commission-cutting threat by restructuring their businesses from commission-based remuneration to management fees. Carlson Wagonlit and American Express say more than 65 per cent of their remuneration is in the form of a fee (*Financial Times*, 2000a). O'Brien (1998b) sees this development as another factor operating in favour of the major business travel agency chains, rather than the smaller independent agencies: 'Fee-based management is mainly implemented by the big multiple agents because demand for this type of account management is strongly correlated with "open-book partnership management accounting arrangements" which are normally equated with the international companies sector'. Business travel agents are, therefore, turning themselves into facilitators and value-adding consultants rather than mere sellers of airline tickets and hotel rooms. As a result, employing a business travel agency is already becoming more like employing a solicitor – a trend set to continue: instead of business travel agencies' remuneration being based on commission, it has been predicted that there will be a ratecard of charges/fees for the services provided. In this way, business travel agents will be charging for the service they provide, like any other profession.

There appears to be little doubt that efficient travel agents do provide services for which they should be able to charge. More and more, however, the range of services offered is being extended, through necessity. All business travel agents face an operating environment where average agency profit margins are forecast to decline in the short and medium term. 'Average agency profit margins are already precariously low, hence it is essential that travel agents develop new revenue streams if they are to ensure a healthy long term future' (O'Brien, 1998b). Finding new ways of adding value to the travel management process has become a crucial issue for business travel agents. Instead of being simple intermediaries between suppliers and business travellers, travel agents are increasingly repositioning themselves as corporate advisers, not simply working within travel policy compliancy, but actually devising companies' travel policies and monitoring them.

Rapidly, the agent's contribution to the value chain is becoming less about sharing commission and issuing tickets and more about providing strategic advice about supplier selection and managing travel policies for clients. A clearer focus of intellectual capital on managing the best deals and less preoccupation with conventional commissions will shape the future. Although it is principally the airlines whose actions have necessitated these moves by business travel agents to assure their own survival, many commentators believe that it would be a mistake to think that the airlines are entirely hostile towards those intermediaries, or even indifferent to their plight. Airlines still need travel agents. The objective of travel suppliers is to reduce their distribution costs at the same time as increasing the effectiveness of their distribution. As a consequence, it is in their interest to work more closely with agents which can influence their yield and market share. The airlines have an interest in travel agents succeeding in their new role. While they wish to deal with more of their customers directly – as will be seen in the second half of this chapter – most airlines realize that they cannot do without travel agents entirely, as a substantial proportion of their bookings are still made through those intermediaries.

DEVELOPMENTS IN TRAVEL TECHNOLOGY

Reduced travel agent commission rates have been closely linked with the development of 'e'-commerce. Innovations in technology are creating new distribution channels for a wide range of products and services, including travel.

Travel is the second biggest selling product on the web, behind PC hardware, and is set to overtake PC hardware by 2002, according to Jupiter Communications, the IT market research group (*Financial Times*, 1999b). A new electronic marketplace has emerged with its own rules. It is efficient, fast, transparent and border-less. It is a place where everyone can see, and compare, all available prices. For example, Internet-based search agents can locate flights and lowest fares, and these same services can be used to book flights and to generate tickets or electronic ticket surrogates ('e-tickets'). Using this technological solution, suppliers can now reach their customers directly, using online Internet booking services. Already well established in the USA, such services were first introduced in Europe in 1995. That year, British Midland launched the first fully bookable European air travel Internet site, and Holiday Inn became the first hotel chain to provide an online booking service. Despite its obvious business travel distribution applications, growth in the use of the Internet for booking travel and accommodation has been overwhelmingly fuelled by leisure travel, a market in which the traveller's dates, times and even destinations are relatively flexible. There is extensive debate over the suitability of using e-commerce to book business travel. Business travellers can rarely choose their travel dates or destinations. As has already been noted at the beginning of this chapter, business travellers need great flexibility in the service they receive, to enable them to book then cancel and change their itineraries, if necessary. They also often need advice on related topics such as vaccinations and visa requirements, which websites, unlike travel agents, rarely provide.

Because of these limitations, the use of the Internet for booking business travel services is still fairly restricted: 89 per cent of companies taking part in the 1999 Carlson Wagonlit Travel business travel survey (1999) reported that they did not book air travel electronically. Nevertheless, the same survey found that three-quarters of travellers and bookers claimed that they would, in principle, be prepared to book flights on their computer system. Furthermore, four out of ten travellers and bookers said that they had been content to use the Internet as a source of travel information. Reflecting the apparent readiness of travellers and bookers to use the Internet for this purpose, extensive growth in online business travel is widely predicted. Inevitably, the American market will lead the way. The US-based Association of Corporate Travel Executives, which represents suppliers as well as travel managers, predicts that 32 per cent, or $39bn (£24.6bn) of US corporations' travel expenditure will be online by 2003. The figure currently stands at $5bn. Equivalent figures for Europe are very low, by comparison. The research company The Gartner Group estimates that the market for all online travel booking was worth £12m in the UK in 1998 and that this will grow to £1.9bn in 2003 (*Financial Times*, 2000b).

Business travel displays a number of characteristics which make it eminently suitable to purchase through e-commerce. In the area of business travel, information is largely standardized and free of emotional involvement, so that the desired travel products can be completely described by the attributes destination, travel dates and times, quality classification and price (Schertler and Berger-Koch, 1999). The same authors argue that business travel is an example of what are known as 'search goods' – goods that can be entirely judged before purchase (after collecting the adequate information) and after consumption. Goods with a high share of search qualities generally offer a high potential for 'disintermediation', the bypassing of mediators/intermediaries.

Clemons believes that the distribution channel for air travel is very vulnerable to 'e-commerce attack', and that, should that attack be successful, travel agencies will lose much of their straightforward corporate business to direct distribution by the airlines. The airlines' attack strategy should start by developing systems for e-ticketing and should make them available directly to travellers for last-minute changes, especially changes en route. This could be part of a stealth strategy to prevent agencies feeling threatened; agencies could initially be encouraged to use e-ticketing, since it would reduce their expenses, and travellers could be encouraged to use agencies for the sake of familiarity. When airlines are ready to attack agencies, they can encourage rapid adoption of direct booking and e-ticketing through 'payment' to their best accounts. This payment can take the form of upgrades, frequent flyer miles or cash rebates. Agencies will still have a role, but it will increasingly be restricted to serving passengers that airlines do not care to serve directly (*Financial Times*, 1999c).

Is there any indication that suppliers will be tempted to follow this aggressive strategy? It is certainly true that the Internet enables airlines and hotels to sell directly to the public for a relatively low cost. But currently, the use of e-commerce for business travel services appears to be more potential than actual, even though that potential may be very significant. To take British Airways as an example. BAs' aim is that half its tickets will be sold online by 2003. At the moment, however, only 1 per cent of its tickets are distributed online. Travel agents account for 85 per cent of its sales, with the remainder being sold over the telephone (*Financial Times*, 2000a). Ryanair and Easyjet in contrast were selling the majority of their tickets online (up to 85 per cent) by early 2001. Nevertheless, flag carriers are determined to capitalize fully on the Internet's potential. For example, ten European airlines, including British Airways, Lufthansa and SAS, announced plans in 2000 to launch an online ticket service. For the first time, consumers will be able to plan complex itineraries online. The service, to be run as an independent agency, will also help with extras such as car-hire. 'The aim is to bump up the amount of business travel booked online. The vast majority of flights sold online in the UK are to independent travellers, with business fliers making up only a tiny percentage (*Guardian*, 2000).

Hotels, too, have embraced the new technology, with considerable growth in the use of e-commerce. In 1999, the European director of sales and marketing of the Marriott hotel chain announced that: 'online reservations have increased dramatically over the last year, with online generated business growing by 213%'

(*Time*, 1999). However, this growth would appear to have generated its own teething problems. A 1998 survey: 'An analysis of web reservations facilities in the Top 50 international hotel chains' conducted by O'Connor and Horan (1999) found that 55 per cent of the hotel groups covered quoted a cheaper room tariff over the telephone than from their online booking facilities. The survey found that on average, web rates were 12 per cent higher than the rate quoted by the central reservations office. They point out, there is no scope for negotiating with an online booking site that only usually processes bookings at rack rates. By way of contrast, the central reservations office tends to be up to date on supply and demand trends and will adjust the price accordingly. The same survey also highlighted inconsistencies in availability given by both types of reservation systems. Of the central reservation offices contacted, 23 per cent said that there was no availability on the nominated night, even though the company's website had processed the booking (*Financial Times*, 1999b).

Current thinking on the use of e-commerce for business travel, at least in Europe, would appear to be characterized by a combination of resignation and cautious optimism that this will be a major element of distribution in the near future. Nevertheless, the path is far from smooth, and there are a number of challenges still to be met. There are still greater hurdles to be overcome in the business travel environment, like interchangeability of tickets on multi-sector itineraries and compliance with corporate travel policies. Well-paid executives spending company time arranging their own travel may also be considered as a waste of resources.

However, even taking these concerns into account, there does appear to be a degree of unanimity that there is a role for the use of the Internet in the purchase of business travel. Most commentators agree that the Internet is suitable for the booking of simple journeys, such as a single destination return flights, e.g. London to Paris and back, may be straightforward enough to be booked in this way. Moreover, the airlines have everything to gain from using the Internet to sell this simple type of product directly to the client, since the profit margin tends to be quite low, and the further deduction of a commission makes it even lower. Arguably too, business travel agents may not miss this type of business, given how little they earn on low-cost travel. It would, of course, be a mistake to regard e-commerce and business travel agencies as two separate and incompatible intermediaries in the business travel distribution chain. The larger agencies, in particular, have embraced the technology, and put it to use to enhance the service they provide to clients. American Express, for example, has instituted its own online reservation system, AXI, which allows corporate travellers to make policy-compliant trip arrangements from their laptops (*Time*, 1999). The agency's decision to develop AXI for its corporate customers is also important in ensuring that American Express retains its market presence as a progressive travel management company. O'Brien (1998a) believes that 'the development of agency Internet booking capabilities, and the provision of company Intranets featuring travel itineraries and other relevant data will enable corporate travel agents to position themselves as technically advanced providers of travel services to their corporate clients'.

However, business travel agencies are not alone in the development of such products, as Global Distribution Systems (GDS) companies are also developing integrated business solutions for the corporate market. For example, Amadeus' suite of products, Corporate World, has been developed in order to answer what the company describes as the growing demand from companies for integrated business solutions offering self-booking, travel information management and decision support. Using Corporate World, travellers can book online following company policy and with the company's preferred suppliers. The business travel agency issues the tickets and bills the company directly. The travel manager is happy that no-one is going outside policy and the agent is happy because the easy point-to-point bookings are taking care of themselves, allowing them time to look after the management of accounts and effectively deal with complicated itineraries.

CONCLUSION

Whatever the threats posed to business travel agencies by e-commerce, it would appear that it has the potential to bring substantial benefits to clients: In the short term, it seems that the customer can't lose; but what of the long term ? The danger is that the travel agencies, faced with such stiff competition, will join forces themselves, through mergers and takeovers, leaving travellers with even less choice. Consolidation in the travel agency sector has already been taking place across Europe, mainly through strategic acquisitions, and is fully expected to continue. Further consolidation is expected in this sector, and the industry would probably see between ten and fifteen large independents emerging behind the big three (American Express, BTI Hogg Robinson and Carlson Wagonlit). But smaller companies, who may well struggle to get the most attractive rates, will have difficulty surviving commission cuts. Although for large corporations management fees are easy, this is not often the case for smaller companies (Padley, 1998). It looks increasingly likely that in the context of upheavals and innovations in the business travel distribution sector, it is the smaller, independent agencies who will be the victims. The strategy they have adopted in order to defend themselves has included joining agency franchises and marketing alliances to protect their market share. Time will tell if this is effective enough to ensure their long-term survival.

REFERENCES

American Express (1999) *Global T&E Management Survey*. American Express.
BTF/BTAC (1999) 'Business tourism leads the way'. The Business Tourism Forum & The
    Business Tourism Advisory Committee.
Carlson Wagonlit Travel (1999) Business Travel Annual Survey.
Davidson, R. (1994a) *Business Travel*. Addison Wesley Longman, Harlow.
Davidson, R. (1994b) 'European business travel and tourism'. In A. V. Seaton *et al.* (eds)
    Tourism: the state of the art. Wiley, Chichester.
Financial Times (1999a) 'Roles redefined in a changing world'. 6 May.
Financial Times (1999b) 'Bargains slipping through the net'. 1 November.
Financial Times (1999c) 'When should you bypass the middleman?' 22 February.
Financial Times (2000a) 'Extinction is fear of agents around world'. 10 February.
Financial Times (2000b) 'Around the world by mouse'. 13 March.
Guardian (2000) 'The low-down: online flight booking'. 5 June.
Lewis, R. C., Chambers, R. E. and Chacko, H. E. (1995) *Marketing Leadership in Hospitality:
    foundations and practices*. Van Nostrand Reinhold, New York.
Mill, R. C. (1992) *The Tourism System: an introductory text*. Prentice Hall, Englewood Cliffs,
    New Jersey.
O'Brien, K. (1998a) 'The European business travel market'. *Travel and Tourism Analyst*, No. 4.
O'Brien, K. (1998b) 'The future of the UK travel agent'. *Insights*, March.
O'Connor, P. and Horan, P. (1999) 'An analysis of web reservations facilities in the Top 50
    international hotel chains'. *International Journal of Hospitality Information Technology*,
    1(1), 77–87.
Padley, L. (1998) 'Putting their best foot forward'. *Business Travel World*, September.
Rowe, V. (1994) *International business travel: a changing profile*. Economist Intelligence
    Unit, London.
Schertler, W. and Berger-Koch, C. (1999) 'Tourism as an information business: the strategic
    consequences of e-commerce for business travel'. In D. Buhalis and W. Schertler (eds)
    *Information and Communication Technologies in Tourism: Proceedings of the
    International Conference in Innsbruck, Austria*. Springer, Vienna.
Time (1999) 'Trimming the fat: slimmed-down corporate budgets and cost-cutting policies are
    revolutionising the business of travel'. 21 June.

CHAPTER 6

Distribution channels: ethics and sustainability

John Swarbrooke

INTRODUCTION

Of all the four 'P's in the marketing mix – product, price, place, and promotion – place or distribution has perhaps received the least attention from tourism academics. However, in recent years, distribution has become a more fashionable topic for a number of reasons, including:

- the trend towards vertical integration whereby tour operators have been buying travel agencies to reinforce their position in the market
- the increasing role of the Internet as a means of distributing tourism products
- the growing sophistication of computer reservation systems and the rise of Global Distribution Systems
- the trend towards direct marketing and the reduced use of intermediaries.

Nevertheless, while distribution is now receiving more attention from academics and tourism industry commentators, relatively little of this attention has, so far, focused on the ethical dimension of distribution in any depth. This chapter concentrates on the links between ethical concerns and distribution. The chapter will take a broad view of this relationship and will include three main elements, as follows:

1. ethical problems in relation to the traditional distribution channels in tourism, particularly travel agents;
2. ethical concerns with the new distribution channels, notably, the Internet;
3. the potential role of distribution in creating more sustainable forms of tourism.

The chapter will then look at ways in which the distribution function in tourism could be made more ethical, and sustainable, in its own right. It is important to recognize that this chapter, of necessity, involves some generalizations, attempting as it does to cover a broad topic in just a few pages. Therefore the nature and scale of the issues discussed may well vary between different countries or individual destinations. Nevertheless, most of the points made are applicable generally to a greater or lesser extent, throughout the world.

ETHICS

There are many definitions of what ethics means, but the following simple one will suffice as a beginning for our brief discussion of ethics, in general: 'Ethics is a set of rules that define right and wrong conduct' (Frederick *et al.*, 1988). However, this definition raises the question of what is meant by rules. This term could include: statutory legislation, formalized codes of conduct, unwritten but generally accepted guidelines on standard behaviour. Of course, these are all things which operates at the level of a society or community. However, each individual also has their own idea of what constitutes ethical behaviour, based on their own moral values.

Figure 6. 1 illustrates the spectrum of ethics ranging from ideas of ethical behaviour that are shared by just a few individuals to those that are enshrined in legislation. Furthermore, most definitions fail to recognize the fact that ethical rules and values vary between different cultures. This is important for organizations which operate in more than one country or culture. Frederick *et al.* go on to define ethics in business as: '[the] application of general ethical rules to business behaviour' (Frederick *et al.*, 1988).

Again this rather simplistic definition raises certain questions. First, is the application of these ethical rules in business the responsibility of governments or companies or individual managers, or all three? In business, there are also a number of audiences who will both influence, and be affected by, the ethical stance taken by an organization. This range of audiences or stakeholders is identified in Figure 6.2.

Of all these stakeholders, which should, or will, have the most or least influence over the 'ethical rules' that will be applied by the organization? When organizations

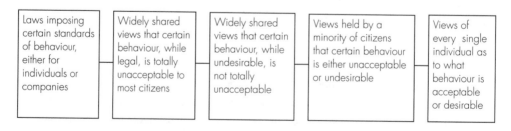

Figure 6.1 The ethics spectrum

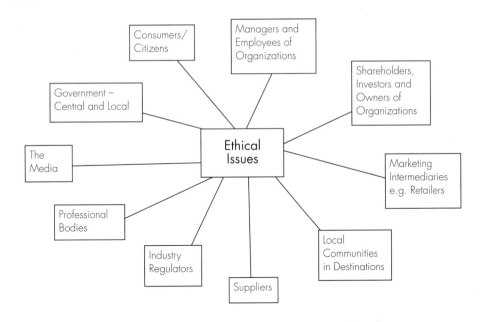

Figure 6.2   The stakeholders in ethical issues in industry

are challenged over ethical issues, they can respond in a number of ways, which are identified in Figure 6.3. There is no doubt that the whole issue of ethics in business is growing in importance whether it be related to product safety, human resource management, or financial propriety. The media is now focusing increasingly on this subject and is raising public awareness of the alleged ethical shortcomings of a wide range of industries and organizations.

The tourism industry as a whole has had its share of challenges in relation to its perceived ethical failings on certain issues, some of which are illustrated in Figure 6.4. In recent years growing attention has been paid by academics, the media and governments to the ethical issues involved in the distribution channels within tourism, specifically. These issues relate to the traditional distribution channels as well as to the new electronic channels that are emerging.

Problem Denial. The organization disputes whether there is a problem, for example, tobacco firms in the USA claiming that tobacco is not addictive

Responsibility Denial. The organization accepts there is a problem but says the task of resolving it is someone else's responsibility. For example, a tour operator may say that it is government's responsibility to tackle the environmental problems caused by tourism

Putting the other side of the argument. The organization stresses the positive impacts of its activities to counter criticism of the negative aspects. For example, it might talk about the jobs created by tourism which is at the same time, damaging the environment

Legal compliance. The organization complies with any relevant legislation but goes no further. An example might be complying with equal opportunities legislation when recruiting staff but not going further, in terms of positive discrimination, for instance

Tokenism. Minor actions are taken to counter criticism and make customers feel better about purchasing a product. For example, the organization might donate £2 off the price of a holiday to a conservation project

Public Relations. This involves just doing those things that offer the best potential, in public relations terms, such as being seen to be helping a popular charity

Cost Reduction. An organization may take quite drastic action but only where it leads to a reduction in costs, such as a hotel introducing energy conservation measures

Competitive Advantage. Organizations that take whatever action is necessary to allow them to use their stance on ethical issues as a basis for achieving competitive advantage, which will bring extra custom. This could mean selling products on the basis that they are not tested on animals, for example

Ideological Conversion. The organization changes its policies and practices radically, even if this can lead to short-term competitive disadvantage, because it becomes convinced that its current activities are morally wrong. This phenomenon is rare!

Figure 6.3 Organizational responses to ethical challenges. *Source*: Swarbrooke, 1999

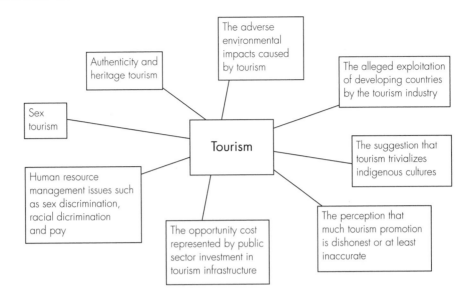

Figure 6.4 Ethical challenges in tourism

ETHICS AND THE TRADITIONAL TOURISM DISTRIBUTION CHANNELS

Figure 6.5 illustrates the diversity of the traditional distribution channels in tourism, although it is clearly a simplification of the real situation. In general, it is fair to say that traditionally tourism products have been distributed indirectly via intermediaries, principally travel agents. This section will therefore focus primarily on the ethical issues relating to the retail travel sector.

Links to producers

In a growing number of countries, there are strong ownership links between tour operators and travel agents. Many tour operators have purchased travel agency chains as part of a process of vertical integration. For example, in the UK, Thomson owns Lunn Poly, while Going Places belongs to Airtours. It is often suggested that such links are not in the interests of the consumer. As demonstrated by Hudson *et al.* in this book, it is argued that customers will be steered towards the products of the parent company by the travel agent, even if these products are not the ones which best meet their needs. Rarely do those travel agents who are owned by major tour operators share the same brand name. Therefore it is impossible for the consumer to recognize the link between the operator and the agent. They will, therefore, be unaware of the risk of their being sold an inappropriate product because of these links. However, at least these owned agents often offer the

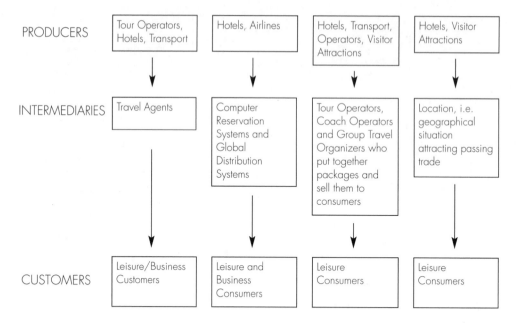

Figure 6.5   Traditional distribution channels in tourism

consumer a choice by distributing the products of their competitors and displaying their competitors' brochures on their shelves. It is inconceivable to think of one supermarket selling the own brand product of a competitor! Nevertheless, there are ethical issues involved in the link between some travel agency chains and major tour operators. In the UK, for instance, these links have attracted the attention of the Monopolies and Mergers Commission. Yet in July 2000 *Travel Trade Gazette* (24 July 2000) reported that after four years of pressure, no agent as yet was displaying their link with a tour operator. However, by October the first agent, Lunn Poly had unveiled its proposed fascia in its shops showing its relationship with Thomson (*Travel Trade Gazette*, 2 October 2000). With the growth of globalization and concentration of ownership, it seems likely that these issues will become increasingly significant in tourism. Figure 6.6 highlights some of the ethical issues involved in the travel agency sector.

Levels of commission

It is well known that levels of commission paid to agents vary dramatically between different organizations and types of product. For example:

* a ferry ticket may pay the agent 8 per cent commission while an airline might pay 10 per cent for a ticket to cross the same stretch of water
* tour operator 'A' may pay 14 per cent commission to a particular agent while tour operator 'B' may pay only 10 per cent airline

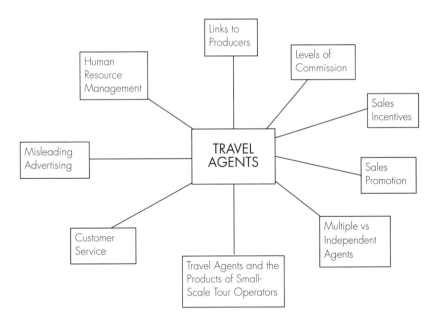

Figure 6.6 Ethical issues and travel agents

- 'A' may pay 12 per cent commission on business class fares but only 10 per cent on economy class tickets.

These differences in level of commission will no doubt influence the sales tactics of travel agency staff. They will have an incentive to sell certain products more than others, or there may be a temptation to sell the customer a second-best product if it will earn a higher commission rate for the agent. Interestingly, travel agent's professional journals such as *Travel Trade Gazette* in the UK, usually carry at least one story per issue about this airline or that tour operator, threatening to cut commission rates, with possible boycotts of such organizations by agents often being suggested.

Sales incentives

The sales tactics of travel agency staff are also affected by the incentives they are offered, directly or indirectly, to sell particular products. An agency may offer its staff bonuses if they sell more travel products in general, or the products of particular organizations. At the same time, as demonstrated in Table 6.1, tourism organizations themselves try to influence agency staff with three main types of incentives, which could lead to customers being sold less satisfactory products because the products bring greater benefits for the agency staff.

Table 6.1 Incentives for travel agency staff

1. financial incentives to sell more of their products
2. educational trips for agency staff where they experience the product for themselves. These trips are ostensibly designed to give sales staff first-hand knowledge of products and destinations, so they can sell them more knowledgeably to their customers. However, they can also seem like a bribe to encourage the travel agent to sell particular products or destinations, particularly given the generally low salaries paid to staff in this sector
3. reduced price holidays for agency staff

Sales promotions

Travel agents make special offers on the services they sell all the time to try to gain a competitive advantage. These offers are widely advertised and undoubtedly attract customers who would otherwise go elsewhere to buy a holiday. Couple 'A', for example, may book their holiday via Agent 'Z' because they are offering the chance to book a holiday with no deposit required at the time of booking. As the couple are in insecure jobs and their financial circumstances could change, this is an attractive offer. However, when inside the agency, and once they have selected a holiday, they are told that if they want to take advantage of this no-deposit offer, they must purchase the agent's own travel insurance at the time of booking. They may well discover later that this insurance is more expensive than that which they could have purchased independently. This practice has attracted considerable criticism but it is still widespread, and is often used to subsidize discounted prices offered to the consumers.

Multiple vs independent agents

It is becoming increasingly difficult for small independent travel agents to compete against the growing multiple chains. The chains can offer bigger discounts and afford major advertising campaigns and investment in new technology. If the independent sector declines or even disappears, the lack of competition could reduce pressure on multiple agents to improve their service. Multiple agents may therefore be tempted to use their strength to try to squeeze the independent agents out of the market.

Travel agents and the products of small-scale tour operators

Travel agents have only limited shelf space on which to display brochures. Therefore, they have to decide which brochures to put on their shelves or which to just keep behind the counter. If a brochure is not shelved and a customer has to ask for it specifically, then the sales from this latter brochure are likely to be much less than those of the former. Often the decision on which brochures to display is, usually sensibly from a business point of view, taken on the basis of which brings the most revenue for the agent. This revenue would be the result of the volume of sales and the level of commission. It is likely, therefore, that the brochures that will be excluded from the display will be those of small-scale specialist agents. This practice denies the customer access to information about the specialist tour operators, and makes it more difficult for those operators to reach a larger market.

Criticisms of agency service

The service offered by travel agents is often criticized on a number of grounds, including the following:

1. the lack of information given to customers about relevant issues that might make them decide not to take a particular vacation or go to a specific destination. This information might include health problems, seasons with extreme weather, and visa restrictions
2. inaccurate information that can lead to consumers purchasing a product that is not suitable for their needs
3. weaknesses in the quality of their service in terms of the time taken to be served and the restricted opening hours of many agencies.

Customers expect that agents will always endeavour to get them the best product at the best price, but because of the issues described earlier in this section concerning commission levels and sales incentives, this may well not be the case. One worrying example of this fact was highlighted in the UK in Spring 2000. Agents were booking flight seats at a particular price. If airlines then offered cheaper seats on the same flights, at a later date to try to fill seats that remained unsold, then the agent was re-booking the original passengers at these lower prices, and not passing on the saving to the client. This kind of practice, again, tarnishes the reputation of travel agents in the minds of the consumer.

Misleading advertising

Agents are increasingly using advertising to sell products, both in their shop windows and via the Internet, for example. They recognize that much of the market is price-sensitive and therefore focus their advertisements on the price of the product. However, when the customer is tempted by these prices, she or he may well find they cannot purchase the product at these prices.

Research by the author in Summer 2000 demonstrated that:

- a flight to Paris advertised at $59 was only available on one flight on one day, in October!
- all flights to Alicante, advertised at $69, had apparently been sold and the only seats now available cost $109!

- a flight to Florida included free car-hire and cost £199. However, the 'free' car-hire did not include compulsory taxes and highly recommended insurance which added another £139 to the price!
- a £99 self-catering holiday in France was based on eight people staying. If a family of four took the holiday, then the price rose to £199 per person!

These examples of rather misleading advertising do little to improve the tarnished reputation of travel agents.

Human resource management

The ethical issues in travel agents are not limited to the link between the agency and its customers. They also extend to the agents' own staff. In many countries, travel agency staff are some of the poorest paid workers, even though they are making bookings worth thousands of pounds every day. Many of these staff are paid little more than the standard minimum wage in those countries which have one. A survey conducted in the UK in early 2000 revealed that the average salary for a travel consultant with between two and five years' experience varied from £9000 to £10000 in Scotland to £13,000 to £15,500 in London (*Travel Trade Gazette*, 6 March 2000). The *Travel Trade Gazette* (4 September 2000) offered further illustrations of the human resource problems being faced by agencies. It reported that:

- the trade union, TSSA, was trying to recruit agency staff but that many agents refused to recognize trade unions
- a Lunn Poly staff survey revealed high levels of dissatisfaction with pay and other issues
- an unfair dismissal case brought against an agency, by a woman who claimed she was sacked because she became pregnant.

There are therefore clearly some major ethical issues involved in the traditional distribution channels in tourism, particularly the travel agents. Growing media interest in tourism and consumer protection in general is raising public awareness of these issues and is leading to a consumer who is increasingly critical of the role of travel agents. However, new technologies are giving consumers a greater choice of how to purchase tourism products.

ETHICS AND THE NEW DISTRIBUTION CHANNELS IN TOURISM

The main trend in tourism in terms of distribution is undoubtedly the growth of direct marketing, where producers sell directly to customers without the use of intermediaries. This is the result of the interaction of two sets of forces, namely:

1. The apparent desire of both producers and consumers to avoid the need to use intermediaries. The producers believe that if they cut out the agents they will

save the commission they pay to agents, which will increase their profit margins. It also allows them to offer lower prices to customers and thus gain market share. Customers are obviously attracted by the prospect of lower prices.

2.   The rise of new technologies, notably the Internet, that make direct marketing a feasible alternative to the use of agents. They allow producers to communicate conveniently directly and cheaply with customers and allow customers to purchase products 24 hours a day, anywhere in the world.

However, the Internet itself and its role in distribution also raises ethical issues. Figure 6.7 identifies some of these issues which will now be discussed in a little detail.

Risk of fraud

Internet marketing has been inhibited by fears of fraud. There are worries that hackers can gain access to websites and the credit card numbers of customers so that they can take money from their accounts. However, there is also the risk that unscrupulous people could create virtual travel agents to sell non-existent holidays and then disappear with customers' money. After all, the Internet is very difficult to police and there is little way of tracing a trader who is operating fraudulently. In recent months, cases of this phenomenon have begun to receive publicity, in both the press and the professional journals of the retail travel sector. This risk can be exaggerated because there have always been a few unscrupulous operators in tourism but there is no doubt that the Internet will make it easier for such people to operate.

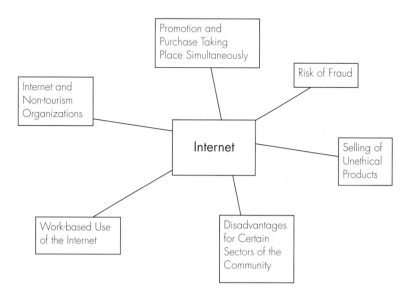

Figure 6.7   Ethical issues and the Internet

Selling of unethical products

The Internet, of course, is a powerful marketing tool that can allow consumers to buy products elsewhere in the world, at any time. They can even purchase them through an assumed identity if they so wish while the seller can also remain anonymous. This fact makes the Internet, potentially, an attractive tool for selling products which may be unethical or even illegal. For example, the Internet is an ideal medium for marketing unethical and probably illegal activities and travel plans:

- sex tourism packages including trips by paedophiles;
- holidays where hunting rare and endangered wildlife is the main attraction.

Disadvantages for certain sectors of the community

There is a danger that the Internet may lead to disadvantages for sectors of the community who are already disadvantaged in some way. Many tourism organizations are offering discounts to those who make bookings via the Internet. However, access to the Internet is not equal among all sections of the community. Currently usage of the Internet is less common amongst the following groups:

- families in the lower income bands
- the elderly living on fixed incomes
- people living in poorer countries.

It is these people who are probably most in need of lower cost holidays but are often denied access to the bargains which are offered via the Internet.

Work-based use of the Internet

Many people now have access to the Internet at work and this is increasing the temptation of workers to plan their holidays while they are at work. It would be interesting to know how much work-based use of the Internet for booking vacations is costing employers, and will cost employers in the future. Some organizations seem to be becoming increasingly aware of this issue, and of questionable uses of the Internet by employees, and are beginning to monitor work-based Internet access.

Misleading advertising

There is a risk that the Internet can become a vehicle for misleading advertising, not only deliberately but also accidentally. If an organization fails to keep its website updated then it may well find itself marketing offers which no longer exist. Several airlines have already experienced this problem and have been prosecuted as a result, notably in the USA. There is, however, no reason to believe that deliberate misleading of customers may be any more frequent with the Internet than with traditional distribution channels.

Internet and non-tourism organizations

The rise of the Internet has brought new organizations into the tourism field. Information technology corporations have seen tourism as a potentially lucrative area in which to operate with products such as Expedia. This trend will give power within the tourism industry to organizations with no previous history of involvement in tourism. This could be a problem because such organizations may have no real allegiance to tourism and could easily simply withdraw if their expectations are not met, leaving suppliers and customers isolated from each other. This could cause major problems for consumers, destinations and tourism organizations.

Promotion and purchase take place simultaneously

Traditionally promotion – brochures, advertising and so on – was generally separated from point of sale in time and even space. People took brochures home from the agent to look at in their own home. They then thought about the various products over a period of time before returning to an agent to make a purchase. The Internet blurs the distinction between promotion and place with customers able – and even encouraged – to gain information, make a decision and purchase all at once. This is undoubtedly convenient but it does reduce the opportunity for quiet consideration and could encourage impetuous purchases which the tourist may not really be able to afford. In a glamorous field like tourism there is a real danger of people making purchases before they have really thought about the financial consequences.

Other ethical issues and direct marketing

The Internet is not the only form of direct marketing that involves ethical issues. The others generally relate to the following:

1. The keeping of personal information on customers on databases for direct marketing campaigns. This is obviously the same in many other industries but this does not lessen the seriousness of the issue for the tourism industry.
2. The growing use of telesales and the issue of unethical phone sales campaigns. This is evident with the growth of telephone selling of timeshare property, for example. Potential customers are often subjected to either high powered sales techniques and/or rung on the pretext that they have won a 'free holiday' which they simply need to claim at a timeshare 'seminar'.

Both of these issues pose ethical dilemmas, but both techniques are found in other industries too.

The newly emerging distribution channels, and in particular the Internet and direct marketing, also raise ethical questions which need to be explored and debated. The potential role of distribution in the development of sustainable tourism also raises several critical points for discussion.

DISTRIBUTION AND SUSTAINABLE TOURISM

Everyone agrees that more sustainable forms of tourism are needed but almost nobody is quite sure how to achieve it or even what it is. Sustainable tourism is often thought to be small scale, well controlled and designed to meet the needs of the host community, as well as those of the industry and the tourist. It is believed that sustainable tourism is about maximizing the social, economic and environmental benefits of tourism while minimizing its costs. Little attention has yet been paid to the potential role of distribution in achieving more sustainable forms of tourism. However, there are a number of ways in which distribution could play such a role, particularly with the growth of new technologies such as the Internet.

For example:

1. The Internet, with its low costs and ability to allow direct communication between producer and customer can allow small tour operators and new destinations to compete on more equal terms with large tour operators and established destinations.
2. The Internet and Global Distribution Systems with their ability to be continually updated, and to make new offers constantly, could help to better match supply and demand and thus prevent wasteful over-supply.
3. Opportunities for educating tourists about sustainability could be incorporated within the distribution process.
4. Sophisticated distribution could also help us to implement de-marketing initiatives to reduce tourist numbers in particular places or in peak seasons or even encouraging less desirable segments such as 'lager louts' not to visit a particular destination.
5. Distribution – whether via travel agents or direct marketing – can also provide information for tourists to help them better understand their destination.

Of course, sustainable tourism can only be achieved if all four elements of the marketing mix – product, price, place [distribution] and promotion – are harnessed together. It will also require all sectors of tourism – and notably tour operators – not just travel agents – to work together and show commitment to this concept of sustainable tourism.

Towards sustainable distribution channels in tourism

Distribution will only be able to play a positive role in the development of sustainable tourism if the whole field of distribution in tourism can achieve a state of equilibrium or steady state itself, albeit that it may look very different to the traditional distribution system of the past. Currently, there is such turbulence in the distribution function that it is unable to help achieve more sustainable tourism. Sustainability requires planning and there is so much uncertainty and change currently that planning is very problematic. Many people are saying that the future will belong to the Internet. If true, this will mean that all the ethical problems discussed earlier in this chapter will need to be debated. It may also mean redundancies in the retail travel sector. Indeed this threat is already being discussed in the professional journals of travel agents. However, this is not likely to happen for three reasons, namely:

1. Some customers will undoubtedly still want to deal with a person in a reassuringly familiar setting.
2. New methods of accessing the Internet may replace the PC such as interactive television.
3. The Internet may well be superseded by other technologies in time.

Furthermore, travel agents will not just watch events. They will, and already are starting to, respond by seeking to enhance service, and integrate the new technologies into their own premises. In terms of sustainable tourism, the best option for the future patterns of distribution could well be as follows:

*   Specialist travel agents working in partnership with small-scale specialist tour operators, accommodation operators and individual destination marketing-agencies, to allow them to compete with the large-scale, vertically integrated tourism organizations.
*   Newly emerging destinations and existing destinations making increased use of the Internet, and complementary technologies to target particular market segment to achieve their marketing objectives whether these be extending the season, re-positioning the image of the destination or educating visitors about the destination.
*   The mass-market multiple travel agency chains focusing on the market they know best, namely the high volume, mass-market, package holiday business.

Whatever happens, in terms of sustainability, it is perhaps to be hoped that tourism distribution will stay in the hands of tourism-based organizations, with a commitment to the future of tourism. However, with globalization, the growth of mega-corporations and the growing power of the IT 'empires', this seems rather unlikely.

CONCLUSIONS

Traditional distribution channels and particularly the use of travel agents, involves ethical problems. However, newer channels such as the Internet also carry ethical risks. It is clear therefore that new channels bring new challenges. The current rapid change in the distribution of tourism products and trends such as globalization and concentration of ownership may restrict the role which distribution may play in the development of more sustainable forms of tourism. If the industry does not put its distribution 'house' in order then the industry, its customers and the tourist destinations will ultimately all be losers.

REFERENCES

Frederick, W. C., Davis, K. and Post, J. E. (1988) *Business and Society: corporate strategy, public policy, and ethics* (6th edn). McGraw-Hill, New York.
Swarbrooke, J. (1999) *Sustainable Tourism Management.* CAB International, UK.

CHAPTER 7

Quality issues in tourism distribution: practices and prospects

Denis Harrington and John Power

INTRODUCTION

Tourism markets are facing unprecedented change because of changing lifestyles and rapidly evolving technologies. The widening range of choice, within and between sectors, combined with growing access to information, has provided opportunities for consumers to exchange one supplier for another. This changing profile of customers has made it difficult for companies to determine future tastes and preferences and the complexity of the market has made the concept of the 'average traveller' redundant. Consumers now require immediate service and products, and services will increasingly be sold on the basis of a company's ability to respond to their customers' needs for flexibility. With consumers shifting loyalties between firms, 'relationships' have proven difficult to develop and nurture. As Bigne *et al.* (1997) remark: 'service quality is a key factor in the development of tourism and travel agencies in particular. The structure and characteristics of the sector, highly dispersed at the retail level, with little room for manoeuvre due to the high concentration of wholesalers, has lead to the identification of quality as a key factor in competitiveness and as a basic element in differentiation and customer loyalty'.

Recent evidence suggests that agents are failing to provide the 'good advice and service' expected of them by customers. A recent survey of 240 British travel agents has shown a lamentable level of customer service. For example, the report reveals that over two-thirds of the companies who participated in the survey were unable to offer the cheapest rail ticket and did not offer impartial or professional advice. Therefore 'agents need to sharpen up their act before they contemplate introducing additional service fees. Consumers will vote with their feet' (O' Connor and Behan, 2000).

Increasingly managers in tourism organizations are looking to the quality dimension in the search for customers and competitive advantage. Quality, it is held, has replaced price as the determining factor in consumer choice, and managing the quality dynamic is more important than ever before. The notion of quality management 'is presented as a comprehensive approach to improving the total effectiveness, flexibility and competitiveness of an organization – in short, the way of running the business' (Rajagopal *et al.*, 1995). Indeed, the research on quality management in tourism has evolved considerably in recognition of the fact that quality customer service is a prerequisite for competitive differentiation in a wide variety of markets. However, while few would dispute the importance of adhering to quality principles, it is also well established that the delivery of consistent quality service is a challenging activity for most operators and particularly for those who operate through service intermediaries.

In response to the above changes and in recognition of the importance of service quality management, this chapter will examine quality-related issues in the distribution of tourist services. Specifically, it focuses on the ways in which quality can be managed in tourism distribution channels. First, the challenges involved in distribution channel management for services will be outlined and discussed. Secondly, the role of intermediaries and, in particular, their responsibilities for the management of quality will be examined. Finally, strategies for incorporating quality in distribution channel management will be considered.

DISTRIBUTION CHANNEL MANAGEMENT FOR SERVICES

In line with wider developments in the service economy, distribution channels for tourism services have increased in significance in recent years. As well as significant developments in the area of e-commerce/business, technological advancements have led to major changes in the ways in which services are delivered to customers. In response to customer demands for flexibility and greater convenience, separate customer service centres have evolved to deal with a whole range of customer queries. Services are also being delivered through both national and international chains. Airlines that were formerly domestic in scope and operation have developed extensive foreign route networks. Hotel chains, travel companies and fast food restaurants now operate on several continents. As Lovelock *et al.* (1999, p. 13) point out: 'This strategy may reflect a desire to serve existing customers better, to penetrate new markets, or both. The net effect however is to increase competition and encourage the transfer of innovation in both products and processes from country to country.'

However, in transferring innovation there are inherent challenges for the effective delivery of tourist services. Ensuring that all channel members adopt exactly the same priorities and procedures is difficult but is critical if consistent quality standards are to be maintained. Indeed, even in situations where service is delivered to standard there are additional concerns regarding overall strategic positioning. These are some of the issues explored and discussed in the sections that follow.

The two parties involved in delivering services to customers are referred to as namely, the *principal* and *intermediary(ies)*. The principal develops the concept that is ultimately sold to the end-consumer while *intermediaries* assist in the implementation and delivery of the services to customers. Principals are therefore dependent on intermediaries to represent, promote, explain and ultimately distribute their products to customers. For example, airlines rely to a large extent on travel agents to handle customer interaction such as information distribution, reservations, payment facilities and ticketing. These channel relationships provide an excellent opportunity to develop a superior offering from the customer's perspective as quality distribution can add significantly to the firm's offering.

However, such relationships depend on intermediaries to deliver to specifications agreed between them, particularly in ensuring consistent quality of provision. The inherent characteristics of services suggest that providers must either be present themselves when customers receive service or identify ways to involve others in the process. This can be problematic in that customers judge service on the basis of their interactions or encounters with a particular provider. Hence, if the product received is sub-standard, then this reflects poorly on the principal and influences customer perceptions of the organization. In this sense it is critical that intermediaries are given the necessary support and motivation to perform their role effectively and maintain the highest possible quality standard in service provision. There are also additional challenges for the contemporary provider of services. While traditionally the notion of a distribution channel conjured up images of a passive approach to delivering products and services to customers, today the situation is somewhat different. The advent of e-businesses and e-commerce together with huge advancements in technology has made many existing approaches redundant. For example, the emergence of low-cost carriers and the Internet are both having a significant impact on the ways in which services are provided to customers. The Internet enables airlines and hotels to sell direct to the public for a relatively low cost and in the process bypass traditional suppliers of tickets and services. While such developments may not spell the end of the travel agency network, as we know it, they will bring significant changes to the ways in which agents conduct their business.

Modern distribution channels are also complex behavioural systems that bind both companies and individuals together to accomplish a variety of goals. The processes of promotion and distribution are critical to service delivery and it is through the service distribution system that companies ultimately develop and manage relationships with customers. This is because the distribution system provides essential information for customers helping them to make decisions regarding company products and services. Indeed, it is through such detailed interaction that many organizations develop, build and sustain relationships with customers. This is because customers generally interact with intermediaries and the importance of this dynamic between intermediary and customer is such that if the customer is dissatisfied with the service provided then the principal risks losing important customers and potentially long-term business. Hence, careful account needs to be taken of relationships with both customer and intermediary when distributing tourism products.

In a tourism context, distribution channels take on a particular significance since the tourist's decision-making is for the most part not a standardized process. As Hanefours and Mossberg (1998, p. 148) point out the tourist is 'actively seeking more information, developing criteria for the choice, forming attitudes to various offered alternatives and arriving at preferences for certain tour operators'. The consumer is influenced greatly by previous experiences of particular operators, word of mouth, advertising and other aspects of the distribution process. As a consequence, the closer and more integrated the linkages between the various players in the distribution process, the greater the opportunity for the provider to build strong and lasting relationships with customers. While this fact has been acknowledged by tourism operators, there is still much to be accomplished in the area, particularly given the current competitive pressures reported upon earlier.

Strains in distribution channel relationships

Consolidation has been a major feature of the industry in recent years. Increased competition and the drive towards globalization have forced companies to increase the size of their operations so as to achieve greater clout in marketing terms and gain scale economies by combining sales, systems, marketing activities and administration. Indeed, today some of the most familiar travel agents are owned by large tour operators, with the result that the company is in effect an integrated business system (Laws, 1997). For example, Nouvelles Frontières has a totally integrated approach with the acquisition of its own airline and expansion into other European countries. Within the industry the market leaders tend to be the big players where the pattern of mergers and acquisitions has been witnessed on an increasing scale. For example, Carlson, the US travel, hotel and restaurant business, has recently merged its travel division in the UK with Thomas Cook. This merger has lead to the creation of one of the largest groups of vertically integrated travel agencies in the UK. Within the sector it is also clearly evident that companies are moving at different rates and much depends on the level and intensity of competition from Internet-based newcomers. Recent experience shows that Internet-based competitors can quickly establish a strategic market position and through web presence can dominate a chosen market sector.

These developments will have a significant influence over the relationships between principal and intermediary. For example, in the past, customers were forced to patronize traditional travel agents because of tight regulations in the transportation industry. Today, however, many consumers believe they can save time and money and possibly gain additional convenience by bypassing the traditional travel agent. Major airlines, for example, are starting to use electronic ticketing (or 'e-ticketing'), which increases the convenience and the services passengers receive. Lufthansa expects to make over £60m in online sales in Germany in 2000 and has set up a separate online company to control its Internet businesses. Low-cost airline Buzz claims that fares are up to 40 per cent lower than traditional airlines and that the implementation of 'e-ticketing' is a key method of containing costs within the company. In addition, airlines expect to see profits grow owing to the resulting marketing edge it provides, coupled with expected accounting savings. For example, the four major US airlines, United Airlines, Delta Airlines, Northwest Airlines and Continental Airlines, have recently joined forces in the creation of one of the largest Internet travel agencies on the web. At least 23 additional airlines have signed on and will be included in an all-inclusive website that will eventually encompass hotel, car rental, cruise line and vacation package booking capabilities. The suppliers in this consortium share a view that they will be able to achieve significant market share with the one-stop shopping site. In response, the traditional travel agents (as represented by the American Society of Travel Agents) have claimed that such a site will lead to less competition among the airlines, to price fixing and may raise antitrust issues. However, as significant segments of the travel market begin to believe that they can make wise and informed decisions in the absence of the service travel agents traditionally provide, the competitiveness of such programmes will grow. As a result, consumers will be able to bypass the traditional travel agent if doing so can result in savings and/or convenience.

Under these competitive conditions, the relationships between tourism intermediaries and principals is coming under increasing pressure, with airlines worldwide reducing the commissions paid to agents for the distribution of travel services. For example, travel agents in the Caribbean recently stopped selling tickets for American Airlines as a result of a reduction in commission payments from 9 to 6 per cent. In fact the American Society of Travel Agents expelled United Airlines as a member in 1999 as the company had repeatedly cut commissions to agents over the last number of years. Even in the UK British Airways has announced that the company intends to cut its 7 per cent commission in favour of booking fees. The airline is aiming to sell half its tickets online by 2003. These are trends that are likely to continue given the growth of Internet use and the application of direct sales by airline companies. For example, customers who book directly with Ryanair, the Irish low-cost airline, are offered an additional £5 reduction on their fare. While this may seem to be small, in relative terms it is quite significant, particularly given the low cost of fares provided by the airline. However, simultaneously service principals also recognize that certain customers enjoy the experience of visiting their travel agent and receiving solutions to their travel queries based on impartial advice.

Increasingly, therefore, principals are aiming to provide services both directly and through intermediaries to end-consumers. In doing this principals recognize the changing nature of the customer base they have to serve.

In response to these changes, travel agents have to refocus their businesses and are placing emphasis on the service dynamic in an attempt to retain business and compete effectively. Increasingly, agents are focusing on the added value that they bring to the travel management process. For example, they are working to ease distribution through the more effective use of customer information. Companies over time accumulate much information on customer preferences and can use this information to assist customers even further with their choices. The agent can make suggestions to the customer based on the quality of the information available. For example, they may suggest suitable restaurants in which to dine, bars in which to drink, department stores in which to shop, etc. Clearly, the provision of such service warrants the additional charge. In many countries corporate customers value the additional service that travel agents provide and have showed a willingness to pay for such services.

SERVICE QUALITY MANAGEMENT IN DISTRIBUTION CHANNELS

The management of quality has thus emerged as an important concern in tourism distribution channel management as operators strive to reinvent themselves and identify opportunities for competing on service delivered to the customer. As a recent commentator remarks: 'Future competition among tourist destinations in the world and accordingly among tour operators on the generating markets will need to focus more on the innovation of the product, on specialization and on the price and quality ratio of services offered' (Calvek, 1999).

Consumers look upon international travel as an opportunity to experience and also to participate in a wide variety of tourism activities. It would appear that most forms of special interest vacations are set to prosper, from working holidays in the Gobi desert to eco-tourism and war zone travel. It is also evident that few zones in the world will remain tourist-free (World Tourism Organization, 1998). Even areas such as the North and South Poles and inner space will open up to tourism. Customers have become more discerning and are shifting their loyalties between companies in the anticipation of continuing improvements in product and service quality. As a consequence, the management of quality has emerged as a fundamental component of an organization's overall strategic efforts (Harrington and Lenehan, 1998). Indeed, the improvement of product and service quality has been widely discussed in the literature as an appropriate competitive strategy for achieving sustainable competitive advantage (Morgan and Piercy, 1996). Heskett *et al.*(1990), for example, argued that internal processes should be managed consistent with the firm's 'internal strategic service vision'. This strategic vision should be viewed as a way of bringing together the firm's target market, service concept, operating strategy and service delivery system so as to enhance the value of service provided for customers. In this way, managers are encouraged to continuously examine current processes against the demands of customers in the marketplace and to update their operations in line with market requirements.

Recent commentators have thus began to emphasize the importance of developing service quality so as to provide a differential advantage over the competition and have attempted to examine managerial perceptions of the strategic importance of quality to the organization (Clark *et al.*, 1994). Kerfoot and Knights (1995), lend credibility to the requirement for adopting such an approach, claiming: 'The pursuit of quality in recent years . . . could be seen essentially as a search for competitive advantage through differentiation strategies. This has occurred largely as a result of a concern among companies to differentiate themselves from competitors . . .'.

The growing interest in quality issues also reflects the need across all sectors to respond to a more volatile and discerning customer base. Customers of tourism companies now require a broad spectrum of convenient services at almost any time and at any place. The challenge to provide a flexible and convenient service has thus never been greater. With the influx of foreign operators, this requirement has intensified. Service expectations are now global and consumers are more willing to compare offerings not only between companies but also across countries.

Greater consideration has been given to the need to define the quality construct carefully and conceptualize quality management within a services marketing context (Reeves and Bednar, 1994; Spencer, 1994). Work in this area has emanated primarily from the contributions of the American and Nordic schools of research. The Nordic approach suggested that the quality concept was a subjective one whose effective management was dependent on an understanding of how the customer thinks about service quality. The general consensus was, therefore, that service quality was a function of the comparison which customers make between expectations of what an organization should provide and perceptions of actual performance. In this sense, quality was a measure of how well the organization's service level matched customer expectations. As Gronroos (1988), remarked: 'what counts is quality as it is perceived by the customers. Only customers judge quality: all other judgements are essentially irrelevant.' The American school of thought on service quality is represented by Parasuraman *et al.* (1985, 1988), and has been concerned to determine the criteria that customers use to evaluate service quality. This chapter examines the Parasuraman model as it is widely used in companies to evaluate quality service and to assist in the more effective management of customer expectations.

Table 7.1   Quality gaps in the Parasuraman model

Gap 1 Difference between customer expectations of service and company understanding of those expectations	This may occur because of a lack of interaction between the organization and its customers; unwillingness to inquire about expectations; and/or unpreparedness in addressing them
Gap 2 Difference between company understanding of customer expectations and development of customer-driven service designs and standards	This gap may exist because those responsible for setting standards sometimes believe that customer expectations are unreasonable or unrealistic or that the degree of variability inherent in service defies standardization and therefore setting standards will not achieve the desired goal
Gap 3 Discrepancy between development of customer-driven service standards and actual service performance	This sort of gap occurs because of the following – employees do not fully understand the role which they play in the company; inappropriate compensation; or lack of empowerment
Gap 4 Difference between service delivery and the service provider's external communications	This gap can occur due to overpromising in advertising; inadequate co-ordination between operations and marketing; and differences in policies and procedures between different outlets
Gap 5 Difference between perceived service and expected service	This gap occurs because of one or more of the previous gaps. The way in which customers perceive actual service delivery does not match with their initial expectations

The SERVQUAL Model

The SERVQUAL Model was developed by Parasuraman *et al.* (1988) as a means of assisting companies in anticipating and measuring customer expectations. Their research focused on two main aspects of quality – process and outcome – and posited that the only factors that are important in the measurement of quality are those emphasized by customers. Only customers judge quality, all other judgements are considered irrelevant. Initially the writers suggested a model of ten criteria for the evaluation of service quality; however, through further focus group research, they refined the model to five criteria known as SERVQUAL: tangibility, reliability, responsiveness, assurance and empathy. The model aims to determine what customers expect from services and the characteristics that determine the quality of such services. In their view, a service can be regarded as 'high quality' when consumer's expectations are confirmed by subsequent service delivery. Parasuraman *et al.* (1988) further identified five gaps where there may exist discrepancies between service expectations and perception of actual service delivery. These gaps can be outlined (see Table 7.1) and are presented diagrammatically in Figure 8.1 in the next chapter.

Although the model has been criticized on theoretical and operational grounds (Carmen, 1990 and Cronin and Taylor, 1994), it has nevertheless been used extensively by service companies worldwide. Given length constraints on the chapter in this book, it is not our intention to review the criticisms. The model is of practical value because it provides an organization with an opportunity to establish the causes of poor service quality. It also suggests that the key to closing the customer gap is to close gaps 1 through 4 and keep them closed. In the event that one or more of gaps 1 through 4 exist then customers perceive service quality shortfalls. The approach is thus all-encompassing in that organizations can include a number of different elements and weights in assessing customer expectations, emphasizing the notion that firms will typically compete on different aspects of quality. Also the customer expectations approach allows the organization to maintain a strong focus on the marketplace and respond effectively to customer needs and wants.

USING 'SERVQUAL' TO MANAGE QUALITY
IN DISTRIBUTION CHANNELS

The SERVQUAL Model is of particular significance to the current discussion concerning the management of quality between service principals and intermediaries. Intermediaries have a strong influence on service performance and in particular on gap 3 – the difference between customer-driven service standards and actual service performance. As service intermediaries design the procedures and standards that guide services delivered to customers, gaps can occur when delivery does not meet the specifications of the principal. Intermediaries can also influence some of the other gaps identified. For example, as intermediaries are contact persons for service principals, they have responsibility for the effective interchange of information between the customer and the service principal to ensure that policy matches customer expectations. In this sense, the customer is influenced greatly by the quality of information provided by intermediaries (gap

1). For the purposes of the current discussion particular attention is given to gap 3 and the challenges facing principal/intermediary relationships in managing quality. This performance gap is of immense significance for principal/intermediary relationships. The great challenge for both principals and intermediaries concerns the requirement to deliver consistent and uniform quality across a wide number of different outlets. While it is possible to lay down quality control standards for each stage in the service process, the human interaction and real-time environment of simultaneous production and consumption suggest that it is much harder to standardize services than it is for manufactured goods. For example, in the event that an outlet underperforms, then the service principal suffers because the entire brand and reputation are jeopardized.

There are a number of approaches open to tourism organizations that assist in motivating employees and intermediaries to adhere to desired standards. First, research can be undertaken to identify opinions concerning the work environment and the ways in which work activities are carried out. The acquired information will assist management in improving employment conditions and arrangements for employees. Secondly, communications can be used to explain policies and improve co-operation between principal and intermediary. Finally, the application of internal marketing strategies can be appropriate, particularly when specific changes are being implemented and new policies introduced. The use of such approaches enables intermediaries to behave in ways that will maintain and improve service standards, thereby increasing overall customer satisfaction levels (Lovelock, 1996).

Service principals have an interest and a motivation to manage intermediaries so as to provide strong service performance. Specifically, there is a clear require-ment to develop strategies that capitalize on the skills and capabilities of both parties in an effort to improve overall service for the customer. The SERVQUAL Model is useful in that it allows for the review and evaluation of the stages necessary for the delivering of quality service to the customer. Using this model strategies that assist the principal/intermediary relationship and allow for the more effective distribution of tourism services to the end-user can be identified.

RELATIONSHIP AND IMPORTANCE OF EMPOWERMENT FOR QUALITY

The notion of empowerment has therefore taken on particular significance within the principal–intermediary relationship. While technological advancement has lead to progress and improvement in work operations (Waldman, 1994), it has not replaced the need for empowered staff who will engage and respond quickly to customer needs. In many companies, the calibre and commitment of staff has become a major source of competitiveness. As noted earlier, the need for effective co-ordination between principal and intermediary is crucial if quality is to be managed within the relationship. Where this co-ordination is absent, service performance gaps can occur when actual service performance falls short of standards agreed between principal and intermediary. As Lawlor (1996) suggests, intermediaries should be allowed to add value by co-ordinating and controlling their own work, thereby reducing the need for bureaucracy. He points out that while this should not mean the elimination of co-ordination, at the same time it is important to put individuals into structures that allow them to exercise self-control so that they can add value.

Empowering intermediaries allows for flexibility and participation in the service delivery process (Bigne and Andreu, 1999). This in turn acts as a motivator for intermediaries, encouraging them to perform to a high standard in service interactions with customers. It also enables trust to develop in the relationship and allows a greater flow of ideas and information between the parties concerned. This is an important consideration as employee-managed service encounters can deliver high levels of personal service for the customer. It has elsewhere been established that three of the five dimensions of service quality – responsiveness, assurance and empathy – all relate directly to the quality of employee performance in the service delivery process (Parasuraman et al., 1988). Bowen and Lawler (1992) have pointed out that there are four criteria that can be used to establish an empowerment-based strategy. These are as follows:

- information about the organization's performance;
- rewards based on the organization's performance;
- knowledge that enables them to understand and contribute to organizational performance;
- power to make decisions that influence organizational direction and performance.

The benefits of empowerment centre around the ability to facilitate faster and more flexible responses to customers' needs and the improvement it makes on levels of employee motivation and satisfaction. Moreover, in situations where problems do occur, a trained and empowered staff is more likely to be in a position to take the necessary corrective action and retrieve the situation accordingly. This point is made by Hales and Mecrate-Butcher (1994, p. 313) when they state: 'only employees with a good level of knowledge of products and services available, a degree of initiative to seize marketing opportunities, the autonomy to seize opportunities and the commitment to do so, will be willing or able to take advantage of service encounters with customers'. In fact, it has been shown that satisfactorily resolved situations can serve to enhance the customers' perceptions of quality for the benefit of both principal and intermediary (Hart et al., 1990).

However, in situations where this participation and motivation on the part of the intermediary is not evident, then quality problems relating to SERVQUAL gap 2 can arise. These deficiencies may be viewed as differences between company understanding of customer expectations and development of customer-driven service designs and standards. Lack of co-ordination between the parties allows for misunderstandings and variability to occur in the service delivered to customers. Over time this problem can manifest itself in loss of customers for the intermediaries and ultimately loss of long-term business for the principal involved.

Encouraging the principal and the intermediary to adopt customer-oriented practices

Tourism is poised to develop from mass-market to made-to-measure packages and in this environment, principals and intermediaries will need to be coached to develop customer-oriented service processes so as to provide the specialized services demanded by clients. Thomas Cook was one of the first high street agents to recognize the need for intermediaries to develop the services provided to customers. However, the company was also keenly aware of the costs involved. For example, in 1998 the company started to charge for its services, introducing a transaction fee of between £10 and £20 on bookings worth less than £100. Other companies have followed suit, e.g. Going Places and Travelchoice. Most fees are levied on low-value bookings such as rail and ferry tickets and do not yet apply to inclusive holiday packages or charter flights. These fees it is argued will allow agents to provide added value for customers and to improve overall service offered by the principal.

Better information through the Internet will make it easier for individuals to create a leisure package suited to themselves. Better communications will enable small specialist companies to reach their markets and potential customers more easily (Buhalis, 1998). Holidays will be designed to meet lifestyle needs and will be based more on culture, special interests and activities (World Tourism Organization, 1998). Given that tourists will take several holidays per year, they will want variety. For example, offerings now range from olive picking in Tuscany to holidays based on activities such as golf, fishing or sailing on ancient vessels in Croatia.

Assisting the intermediary to develop a service-quality approach

Across all countries customers are becoming more knowledgeable and aware about the service they receive. If their expectations are not met by operators then they will complain and demand a better service. The new mature tourists are travelled, better off and more highly educated than in the past. They are more demanding of the unique and more demanding of convenience. For these tourists, vacations are opportunities to pamper themselves with treatments and surroundings they have not realized in their day-to-day lives. The trend towards seeking greater quality and value for money in tourism products has been widely identified (Harrington, 1999). In a recent report, it was noted that international consumers have become better informed and pay closer attention to the quality of tourism products. Tourists have become skilled at seeking out destinations where they will find the best product at a competitive price (Joint Hospitality Industry Congress, 1998).

These developments carry important implications for principals and intermediaries. The availability of highly skilled and trained staff in tourism enterprises and with a high degree of customer service skills has never been as important as it is now. To respond quickly and efficiently to customer queries, companies must recognize the need to invest in their staff. In particular, staff must be equipped with the skills and capabilities to work in this new dynamic market-place. What this signifies is a need to shift the focus from managing technology to managing organizational change with a strong emphasis on what this change will ultimately mean for the people involved.

For example, CERT, the Irish state tourism training agency, in its recent employment report suggests that Ireland needs 105,000 additional persons by 2005 to accommodate the increased demand for tourism services in this country (CERT, 2000). As most commentators agree, excellent service at a competitive price can only be provided by competent, well-managed and well-motivated people. Essentially, this means recruiting the right people in the first place, equipping them with the skills they need and managing staff so as to create motivation, job satisfaction and high productivity. This poses challenges not only for individual managers but for the entire tourism industry as it shifts the debate from merely training front-line staff in the 'have a nice day' approach to quality service to incorporating service and training issues into management practice. As a consequence, substantially more money will be spent on training and development of staff in Ireland under the new National Development Plan. Under the plan, the Government will commit £350 million to tourism marketing, product development and training over the seven years of the new plan. This, in addition to the Bord Failte budget of £30 million a year, will help ensure the continued growth and expansion of the industry in the years ahead.

With the pace of change quickening and competition intensifying, obsolescence of employee skills and abilities is emerging as a critical issue in many companies. To address this problem, European companies must foster a learning-oriented culture where the emphasis should be placed on lifelong learning for everyone. Such initiatives should not only focus on the 'hard' system components but also the 'softer' process skills associated with managing change, innovation and learning. These issues should not be discarded as overworked buzzwords, but instead they should be incorporated as important components of the training intervention so as to improve overall customer service. Organizations must therefore strive for more proactive, credible and transparent quality management approaches if they are to remain competitive under present conditions of uncertainty (Calingo, 1996). With the challenge of direct sales due to technological innovation, the requirement for increased consultation between principal and intermediary on marketing strategy has never been more critical.

Monitoring pricing to ensure the quality approach

The issue of pricing has also assumed importance in the management of quality in services distribution. In most cases agents are given a role in negotiating and determining price levels for particular services. The intermediaries also have an input into the marketing of the services provided so as to anticipate and respond to customer requirements. However, from a quality perspective, it is possible that discrepancies may arise between prices deemed appropriate by the service principal and those eventually negotiated with customers (Knowles and Grabowski, 1999). This can be particularly significant if the service principal trades on the basis of a high price so as to convey service quality. In such instances, the primary concern of the principal is to deliver a premium service that is supported by a strong brand and communications strategy. If the price is negotiated or changed in any way then it can undermine the image of the brand and ultimately the service that is delivered to the customer.

There may be additional problems when the intermediary decides to offer different prices to customers in a particular region. It may prove beneficial to offer different prices to customers if those customers are geographically dispersed. However, if intermediaries negotiate and arrange different prices for customers in the same region, this can cause problems for the service provider. This is because customers like to exchange details and information on the deals arranged with intermediaries. For example, if one customer pays a high price for a holiday in the expectation that the package is of a high quality then he/she will not be impressed if another customer acquired a similar holiday deal for a lower price. This affects the service provided by the principal in two main ways. First, it raises questions about the quality of the service provided by the principal via intermediaries. Secondly, it suggests that the provider is overpromising on the quality of the service given. This refers in particular to gap 4 of the SERVQUAL Model (difference between service delivery and the service provider's external communications). As outlined earlier, these gaps can occur when intermediaries overpromise in advertising or pricing of the product; where inadequate co-ordination exists between operations and where there are marketing discrepancies in policies and procedures between different outlets.

CONCLUSIONS

The adoption of quality management techniques is generally regarded to have positive implications for business performance and is to be viewed as an effective means by which an organization can achieve competitive advantage through differentiation. In line with other service industries, competition within the tourism industry has intensified in recent years with the growing sophistication of customer demand and the pressures for technological advancement and globalization. These developments have encouraged European tourism companies to embrace quality as a medium through which they can appeal to a discerning public.

In the future, customers will increasingly look for innovation in destinations and activities and will seek fulfilling experiences. They will find more transparent price structures (especially with the Euro) and as users of the Internet will seek immediate information and interactive reservations facilities. To compensate for the increase in direct sales by airlines to the public and the growth of importance of the Internet, intermediaries such as travel agents need to evolve effective quality service strategies to meet changing customer expectations. As Buhalis (2000) remarks, a large proportion of existing tourism organizations have failed to address the requirements of the marketplace. These organizations increasingly lose market share and will eventually be forced out of the market as they will be unable to compete with the value-added and the interaction benefits offered in the new global market. Many companies have in recent years undergone a quiet revolution in their thinking and approaches to managing quality. However, there is still much to be accomplished. The globalization of service expectations suggests that quality will emerge as a key differentiating factor in European and world markets. Either companies accept this reality or they face being forced out of the market by their more sophisticated, quality-driven rivals. With the boom in online business, the management of change in tourism markets has taken on a whole new significance. The rewards await those who can respond to the challenge.

REFERENCES

Bigne, J. E. and Andreu, L. (1999) 'Strategic marketing in the travel agency sector'. In F. Vellas and L. Becherel (eds) *The International Marketing of Travel and Tourism*. Macmillan, Basingstoke, pp. 265–97.

Bigne, J. E., Martinez, C. and Miquel, M. J. (1997) 'The influence of motivation, experience and satisfaction on the quality of service of travel agents'. In P. Kunst and J. Lemmink (eds) *Managing Service Quality*. Paul Chapman Publishing, London, pp. 53–70.

Bowen, D. E. and Lawler, E. E. (1992) 'The empowerment of service workers: what, why, how and when'. *Sloan Management Review*, Spring, 31–9.

Buhalis, D. (1998) 'Strategic use of information technologies in the tourism industry'. *Tourism Management*, **19**(5), 409–21.

Buhalis, D. (2000) 'Tourism and information technologies: past, present and future'. *Tourism Recreation Research*, **25**(1), 41–58.

Calingo, L. M. R. (1996) 'The evolution of strategic quality management'. *International Journal of Quality and Reliability Management*, **13**(9), 19–38.

Calvek, N. (1999) 'Changes in marketing strategies of European tour operators'. Proceedings of Research and Academic Papers, Travel and Tourism Research Annual Conference, Dublin, 1–5 September.

Carmen, J. M. (1990) 'Consumer perceptions of service quality: an assessment of the SERVQUAL dimensions'. *Journal of Retailing*, **66**(1), Spring, 33–5.

CERT (2000) *Employment Survey of the Tourism Industry in Ireland*. CERT, CERT Publications.

Clark, F., Tynan, C. and Money, A. (1994) 'Senior managers' views on quality: a strategic perspective'. *Journal of Strategic Marketing*, **2**, 61–84.

Cronin, J. J. and Taylor, S. A. (1994) 'SERVPERF versus SERVQUAL: Reconciling performance based on perceptions-minus-expectations measurement of service quality'. *Journal of Marketing*, **58**(1), 124–31.

Gronnroos, C. (1988) 'Service quality: the six criteria of good perceived service quality'. *Review of Business*, **9**, 10–13.

Hales, C. and Mecrate-Butcher, J. M. (1994) 'Internal marketing and human resource management'. *International Journal of Hospitality Management*, **13**(4), 313–26.

Hanefors, M. and Mossberg, L. L. (1998) 'The tourism and travel consumer'. In M. Gabbott and G. Hogg (eds) *Consumers and Services*. John Wiley & Sons, Chichester, pp. 141–62.

Harrington, D. (1999) 'Quality implementation in selected UK hotels: perspectives and future challenges'. *Tourism and Hospitality Research: The Surrey Quarterly Review*, **1**(2), 103–18.

Harrington, D. and Lenehan, T. (1998) *Managing Quality in Tourism*. Oak Tree Press, Dublin.

Hart, C. W. L., Heskitt, J. L. and Sasser, W. L. (1990) 'The profitable art of service recovery'. *Harvard Business Review*, July/August, 148–56.

Heskett, J. L., Sasser, W. E. and Hart, C. W. L. (1990) *Service Breakthrough: Changing the rules of the game*. Free Press, New York.

Joint Hospitality Industry Congress (1998) *Anything They Can Do, We Can Do Better*. Report. London, JHIC.

Kerfoot, D. and Knights, D. (1995) 'Empowering the "quality worker"?: The seduction and contradiction of the total quality phenomenon'. In A.Wilkinson and H. Willmott (eds) *Making Quality Critical*. Routledge, London.

Knowles, T. and Grabowski, P. (1999) 'Strategic marketing in the tour operator sector'. In F. Vellas and L. Becherel (eds) *The International Marketing of Travel and Tourism*. Macmillan, Basingstoke, pp. 249–62.

Lawlor, E. (1996) 'Far from the fad in-crowd'. *People Management*, **2**(21), 38–42.

Laws, E. (1997) *Managing Packaged Tours*. International Thomson Business, London.

Lovelock, C. (1996) *Services Marketing*. Prentice Hall International Editions, London.

Lovelock, C., Vandermerwe, S. A. and Lewis, B. (1999) *European Services Marketing*. Pearson Publications, London.

Morgan, N. and Piercy, N. (1996) 'Competitive advantage through people'. *British Journal of Management*, **7**, 231–45.

O'Connor, J. and Behan, R. (2000) 'Holiday Which Report'. Telegraph Travel, London.

Parasuraman, A., Zeithaml, V. A. and Berry, L. L. (1985) 'A conceptual model of service quality and its implications for future research'. *Journal of Marketing*, **49**, 41–50.

Parasuraman, A., Zeithaml, V. A. and Berry, L. L. (1988) 'SERVQUAL: A multiple item for measuring consumer perceptions of service quality'. *Journal of Retailing*, **64**, 12–40.

Rajagopal, S., Balan, S. and Scheuing, E. E. (1995) 'Total quality management: quick fix or sound sense'. *Total Quality Management*, **6**(4), 335–44.

Reeves, C. A. and Bednar, D. A. (1994) 'Defining quality: alternatives and implications'. *Academy of Management Review*, **19**(3), 419–45.

Spencer, B. A. (1994) 'Models of organization and total quality management: a comparison and critical evaluation'. *Academy of Management Review*, **19**(3), 446–71.

Waldman, D. A. (1994) 'The contributions of total quality management to a theory of work performance'. *Academy of Management Review*, **19**(3), 510–36.

World Tourism Organization (1998) *Tourism 2020 Vision – Revised and Updated 1998*. World Tourism Organization, Madrid.

CHAPTER 8

Service quality and the distribution chain for inclusive tours

Øystein Jensen

INTRODUCTION

An essential part of service production in tourism is described by the term co-production where many producers are in charge of limited portions of the product. Co-production has been scarcely illustrated empirically within tourism research and particularly within the perspective of a vertical value chain. In the co-production and distribution of organized tourism products, a number of exchange relations and transactions between different participants within the distribution system will arise. One of the problems that results is how service quality can be controlled when many participants are involved in the distribution and production process.

This chapter focuses on the transactions connected to distribution of a round-trip product. The product units which are focused on are services offered by local tourist firms as partial elements of a tour package. Attention is directed at the distribution process towards the consumer market via different intermediary links and at the consequences this can have for interactions in the distribution chain. More specifically, the elaboration embraces the transfer of service-quality specifications within the complicated production and distribution process and how service-quality perceptions of the end-users can be influenced in this process. In order to identify the various steps of such a process and the points where the delivery of service quality can be disturbed, an interorganizational Gap Model that identifies the potential for gaps between expected and perceived service-quality specifications is introduced. Also the implications of this model on service quality is discussed. The model and its implications are mainly based on a research study (Jensen, 1998a) accompanied by data from service providers in the tourism industry

CONSUMER

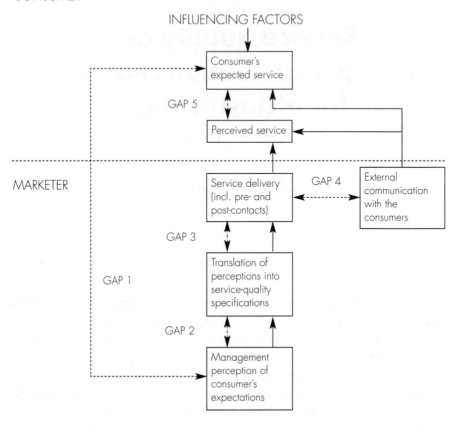

Note: The influencing factors are word-of-mouth communication, personal needs and past experience

Figure 8.1 Conceptual model of service quality. *Source*: Simplified version from Parasuraman *et al.*, 1985, p. 44

$$P \rightarrow TO \rightarrow TA \rightarrow EC$$

Notes: P = service product (of a service element), TO = tour operator, TA = travel agent (detailed link), EC = end-consumer

Figure 8.2 A simple distribution channel for organized tourist trips

of Norway and European tour operators distributing and partly producing inclusive round-trip products to Scandinavia.

SERVICE PRODUCTION AND THE DELIVERY OF SERVICE QUALITY

Based on the special characteristics of service production and the overlap between production and consumption, service production has been designated 'servuction' (Gummesson, 1991). An intangible service-production process or 'servuction' has many characteristics that make the process difficult to control and standardize. Shostack (1987) illustrates how individual phases and aspects of service delivery can be divided up into elements to a 'blueprint'. Troye et al. (1994) point out that the 'backstage' elements (Goffman, 1959; Grove and Fisk, 1983) and the structural elements such as building, inventory and facilities, are relatively easy to standardize. However, it can be shown that to a lesser degree this is also true for the interaction elements and consumer's own participation as 'prosumer' (Toffler, 1980; Troye et al., 1994). In inclusive tour products where different and heterogeneous parts of the total product are delivered by a number of service producers, the control of service delivery represents a critical task in the co-ordination of the production process, which usually falls to the tour operator.

From a macro perspective a co-production system can be regarded as a business network where various business actors interact with each other in economic exchange processes (Webster, 1984; Johanson and Mattsson, 1987; Haakansson and Johanson, 1992). The members of the network perform specialized functions and additionally control scarce tangible and/or intangible resources that are valuable for the others. The stability of such a network depends on the loyalty of the participants, the degree of interdependence between various actors and the development in the business environment. The conditions for exchange can be dominated by the price mechanism and formal contracts, but normally some social norms with particular emphasis on sufficient level of mutual trust represent a basis for co-operative involvement between the parties. Within relationship marketing in the service sector the development of confidence and good reputation is not only of importance in business-to-business markets but also in business-to-consumer markets. Tour operators are usually involved in and have a central co-ordinating role at both market levels. Confidence in their sub-suppliers' capacities to deliver appropriate service quality are thus fundamental to their abilities of earning the confidence and the reputation needed to be successful in international tourist markets.

One of the best known models with focus on the delivery process of service quality is Parasuraman et al. (1985), also known as the 'Gap' Model. Service delivery is primarily regarded from a contractual perspective (Oliver, 1980, 1997; Deighton, 1992) with emphasis on the service company's compliance with 'product promises' to the customer. A primary function of this model is the overview of 'areas' where adjustment problems related to customers' needs, expectations and actual experience encounter the service offer related to different phases of the providers' planning and delivery process. It specifies areas of deviation or gaps that can occur during the service planning and delivery process and illustrates how such discrepancies eventually will influence the customer's perception and evaluation of the service quality based on definite, measurable dimensions (Zeitham *et al.*, 1988). Perceived service quality is generally depicted as a result of the degree of accordance between the customer's expected service and the offered service (Grönroos, 1984). The GAP Model generally reveals some of the difficulties of delivering consistently good service quality and can thus be used as a frame of reference for demonstrating how such difficulties occur in more complicated co-production processes between firms involved in the production and the distribution of organized round-trip products in the tourism industry. A simplified Gap Model (Figure 8.1) identifies four distinct gaps occurring in a service organization and illustrates how perceived service quality of the consumer (defined as the difference between consumer expectations and perceptions – marked as a fifth gap) can be influenced by these gaps.

DISTRIBUTION AND PRODUCTION OF ORGANIZED ROUND-TRIP PRODUCTS

The service-delivery process of inclusive tours within the organized tourism industry differs in many respects from the service-delivery process within a single organization, and this section will describe some of the contextual characteristics of this more complex service-production form. While the Gap Model has its point of departure in one service company, the service quality of more complicated products must often be evaluated based on a co-ordinated meeting between many independent individual businesses that separately produce a discrete part of a composite total package, for example an inclusive tour (Figure 8.2). Each of the service firms represents individual firms that have a more or less discrete contractual relationship with at least one tour operator. In this distribution process, the point of departure starts with a local service product, for example, a hotel or transport company that distributes its partial service (overnight stays or local transport) as an element in a larger product package that is prepared by a tour operator. The finished product package is further distributed via a travel bureau (detailed level) on to the end-consumer level. Organized round-trip products will be combined with a number of different elements, and service delivery will occur in a variety of ways and at many places in the total product's individual elements. Consumption of the product presupposes that the tourist personally relocates himself to the destination. The tourist will therefore not only experience the individual service firms, but will also 'consume' a number of special features of the local communities (Kaspar, 1982). In a number of the partial services, the tourist himself must make the initiative. This depends upon, among other things, how strongly the product package is organized beforehand regarding fixed elements. Based on a comparison with Lovelock (1991), the end-user seeks out, by means of a round trip, not only different places ('*multiple sites*'), but each phase involves both a new firm and a new geographical and cultural setting.

Distribution processes between different intermediate links in the distribution channels generally can be divided into a number of functions and streams. It can be difficult to track down what is really being distributed, in as much as physical possession of services is precluded. Bowersox and Morash (1989) depict transfer of ownership (Grether *et al.*, 1952) of the distribution object as 'title transfer'. In tourism the wider designation, 'transfer of rights', occurs as a more appropriate term for describing what is distributed with particular emphasis on the providers' promises of a specified service performance (Jensen, 1997). This implies that the right to a significant degree is to be understood in a normative way as a moral duty more than a purely judicial duty. The central object in the distribution process for organized trips is based on this transfer of service rights. A service right is defined here as a right or a demand for a specific service output (or many outputs) at a definite point in time (or period) at a definite place (or many places). Specifications of the service rights and additional conditions are a result of agreements between contract partners. A hotel can, for example, transfer the right to a tour operator for 35 beds and breakfasts for a tourist group that arrives 15 July 2000 at 6 p.m. This right can be transferred further in the distribution channel between different intermediate links and the right will not be finally utilized before the actual consumption has occurred. The timespan between the first transfer of rights and consumption represents an important contextual factor connected to the participants' interactions, and can vary from a couple of months to almost two years. The risk, that unexpected circumstances can influence the interactions and the service production will occur, can be assumed to increase with increased duration of this timespan (Jensen, 1998a, 1998b).

A specific service right is not in principle finally distributed before the end-user (consumer) purchases a round trip at a travel agency. It is, however, not until the moment that consumers consume service products that the right is realized and the service delivery takes place. Based on a service perspective, a simultaneous process can occur here in that the production begins just as the right is being realized. The heart of this service delivery process, 'the moment of truth' (Normann, 1983), lies in the social encounter between the service provider and the customer. The entire process from transfer of specific service right from a local service producer and further onward to completed consumption can, based on this, be specified in three phases:

1. Transfer of the service right
2. Completion of transfer of right (final purchase)
3. Realization of the service right (consumption).

In a great number of organized round trips to Scandinavia in comparison with other national markets, the tour operator level can be expanded with an extra intermediate link which within the business sector is generally designated as agents or incoming operators (see also Holloway, 1989). The difference between 'ordinary' tour operators and agents originates from which distribution functions they perform, to what degree they themselves participate in service production and at which level they are to be placed in the distribution chain. One can place the different operators' functional activities on a continuum ranging from primary to secondary tour operators on a scale between two extreme points represented by two main categories of operators:

1. The *'full-scale' tour operators* (or primary tour operators) brand their product and have product responsibility, i.e. they bear the risk of the finished, composite product and its quality. Product responsibility is connected to the producer brand and is related to the consumer level. The role as producer is primarily related to the operating of the tour and normally to interaction with the consumer through the tour operator's tour guide as well as through possible contact with the consumer after the tour.

2. *'The agents'* (or secondary tour operators) do not have primary product responsibility and do not sell to consumers. They let the full-scale tour operator place its brand name on the product. The main function is to provide individual product elements or clusters of individual elements, e.g. reserved hotel rooms at specific points of time within specific locations. The agents mostly carry out comprehensive wholesale functions such as the provision of certain pre-designed service elements, according to another tour operator's customer's inquiry. Agents also include 'incoming tour operators' that are specialists of 'their own' geographic area, i.e. Scandinavia.

A CASE ILLUSTRATION OF AN INCLUSIVE
ROUND-TRIP TOUR TO NORTHCAPE

In order to illustrate the different levels of actors and activities that can be involved in the production of an international inclusive tour, a hypothetical case of a round trip to Northcape is presented (Figure 8.3). Casarin Viaggi produces round trips to various destinations in Europe and would now like to include an inclusive tour to Northcape in Nothern Norway in its programme for its prosperous Italian market segments. It therefore needs to reserve hotel rooms, local transport and local activities in the area. As it does not have all the information needed about local tourist firms it makes contact with an incoming tour operator (agent), Scandinavian Focus (B), that participates at the annual international travel workshop BIT in Milan in February, 1999. Scandinavian Focus specializes in booking hotel rooms and providing other facilities in Scandinavia for sale to interested tour operators from all over the world. Based on its experience in the area and on the global market, Scandinavian Focus generally makes reservations two years before the actual season with a number of local service providers in Scandinavia, among them Artico Hotel (C) in the village of Lakselv not far from Northcape. This local hotel wants to reserve most of its 65 rooms for tourists during the summer season. As Scandinavian Focus is known as one of the biggest incoming operators in Scandinavia, Artico Hotel has made a contract putting a significant proportion of the room capacity at the disposal of this agent for the summer season of year 2000.

Based on the capacity of hotel rooms and other types of services aquired from Scandinavian Focus as well as from a number of other Scandinavian operators and local tourism firms, Casarin Viaggi is now able to design a ten days' round trip for 30 persons with tour guide using various means of transport through Scandinavia up to Northcape starting on 21 July 2000. This inclusive trip is marketed in catalogues and advertisements (E) and is distributed to the Italian market through a system of travel agents, among which the travel agent Mariotti (D) in Novara is one. A retired couple, Mr and Mrs Acappella (F), who would like to celebrate their golden wedding in the north, are some of the customers that buy this inclusive round trip at Mariotti. Casarin Viaggi's round trip actually starts from Milan by plane to Copenhagen as scheduled and contains various activities and nine overnight stays in different places in Scandinavia. After having received a set of service deliveries on the trip so far (G), the travel group arrives at Artico Hotel in Lakselv at 7 p.m. on Thursday, 27 July 2000 (H). During these first seven days of travel, a number of incidents may have influenced the perceived service quality of the trip so far (I) and of this particular hotel in Lakselv (J). Later on Mr and Mrs Acappella are back in Milan with their travel group on Sunday evening, 30 July. A number of actors and contextual factors may have influenced the perceived service quality of Mr and Mrs Acappella, and the evaluation of the experience may even continue long after the return home.

DEVELOPMENT OF AN INTER-ORGANIZATIONAL 'GAP' MODEL

Figure 8.3 is an expanded Gap Model (Parasuraman *et al.*, 1985) and demonstrates the complexity in the value chain's endeavours to maintain service quality with reference to organized round trips in Scandinavia. The model begins with transfer of a discrete service right through the distribution system. The focus of the model is actually directed toward the consumer's perceived service quality of the service producer which is the primary outcome of the discrete service element, that is, the

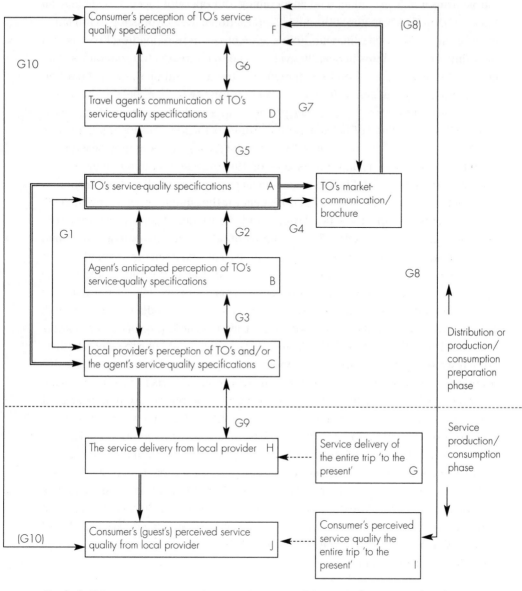

Figure 8.3 Inter-organizational 'Gap' Model concerning transfer of service-quality specifications for a discrete service claim through a value chain. *Source*: Inspired by Parasuramen *et al.*, 1985

local service producer (in co-production with the tour operator). This indicates that the range of the product and the service specifications primarily focused on in our model are initially less comprehensive than those undertaken by the GAP Model of Parasuraman *et al.* (1985). The central problems are to show how one can identify 'gaps' relative to expectations, understanding, service specifications and experience of the service quality of the service element in this process, as well as how the majority of the decisive processes lie outside of the local service producer's scope. This model represents the producer's view in contrast to the customer's perception. The model can here be understood as a 'sketch' or illustration of the complex structures and processes in this part of the business sector. The various phases in the model (Figure 8.3) can be divided into two main phases:

1. The distribution phase or production/consumption preparation phase (included 'steps' A through F).
2. The service production/consumption phase ('steps' G–J).

In the model the process starts with tour operator's [Casarin Viaggi] design of a (round) trip with corresponding service-quality specifications (position A). From position A two directions are indicated in the further transaction processes: one process upward in the direction of the end-user and one process downward towards the co-producer (that is to say 'backward' in the value chain). The downward process starts first and includes interactions with agents and service suppliers. As many incoming agents systematically make reservations at hotels and other service suppliers within a region a considerable time before (up to two years) potential round trips are actually produced, important preparatory 'ground work' has already been done at this stage. Parts of the trip are therefore frequently anticipated by an incoming agent within a definite destination area based on estimations of future demand. These parts can be sold to the tour operator. In the previous case the agent (incoming tour operator) Scandinavian Focus has already made arrangements with and reservations at several local service producers in Scandinavia, *inter alia* with Artico Hotel in Lakselv, and is able to offer a proportion of these rooms to the Italian tour operator Casarin Viaggi at the international sales workshop in Milan in February 1999. When the tour operator purchases pre-arranged elements, it is the agent that exerts the greatest influence on the service-quality specifications relative to the local service producer (B–C), but the tour operator has the opportunity of coming in at a later point in time (A–C), potentially through the agent, in order to exert a certain influence on the local service producer.

In the distribution system towards the market from the tour operator (position A) the product is sold via a travel agent (A–D). This is illustrated by the sale of retailing travel agent Mariotti in the North Italian town, Novara, to Mr and Mrs Acappella in Winter 2000. Sales personnel communicate their understanding of the service specifications to the consumers in the form of 'product promises' (D–F). The consumers also receive specifications (promises) from the tour operator's brochure

(E–F). During the consumption many discrepancies connected to identifiable gaps may have arisen. Consumer's perceived service quality from the local service producer (J) [Artico Hotel] presumes that it is being influenced by the relationship between expectations created by 'product promises' before the trip (D/E–F) and in the service delivery process at the local service producer (H). Element G is 'stuck in' the model to illustrate that the service delivery from the local service producer can be influenced by incidents en route (service delivery 'up to now') that may produce unexpected changes in the programme operated, for example because of transport delays. Consumers' experiences of the actual programme and other events to this point are presumed to influence the remaining perceived service quality from the local service producer. In the actual example, the round trip to Northcape of Mr and Mrs Acappella started on 21 July 2000, and a number of unexpected incidents may have occurred up to the moment, on 27 July, when their travel group is supposed to enter Artico Hotel in Lakselv close to Northcape. The steps within 'the distance' C–F (exclusive of E) in their structure illustrate a traditional distribution chain. The order of the individual processes does not need to follow the individual links in a parallel way. By booking on the Internet, consumers can also jump over the retail level [travel agent Mariotti] and order directly from the tour operator.

DISCUSSION AND ADDITIONAL PROBLEM AND HYPOTHESES

The processes and the structures that are illustrated by means of the inter-organizational Gap Model reflect a number of problems of both a theoretical and a practical character. If one focuses on the structural relational aspect, the transition of the distribution and production process in principle shows that transactional-type

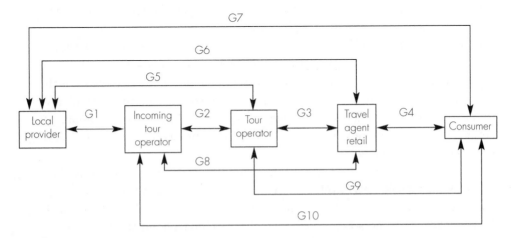

Figure 8.4 Overview of the single transaction relations in the transaction process

relations can arise between participants connected to different types of functions and exchange. Even if we use the exchange relations between the local service producer and the tour operator agent (relation 1) as our point of departure, nine other exchange relations with varying degrees of closeness can arise, and each of these will be able to influence interactions within such a focus dyad. Figure 8.4 illustrates the complex relational structure that is the foundation for transfer and understanding of service-quality specifications in the interorganizational production and distribution process.

Among the various factors that have a significance for the perceived service quality of the performance by the local service producer, for example, a hotel, in connection with a round trip for a travel group – four categories can be distinguished in Figure 8.3 (Jensen, 1998a):

- Local producer-influenced factors (related to both main preparation and consumption phases)
- Tour operator-influenced factors (related to both main preparation and consumption phases)
- Interaction-influenced factors (between provider and consumer) (related mainly to consumption phase)
- Factors caused by external contextual circumstances (such as 'accidental incidences en route') (related mainly to consumption phase).

The different categories come into play in various ways before the trip and en route. The different categories of factors can also be identified in tours of individual travellers who buy parts of pre-arranged tours from tour operators. Here the tour operator's role in setting the travel programme and especially its chances of influence en route is clearly more limited. Factors such as group dynamics within the individual travel group is in this context basically outside the tour operator's scope of influence. The local service producer-influenced factors here entail all the planned activities that a local service producer carries out before the arrival of the tourists or guests (see G), as well as the performance during the stay (H), and possibly also in the post-performance phase (not included in the model). These factors are closely related to the dimensions of service quality that have already been elaborated by earlier research (for example, Zeithaml *et al.*, 1988; Troye *et al.*, 1994; Zeithaml and Bitner, 1996). The chances of local service producers to influence the product increase with the degree of differentiation and are greatest in complicated adventure offers (for example, dog-sledging in the winter). At the other end of the scale, for example, strictly standardized hotel services for group travellers can be characterized as purely 'cookbook style'. The local service producer's understanding of his or her role in the co-production influences his or her abilities or willingness to adjust the design parameters relative to individual customers. This especially involves emphasis on secondary services such as an offer of adventures in the local area. The chances of gaps (particularly gaps 9 and 10 in Figure 8.3) are assumed to increase with increased degree of product differentiation.

Relative to the tour operator-influenced factors, the tour operator's input as a dramaturge (Grove and Fisk, 1983) and 'dream packages' (Reimer, 1990) concerning design (A) and execution (G) of the entire trip, represent an important aspect in influencing the tourists' perceived service quality of a local service producer's performance. For example, tourists will be able to give another evaluation of a hotel from that which the hotel's general standard or type 'should' promise. Basically, the agent's influence on the service quality (gaps 2 and 3) should be separated into a distinct category of factors. However, for the sake of simplification, we will include these factors in the tour operator-influenced factors in this discussion. Tour operators have a number of design parameters in order to influence a round trip's contents and customers' service-quality expectations of the product. This extends out from the tour operator's promotional initiatives and also includes decisions of thematic content, technical execution, technical quality, composition of travel groups, degrees of individual adjustments and complaints.

Even during the trip (the service-delivery process) the tour operator will influence the group atmosphere and total experience. This occurs by means of the travel guides input (Albrecht, 1982) and by means of group dynamic process where the interaction between everyone in the group comes into play (see G). The interaction-influenced factors can, however, only partly be controlled (Troye et al., 1994) and will, to a certain degree, be driven by their own dynamics.

Some of the contextual factors, for example 'events en route', that can be experienced as positive or negative by individuals or a group, could be influenced by the perception of a local service producer's performance (I and J). Such variations in group atmosphere are often registered by the local service producers, for example, with the guests' arrival at the hotel (G). Such variations in atmosphere have significance for the guests' perception of the hotel's service (J) based on immediate observable behaviour, complaints, etc. (Troye et al., 1994). The character of the relationship between the tour operator and the local service producer can also create an atmosphere that can be contagious for the tourists/guests. Such relation-specific characteristics involve, on the one hand, the degree of mutual involvement in the co-operation and long-term arrangements and on the other hand, characteristics in the individual social relations, for example between the assigned contact person or trip leader from the tour operator and person(s) from the local service producer. A long-term letter of intent for co-operation can lead to what an interviewee characterized as 'sharpened preparedness' for preferred customers.

An aspect that highly influences the participants' expectations and interactions in the distribution or value chain is the importance of reputation or image within the business sector. The reputation or image of an individual firm stands out as one of the most important competitive factors influencing the production and distribution processes. Except for highly standardized trips to one particular destination, for example to a sand-sea-and-sun resort or a trip to a main capital, or certain repeated trips for an individual, an international vacation trip can mainly be regarded as a high-involvement product (Schiffman and Kanuk, 1991) connected to extensive problem solving (Howard and Sheth, 1969) and accomplished with a relatively high level of uncertainty. Uncertainty is principally connected to difficulties for the customer in inspecting the product beforehand (Nelson, 1970), or during and even after consumption (Darby and Karni, 1973). A vacation trip's immaterial character involves an accentuation on adventures and dreams. Reimer (1990) suggests that feelings can have great significance for the consumer. A firm's reputation or image here can represent an important indicator in a credible product for consumers. There are indications that the more differentiated the product is, the more important is the reputation of the seller in the purchase decision phase (Jensen, 1998a). Frequently the closer the personal contact the tour operator has with the consumer level, the greater the responsibility for making the customers satisfied. This can be illustrated by the quotation of a leader in a tour operator's literature: '*I have been responsible for three weeks of my customer's life*' (Jensen, 1998a). The responsibility in influencing the formulation of these three weeks is felt by this tour operator's leader as a vote of confidence from the customer. His task is to fill these three weeks with travel experiences that will give the customer satisfaction.

The risk of damage to image is a central problem for firms in the distribution chain for organized trips. Risk of damage to image is connected with the devaluation of image or reputation concerning the product, especially in connection with the destination, but also in connection with product-element mixes and forms of travel and/or producer (provider), that is, both in the consumer market and involving the middleman. This especially refers to the provider's reputation with respect to general service quality, to the means of conducting assignments and chiefly to that which is promised. Errors caused by a co-vendor will, as a rule, produce the greatest damage to image to the link that is closest to the consumer in the area of sales, that which by means of promotion is most strongly connected to the product or that which has officially had the product responsibility. As a rule, this is a tour operator or a travel bureau. The tour operator's quality assurance of the partners involved in the co-production is made primarily on the basis of reputation (as a preliminary indicator), by checking the degree of product-profile responsibility, by attempts to control partners' professionalism and by pre-inspections, and, not least, by the experience and testing of trust at an individual level.

With the business sector, there is a difference in the connection between especially high-risk products and less risky products, whereof the first is bound to production conditions that are difficult to control and high service demands on the part of the consumers. The concept of 'product-sensitivity' consists of those two aspects of risk (see Sako, 1992; Nooteboom *et al.*, 1997):

1. Uncertainty in the outcome of a definite production/consumption process.
2. Risk connected to consequences of the outcome (the market reactions).

A 'sensitive product' can be described as a product bound to large marketing consequences connected to the outcome of the service-production process.

Examples of highly differentiated products are activity-based adventure products (driving dog teams or reindeer, rafting, etc.). The danger of damage to image is great in these cases. The danger of gaps arising by means of the entire distribution and production process generally can be assumed to increase with higher product-sensitivity, because the tour operator's need for quality assurance of the co-producers is also higher. A way to reduce uncertainty and the danger of misunderstandings is to eliminate the intermediate link and to establish direct contact with the co-producer.

A tour operator's feeling of 'duties' towards his end-customers, on the one hand, can be connected to a professional-ethical aspect (professional pride and necessary hospitality obligations) and, on the other hand, to social bonding between providers and customers. Social bonding leads, among other things, to tangible social costs wherein the customer perceives that the tour operator has done a poor job. The closer the tour operator's personal contact with the consumer is, the greater emphasis the tour operator has placed on assuring the service quality of the local service producer's co-product, especially by means of cultivating good personal contact between co-operating individuals in each firm.

CONCLUDING COMMENTS

An essential part of service production in tourism can be characterized by co-production where many producers are in charge of discrete parts of the production. This chapter has focused on co-production viewed from a vertical perspective related to a distribution channel for organized round trips. The inter-organizational 'Gap' Model that is developed from the Gap Model of Parasuraman *et al.* (1985) directs the spotlight on to the transfer process of service specifications by means of a vertical co-production and distribution chain with the point of departure in co-producers. The focus on the end-users' perceived service quality directs attention to the dangers of specification-type gaps that can arise in the transfer process and individual factors that can influence perceived service quality of an individual element and the total experience for the end-users. A classification of such factors in this chapter is presented by means of the division between tour operator-influenced factors, local service producer-influenced factors, interaction-influenced factors and contextual factors.

The participant that has the greatest influence on the end-product in a tour operator-organized round trip is, quite naturally, the tour operator. If one considers the producer structure of the composite trip as a network, the tour operator's position in the network can be compared to a spider's position in a spider web. As a rule it will also be the tour operator that has the greatest interest in 'guiding' the entire service-production process in the most reliable way possible because it is usually the tour operator that bears the greatest risk if something goes wrong. One of the most important risk components for the tour operator is the danger of damage to image. This has a connection in that the image/reputation and trust represents especially critical factors in the choice of organized vacation trips across country borders because they revolve around high-involvement purchases (Schiffman and Kanuk, 1991) or products with a major dominance in 'search qualities' (Nelson, 1970) and 'credence qualities' (Darby and Karni, 1973), as service quality can be difficult to control beforehand and/or sometimes after consumption. Risk connected to damage to image is also presumed to increase with higher degrees of differentiation of the product or the service production.

The inter-organizational 'Gap' Model should be regarded as an overview model sketching out a frequent pattern of processes and inter-firm structures in the production of an organized round trip. There are, however, a number of questions that still are to be elaborated, i.e. how different dimensions of service quality can be influenced or controlled within the different phases in the model. An example of a particular area of interest in the future is the influence of bookings via the Internet and other forms of IT-based reservation and communication system on service quality. By mapping and identifying the factors and the processes that influence service quality by the production of inclusive round-trip products on international markets, increased awareness of the points of danger as well as of the need for co-ordination by the delivery of service quality can still be obtained.

REFERENCES

Albrecht, U. (1982) 'Konzepte der Studienreise. Die traditionelle Studienreise'. In W. Günter, *Handbuch für Studienreiseleiter. Pädagogisher, psychologischer und organisatorischer Leitfaden für Exkursionen und Studienreisen.* Studienkreis für Tourismus, Starnberg (Tyskland).

Bowersox, D. J. and Morash, E. A. (1989) 'The integration of marketing flows in channels of distribution'. *European Journal of Marketing*, **23**(2).

Darby, M. R. and Karni, E. (1973) 'Free competition and the optimal amount of fraud'. *Journal of Law and Economics*, **16** (April), 67–86.

Deighton, J. (1992) 'The consumption of performance'. *Journal of Consumer Research*, **19** (December), 362–72.

Goffman, E. (1959) *The Presentation of Self in Everyday Life*. Doubleday Anchor, New York.

Grether, E. T., Cox, R. and Vaile, R. S. (1952) *Marketing in American Economy*. The Ronald Press, New York.

Grönroos, C. (1984) *Strategic Management and Marketing in the Service Sector*. Studentlitteratur, Lund.

Grove, S. J. and Fisk, R. P. (1983) 'The dramaturgy of services exchange: an analytical framework for service marketing'. In L. L. Berry, G. L. Shostack and G. D. Upah (eds) *Emerging Perspectives on Service Marketing*. American Marketing Association, Chicago.

Gummesson, E. (1991) 'Kvalitetsstryrning i tjäneste- och serviceverksamheter) Del 1'. Preliminary version. April, Högskolan i Luleå.

Haakanson, H. and Johanson, J. (1992) 'A model of industrial networks'. In B. Axelsson and G. Easton (eds) *Industrial Networks: A new view of reality*. Routledge, London.

Holloway, J. C. (1989) *The Business of Tourism*. Pitman Publishing, London.

Howard, J. A. and Sheth, J. N. (1969) *The Theory of Buyer Behavior*. John Wiley and Sons, New York.

Jensen, Ø. (1997) 'Reiselivets distribusjonssystem'. In Jacobsen og Viken (eds) *Turisme. Fenomen og næring*. Scandinavian University Press, Oslo.

Jensen, Ø. (1998a) 'Kjøper-selger-relasjoner innenfor internasjonal reiselivsnæring). En studie av samspillet mellom bedriftene ut fra ønske om utvikling av varige konkurransefordeler'. PhD thesis at the Aarhus School of Business, Faculty of Business, Denmark.

Jensen, Ø. (1998b) 'An analysis of the distribution process of service elements within an inclusive tourist product'. Paper presented at the 1998 Australian Tourism and Hospitality Research Conference at Griffith University, Gold Coast, 11–14 February.

Johanson, J. and Mattsson, L. G. (1987) 'Interorganizational relations in industrial systems: a network approach compared with the transaction-cost approach'. *International Studies of Management and Organization*, No. 1, 34–48.

Kaspar, C. (1982) *Die Fremdenverkehrslehre im Grundriss*. Verlag Paul Haupt, Bern.

Krippendorf, J. (1980) *Marketing im Fremdenverkehr*. Peter Lang A.G., Bern.

Lovelock, C. H. (1991) *Service Marketing*. Prentice-Hall International Editions, Englewood Cliffs, New Jersey.

Nelson, P. (1970) 'Advertising as information'. *Journal of Political Economy*, **81** (July-August), 729–54.

Nooteboom, B., Berger, H. and Noorderhaven, N. G. (1997) 'Effects of trust and governance on relational risk'. *Academy of Management Journal*, **40**(2), 308–38.

Normann, R. (1983) *Service Management*. Bedriftsøkonomens forlag, Oslo.

Oliver, R. L. (1980) 'A cognitive model of the antecedents and consequences for satisfaction decisions'. *Journal of Marketing Research*, **47** (Winter), 68–78.

Oliver, R. L. (1997) *Satisfaction: A behavioral perspective on the consumer*. McGraw-Hill, New York.

Parasuraman, A., Zeithaml, V. A. and Berry, L. L. (1985) 'A conceptual model of service quality and its implications for future research'. *Journal of Marketing*, **49** (Fall), 41–50.

Parasuraman, A., Zeithaml, V. A. and Berry, L. L. (1988) 'SERVQUAL: A multiple-item scale for measuring consumer perceptions of service quality'. *Journal of Retailing* (Spring), 12–39.

Reimer, G. D. (1990) 'Packaging dreams. Canadian tour operators at work'. *Annals of Tourism Research*, **17**, 501–12.

Sako, M. (1992) *Prices, Quality and Trust*. Cambridge University Press, Cambridge.

Schiffman, L. G. and Kanuk, L. L. (1991) *Consumer Behavior*. Prentice-Hall International Editions, Englewood Cliffs.

Shostack, G. L. (1987) 'Service positioning through structural change'. *Journal of Marketing*, **51** (January), 34–43.

Stern, L. W. and Reve, T. (1980) 'Distribution channels as political economies: a framework for comparative analysis'. *Journal of Marketing* (Summer), 52–64.

Toffler, A. (1980) *The Third Wave*. William Morrow, New York.

Troye, S. V. (1990) *Markedsføring og styring av kvalitet*. Scandinavian University Press, Oslo.

Troye, S. V., Øgaard, T. and Henjesand, I. J. (1994) 'Service and product quality: an alternative perspective and empirical findings'. In A. W. Falkenberg (ed.) *Marketing Perspectives*. Fagbokforlaget A/S, Bergen.

Webster, F. (1984) *Industrial Marketing Strategy*. Wiley, New York.

Zeithaml, V. A. and Bitner, M. J. (1996) *Service Marketing*. McGraw-Hill, New York.

Zeithaml, V. A., Berry, L. L. and Parasuraman, A. (1988) 'Communication and control processes in the delivery of service quality'. *Journal of Marketing* (April), 35–48.

PART 2

Tourism distribution structures

CHAPTER 9

Tourism distribution channels in Europe: a comparative study

Francesco Casarin

INTRODUCTION: THE INDUSTRIALIZATION
OF TOURISM IN EUROPE

The economic expansion of the post-war years in Europe saw tourism transform itself into an industry. In the 1950s and 1960s increasing demand for holidays in the northern countries led first to the development of seaside resort areas in domestic regions, while the proliferation of locations along the Mediterranean coast kept pace with advances in air and rail transport (Laws, 1997). The chain of production in tourism was industrialized as package travel became a product for mass consumption. The main flow of mass tourism originates in the urban, industrialized areas of Central and Northern Europe and heads toward the sun-sea-sand destinations of the Mediterranean, with their added cultural and historical appeal. Millions of workers in manufacturing industries throughout the UK, Germany, Scandinavia, the Netherlands, Belgium and Austria share commensurate standards of living and leisure styles, and largely opt to spend their holidays at the sea. The greater the distance between the source of the tourism flow and the seaside destination, the more substantial the opportunities for the industrialization of distribution become. Countries with the most internal demand have produced the most sizeable industrial tourism groups, often vertically integrated both forward and backward. These are groups that are capable of transporting vast numbers of the population across Europe.

Differences in climate and geographical distances have proven strong enough to establish asymmetries between Northern Europe and the Latin world in the travel package industry. Central and Northern Europe particularly need the organizational capacities for production and distribution offered by tour operators and travel agencies. The UK and the Nordic countries encounter limited choices for internal consumption and the complications of making travel arrangements for distant locations. German tourists, however, demonstrate a greater degree of autonomy. Higher levels of disposable income and a more advanced post-industrial economy generate a demand with more complexity. Tourists are less bound to the stereotypes of past decades, while the mass tour operators are not always ready to respond. Areas such as Bavaria face significantly fewer geographic obstacles as well.

The drop in traffic volumes for the once popular northern destinations was checked by aggressive campaigns to promote regional attractions. Historic sites, urban centres, national parks and rural settings provided the basis for initiatives that played up the natural, cultural and historical values of the northern regions. Despite attempts to boost incoming flows, the North never fully recovered the prominent role it played following the Second World War (Middleton, 1998, p. 27).

THE TOURISM INDUSTRY IN NORTHERN EUROPE

The tourism industry in Northern Europe continues to make strides toward a definite structural maturity: vertical integration, concentration, extension on a continental scale, building synergies with non-tourism industries and mass distribution techniques. The maturity of supply corresponds to a maturity of demand. The majority of people wishing to travel at home or abroad do so already, and, as a result, market expansion takes place principally through an increased frequency of consumption. The presumed crisis of the traditional leisure travel package was less a rejection of package travel than a request for a new form of packaging by more knowledgeable, and therefore more self-confident, tourists (Horner and Swarbrooke, 1996). The large tour operators (Table 9.1) have all been responding with more flexible packages. Tourists have greater freedom and flexibility in their choices for the use of their time and space, while the underlying demand-side motivations for justifying the role of the intermediary are met. Cost savings over do-it-yourself arrangements and reduced risks for less familiar destinations remain the basic rationale which propels the industrialization of tourism. Demand in the Mediterranean countries – Italy and Spain, but also France – is, instead, strongly characterized by internal consumption and self-organized travel. In the three countries, similarities in the styles and approaches towards tourism are emerging and suggest that cross-border target groups may be considered. Substantial differences, however, persist between the Northern European markets, in which industrialized tourism packages predominate, and the Southern European markets, where standardized packages clearly represent a minor form of travel.

138

Table 9.1   The tour operator groups in Europe (1999). *Source: TTG Italia,* 26.06.2000

Rank	Tour operator	Country	Turnover (millions of Euro)	Holidaymakers (000)
1.	TUI – Touristik Union International	D	6,083	12,906
2.	Airtours	UK	5,468	10,299
3.	C&N Touristic	D	4,365	9,171
4.	Thomson Travel Group	UK	4,234	7,700
5.	First Choice	UK	2,262	n.a.
6.	Kuoni	CH	1,909	n.a.
7.	Rewe Gruppe	D	1,635	n.a.
8.	Nouvelles Frontières	F	1,585	2,722*
9.	LTU Touristik	D	1,524	2,610
10.	Club Méditerranée	F	1,476	1,767
11.	SLG – Scandinavian Leisure Group	S	1,245	2,051
12.	Dertour	D	1,063	n.a.
13.	Hotelplan	CH	1,000	1,912
14.	Gruppo Alpitour	I	906	1,700
15.	FTI	D	897	1,935
16.	Thomson Scand (Fritidresor)	Scan.	856	n.a.
17.	ITS	D	784	1,510
18.	Alltours	D	685	1,021

Note: *1998

In fact, numerous push factors in Northern Europe have played a vital role in creating a favourable environment for the development of the mass tourism market: increases in leisure time and per capita income, recent national legislation regulating the length of work holidays, advances in technology (especially in the aviation and automobile industries), and structural changes in the labour market. Regulations governing the length of holidays, and therefore increasing employees' leisure time, have been the most determinant factor (Steinecke, 1993). In Germany, for instance, the number of holidays permitted the individual employee has increased from 16 in 1960 to 30 in 1990. These trends have followed in Southern Europe with a negative time lag. Other structural factors, such as the proximity to seaside locations, have also slowed an evolution towards outbound mass tourism. Compared with the North, the development of intermediation and the concentration in tourism distribution channels are, consequently, less advanced in the South. Another factor, which has contributed significantly to the sluggish growth of outbound tourism, were the eroded currency rates against the dollar and the strong

Northern European currencies that characterized the Southern economy for most of the 1980s and 1990s. The deflated exchange hindered the development of intermediation in the geographic areas with lower per capita income, since margins of return from intermediation for domestic destinations are normally limited compared to those of foreign destinations.

An analogy of the differences in demand between Northern and Southern Europe can be found in the Italian market. During the 1990s, mass demand in Northern Italy and Rome was not unlike that of the rest of Europe. Central and Southern Italy, however, lagged considerably far behind. Looking at the supply of accommodation, the needs of tourism flows from northern countries were met by the small family enterprise. Small firms have performed a crucial role in sustaining the national economy in periods of crisis, as in the 1960s, both monetarily and in employment levels. As an organizational response, however, they have demonstrated themselves to be structurally incapable of satisfying the large volumes coming from Northern European mass tourism. Large northern players have therefore not invested in Italy, but in resorts in Spain, followed by Greece and North Africa.

At the beginning of 2000, tourism production in Northern and Southern Europe exhibits marked differences in industrialization, which have grown out of the disparate maturity levels for supply and demand. The distribution structures reflect this contrast. Accordingly, a more detailed examination of the distribution channels in the most advanced countries will delineate the different models of development. In particular the three main Northern European markets (the UK, Germany and Scandinavia) and the three most important Latin markets, France, Italy and Spain, are analysed.

TOURISM DISTRIBUTION CHANNELS IN THE UK

The British tourism industry is marked by a high rate of concentration and vertical integration, and the predominance of outgoing tour operators linked to networks of agencies. The leisure tourism market is undergoing substantial growth, owing in part to the general good health of the British economy. The English tourist tends to take more than one holiday per year, while the market has seen increases in city breaks, short breaks and cruises. According to the Civil Aviation Authority, in the summer of 1997 alone, 14.2 million packages and flights were sold, an increase of 10 per cent with respect to 1996. Two operators, Thomson Travel and Airtours, together meet 36 per cent of summer holiday package demand (Bywater, 1998). The two groups are internationalized and vertically integrated. In addition, Thomson Travel was acquired by the German holding Preussag in August 2000. Airtours is presently rated the second largest European tour operator and is noted for acquiring aggressively: tour operators in Scandinavia and Belgium, airline companies and cruise lines (for example, of Costa Crociere, bought jointly with Carnival). The first three British producers Airtours, Thomson Travel and First Choice, command over 60 per cent of the outgoing British market.

The first agency networks were formed in the UK. In 1998 there were more than 7000 travel agencies. The clearest trend in recent years is represented by the observable consolidation of large retail agency networks (Lunn Poly – 800 outlets, Going Places – 700, Thomas Cook – 400, Co-op Travelcare – 300) and of Advantage Travel Centres, a consortium of 500 independent agencies. The largest agency networks are controlled by the leading tour operators (Thomson Travel – Lunn Poly, Airtours – Going Places), who can therefore rely on a fairly homogeneous distribution channel capable of guaranteeing a continuity of commercial activity. The large agency networks are, for example, able to satisfy the average English tourist's extreme attention toward discount pricing. The small to mid-sized independent agencies instead serve customers with personalized service and advice.

British intermediation also tends to be ahead of other countries in addressing the drastically reduced commissions coming from suppliers. Especially for the business market, the response has consisted in redirecting the contracts along the value chain, in the form of management or transaction fees, through which the client is then charged for the services rendered (a step taken by Thomas Cook, for example, on transactions of limited economic value). This contractual fee, which guarantees greater price transparency, makes English intermediation a reality to watch carefully, as it may well anticipate European trends for the coming years.

During the 1990s the business travel market saw large operators (American Express and Carlson Wagonlit) come away strengthened, but also found the minor agency networks an active presence. The networks have adopted a strategy of joining broad international networks in order to promote services on a worldwide scale. Britannic is a member of the First Business Travel International network, Portman and P&O Travel of Woodside Travel Trust, and Gray Dawes Travel is part of the global Internet Inc. The concrete objective is to provide 24-hour service internationally.

The leaders in British tourism stand out for their model of vertical integration, and for exercising a controlling interest at every level of the value chain: airline companies, accommodation providers, tour operators, agencies. In recent years the model seems to be completing itself through the acquisition of accommodation establishments. Until a short time ago, the relationships between tour operators and accommodation structures excluded strong equity investments. Tour operators preferred a degree of freedom in negotiations with hotel groups in order to:

- take advantage of difficult periods in the accommodation industry;
- quickly transfer their own investments from destination to destination in response to demand preferences;
- avoid risks associated with certain destinations; and

- mitigate the effects of their own sectors' seasonality.

In a market with stable growth and an increasingly mature tourism supply, the strategy of the large British groups now seems to be more directed towards the integration of the hotel chains and the profit margins derived from backward vertical integration. The profit margins are considerably greater than those found in forward vertical integration and allow the tour operator to exercise tighter control over the quality of the final product. Vertical integration grants the various players in the channel a series of advantages. Part of the cost savings from lower transaction costs can be transferred into final prices. Managing the information attained from forward integration also permits a series of benefits: finely tuned yield management systems, an effective management of last-minute sales, products that are easier to sell across the agency network, reduced distribution costs due to decreased commissions and a more efficient distribution of brochures. In France, for example, 20 to 30 brochures are needed to obtain a reservation, in the UK 15 are sufficient (Chaintron, 1995). In the UK, the rewards from vertical integration have been invested in the standardization of the product, that is, towards price reduction and quality control, rather than an enhanced quality of the components. This has opened a niche for small operators to specialize in the upper segment of the tourism market.

TOURISM DISTRIBUTION CHANNELS IN GERMANY

Germany is the largest European tourism market, not only in terms of demographics, but also in terms of the number and length of holidays each year per capita, which are greater than those of other countries generating tourism flows. As demonstrated in Table 9.2, the structural evolution of the German tourism industry has been characterized by investments from large commercial and financial groups operating outside the tourism industry, such as Westdeutsche Landesbank and Preussag. During the 1990s market expansion was additionally sustained through the impact of political unification, which opened vast areas of demand for tourism consumption. The distribution channels have been developed and extended towards the East. With the acquisition of Thomson, Preussag, owner of Hapag Touristik Union (HTU), has created the world's largest tourism group. Vertical competition in the distribution channels in Germany, as in the UK, has witnessed travel product suppliers prevail over intermediaries.

Historically the main agency networks were tied through intense, even exclusive, collaborative relationships with one of the large tour operators (i.e. TUI or Neckermann). On the one hand, this did not encourage investment in a proprietary network of agencies. On the other hand, the situation did not prompt independent agencies to start voluntary associations (Pompanon, 1995, p. 18). The strategy of vertical integration was, therefore, initially directed backwards, toward those accommodation chains with a strong presence in the Mediterranean basin (for example, Iberotel, Riu, Prinsotel), and only later towards airline companies. After the deregulation of the mid-1990s, some of the largest tour operators preferred to build their own agency networks, using franchising, privileged accords, and proprietary outlets. At present the vertical integration model is still in a phase of implementation. Two groups, Hapag Touristik Union (HTU) and Condor & Neckermann (C&N), have already completed integration, while other groups, such as LTU, FTI and Rewe, have not yet achieved forward integration of the agency network. Between the two completely integrated groups there exist, however, considerable differences in the management of the network. HTU favours a centralized management model, while C&N consents a greater degree of autonomy to its networks (FVW International, 1999).

Table 9.2   The top ten German tour operators (1999)

Position	Tour operator	Participants (000)	Turnover (bill. DM)	Marketshare (%)
1.	TUI Group Deutschland	6,043	7.6	21.1
2.	C&N	5,885	6.4	17.8
3.	LTU	2,610	3.0	8.3
4.	Dertour	2,927	1.8	5.0
5.	FTI	1,935	1.8	5.0
6.	ITS	1,510	1.5	4.2
7.	Alltours	1,021	1.3	3.6
8.	Öger	751	0.77	2.1
9.	Studiosus	100	0.37	1.1
10.	Arkona	041	0.28	0.8

In the business travel sector, the concentration is higher. In 1998 the first six groups (Hapag-Lloyd, First, LCC, DER, BTI Euro Lloyd and American Express) received 68 per cent of all business travel handled through agencies. Major corporate clients demanding worldwide service also pushed the agency networks operating in this sector to form agreements with international reservation systems. In the late 1990s the process of integration progressively reduced the number of independent travel agencies, which had multiplied following deregulation. In 1998, 47 per cent of the 14,000 German travel agencies were still independent, although generating only 20 per cent of the total agency market, an estimated 44.92 billion DM (DER figures). The independent agency market share had amounted to 29 per cent in 1997. As a result of this trend the appeal of agency networks rose: the number of agencies joining chains or franchised networks increased by 5 per cent between 1997 and 1998, while those adhering to voluntary associations (co-ops) increased by 9 per cent, evidence that independent owners primarily sought weak ties. Confronting the numerical growth of the agencies with statistics on turnover, however, highlights the weakness of the distribution channel network: average turnover per agency decreased from 4.5m DM to 4.4m DM, and the reduction is even more striking for chains or franchised agencies. Since the co-ops do not handle the steadily growing business travel market, this gap will most likely continue to expand in the future. Moreover, turnover for the overall retail market in 1998 increased by only 2.4 per cent, while that of the tour operators grew by 5 per cent. It is expected that the development of direct online sales channels will widen this gap further.

In Germany the dominant position of the distribution channel has for some time permitted tour operators to engage with tourists in customer loyalty campaigns and initiatives of vertical cooperation. TUI, for example, introduced the TUI-Card in 1994, Kuoni instituted the Gold Club in 1995 and LTU launched the LTU-Card in 1996 (Kärcher, 1997). These programmes are opposed by the tourism agencies, but they produce various benefits. Not only do they create greater customer loyalty, but detailed information on clients' travel and holiday behaviour can also be gathered. Tour operators can then tailor products for the following year based on complex marketing data. It will be interesting to see, however, if the large groups that are not forwardly integrated will be able to profit from online sales more easily. These groups will not have to face disintermediating or repositioning their own networks of agencies.

TOURISM DISTRIBUTION CHANNELS IN SCANDINAVIA

In Scandinavia (Sweden, Norway and Denmark), distribution displays a high rate of concentration. The three main tour operators, SLG, Spies/Tjaereborg and Transpool possess 75 per cent of the total outgoing leisure market. The English group Airtours has acquired the first two and has now obtained 50 per cent of the Scandinavian market. In Finland, on the other hand, the whole tourism channel is dominated by subsidiaries of the group Finnair, which has achieved complete integration. SLG and Spies/Tjaereborg distribute their own brand products mainly through exclusive agencies. This strategy facilitates the management of last-minute sales, and responds to what has proven to be one of the main trends in Scandinavian demand.

Another aspect which characterizes demand in Scandinavia is the presence of a substantial youth market of frequent travellers. This segment demands more flexible, less packaged products, typical of the experienced traveller, but on a more limited budget. The product requirements specific to this youth market stimulated the entrance of new specialized players, such as, for example, Kilroy Travels. In the business tourism market the competition is stable and limited to the three main international groups which divide the market: American Express, Carlson Wagonlit and Hogg Robinson.

Perhaps the most interesting aspect of the Scandinavia market regards the prospects for online tourism. The Nordic countries are contending as leaders in the IT revolution in Europe, especially in mobile telephony and wireless communications infrastructure. With 82 per cent of the population online, Internet penetration is the highest in Europe. That direct online distribution will develop more rapidly than other countries is, therefore, certain. Perhaps for this reason, strong investment in the travel agency sector has not been seen from the mid-1990s on.

TOURISM DISTRIBUTION CHANNELS IN FRANCE

French distribution channels are distinctly different from those in the UK and Germany. They have high levels of concentration (although somewhat lower than in Germany and the UK) and, more notably, the agency networks dominate over the tour operators in the tourism value chain. The networks, both chains and co-ops, therefore govern the distribution channels. There are no large vertically integrated groups (with the exception of Look Voyage and Nouvelles Frontières which, apart from owning suppliers and tour operators, also possesses 125 agencies with exclusive distribution). The networks are able to impose heavy commissions on the tour operators, approximately 12 to 20 per cent, as opposed to the 9 to 18 per cent in the UK. In France the practice of discriminatory discounts does not exist. During high tourist season in the UK, the share of sales volume the tour operator earns from the home agency network is increased through discriminatory actions against competing products. The final prices paid by the British tourist are therefore lower than French prices.

The leading chains are Havas Voyages (550 outlets, wholly owned or franchised), Carlson Wagonlit (350, business travel), Frantour (100); among the co-ops of independent agencies Selectour (450 outlets), Afat Voyages (350), Manor (300, business travel), and Tourcom (100) stand out. Over half of the agencies are still independent, but, as in Germany, their share of the market is diminishing: the possible alternative remains niche positioning, especially in the cities of the provinces, or joining agency associations. Another characteristic of the French travel agency market is the presence of small, aggressive chains owned by large French commercial distribution groups, such as PPR and Carrefour, who, adopting a strategy of differentiation, have not overlooked the high growth rates of the tourism industry. None of the nearly 350 French tour operators owns a network of agencies. Partnership agreements with independent agencies, however, or their direct acquisition, can be found. Based on sales, the two principal tour operators, Nouvelles Frontières and Club Med, together control only between 18 and 20 per cent of the market.

In business travel, the degree of concentration is higher. Three operators, Havas Voyages/American Express, Carlson Wagonlit Travel and Via Voyages dominate the segment. On the supply side, the separation between the leisure and business target markets is less clear cut than in Northern Europe: many operators compete in both markets. It is interesting to note that, as in the British market, some agencies specialized in business travel have begun to require a management fee from the client.

TOURISM DISTRIBUTION CHANNELS IN ITALY

Compared to the tourism industry in Northern Europe and, to a degree, in France, Italy lacks market maturity. Chronic under-capitalization and family ownership have hampered the dimensional growth of small firms, and fragmented the tourism supply. The result is an overcrowding of small chains and disconnected, independent agencies rooted in the local territories. Levels of vertical integration and the degree of concentration are still low among accommodation structures, tour operators and travel agencies, as demonstrated in Table 9.3.

Some trends, however, have begun to appear in Italy. A number of non-tourism-related financial and industrial groups have started investing in the distribution channel, intent on quickly reaching the critical mass necessary for operating in the European market. According to statistics from the Italian Tour Operators Association, in 1999 Italian tourism distribution channels consisted of approximately 110 tour operators and 7000 travel agencies. The top 45 per cent of the tour operators commanded 77 per cent (6000 billion lire) of total business, which in 1998 was estimated at 7800 billion lire (39 billion euro). One single group, Alpitour, which holds a 23.5 per cent market share, or 1591 billion lire in sales (in 1998), already appears capable of performing at European levels, having evidently benefited from the involvement of IFIL, the Agnelli family's financial group. The number of Italian travel agencies grew steadily during the 1990s, helped by the liberalization of trade under the Bersani reforms of 1998. Statistics from the Italian Travel Agents Association show that the number of agencies increased from nearly 4000 in 1996 to 6088 in 1999, of which 1450 participate in some form of network membership. Over half of the networks were established after 1995. Table 9.4 shows that two networks are reaching viable proportions: Giramondo, with 510 franchised agencies, and Buon Viaggio Network, with 270 agencies, which groups chains of agencies into purchasing groups and consortia.

In the business travel segment, the four leading players are Carlson Wagonlit Travel, American Express, Uvet Viaggi and Kuoni (the BTI representative in Italy). The two leading networks in leisure tourism are widely present in the north of the country, both having designs on controlling the national market. Giramondo is also adopting a strategy of internationalization, with expansion into both the Spanish

Table 9.3 The principal tour operators in Italy (1998)

Rank	Tour operator	Turnover (billion lira)	Market share (%)
1.	Gruppo Alpitour	1,591	23.5
2.	Costa Crociere*	500	5.9
3.	HIT	500	5.9
4.	Viaggi del Ventaglio	441	5.2
5.	Valtur	370	4.3
6.	Hotelplan – Turisanda	346	4.1
7.	Kuoni – Gastaldi	310	3.6
8.	Teorema	210	2.5
9.	Club Med Italia	152	1.8
10.	Eurotravel	138	1.6
11.	Olympia Viaggi	135	1.6
12.	I Grandi Viaggi	116	1.4
13.	Nouvelles Frontières	112	1.3
14.	Orizzonti	110	1.3

Note: *only Italy

Table 9.4 Retail travel networks in Italy. *Source*: Specialized press

Networks	Number of travel agencies (1999)	Turnover (1998, billion lira)
Giramondo	510	1,100
Buon Viaggio Network	270	800
Itn Italia	110	n.a.
Sestante Travel Network	74	500
Fabretto Travel Network (now Welcome Partner)	60	110
Robintour	38	300
Noi le vacanze	33	120
Pool 7	23	70
Cisalpina tours	22	240
Lufthansa city center	22	n.a.
Con.Te	21	n.a.
Carlson Wagonlit	18	500

and American markets. Their strategy is based on a strong investment in training and advertising, and they allow new entrants to the network. In contrast, the Buon Viaggio network is selecting only well-established agencies that are managed by an experienced staff. Networks must provide agencies with information, general and specialized training (Casarin and Zampese, 1997), marketing services, advertising support, software programs and preferential relationships with suppliers. The management culture of the smaller networks, however, is not exceptionally advanced. Smaller purchasing groups will often limit themselves to negotiating on commissions from tour operators. Moreover, the groups generally tend to involve agents in open agreements with loose commitments. The tour operators, therefore, form with these groups the thin relationships they maintain with the large independent agencies. The average size of the Italian network is destined to grow over the next few years. The increase is due to the existence of greater numbers of independent agencies capable of successfully entering the network, and some rationalization effects that should reduce the total amount of the national networks.

The prospects of direct channels are tied to the Internet penetration rate. Internet usage will be spurred by the widespread diffusion of cellular phones, which in Italy represents one of the highest rates in the world. Recent progress in the levels of postal service will also facilitate strategies for direct marketing. Only the largest agency networks will be able to integrate online sales with the widespread points of sales. The transformation of the major networks, such as Buon Viaggio and Giramondo, into Internet portals could represent a natural evolution of the network concept, and come into conflict with the portals of the GDS and the large, vertically integrated tourism groups. These changes, however, will come up against strong technological resistance in the travel agency environment. Consequently, the networks will seek the organizational and technical know-how of international allies even from service sectors outside the tourism industry (mobile telecommunications firms, large commercial retailers, credit card companies, insurance companies, banks, former state-owned groups such as the PTT, ENEL and others).

TOURISM DISTRIBUTION CHANNELS IN SPAIN

Spanish tourism is still characterized by strong domestic flows (in 1999, 32 million holidays were taken within national borders, as compared to 3 million holidays abroad), and by incoming tourism from foreign Spanish-speaking markets, especially in South America. In 1999 outgoing sales of the main 100 tour operators amounted to approximately 2.5 billion Euro, with the top ten tour operators realizing 50 per cent of these profits. Nevertheless, the distribution channels are dominated by a few vertically integrated groups, which developed as the agency networks progressively bought out airline companies, hotels and tour operators.

As in many other Latin countries, the development model favoured the agencies over producers of outgoing holidays.

The high rate of concentration of the travel agencies allowed for strategies of vertical integration. Groups such as Halcòn Viajes and Grupo Viajes Iberia have integrated all their tourism package components, but do not yet have international dimensions. The expansion of these groups towards the broad Spanish-speaking market is, however, expected. Each of the principal groups operates in both the leisure travel and business travel segments.

CONCLUSIONS

Tourism distribution in Europe reveals pronounced differences in approaches to holiday taking. In Northern Europe cultural, economic and environmental factors have encouraged the standardization and industrialization of package travel, which in turn has allowed large tour operators to assume the lead in the distribution channels. Southern Europe, in contrast, has seen these same factors strengthen the trend for self-organized holidays and the intermediation of product packages. In Italy, moreover, legislative restrictions in place until 1998 further retarded the maturity of retail agencies.

The large German and English groups will most likely achieve total vertical integration, both forward and backward, by the end of 2001. Such a strategy ensures them control over the entire chain of production and distribution. In the South, strategies of concentration will predominate in order to achieve economies of scale. In the coming decade, the impact of new technologies will decide the future direction of the distribution channels (Buhalis, 1998). The question remains whether the large northern groups will have difficulties in exploiting the potential of the Internet compared to groups that are not forwardly integrated, and, consequently, who will suffer from fewer constraints.

Differences in intermediation for the business and leisure markets are more pronounced in the North, where large specialized groups dominate. The distinction is less clear in the South, as many players operate in both segments. Further differences can be found within each of the two markets (North and South). In the UK, tour operators' strategies for vertical integration have first involved airline companies, followed by accommodation establishments. Germany, on the other hand, has focused first on accommodation establishments and then on airline companies. For Southern Europe, the French and Italian markets, with a total absence of completely integrated groups, need to be distinguished from that of Spain, where comparatively small groups, according to continental standards, are already completely integrated both vertically and horizontally. Networks of considerably large dimensions dominate the French distribution channels. The growth of the agency networks in Italy, however, is only a recent event. A hastened process of network consolidation, as a way of bridging the size gap with more advanced countries, seems likely.

In general, the large networks are attempting to compose vast networks of networks, and compete on price. Although still significant in number, independent travel agencies are quickly disappearing in all countries. The choices open to them are two: carving out niche positions, especially for those in outlying cities, or forming associations. The development of a consultancy approach toward the client is, nonetheless, essential, particularly in light of the trend toward management and transaction fees. The business travel segment is leading the way in spreading these practices to the leisure market. Strongly integrated systems hinge on the large tour operators. Large groups concentrating on strategies of brand differentiation will have the option of acquiring small tour operators with a niche position. There does not, however, appear to be much space for mid-sized operators in the mass market.

REFERENCES

Buhalis, D. (1998) 'Strategic use of information technologies in the tourism industry'. *Tourism Management*, **19**(3), 409–23.

Bywater, M. (1998) 'Who owns whom in the european travel industry'. *Travel & Tourism Analyst*, **3**, 41–59.

Casarin, F. and Zampese, E. (1997) 'Quality and tour operator services: an application of the Analytic Hierarchy Process with feedback'. In J. Lemmink and P. Kunst (eds) *Managing Service Quality*, vol. III. Paul Chapman, London.

Chaintron, B. (1995) 'Industrie touristique: le choc des modèles anglais et français'. *Cahier Espaces*, **44**, 31–6.

FVW International (1999) *Reisebüro-Ketten und Kooperationen, Dokumentation 1998*, 11 June.

Horner, S. and Swarbrooke, J. (1996) *Marketing Tourism Hospitality and Leisure in Europe*. International Thomson Business Press, London.

Kärcher, K. (1997) *Reinventing the Package Holiday Business*. Deutscher Universitäts-Verlag, Wiesbaden.

Laws, E. (1997) *Managing Packaged Tourism*. International Thomson Business Press, London.

Middleton, V. T. C. (1998) *Sustainable tourism: A marketing perspective*. Butterworth-Heinemann, Oxford.

Pompanon, L. (1995) 'Le secteur de la distribution des produits touristiques en France'. *Cahier Espaces*, **44**, 14–30.

Steinecke, A. (1993) *The Historical Development of Tourism in Europe: Structures and developments*. CAB International, Wallingford.

CHAPTER 10

Who owns whom in the European travel distribution industry

Marion Bywater

INTRODUCTION

The last ten years have seen major shifts in ownership in the European tour operator and travel agency industry. The market leaders have remained largely the same, but mergers and acquisitions of and by the major players have radically changed the landscape, not only in terms of who owns which companies within the industry, but of who pulls the strings. This is the result of the large tour operator groups outgrowing the potential of their domestic markets, the differentiation of business and leisure segments, and a rationalization of cross-shareholdings in Germany, Europe's largest market.

It is also due to a total rethink of the business strategies of two large international companies: Thomson, the Canadian media group, which has withdrawn from the sector; and Preussag, the German logistics and industrial group, which entered it in the late 1990s. The former withdrew by floating its holidays' subsidiary in the UK and then selling its minority stake; the latter entered the industry on a large scale through its acquisition of Germany's largest travel group followed by acquisition of Thomson Travel Group. These are just the major developments among a raft of changes. This chapter looks at the structure of the industry in early 2001, at where these primary players may go from here, at how and where the secondary players fit into the picture, and at the initial impacts of the Internet.

A handful of dominant international groups have emerged, or strengthened their positions, in the leisure and business markets in Europe over the last five to ten years. These are, in the leisure sector, Preussag (TUI, Hapag-Lloyd and Thomson Travel and a stake in Nouvelles Frontières), C&N and Rewe of Germany, Airtours of the UK, First Choice of the UK, Kuoni of Switzerland and, in the corporate travel sector, Carlson

Wagonlit, Business Travel International/Kuoni and American Express. At the same time, the industry has become much more international and much more likely to look to stock markets to funds its expansion, with the notable exception of Hogg Robinson, which de-listed in 2000 following a management buyout.

A decade ago, only a handful of companies operated outside their own countries – notably Club Méditerranée, the German companies with operations in the Benelux, and Kuoni. Now cross-border operations are the norm. The deregulation of air transport in Europe, which has stimulated charter operations, and the ability of technology to achieve back-office economies of scale in international operations and negotiations with suppliers have so far been the main drivers of the change. Internet strategies are now also shaping developments.

In the process, some of the French travel companies that were pioneers of the industry have increasingly been left behind, while large Italian and Spanish companies have expanded to a size comparable to that of the French groups. Until 2000, the Italian and Spanish groups had generally remained within national borders or – in the case of the Spanish groups – restricted expansion to Portugal and the Caribbean but this is now changing. Some of the major North European companies, and in particular TUI and C&N, have bridgeheads in the Italian, Spanish and French markets, however, which threaten to isolate these local groups unless they counter-attack. That threat has been heightened with the announcement that Preussag is progressively to acquire a 34.4 per cent stake in Nouvelles Frontières.

KEY MARKET FEATURES AND TRENDS

One of the distinguishing characteristics of the industry is the dominant position of German companies and Airtours of the UK in the leisure markets of the UK, Germany, the Nordic countries, Ireland, Austria, Belgium and the Netherlands. In most of these countries – the notable exceptions being Belgium and the Netherlands – this was not the case prior to the mid-1990s. Another is the emergence of the corporate travel specialists. This trend has been enhanced by the clearer differentiation by American Express of its leisure and corporate travel businesses, notably in France, Belgium and Germany. The major corporate travel players in Europe are:

Carlson Wagonlit,
American Express,
Business Travel International (BTI), which is a joint venture of World BTI and is a subsidiary of BDC Holdings of the Netherlands) (with 46 per cent),
Hogg Robinson (46 per cent) and
Kuoni of Switzerland (8 per cent), which is the owner of Euro-Lloyd in Germany,

as well as corporate travel agencies in a number of other countries, FAO Travel in Germany, Protravel, and alliances e.g. Radius, formerly Woodside Travel Trust, GTM Global Travel Management, First Business Travel International, and franchises, such as Uniglobe and Rosenbluth International.

There have been a number of other striking developments. One has been the adoption, on the leisure side of the industry, of the vertically integrated model, where a single group is a full owner of, or has equity in, airline operations, tour operating, travel agencies and accommodation. A few years ago, the UK operators eschewed investment in accommodation, but they are now far less categorical about this. Airtours became hoteliers perforce when it acquired the Scandinavian Leisure Group (SLG), but has since embraced accommodation ownership, with, for example, the purchase for £63.4m in January 2000 of the Bellevue complex in Mallorca, which is the largest apartment-based leisure complex in Europe. The Germans, on the other hand, were previously not as consistently integrated at the charter airline end and to a lesser extent in the travel agency side of the business. This is no longer the case since Preussag brought TUI and Hapag-Lloyd into a single group, Neckermann teamed up with Lufthansa charter subsidiary, Condor, to form C&N which bought Thomas Cook in December 2000 and Rewe went into joint venture with LTU.

Within the leisure market, a clear sub-segment has emerged over the same period. These are the seat-only operators, which provide airline tickets for the independent traveller and only limited additional services. Some cater exclusively to the youth and student travel market, which has its own specialists (such as STA Travel, a UK/Australian company, Kilroy, headquartered in Denmark, and USIT/Connections, headquartered in Ireland). Others also target experienced travellers and/or those visiting friends and relatives (VFR travellers), particularly in long haul destinations. In its operations outside France, Nouvelles Frontières falls predominantly into this category. The 'bucket shops' of a decade ago, which sold tickets obtained on the 'grey' market, have been largely replaced by mainstream operators, including consolidators. Deregulation of airlines and fares has removed the need for 'bucket shops' using practices the airlines were aware of but with which they did not want to be directly associated. These included sales by these agents of sufficient volumes to enable them to offer group tour rates to individuals even though the members of these pseudo-groups were not aware of each other's existence. Another practice was to bundle with those fares which can theoretically only be offered in conjunction with accommodation which existed should there be checks, but which the airlines were well aware the passenger would not use, e.g. in basic dormitory accommodation away from the city centre. Airline deregulation has removed the need for these practices, though airlines still have a requirement to offload surplus seats as part of their standard yield management. Frequently, they use specialist travel agents (and increasingly those operating via the Internet) for this in order to mask to those paying higher fares the availability of cheap last-minute deals.

Increasingly global corporate sector

A catalyst of change has been the growing importance of global reach for corporate travel agents. This might seem like a self-evident requirement for a corporate travel agent, but it is only in the last five to ten years that it has become essential for the sector to be able to provide round-the-clock service virtually anywhere. The different skill sets and types of service which the business and leisure markets require mean that they are now clearly going their separate ways. Finding a corporate travel agent with a street-front outlet is becoming increasingly difficult as these companies follow the example of many airlines and tourist offices in discouraging passing trade. Corporate travel agents handle more and more business from centralized corporate travel centres which do their business by phone, e-mail, satellite ticket printer, via 'implants', i.e. agencies, on corporate premises or via a team specifically working for a single corporate client within the travel centre. The number of companies which now combine leisure and business travel under a single umbrella is small. In such companies, there are distinct business functions. This does not mean that corporate travel agents do not provide leisure travel for their clients, or that retail travel agents do not provide business travel services, particularly for small and medium-sized travel agencies. However, they both have a clear understanding of their main function.

National differences

There are still some marked national differences – e.g. in attitudes to stock market listing, or in the appropriate level of involvement of airlines and railways in the package tour and business travel markets. For a long time, there were only three listed stand-alone companies in this sector: Airtours and First Choice of the UK and Club Méditerranée of France. Kuoni of Switzerland listed in the mid-1990s and Thomson Travel of the UK, not until 1998.

The leading German travel companies, on the other hand, are within much larger listed (and in some cases unlisted) groups, which would probably be shunned by Anglo-Saxon investors as not belonging to a well-defined sector. This is particularly true of the range of activities within Preussag, the new parent of Europe's largest travel group, TUI, inclusive of Hapag-Lloyd and Thomson, which has been de-listed as a result of the takeover by Preussag. While Preussag has begun hiving off some industrial activities and plans to focus more and more on tourism, the markets still regard it as a hard-to-categorize hybrid. Nevertheless, it has dropped plans for a separate listing of TUI on the grounds that tourism will within two to three years be the predominant activity. C&N (which is a joint venture of retailer Karstadt and airline Lufthansa) is expected to list when stock market conditions are favourable. LTU Touristik is a wholly owned subsidiary of co-operative retailer, Rewe, which since January 2001 has not only acquired the totality of LTU Touristik from SAir Group (the parent of Swissair), but also been in joint venture with SAir and WestLB in the LTU Leisure airline. Rewe's interests also include Atlas Reisen (including tour operator, ITS), and the formerly railways-owned DER travel agencies and the DerTour tour operator.

The UK-run groups are differentiated from most of the other leaders not only by being listed but by having in the case of Airtours and First Choice developed synergies with the Canadian market. This improves the spread of their business over the year because Canada is a strong winter market to the Caribbean. The process has been reversed by Transat of Canada which became a major player on the market with its purchase of France's Look Voyages. Transat also has a number of other subsidiaries in France which include travel agencies and an airline (Star). It is still possible, but increasingly rare, for a family or founder-run business, where the business appears to hinge on the presence of one person, to be a market leader. Exceptions are Fram of France, Alltours of Germany (which is, however, talking of listing) and Grupo Barceló of Spain (which is also talking of listing and has concluded a strategic alliance with First Choice).

Divergent airline philosophies

Airlines continue to have mixed feelings about their role in the travel business and, in 1997, Air France disposed of Jetours, the tour operating subsidiary for which it had struggled for a decade to find the right formula. Since 1999, Jetours has been owned by Club Méditerranée (though not all the non-French arms of the business were part of this acquisition). Swissair was unable to turn around LTU and went into joint venture with Rewe in 2000. Other European airlines with tour operating subsidiaries appear to see them as a means of filling the seats in the economy sections of their planes rather than as a fully fledged business activity. For many years, Finnair had a clear vision of tour operating and travel agencies as part of its core business, but has made a number of sales since 1999, including the sale of Finntours to Thomson Travel Group. Austrian Airlines also has a clear vision of tour operating and travel agencies as part of its core businesses, although it now holds only minority stakes, where in the past it was in some cases more more hands-on. It has a 25 per cent stake in Gulet Touropa and a minority stake in Österreichisches Verkehrsbüro. In Finnair's case, this is mainly through Suntours and the Finland Travel Bureau. Some other airlines have tour operating subsidiaries – e.g. British Airways Holidays, Virgin Holidays or Offshore and Italiatour (Alitalia) – but these are not part of the airlines' mainstream operations to the same extent.

The railways generally believe that this is niche business for them, with the notable exception of the Swiss railways. With the sale to retailer Rewe's travel subsidiary Atlas of its DER subsidiary in 1999, the German railways have pulled out of the travel agency and tour operating business except for the rail tour operating business, Ameropa. The French railways have also pulled out of non-rail tour operating.

Table 10.1   Major groups with European travel interests, April 2000

Parent group	Annual sales	Description of group	Travel sector interests in Europe
Carlson Companies Inc./Groupe Accor	In excess of US$22,00m (Carlson) EUR 6.1bn (Accor)	Hospitality including cruises (Carlson), hotels and catering, tour operating (Accor)	Carlson Wagonlit Travel. Predominantly a corporate travel agency. In the top three in this segment in most European countries. Global sales of US$11m. Accor has tour operating interests and was reported in late 2000 to be interested in a major expansion of these through acquisition.
Rewe	EUR 34.26bn (1999)	Co-operative, supermarket, do-it-yourself, garden centre operator. Claims to be Europe's largest grocery retailer. In Germany, it has a sixth of the market. It operates in Austria (where it owns Billa), Italy, Spain, France, Hungary, Poland, the Czech and Slovak Republics, Croatia and Romania	Atlas Reisen, largest chain of German travel agencies by number of outlets. ITS Reisen, number five German tour operator. Specialist in the medium haul sector. Also operates in Austria. DER, major travel agency chain. Leading issuer of rail tickets. DerTour, major upmarket, long-haul and city break tour operator. Adac-Reisen, purchased by DER in early 2000, from the Adac motoring association. Travel agencies and tour operating. Accommodation operator through hotels Club Calimera. LTU, charter airline and tour operator, in joint venture with SAir. Brands include Jahn, Tjaereborg, Meier's.
American Express	EUR 21bn (1999)	Financial services and travel	American Express travel agencies and representative offices throughout Europe. Joint venture with BBL Travel in Belgium. Generally trades under own name. Major exception is Nyman & Schultz, number one corporate travel agency in Sweden with operations also in Norway and Denmark. Has a 1 per cent stake in Club Méditerranée of France.
Karstadt Quelle	DM 10.74m (1999) (exclusive of C&N Touristic)	Karstadt Quelle as of 2002; previously Karstadt Hertie and Karstadt. Department stores (Karstadt and Hertie) and mail order in Germany and several other European countries (Neckermann). Quelle-Schickedanz, the other major German mail order firm has a 26.77 per cent stake and further amalgamation is under way	C&N, joint venture with Lufthansa (qv) and Condor, charter airline. Neckermann, number two German tour operator; number one tour operator and travel agent in Belgium; leading tour operator (Neckermann) and travel agencies (Neckermann and Broere) in Netherlands and Austria (Neckermann and in conjunction with Kuoni). Purchased Havas travel agency chain in France, 2000. Purchased Thomas Cook in the UK in December 2000 (see below). Accommodation chains: Club Aldiana, Paradiana.

Table 10.1 Major groups with European travel interests, April 2000 (continued)

Parent group	Annual sales	Description of group	Travel sector interests in Europe
Preussag	EUR 20bn	Energy, metals trading, construction technology, and logistics services	Hapag-Lloyd, corporate and leisure travel agency and charter airline. TUI, leading European tour operator, travel agent and charter airline. A total of 60 brands. Leading Dutch (Travel Unie International, ex-Arke and Holland International; Kras) and Belgian travel agency and tour operator (VTB-VAB Reizen, JetAir); tour operator in Austria (TUI); travel agent in Club 18-30; fledgling tour operating business in Switzerland (ITV). Thomson Travel Group, UK (including Britannia Airways and travel agent, Lunn Poly, purchased 2000). Operations in Nordic countries (Fritidsresor, Finnmatkat) Accommodation chains, notably in Austria, Greece and Spain. Ground handling businesses in major destinations. Major hotel owner in Mediterranean (Riu, Iberotel, Grecotel, Club Robinson, Dorfhotels).
Deutsche Lufthansa	EUR 12.8bn	Airline	C&N (see also Karstadt). Lufthansa City Centre (LCC) travel agencies – 300 in Germany, 80 elsewhere, notably in Italy and Austria. Rationalized travel agency holdings in 1997 with sale of stakes in Euro-Lloyd and stakes in Hapag-Lloyd and DER.
Migros	EUR 9.9bn	Supermarkets, department stores (Globus), petrol stations, food processing, road haulage, primarily in Switzerland	Hotelplan, a leading tour operator and travel agency in Switzerland, together with its Esco and Tourisme pour Tous tour operating businesses and the M-Travel agencies and tour operating brand. Owns Interhome, major holiday rental agency. Number five tour operator in the Netherlands (Hotelplan). Small travel agency chain in the Netherlands (Brooks). Small tour operating business in Italy (Hotelplan) and the UK (Inghams). Corporate travel business. Is a member of First Travel Management. Total turnover EUR 1.2bn.
Airtours	EUR 5.52bn	Travel only	Airline, travel agency (Going Places) and tour operator in the UK. Tour operating in Scandinavia including through direct sales (Tjaereborg, Spies, SLG Group, inc. Ving). Tour operating, charter airline and travel agencies in Germany through Frosch Touristik International (with some operations in Austria). Closed Belgian tour operator (Sunair) Autumn 2000.

MAJOR GROUPS WITH TRAVEL INTERESTS
AND LEADING TRAVEL GROUPS

The major relationships between leading international and European travel companies and large European non-travel agency, non-tour operating groups are illustrated in Table 10.1. This lists the main groups by size of their respective parent companies rather than simply by their travel interests. However, the list includes only those groups whose travel industry interests are considered to play a decisive role. Borderline cases are French retailer, Carrefour, which has several dozen travel agencies in France, and German-based mail order company, Otto Versand, which is the world's largest mail order house. Otto owns two chains. One is a general travel retailer, Reiseland. This was initially strongest in Eastern Germany, but has been expanding westwards. In early 1998, it expanded further through its acquisition of 25 American Express leisure outlets, which it rebranded Reiseland American Express. The other Otto travel subsidiary is the Travel Overland chain for independent travellers, which bought Neue Reisewelle in 1997.

Ranking the leading companies in this sector has historically been complicated by the fact that there is no common agreement on how to measure size. In strict accounting terms, the true measurement of a travel agency's business is the value of the commissions it collects – not the sales volume, or the total face value of the tickets or packages it sells. Not every company follows this convention, however. For many years, continental European travel companies produced little meaningful financial data at all and benchmarked themselves solely on passenger numbers – a measure which has always been rejected by their UK counterparts except in the broadest terms. Even in continental Europe, it is now recognized that this is not an acceptable measure. When most holidays were to the Mediterranean and most sales were of all-inclusive packages, it may have provided a reasonably homogeneous substitute for sales figures. The value of a package holiday and the package element within it are now too variable for use of passenger numbers to have much justification.

Using the *number of travel agencies* to assess the importance of travel retailing is equally increasingly unscientific. Per outlet sales of corporate travel agents have always tended to be higher than those of 'corner shop' operations. In addition, corporate travel agents are consolidating their operations in business travel centres. Large numbers of agencies are now, arguably, in some cases a sign of a group that is not showing leadership. Probably the same will become true in future years of retail agents as more sales are made over the phone and electronically.

Financial data is much better than it used to be, but there are still some major difficulties with travel companies which are subsidiaries of major groups. Thomas Cook (and its tour operating subsidiary JMC) when it was still an independent company, American Express and Carlson Wagonlit Travel are the best (or perhaps

Table 10.2   The top European travel and tourism groups, September 2000

Group	Country/ies
Carlson Wagonlit Travel	USA, Netherlands
American Express	USA
Preussag (TUI/Hapag-Lloyd/Thomson)	Germany
Rewe/LTU	Germany
C&N Touristic (inc Havas and Thomas Cook)	Germany
Kuoni/Hogg Robinson/Business Travel International	Switzerland, UK
Airtours	UK

Table 10.3   Turnover of the top ten European leisure travel groups, 1999. *Sources*: FVW International and respective companies

Company	Turnover 1999 (EUR bn)
TUI	7.27
C&N Touristic	4.65
Airtours	5.52
Thomson Travel	5.00
Rewe Touristik[a]	3.60
Kuoni	3.50
First Choice	2.44
LTU	2.04
Club Méditerranée	1.48
Nouvelles Frontières	1.41

Notes: Excludes groups which are predominantly travel agents and which are difficult to rank because of the lack of data

[a] Non-consolidated figures based on grossing up 1999 acquisition of DER/DERTour as if it had been purchased in that year. Without that purchase, Rewe (Atlas and ITS) was in ninth slot

159

worst!) examples of this. The emergence of alliances, particularly in the corporate travel sector, has complicated the picture. Because of these difficulties, it is not possible to attach figures to the list of the overall leaders in the sector. Nevertheless, it is quite clear which groups now lead the industry across Europe. These are shown in Table 10.2. The leisure companies, which are a more homogeneous group, are ranked in Table 10.3. The eight leading groups in Table 10.2 are then profiled in greater detail. These are the eight which stand out for their combination of size and international presence in terms of reach and depth in the tour operating and travel agency markets.

Carlson Wagonlit Travel

This is a 50:50 joint venture. It was set up in loose form in 1996 and finalized the following year. It combines the travel agency interests of Carlson Companies Inc. of the USA and the French Groupe Accor. Sales volume in 1999 was in excess of US$11 billion. The author's estimate of actual turnover (on the basis of Accor's figures for its share of turnover, i.e. EUR 434m in 1999) is around US$1 billion. Accor has a separate tour operating activity, Accor Tour, with a turnover of around EUR 100m. It is dubious whether an operation this size is viable and Accor was said at late 2000 to be looking for an acquisition.

Carlson Companies is still a family-run business despite its size. Its best known activities, apart from Carlson Wagonlit Travel and its Travel Agents International brand, are Regent International Hotels, Radisson Hotels, Country Inns and Suites, Friday's Hospitality (the TGI Friday restaurant chain) and Radisson Seven Seas Cruises. The Carlson interest in Carlson Wagonlit Travel comes under the Carlson Leisure Group. This also includes Neiman Marcus Travel Services, Carlson Vacations and an incentives arm. In addition, the Leisure Group incorporates Carlson Worldchoice in the UK, which is not part of Carlson Wagonlit Travel. Carlson Worldchoice is the brand name for the alliance forged in 1997 between the Carlson-owned AT Mays leisure travel agency chain (which is number four in the UK) and the Worldchoice franchise for independents. Carlson Leisure Group divested itself of its stake in Thomas Cook in late 2000 as part of the process by which C&N Touristic acquired Thomas Cook (and its tour operator JMC) because Preussag could no longer control Thomas Cook after it had purchased Thomson Travel. Groupe Accor is a listed company best known for its Sofitel, Novotel, Mercure, Ibis, Libertel and budget hotel brands and for its luncheon voucher and catering businesses. It has a long-standing strategic interest in Ifil, which in early 2001 acquired total ownership of Italy's leading tour operator, Alpitour. Accor has a strategic alliance in the leisure travel agency business with the Selectour alliance. It has recently been strengthening its tour operating side.

Carlson Wagonlit Travel operates in more countries than any other travel agency and is second worldwide in size to American Express. The merged company is nominally headquartered in the Netherlands, but the executive offices are in New

York, USA, and the European operation is run from Paris. In Europe, Carlson Wagonlit Travel's weak spot is Germany. The number of agencies a group has is not everything, particularly in a market where Carlson Wagonlit Travel is concentrating on the business market, but it is striking how few agencies it has in Germany compared with its presence in other countries. It has significantly more agencies in the Netherlands, Norway and Finland and as many, or more, in Denmark, Italy and Belgium. These are all countries where – as in Switzerland – Carlson Wagonlit Travel is the number one or two of corporate travel agencies. It occupies the same positions in France and Spain but in those countries it also has a strong leisure presence for historic reasons – well over 100 agencies in each country. France was one of its original core markets (together with Belgium and the Netherlands), for Wagon-Lits as it was then called. Its strong presence in Spain is the result of its having purchased Viajes Ecuador at the end of the 1980s. The Spanish subsidiaries have been consolidated into a single company, but the leisure side of the business still trades under the Viajes Ecuador name. A major expansion of this chain is under way. Many of the US agencies in the Carlson group are franchises. There are far fewer among Carlson Wagonlit Travel outlets in Europe, but France has a relatively significant share. Carlson Wagonlit Travel generally steers clear of packaging travel except in specialist niche markets. However, in Europe – first in Belgium and now in other countries – it does, on the other hand, play a major role as an air ticket consolidator in the leisure market through its Airtip operation.

American Express

American Express is the world's largest travel agency group and part of the listed US financial services group of the same name which includes credit card and travellers' cheque services. The focus of American Express' travel activity in Europe is the corporate travel market. It does not publish figures, but it is certainly in the top three in this segment in the UK, Belgium and Switzerland and is the market leader in Sweden. Its position in both the UK and Germany was significantly strengthened in 1995 when it purchased from Westdeutsche Landesbank (WestLB) the corporate travel business of Thomas Cook. Traditionally, American Express has been present in the retail, inbound and business travel markets in Europe. On the retail and inbound travel side, the activity grew out of a desire first and foremost to support its cardholders and tourists familiar with the brand. The result was a network of retail outlets in cities on the major tourist trails, often in prestigious locations, but with no depth in leisure markets. This has frequently led industry observers to query its strategy on the leisure travel side.

American Express generally sells under its own name. The major exception is Sweden, where it has not changed the name of Nyman & Schultz which it bought in the early 1990s. Nyman & Schultz dominates the Swedish corporate travel market. It is also a solid force in Norway, while there is a relatively much smaller operation in Denmark. The Nyman & Schultz purchase in 1993 was the first in which American

Express tacitly acknowledged that there were markets in which it was better off with a local brand. The next example of this was announced in 1995 and implemented in 1996. This was the merger of its business travel activities with those of the business travel activities of Havas Voyages in France. At that point, American Express had 19 per cent of Havas Voyages American Express and also had preemptive rights as a result of its 1995 deal.

In mid-June 1998, American Express announced that it had agreed to pay around FFr850 million (US$141 million) to acquire the outstanding 81 per cent of Havas Voyages American Express and 100 per cent of Havas Voyages from its owners, Vivendi. The deal, which gave it the biggest network in France, involved 632 agencies generating total sales of FFr13.5 billion in 1997 and an operating profit of FFr13 million. It covered all parts of Havas Voyages except its 50.1 per cent stake in Maeva, a network of self-catering holiday apartments, which will be acquired by CGIS, parent company Vivendi's property division. The Havas Voyages stake was onsold to C&N in 2000.

Talks between American Express and Hapag-Lloyd in late 1995 for a similar deal in Germany in the corporate travel sector to the Havas Voyages American Express deal signed the same year were unsuccessful. In late 1997, on the other hand, it entered into a joint venture in Belgium with BBL Travel. BBL Travel is the leading Belgian-owned travel agency group and one of the top three in business travel. It is a subsidiary of the Banque Bruxelles Lambert – itself now a subsidiary of ING. The joint venture ousted Carlson Wagonlit Travel from its number one position in the corporate travel sector in the Belgian and Luxembourg markets. It should ease the path into Belgian companies and European institutions needing global corporate travel management but feeling more comfortable with a European brand.

Preussag(Hapag-Lloyd/TUI/Thomson)

TUI in its current configuration, after a decade of reshuffling in its ownership structure, is now a wholly owned subsidiary of Preussag. Preussag also owns Hapag-Lloyd, which is a shipping and cruise company and travel agent. Following restructuring, TUI and the travel side of the Hapag-Lloyd business have become arms of Preussag and Hapag-Lloyd's shipping business is run as a stand-alone entity. In the process of this consolidation, mail order group Quelle-Schickedanz and the bank WestLB have divested themselves of their stakes in TUI. Quelle-Schickedanz had a conflict of interest after buying a 20.3 per cent stake in Karstadt in 1997 from the Deutsche Bank and the Commerzbank. WestLB had a conflict because of its stake in LTU. There is, nevertheless, a close relationship between WestLB and Preussag as WestLB is a strategic shareholder in Preussag. The German railways have also sold their stake in TUI.

The rationale for Preussag's entering the travel business is that it is moving out of traditional engineering and metalworking industries into sectors it believes offer better potential for growth, thus becoming more of a service provider and reducing its dependence on raw material processing. It sees the tourism sector as a growth area and as a good fit with its view of logistics as one of its core businesses. Part of the funding for the Hapag-Lloyd purchase came from selling its steelmaking subsidiary. Its purchase of Thomson Travel Group was funded by the sale of housing estates. In taking control of Hapag-Lloyd and TUI, Preussag has combined into a vertically integrated group two businesses which have long been allied both as business partners and through cross-shareholdings. This group initially comfortably outstripped its competition in Europe in terms of size. It was soon threatened by the expansion of C&N Touristic but then took another quantum leap with the purchase of Thomson Travel Group.

The travel side of Hapag-Lloyd – as opposed to the shipping arm – owns a charter airline which works closely with TUI, and is a leading corporate and leisure travel agent that is particularly strong in northern Germany, but has been extending its geographic reach. It also has some niche tour operating businesses and has a cruiseship subsidiary. TUI is the largest tour operator on the German market – mainly under the TUI brand, but also through Airtours, Air Conti and L'Tur, a last-minute travel specialist. It traditionally did not own travel agencies in Germany, but has been building up the numbers through ownership, franchises and alliances. It also has retail travel agencies in Austria and Spain, among others. It owns a score of ground-handling firms at major destinations. Some of these provide services to other groups or operate independent travel operations, e.g. Ultramar Express in Spain and Dr. Degener in Austria. It has chains of hotels and holiday villages in Greece, Spain, North Africa, the Caribbean, Switzerland and Austria. The Riu and Iberotel chains are among the largest in Spain. A relatively late and seemingly serendipitous entrant to the corporate travel market via its acquisition of Holland International, TUI has since built this side of the business through other acquisitions and through choosing not to divest their business arms. Its major brands are First and First Travel Management. TUI rose to be the number three tour operator in Austria in two years after being forced to go it alone when Austrian Airlines insisted on adding TUI's 50 per cent of leading tour operator, Touropa, to the 50 per cent it already held. TUI has gone back to number one (ahead of Neckermann's joint venture with Kuoni). In February 2000, TUI acquired 75 per cent of Gulet Touropa, Austria's largest travel business. The remainder stays in the hands of Austrian Airlines. This operation has brought TUI virtually full circle.

Through the relatively recent purchase of JetAir and VTB-VAB Reizen in Belgium and with the acquisition of travel agency, Belgium International, when it acquired Holland International in 1995, TUI has become number two on the Belgian market behind Neckermann. In the Netherlands, TUI's local subsidiary, Travel Unie International, is the market leader in tour operating, business travel and inbound travel. It is the result of the merger of the Holland International business purchased from German retailer Kaufhof, and of the Arke Reizen businesses of which it acquired total control the same year after some years of minority ownership. Through Holland International, TUI acquired 10 per cent of Business Travel International (BTI), the business travel alliance, which is now dominated by Kuoni and Hogg Robinson. TUI entered Switzerland in 1996 and from early 1998 has been in a joint venture with a direct-sell tour operator, Vögele, and number three tour operator, Imholz. This is known as ITV. Imholz includes the Travac range. TUI Suisse has a strategic alliance with Kuoni. It has entered the UK market with the reorganization of shareholdings by WestLB which has left TUI with stakes in Thomas Cook, JMC, Neilson and Club 18–30. All of these were sold to C&N Touristic in late 2000 to satisfy the competition authorities that the purchase of Thomson Travel Group would not give TUI too strong a position on the UK market following its purchase of Thomson Travel.

Thomson Holidays (the name of the tour operating subsidiary and of its main brand) is the leading tour operator in the UK with around one-fifth of the summer holiday package market – compared with 15 per cent for Airtours. In the 1980s, when package tour companies operated only from their domestic market, Thomson vied for the position of European leader with TUI, although the two operations have never been easily comparable. Thomson has an inhouse charter airline, Britannia Airways, and an inhouse travel agency chain, Lunn Poly – now the largest chain in the UK. Through acquisitions, it now trades in the retail market under other names as well – a break with the past, but one which affects only a small proportion of the total number of outlets. Thomson Travel had no destination investments until it purchased Fritidsresor of Sweden and then Finntours of Sweden. International expansion by the Thomson Travel Group from late 1997 on, and, in particular, the late-1997 purchase of Fritidsresor of Sweden enabled Thomson to recover ground lost to arch rival, Airtours. Thomson Travel Group was listed in April 1998. The original parent, the Canadian Thomson media and publishing group, retained a 23 per cent stake, but sold this to Preussag as part of the latter's 2000 takeover of Thomson Travel. Thomson Travel was the slowest of the European majors to venture outside its original borders, or outside the air charter package sector which it perceived as its core business. Since the mid-1990s, however, it has bought the largest UK domestic rental accommodation business, Country Cottages, as well as Blakes Cottages and Country Cottages in France, and Chez Nous, a directory of properties to rent in France; acquired an Irish tour operator with some retail outlets, Budget Travel; and made a number of other significant acqusitions. These include ski specialist Crystal; long haul ticketing specialist Austravel, which mainly sells travel to Australia and New Zealand; Magic Travel, a specialist in Spain and Italy, particularly self-catering; and Simply Travel. Other key brands include Portland Direct and Skytours.

The second largest leisure travel group in Scandinavia, Fritidsresor, is what survived as a homogeneous leisure business from a group of businesses which included corporate travel agencies sold to Hogg Robinson (Bennett), hotels (Reso and Sara) and an airline (Transwede). The tour operating group was known variously over that period as NRT Nordpool, Nordpool, and as part of the Borgtornet group. This, and the airline, were bought by a group spearheaded by former SAS chief executive, Jan Carlzon, in 1995. It was on-sold to Thomson under the Fritidsresor name, but the charter side of the airline had been given a distinct identity as Blue Scandinavia. This was part of the sale to Thomson. Thomson expanded further in Scandinavia in 1999 with the purchase of Winge (travel agents) and Prisma Tours. In 1999, Thomson also added Scan Holiday to its foreign portfolio. This is Poland's largest air-inclusive tour operator. Fritidsresor has an obvious affinity with Thomson in that it does not sell through dedicated outlets – unlike the Scandinavian Leisure Group owned by Airtours. On the other hand, it owns no agencies at all. The main tour operating brands are Star Tour, Fritidsresor, Royal Tours and Tema. The group owns hotels and the Blue Village holiday villages. At October 2000, TUI had 3628 travel agencies in seven European countries, 39 tour operating brands, 62 planes (in Germany and the UK), 18 incoming agencies and 187 hotels. It carries 12.9 million passengers a year and employs 49,000 people.

C&N Touristic

C&N Touristic was created in late 1997 when German national carrier Lufthansa and Karstadt, operator of the Karstadt and Hertie department stores and owner of the Neckermann mail order businesses, pooled 90 per cent of their stakes respectively in charter airline, Condor, and NUR Touristic (now branded Neckermann). They have each retained 10 per cent of the company they brought into the joint venture. Condor has more than one-quarter of the German air travel charter market. Travel interests which remained outside were the Euro-Lloyd chain of business travel agencies – a 49:51 joint venture since sold to Kuoni, and the Lufthansa City Centre chain of travel agencies. This is owned directly by the airline rather than through Lufthansa Commercial Holding, the parent of Condor. C&N Touristic has created a vertically integrated leisure travel group to vie with Preussag and Rewe for the top slot on the German market. The NUR Touristic side in Germany consists of the Neckermann tour operating businesses. Condor had previously acquired Kreutzer and Air Marin. Neckermann had acquired Fischer and Bucher. In some cases, they initially acquired stakes, but now all are wholly owned subsidiaries. Terramar has also been acquired. Neckermann owns and has franchised travel agencies in its portfolio, but so do Karstadt Hertie and Lufthansa. Neckermann owns hotel and resort accommodation (the Club Aldiana holiday villages and Paradiana hotels), and ground-handling agencies. This includes a key 40 per cent stake in Iberoservice with Grupo Viajes Iberia of Spain, a major hotelier (Iberostar), but also a travel agent and tour operator.

Outside Germany, Neckermann is the leading tour operator in Belgium under the Neckermann name. This was introduced into Belgium in the 1980s and is sold through dedicated Neckermann travel agencies and through Sunsnacks, AllAir and other tour operations acquired since the beginning of the 1990s. Neckermann also has a strong position in the Netherlands as both tour operator and travel agent – through a cross-shareholding arrangement with Broere Reizen – and in Austria, where it is in joint venture with Kuoni. The Belgium and Dutch operations are run as a single unit. This operation also has a small tour operating activity in northern France. In April 2000, C&N purchased Havas Voyages of France from American Express. This gave it 380 French leisure travel agencies (including franchises) and made it the largest travel agent in France. At the same time, it bid for Thomson Travel of the UK but was unsuccessful. It then looked at Airtours, but a deal failed to materialize because of a failure to agree on price. First Choice, the fourth largest tour operator, was another potential target. In early December 2000 it bought Thomas Cook for £550m cash and announced that it will play a main role in the UK. It has indicated that its next priorities are in Southern Europe, but an opportunistic purchase in another market cannot be ruled out. C&N is expected to become a listed company within two to three years.

Airtours

After making rapid inroads into the UK market in the 1980s and early 1990s, and overtaking First Choice (formerly Owners Abroad) in the process, Airtours was consistently a step ahead of the UK number one, Thomson Travel, in expanding outside the borders of the UK and becoming for a while the number three European group. By taking total control of Frosch Touristik International (FTI) in late 2000, it made a quantum leap forward in consolidated terms, although this did nothing for its results as it brought forward its acquisition of all FTI shares in order to accelerate restructuring at the loss-making German group. Closure of Sunair in Belgium in late 2000 was also a blow to its results and its image. The UK is still by far the largest market for Airtours, where it is a vertically integrated operator which has its own airline, Going Places – the UK's second largest chain of travel agencies (plus a smaller chain, Travelworld) – and tour operations. Airtours is the flagship tour operating brand, but it also trades as Panorama, Direct Holidays, Bridge Travel Group, Cresta Holidays, Tradewinds and Eurosites as well as under more recently acquired brands.

Airtours' first foray outside the UK was in 1995 when it purchased the Scandinavian Leisure Group from SAS. This gave it the Ving tour operating brand, which sells through dedicated Ving agencies in Norway and Sweden, and the Saga and Always brands, which are sold in Norway and Sweden respectively through third party agencies and resort hotels. In 1996, it purchased the Danish Spies/Tjaereborg group. This sells through dedicated agencies across Scandinavia. It acquired a 50 per cent interest in a charter airline, Premiair, at the same time. It subsequently purchased Trivselresor, a Swedish scheduled tour operator. After the purchase of SLG, it followed this with the purchase or launch of tour operations in North America and a strategic alliance with Carnival Cruises. Carnival became Airtours' largest individual shareholder, with around one-quarter of the shares. In

1997, the two companies together bought Italian cruise-ship operator, Costa Crociere, as a 50:50 joint venture, but Carnival bought out Airtours in mid-2000. Airtours was the first European company to exploit through direct investment the rapid growth in the market for cruising.

In early 1998, Airtours finalized its purchase of Belgium's Sun International. After the inroads TUI and Neckermann had made into the Belgian market, this was the sole surviving major Belgian operator. Until the early 1990s, both Sun International and its holiday village arm were in a strategic alliance with German retailer Kaufhof. At that time, Kaufhof also owned German tour operator ITS (since sold to Rewe – see Table 10.1) and Holland International (see under TUI). It had difficulty locating a buyer for Sun International because the holiday village side of the business was making a loss. In addition, it was a family-run business, which the older generation was originally reluctant to see go out of the family. Airtours acquired the tour operation, a small chain of travel agencies, the two-plane airline (Air Belgium), which subsequently added an additional plane to the fleet, and the UK short-break operators (Bridge Travel and Cresta Holidays). Bridge and Cresta have been among the most successful parts of the business in recent years. The holiday villages were not part of the deal. Airtours struggled to turn Sun around in the face of the competition from TUI and C&N. It first sold the coach tour subsidiary (West Belgium Coach) and then closed the tour operating business.

Airtours' German bridgehead was Frosch Touristik International (FTI), a multi-brand operation with a number of niches. The tour operators in the group include CA Ferntouristik (long haul), Frosch Touristik, LAL Sprachreisen (language holidays), Club Valtur and Sport-Scheck Reisen. It is building a travel agency presence via Flugbörse, Allkauf (both acquisitions), Fti Ferienwelt and 5 V Flug. It is one of the market leaders for holidays to Malta. Several of its subsidiaries also sell in Switzerland and Austria. In Austria, it also has a stake in Merlin. The link with Airtours has led to a launch of its own charter airline, Fly FTI. The German market has proved difficult for operators from other countries to buy into and FTI was one of the few, if not the only, major tour operator which was an exception to the rule. However, Airtours found it had bought trouble because FTI produced very poor results in 2000, which were attributed to its overestimating its capacity requirements in the summer season and being left with unfilled allocations. Brands in the North American market (which account for 10 per cent of sales) include Vacation Express, Suntrips and Sunquest. Other recent purchases have been Jetset, Manos and Sunway Travel in the UK, 50 per cent of the Hotetur hotel group in Mallorca, purchase of the Bellevue apartment-hotel in Mallorca, and Travel Services International in the USA, an Internet leisure travel distributor.

Kuoni/Hogg Robinson

There are virtually no formal ties between Kuoni of Switzerland and Hogg Robinson of the UK, but they are increasingly acting in concert in the business travel market.

Moreover, their actions in this market have had some spillover effects into Kuoni's other activities. What has brought Kuoni and Hogg Robinson together is Business Travel International (BTI). BTI has annual sales of US$20 billion in twenty countries. This is an international alliance, but these two were originally the dominant partners and shareholders. Kuoni now has an 8 per cent stake and Hogg Robinson and WorldTravel are the principal shareholders. Kuoni tends to own the Central European (including Swiss, Austrian and German) members of BTI, whereas Hogg Robinson has those in the UK and the Nordic countries (Bennett), while WorldTravel's strengths are in the Netherlands and North America.

Kuoni is by far the larger of the two companies as it is an integrated travel group, listed on the Swiss stock exchange in 1995, and is a major player in its own right. However, it has less depth across the European market than other groups profiled here. It also stands out by combining leisure, business and incoming businesses. Kuoni (together with its Polaris brand, which is a 65 per cent-owned joint venture with the Co-op retail chain) has the largest chain of travel agencies in Switzerland – ahead of HP Swiss, formerly Hotelplan. It is the leader in the Swiss tour operating market, with brands such as Helvetic Tours, Manta and Private Safaris as well as the core Kuoni Reisen brand. It has a minority stake in the railways' Railtour and a strategic alliance with Kuoni. It is also the number five operator in the UK. There, it specializes in upmarket medium to long haul travel and long haul ticketing through the Far East Travel Centre. Other brands include The Travel Collection, Voyages Jules Verne and Sport Abroad. It also has a small stake in TV Travel. It has a small chain of travel agencies and a tour operating business in France (including Voice and Scanditours). There is also tour operating activity in Austria (with C&N), in the Netherlands (Special Traffic), Spain and Italy. More recent acquisitions (apart from strengthening of the Italian operation through a joint venture with Gastaldi Tours) have been in Denmark and Sweden. There is a strong travel agency business in Austria. It disposed of its business travel activities in those countries to Hogg Robinson in 1997. Outside Europe, it is strong in tour operating in India and has a niche presence in the USA.

In business travel, Kuoni is focusing on central Europe. It owns a chain of travel agencies in Austria – where it also sells leisure travel and is in a joint venture with Neckermann in tour operating. There are fledgling operations in Eastern Europe. After several sorties designed to improve its weak position in Germany, including a short-lived franchising arrangement with First, Kuoni made a major breakthrough in late 1997 with the purchase from Karstadt and Lufthansa of Euro-Lloyd. It has been rebranded BTI Euro-Lloyd. Together with its existing agencies, this gives Kuoni a chain of 160 outlets. Kuoni has an airline, Edelweiss, and is also a major inbound tourism operator.

Hogg Robinson is a UK company increasingly focusing on the corporate travel business – its sole area of travel activity for a number of years. It sold its transport division in 1999 to allow it to concentrate on corporate travel and financial services.

The corporate travel side is by far the major part of the business, however. The main components of this business are the Hogg Robinson operation in the UK (Business Travel UK) and the Bennett travel agencies in the Nordic countries (Business Travel Nordic). These were acquired in 1995 and added to in December 1997 when Hogg Robinson acquired Matkapiste of Finland. This made it number four in the Finnish business travel market with an 8 per cent market share. It is in the top three in Sweden and Norway. It also acquired the business travel interests of Kuoni in Italy and France in late 1997, Destination Services Russia in March 1998 and first 51 per cent and then control of Rider Travel Corporation of Canada in May 1998. Most of its travel business is carried out through implants and off-street business travel centres.

CONCLUSIONS

There are certainly more changes to come. To fulfil an ambition to overtake Preussag/TUI/Hapag-Lloyd, C&N acquired Havas Voyages in early 2000. C&N feels the French market is ripe after years of unfulfilled promise for the outbound package tour market to take off. Ownership of France's largest leisure travel agency (as opposed to owning Havas Voyages American Express for business travel) never did fit with the logic of the other American Express operations in Europe. TUI hit back with the alliance with Nouvelles Frontières. But neither was the perfect deal for either company. C&N still lacks tour operating depth in France. The corporate cultures of TUI and Nouvelles Frontières are very different. In late 2000 C&N bought Thomas Cook, giving it a significant foothold in the UK, but it still lacks a presence in the Nordic countries. Airtours is looking vulnerable following its failure with Sun International of Belgium and in light of the difficulties of FTI in Germany. The German market continues to look overcrowded just below the top where FTI and Alltours, for example, sit. The market has continued to grow strongly, but is likely to be hit by a weak Euro at least in 2000. As a result, more mergers and acquisitions are inevitable. Rewe/LTU will also have to decide whether a strong German/Austrian base is adequate in the face of pan-European competition, though its options for moving into other markets (other than in Eastern Europe) have largely been foreclosed by the moves of those who have gone before it.

A situation in which some companies could rely for growth on the continuous appreciation of the Deutschmark against South European currencies is a thing of the past. It is, consequently, hard to envisage new entrants without new exits. In addition, the markets of Spain, Italy and France are likely to hold increasing attractions for the North Europeans. In the countries with Mediterranean coastlines, several major travel groups have been struggling in recent years, e.g. Club Méditerranée. This has been turned around but may still not have enough depth in certain markets, such as Germany, or even in its own market as long as it cannot achieve greater global size to deliver economies of scale on its home market. Others, e.g. Alpitour in Italy, Barceló and perhaps Halcón/Globalia of Spain, have grown to a point where they may be exhausting their domestic potential. The Spanish have already begun to expand into Latin America. Others operators in these countries have recognized the need to achieve critical mass. There have been a number of domestic mergers and acquisitions in Italy. Alpitour has tied up with Francorosso (among others); Kuoni has linked with Gastaldi and Hotelplan of Switzerland has taken over Turisanda. There could also well be a reshuffling of the cards in Eastern Europe. Most major companies have a toehold in that market, but trading conditions have been difficult. That applies also, however, to local firms which may start succumbing to the charms of the international groups over the next five years.

TUI has never shown any inclination to expand beyond the Spanish operations it has had for some years, but this appears to be changing. In addition, it has resort and ground-handling operations in Italy which could act as a toehold for further expansion. TUI's caution can possibly be traced back to having had its fingers burnt in France in an unsuccessful incursion in the late 1980s and early 1990s. It also tried the temperature of the Swiss waters in the late 1990s and then sold out to Kuoni.

C&N, on the other hand, appears determined to take on the French market despite the entrenched positions of the incumbents. It has a small operation in northern France run from the Benelux, which it had been using as a bridgehead and a means of gaining experience of the market prior to the Havas Voyages purchase. Airtours has forfeited scope for expansion into France via activities in northern France acquired with its purchase of Sun International.

Some companies stand out as loners surrounded by alliances. They are Alltours of Germany, Fram of France and First Choice of the UK. The first two have in common that they are still firmly in the hands of their founders, though Alltours has now recognized that it needs additional capital from outside, which it hopes to raise from the stock market. First Choice, a tour operator and airline, and the purchaser in June 1998 of the Unijet and Hayes & Jarvis groups in the UK, was thwarted in an attempt to merge with Kuoni in 1999 by a counter-bid by Airtours. By the time that had been rejected by EU competition authorities, in a move which many regarded as predictable, Kuoni had withdrawn from the fray. Airtours appealed the decision. Until the outcome of that is known, potential suitors may stay clear of First Choice for fear of suffering a similar fate to Kuoni's. In 2000, it did conclude a strategic alliance with Barceló, with which it had anyway long worked closely on the ground in Spain.

The imponderable for all the firms, however, is how important e-commerce will be to the industry. In business-to-business dealings, there is little doubt of its impact. The debate still rages on whether consumers will want to book via the Internet (or alternative forms of e-commerce, e.g. TV channels devoted to holiday sales, or interactive TV). The question if they do is whether they will become more independent of the organized industry in the process and whether they will remain loyal to the existing companies or will switch their loyalties to new entrants. It may be that telecommunications companies, global computerized reservations systems or software developers – or even hotels groups or airlines – have comparative advantage in this area over the conventional players.

ACKNOWLEDGEMENT

This chapter has been extensively revised and updated by Marion Bywater from her article which originally appeared in the *Travel and Tourism Analyst* (No. 3, 1998). The Editors are grateful to her and to Travel Tourism Intelligence (http://www.t-ti.com/) for their permission to use the original article as the basis for the update.

CHAPTER 11

Travel retailing: 'switch selling' in the UK

Simon Hudson, Tim Snaith, Graham A. Miller
and Paul Hudson

INTRODUCTION

Expenditure on holidays by the British came to £22.5 billion in 1998 (Mintel, 1999), representing a 4 per cent share of all consumer spending. In terms of the type of holiday taken by UK consumers when they travel abroad, the package holiday or inclusive tour is at the core of the leisure travel industry's business. In 1997, 28 million holidays abroad were taken, of which 15 million were inclusive tours and 13 million were independently organized.

Travel agents represent a major communication channel for British travellers (Hsieh & O'Leary, 1993). Between 80 and 90 per cent of inclusive tours are sold through travel agents, where vertically integrated tour operators are also the dominant retailers (Mintel, 1999). The Monopolies and Mergers Commission (MMC) have suggested that the traditional mechanism of visiting travel agent, taking away brochures for perusal at home, and returning to the agent to confirm the booking, remains the main retail channel for holidays abroad (MMC, 1998). The distribution of inclusive tours has come under close official scrutiny in recent years, and after a recent investigation, the MMC came to the conclusion that the vertical integration of tour operators, charter airlines and major travel agents did not affect consumer choice adversely.

PACKAGE TOUR DISTRIBUTION IN THE UK

The largest three tour operators, Thomson, Airtours and Thomas Cook, control about 75 per cent of the market, and each has their own chain of travel agencies. Thomson own 791 Lunn Poly agencies, Airtours control 717 Going Places branches and Thomas Cook have over 700 retail outlets under the Thomas Cook and Carlson brand names (Buckingham, 1999). Forty per cent of Lunn Poly's bookings for 1999 are for its parent company, Thompson holidays, 38 per cent of Going Places' sales are for Airtours' holidays and 31 per cent of Thomas Cook's sales for Sunworld (Heape, 1998). In addition to travel agents, each of the main tour operators has their own airline through which they process as much of the holiday traffic as possible (Table 11.1). In 1998, the Monopolies and Mergers Commission (MMC) ruled that a vertically integrated travel industry did not compromise consumer choice. However, one of the key concerns of the report was the potential for 'directional' or 'switch selling' by travel agencies in favour of their allied tour operators. Were this to happen, they suggested that ultimately consumer choice would be diminished.

Table 11.1 Integration between UK operators, airlines and travel agents. *Source*: Adapted from Holloway, 1998, p. 200

Airline	Tour operator	Travel Agent
Brittania Airways	Thomson Travel	Lunn Poly
Airtours Aviation	Airtours	Going Places
Air 2000	First Choice Holidays	Travel Choice
Airworld	JMC	Thomas Cook
Monarch Airlines	Sunworld	
Flying Colours	Cosmos Holidays	
	Flying Colours Group	

The research contained within this chapter seeks to explore the reality of consumer choice at the high street retail outlet. This is achieved by briefly outlining the structure of the UK tourism industry and more specifically, exploring the holiday recommendations made by the agents of the three main vertically integrated tour companies. In order to achieve this, focus groups, mystery visitors and telephone interviews were employed. Results show that contrary to the MMC's findings, the industry is guilty of 'switch selling'. Differences were found between the main companies in the extent to which their employees engaged in 'switch selling'. This finding has potentially serious implications regarding the level of control and therefore choice which the consumer wields in the UK holiday market.

One practice that was of some concern to the MMC was 'directional selling', which they define as 'the sale or attempted sale by a vertically integrated travel agent of the foreign package holidays of its linked tour operator, in preference to the holidays of other operators' (MMC, 1998, p. 4). The practice was seen as being facilitated by the lack of transparency of ownership links. Independent travel agents and smaller tour operators argue that the vertically integrated travel agents deceive customers by posing as impartial agents when primarily selling their parent company's holidays. However, in their investigation, the MMC found no evidence that directional selling has resulted in less value for money for consumers, and therefore did not rule it to be against the public interest. This has frustrated smaller agents and operators, as well as consumer groups who argue that the practice is anti-competitive and leads to limited and biased choice for the consumer when buying a holiday. They also argue that the practice is more widespread than the MMC or the larger operators prefer to admit. The MMC ruled that vertical integration in the travel business would not compromise consumer choice so long as the agencies clearly spelled out their ultimate ownership (MMC, 1998).

CHOOSING A HOLIDAY

Understanding the consumer's needs and buying process is the foundation of successful marketing. By understanding how buyers proceed through the decision-making process, the various participants in the buying procedure and the major influences on buying behaviour, marketers can acquire many clues as to how to meet buyer needs. The 'grand models' of consumer behaviour have been transformed by authors interested in the tourism choice process. However, this 'borrowing' of theories from those who have concentrated on more tangible products, has hampered the process in developing more realistic models (Gilbert, 1991). Tangible products can be assessed prior to purchase, but it is more difficult to develop and construct models of the decision process that relate to the purchase of tourism products. Mansfeld (1992), in a review of the body of knowledge forming the basis of a theoretical framework for tourist destination choice processes, found a lack of a sound theoretical base for the issues involved.

The need to study the destination choice process has become more important in recent years as a result of the rapid growth of both travel demand and the tourist industry. Recommendations are generally viewed as an important type of information considered by consumers during the decision-making process (Howard, 1963; Beaver, 1993; Buhalis, 1995; Peter and Olson, 1993; Renshaw, 1997). Some researchers have discovered that rather than simply consulting with others (opinion leaders) for opinions or recommendations, consumers often relinquish control of all or part of the decision process to external experts, agents or surrogates (Solomon, 1986). In the travel industry, travel agents represent a key influence in the tourism marketing system (Bitner and Booms, 1982). In addition to helping travellers book reservations and obtain tickets and vouchers, they influence tourism planning decisions and outcomes. Recommendations of which operator to travel with may be critical to the success of various tourism businesses.

For marketers it is thus critically important to develop an understanding of

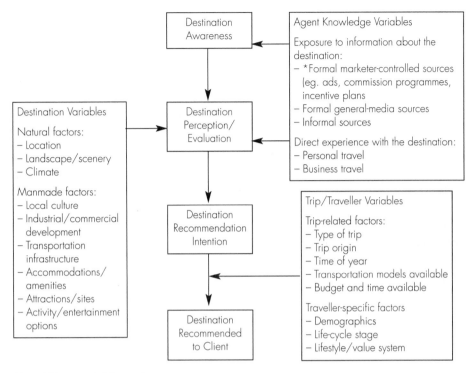

Note:* Focus of this study

Figure 11.1   Conceptual model of the process and factors influencing travel agents' destination recommendations. *Source*: Adapted from Klenosky and Gitelson, 1998

the factors that might influence travel agent recommendations. However, given the size and the economic impact of the travel intermediary sector of the tourism industry, surprisingly little research has been reported on travel agencies (Kendall and Booms, 1989; Goldsmith *et al.*, 1994). Most previous research has focused on travel agents' customers, dealing with either their search for information and services (Gitelson and Crompton, 1983; Snepenger *et al.*, 1990; Gilbert and Houghton, 1991; Hsieh and O'Leary, 1993; Goldsmith *et al.*, 1994); or with factors which influence their perceptions of and response to travel agency advertising (Kendall and Booms, 1989; Laskey *et al.*, 1994). In contrast to these studies, which focus on potential tourists, only a few studies have focused on travel agents themselves. One study contrasted travel agents' perceptions of destination attributes with those of their clients (Michie and Sullivan, 1990), and another (Contant *et al.*, 1988) examined travel agents and the impact of terrorism on destination recommendations.

A more recent study by Klenosky and Gitelson (1998) presented a conceptual model describing the recommendation process of travel agents (Figure 11.1). They empirically examined the impact on agents' destination recommendations of two factors from the model: trip type and origin. Although the study focused on destination choice as opposed to brochure/tour operator choice (as in this piece of research), it was acknowledged that the role of travel agent recommendations is a neglected but critically important area for study, especially in the current environment of increasing competition and reduced promotional resources.

TACKLING THE QUESTION

In order to explore the reality of consumer choice at the high street retail outlet, a mixture of focus group, interview and 'mystery shopper' methodologies were employed. Consumer behaviourists are increasingly embracing qualitative techniques and models in order to deal with relevant topics in meaningful and pragmatic ways (Hodgson, 1993; Walle, 1997). The research design had two main stages, and because the results of the first stage determined the structure of the second, the details of each will be discussed in turn.

Interviews and focus groups

In order to gain a clearer insight into travel agent recommendations, it was first necessary to investigate the role of the brochure within the buying process, for both the agent and the potential holidaymaker. Exploration into the consumers' perspective of the process of choosing a holiday showed that the brochure plays an important role. There appeared to be two distinct routes to booking a holiday using the brochure. One group would have a country or resort in mind and then gather all the relevant brochures. Having looked at the information, they would narrow it down to a few holidays. They would then go into a travel agent with their options to see what is available. The second group – which seemed to be mainly 'families on a budget', would get *all* the brochures before consulting the family. They would then look at prices and decide which destinations were possible. They would then either go into the travel agency to book a holiday, or telephone the agent to avoid certain inconveniences such as taking small children to the shop. For them, the travel agent was a key influence on their final decision, especially in choosing which tour operator to travel with.

Findings from the travel agent focus groups indicated that the brochure was of a low priority, and often just used as a reference tool. Other factors, such as vertical integration, tour operator commission levels, habit, availability, an efficient View Data system and pricing, were found to have considerable influence. The key determining factor appeared to be the level of integration, and whether or not the agent was owned by one of the large tour operators. Based on this finding, a model was developed which enabled us to test the day-to-day reality of choosing a holiday at the high street retail outlet (Figure 11.2).

The model suggests that the influence of an agency, and therefore its propensity

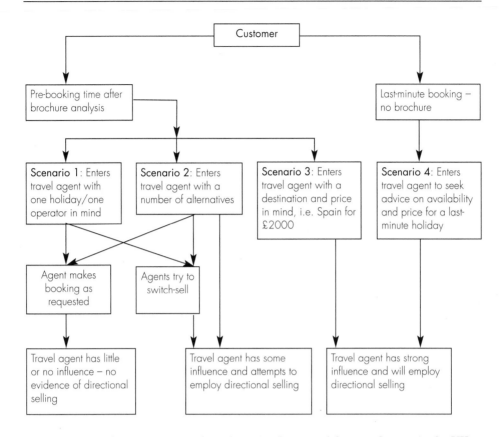

Figure 11.2 Model indicating the role and influence of the travel agent in the UK

to employ 'switch selling', will depend upon the request of the customer. From the research, four typical scenarios become apparent:

Scenario 1: customer has one specific holiday in mind
The customer has one specific holiday from one brochure/operator in mind. Here it is hypothesized that the agent has little influence and will most likely make the booking as requested. However, the agent may attempt to switch-sell and direct the customer towards the holiday of their parent company.

Scenario 2: customer has alternatives from different brochures
The customer has a number of alternatives chosen from different brochures. Here it is hypothesized that the agent will make an attempt to push the holiday of their parent company.

Scenario 3: customer has a budget in mind as well as a destination
The customer has a budget in mind as well as a destination. In this case it is hypothesized that the agent will attempt to exert a stronger influence than

in the first two scenarios and will recommend the holiday of its parent company.

Scenario 4: customer is looking for a last-minute holiday
The customer is looking for a last-minute holiday and calls the agent to see what is available. Again, the agent has a strong influence over the decision the customer makes and it is hypothesized that the travel agent is more likely than in any of the other scenarios to employ directional selling of parent company products.

Hence, the research hypothesis posits that the fewer concrete plans that consumers have determined prior to entering the travel agency, the more inclined travel agencies will be to switch-sell and to influence consumers. In the second stage of this research, the above scenarios were tested using mystery shoppers.

Mystery shopping

Mystery shopping is used quite extensively by organizations in financial services, leisure services, retailing, motor dealerships, hotels and catering, passenger transportation, public utilities and government departments. Mystery shopping is a form of participant observation where the researcher interacts with the subjects being observed, and stems from the field of cultural anthropology. In the services context, mystery shopping is able to provide information on the service experience as it unfolds (Grove and Fisk, 1992). Participant observation of this type helps to develop a richer knowledge of the experiential nature of services. The participant can identify dimensions of the service encounter unlikely to be discerned by a distant or non-participant observer. Concealment of this observation, although raising ethical issues, can ensure that the experience is natural and not contrived for the sake of the observer.

The main benefit of mystery shopping as a research tool is that it gives a clear insight into the reality of what is happening from a consumer perspective as opposed to the strategists' perspective of how they believe their policies are being implemented. In 1998, mystery shopping was worth over £30 million a year to British marketing research companies. It is a common technique used in travel retailing to compare the presentation of agencies and to assess the skills and techniques of sales staff. However, research on mystery shopping is limited to a small number of papers that have mainly focused on its use in specific sectors. Mystery shopping has been used in many service industries to find out if the institution is addressing the customer's needs, preferences and priorities (Grove and Fisk, 1992; Morrall, 1994; Wilson, 1998).

'Mystery shoppers' were used to test travel agent recommendations across the country, within the three main vertically integrated travel agency chains. One hundred and fifty-six agencies from Lunn Poly (owned by Thomson), Going Places (Airtours) and Thomas Cook or Carlson (Thomas Cook) were contacted. This contact included a mixture of actual visits (n=36) and telephone calls (n=120) to gain an insight into what happens when potential holidaymakers contact a travel agent to book a holiday. Researchers were given the four different scenarios and required to make enquiries regarding the availability of holidays as advertised in the holiday brochures.

EVIDENCE OF SWITCH SELLING

The results in Table 11.2 indicate the level of 'switch selling' employed, as well as the level of transparency (agents indicating that they were owned by a tour operator). Taken as a whole, of the 156 travel agents approached, 95 (60 per cent) clearly employed 'switch-selling' tactics. However, only 9 of the 52 Thomson-owned Lunn Poly agencies attempted to steer the researchers towards the Thomson product. So aside from Thomson, 86 of the other 104 agencies (82 per cent) owned by Airtours and Thomas Cook gave biased advice. This consisted of 90 per cent of Going Places agencies pushing the Airtours brand, whilst 75 per cent of agencies owned by Thomas Cook tried to sell their own brands such as JMC Holidays, Thomas Cook (mainly long haul) and Inspirations.

With the actual visits, for the first scenario, none of the agents made an attempt to switch-sell and were happy to check availability as requested. Additionally, researchers reported that under this scenario, travel agents were less giving of their time. This is interpreted as recognition of the limited scope for converting these customers into an allied product from which greater income could be achieved. For the second scenario, the mystery shopper provided the agent with three holiday alternatives selected from the holiday brochures of the three main travel companies. Seven out of the nine agents made an attempt to push holidays offered by their parent company. Some of this persuasion was of a more subtle nature (the Lunn Poly agents, for example, gently convinced the researchers that the Thomson holiday was far better value for money than the rest). Going Places, however, were perceived to be more forceful in their attempt to push their Airtours holiday. In the third scenario, the mystery shopper had a hypothetical sum of money and a destination in mind. Every single one of the nine agencies visited employed 'switch-selling' tactics. Thomas Cook, Going Places and Lunn Poly all attempted to sell the holidays run by their parent companies. In the fourth scenario, six of the nine agents asked about late availability pushed holidays belonging to their owners. Surprisingly, two Lunn Poly agencies and one Thomas Cook agency were keen to sell an Airtours holiday! This could be explained by many factors such as poor training, disgruntled staff, or that their parent tour operator did not have any late availability. However, in order to gain a fuller understanding, such conjecture on our part needs to be further examined.

The mystery shoppers were also asked to look for evidence of ownership links, either through printed material or through communication with the agents

Table 11.2 Results of mystery shopping exercise in travel agencies

Mystery shopping scenarios

156 calls/visits were made to agencies around the UK spread evenly amongst the 3 largest linked agencies (52 each). They were asked the following 4 questions (13 agents per question):

	% of agents that tried to persuade researchers to travel with their parent company/linked operators instead of others			If so, did they make it clear that they were owned by the parent company?		
	Lunn Poly	Going Places	Thomas Cook or Carlson	Lunn Poly	Going Places	Thomas Cook or Carlson
Number studied	52	52	52			
Travel agent owned by:	Thomson	Airtours	Thomas Cook	Thomson	Airtours	Thomas Cook
1. Travel agency was asked about the availability of a Cosmos holiday in Majorca. A hotel was chosen where Thomson/Airtours/Thomas Cook go (Cosmos have no travel agencies)	0/13 0%	8/13 61%	4/13 30%	No	No, only when asked, and reluctantly	No, only when asked
2. Travel agency was asked about the availability of two specific holidays from brochures, one a Cosmos holiday and the other a Thomson/Airtours/Thomas Cook holiday	2/13 15%	13/13 100%	10/13 77%	No	Sign on computer in 1 agency	No
3. Travel agency was asked about the availability of a specific hotel and resort chosen from the brochures (where all the major operators go)	5/13 38%	13/13 100%	13/13 100%	No	No	No
4. Travel agency was asked about the general availability in the Canary Islands for the following week	2/13 15%	13/13 100%	12/13 92%	No	No	No
TOTAL % FOR EACH AGENT EMPLOYING DIRECTIONAL SELLING (n=52)	9/52 17.3%	47/52 90%	39/52 75%			

themselves. Only one of the 36 researchers saw a clear sign indicating ownership. In addition, only three of the agencies informed the mystery shoppers of their ownership ties. In these cases, the ownership was used as a selling tactic – 'this is why we can offer you such a good deal on insurance', said one agent. A number of travel agencies used small signs on the computer indicating 'membership' of a corporate group. However, this concession to the MMC (1998) report calling for greater transparency of ownership was weakened on two fronts. The first, mystery shoppers felt, was the use of phrases such as 'bonded by' and 'part of . . . family of companies' which clouded rather than clarified the issue of ownership. Secondly, and perhaps less subtly, the use of piles of brochures, plants and office furniture served to physically conceal an already confusing statement of ownership.

With the telephone calls, the Lunn Poly agencies were unbiased in the information and recommendations they provided. They all gave similar and very helpful answers to all questions asked of them, and at no time made an attempt to push the client towards a Thomson holiday. Their telephone manner was extremely friendly and professional, indicating a high and consistent level of customer service training. In fact 93 per cent of Lunn Poly agents offered completely unbiased information. Those few that did recommend a Thomson holiday did so under the last two scenarios, but this was only 3 from 20 agencies, and could have been based on product knowledge and preference rather than internal pressure to sell the Thomson product.

The agencies from Going Places (owned by Airtours) and Thomas Cook or Carlson (linked to Thomas Cook), showed strong evidence of directional selling. Ninety-five per cent of Going Places travel agents made an attempt to push the Airtours product, whilst not disclosing the identity of their owner. It was only when asked that they revealed (reluctantly) the name of the operator whose holiday they were recommending. Of those agencies linked to Thomas Cook, 80 per cent employed directional selling tactics. Again, they did not freely admit the connection to the tour operators that they have links with, such as JMC, Thomas Cook Holidays and Inspirations.

IMPLICATIONS FOR THE CUSTOMER AND THE INDUSTRY

The results from the mystery shopping exercise support the hypothesized model in Figure 11.2 for two of the vertically integrated companies, but not for the largest operator, Thomson and their travel agency chain, Lunn Poly. Thomson Travel Group have always claimed publicly that they do not have a sales policy of switching customers towards the purchase of Thomson Holidays, findings supported by this research. This contradicts results from a previous consumer group survey (Goldsmith, 1997) that suggested Thomson were just as guilty of 'switch selling' as their competitors. It also supports the possibility that there may be a gap between the strategic policy and operational practices within the companies. Customers entering a travel agent linked to Airtours and Thomas Cook are likely to receive biased recommendations, and a distinct lack of choice. This means that the individual staff of the travel agents are putting their own financial interests and therefore by association, the interests of the large tour operators, before the interests of consumers. Ultimately this could lead to a consumer purchasing a package holiday unsuited to their needs. The main industry implication of this 'switch-selling' behaviour is the development of anti-competitive practices. Supporters of 'switch selling' suggest that it makes business sense to control the chain of supply. However, the real issue is whether the consumer is being left to believe they are getting the best independent advice to suit their holiday needs. The mystery shoppers used for this piece of research did not believe they were receiving such independent advice except from the Lunn Poly agents.

The results showed that the vertically integrated companies are not complying with Office of Fair Trading demands to make their ownership links more transparent. Indeed, Thomas Cook has recently re-branded their tour operations under the new name JMC. For the initiated, this acronym identifies the nephew of Thomas Cook; however, to the general public, the re-branding serves to further obfuscate ownership. The MMC suggest that the lack of transparency means that consumers shop around less for holidays, with the result that there is less competitive pressure on travel agents. Consumers are therefore likely to get less value for money (MMC, 1998).

There were a few subtle differences between the ways in which agencies responded to the mystery shopping visits as opposed to the telephone inquiries. For the visits in the first scenario, none of the agents attempted to switch-sell the mystery visitors, but 12 of the 30 agents called by phone made an attempt to change the caller's plans. Perhaps in person, the travel agent saw more of an opportunity to close a sale. When they did attempt to direct the researcher towards their tour operator, the agents visited in person employed much more subtle tactics, often spending considerable time explaining why the customer should choose another product. This was the case even for the Lunn Poly agents who were reported to use less force than the other two chains. However, when called by telephone, the Lunn Poly agents were completely unbiased, and their telephone manner and professionalism indicated a high and consistent level of customer 'tele-sales' service training.

CONCLUSION

In a mature package holiday market, shareholder demands for constantly improved profits have left the vertically integrated tour operators with three choices. First, they can increase prices, but risk losing market share. Secondly, they could cut prices to gain market share, at the risk of also cutting earnings and perhaps sparking a price war. The third option for operators is to implement 'switch selling' to ensure that travel agents sell their holidays, rather than their competitors'. This means either buying distribution outlets, or influencing travel agents in their recommendations to consumers.

For the time being it is clear that the three main tour operators in the UK have chosen the latter tactic. This research has shown that two of the three largest vertically integrated travel companies actively employ 'switch-selling' tactics. It is not the purpose of this chapter to suggest that this has an adverse affect on the consumer, and the travel industry in general, but the issue clearly requires further debate. More importantly, the study, and its use of mystery shopping as a powerful research technique, has highlighted the critical role that travel agents play in the decision process of consumers. This chapter has identified and explored the potential impact of 'switch selling' on the distribution channels used by UK tour operators. However, this research concerns just one aspect of the interaction between the travel company and its customer. Further research is required which further identifies and explores other forms of information and interaction between the consumer and the travel industry on which tourists rely when making their holiday decisions. In particular, the impact on recommendations, made by travel agents to customers as a result of internal marketing tactics directed at travel agents such as sales incentives and commission payments. Although these promotional tools are widely used, little is currently known about their differential effectiveness in generating business.

REFERENCES

Beaver, A. (1993) *Mind Your Own Travel Business: A Manual of Retail Travel Practice.* Radlett, Herts.

Bitner, M. J. and Booms, B. H. (1982) 'Trends in travel and tourism marketing: the changing structure of distribution channels'. *Journal of Travel Research*, **20**(4), 39–44.

Buckingham, L. (1999) 'Airtours goes back to the singles market'. *Guardian*, 11 June, p. 27.

Buhalis, D. (1995) 'The impact of information telecommunications technologies upon tourism distribution channels: Strategic implications for small and medium sized tourism enterprises' management and marketing'. PhD dissertation, Department of Management Studies, University of Surrey.

Contant, J. S., Clark, T., Burnett, J. J. and Zank, G. (1988) 'Terrorism and travel: managing the unmanageable'. *Journal of Travel Research*, **26**(4), 16–20.

Gilbert, D. (1991) 'An examination of the consumer behaviour process related to tourism'. *Progress in Tourism, Recreation, and Hospitality Management*, **3**(5), 78–105.

Gilbert, D. C. and Houghton, P. (1991) 'An exploratory investigation of format, design, and use of UK tour operators' brochures'. *Journal of Travel Research*, **30**(2), 20–5.

Gitelson, R. J. and Crompton, J. L. (1983) 'The planning horizons and sources of information used by pleasure vacationers'. *Journal of Travel Research*, **21**(3), 2–7.

Goldsmith, N. (1997) 'Who's taking you on holiday?' *Which?*, May, 8–10.

Goldsmith, R. E., Flynn, L. R. and Bonn, M. (1994) 'An empirical study of heavy users of travel agencies'. *Journal of Travel Research*, **33**(1), 38–43.

Grove, S. J. and Fisk, R. (1992) 'Observational data collection methods for services marketing: an overview'. *Journal of the Academy of Marketing Science*, **20**(3), 217–24.

Heape, R. (1998) 'Tour operator league table'. *Tourism: The Journal of the Tourism Society*, **98**, 7.

Hodgson, P. (1993) 'Tour operator brochure design research revisited'. *Journal of Travel Research*, **32**(1), 50–2.

Holloway, J. C. (1998) *The Business of Tourism* (5th edn). Longman, Essex.

Howard, J. A. (1963) *Marketing Management* (2nd edn). Irwin Publishing, Homewood, IL.

Hsieh, S. and O'Leary, J. T. (1993) 'Communication channels to segment pleasure travellers'. *Journal of Travel and Tourism Marketing*, **2**(2&3), 57–75.

Kendall, K. W. and Booms, B. H. (1989) 'Consumer perceptions of travel agencies: communications, images, needs, and expectations'. *Journal of Travel Research*, **27**(4), 29–37.

Klenosky, D. B. and Gitelson, R. E. (1998) 'Travel agents' destination recommendations'. *Annals of Tourism Research*, **25**(3), 661–74.

Laskey, H. A., Seaton, B. and Nicholls, J. A. (1994) 'Effects of strategy and pictures in travel agency advertising'. *Journal of Travel Research*, **32**(4), 13–19.

Mansfeld, Y. (1992). 'From motivation to actual travel'. *Annals of Tourism Research*, **19**(3), 399–419.

Michie, D. A. and Sullivan, G. L. (1990) 'The role(s) of the international travel agent in the travel decision process of client families'. *Journal of Travel Research*, **29**(2), 30–8.

Mintel (1999) *Inclusive Tours*. Mintel International Group Limited, London.

MMC (1998) *Foreign Package Holidays*. HMSO, London.

Morrall, K. (1994) 'Mystery shopping tests service and compliance'. *Bank Marketing*, **26**(2), 13–23.

Peter, J. P. P. and Olson, J. C. (1993) *Consumer Behavior and Marketing Strategy*. Irwin, Homewood, IL.

Renshaw, M. (1997) *The Travel Agent*. Business Education Publishers, Tyne and Wear.

Snepenger, D., Meged, K., Snelling, M. and Worrall, K. (1990) 'Information search strategies by destination-naive tourists'. *Journal of Travel Research*, **29**(1), 13–16.

Solomon, M. R. (1986) 'The missing link: surrogate consumers in the marketing chain'. *Journal of Marketing*, **50**(4), 208–18.

Walle, A. H. (1997) 'Quantitative versus qualitative research'. *Annals of Tourism Research*, **24**(3), 524–36.

Wilson, A. M. (1998) 'The use of mystery shopping in the measurement of service delivery'. *The Service Industries Journal*, **18**(3), 148–63.

CHAPTER 12

Accommodation distribution: transforming YWCA Australia into Travel Ys International

Brian King and Carina Slavik

INTRODUCTION

This chapter outlines a distribution strategy developed by the Young Women's Christian Association (YWCA) Australia to increase the sales and profitability of the organization's travel accommodation services in international markets. It is an instructive case study demonstrating how Internet technology can be adopted as a key channel within an overall distribution strategy. The particular approach outlined here has enabled a domestically focused organization to connect with partner suppliers overseas as well as with international consumers, thereby transforming itself into a genuinely internationally focused organization.

YWCA Australia is a not-for-profit organization which, amongst its diverse interests, owns and operates five budget-style hotels. These hotels provide an important source of income for the fulfilment of YWCA's community service commitments. To sustain this income flow as the supply of budget accommodation increased, YWCA Australia has needed to adopt a more aggressive market-focused approach. As outlined in this chapter, the development of a distribution strategy to increase overall brand awareness and to increase room sales and profitability has been critical to YWCA's emergence as a serious tourism industry player in Australia and to its entry into the global marketplace.

The selection of distribution mechanisms by accommodation establishments is influenced by a number of factors including the style of the relevant establishment, the scale of operation, the location, target audience and size of marketing budget. Larger scale operations have sufficiently large budgets to permit the use of several distribution mechanisms tailored to specific target markets. These may include the organization's own sales force and its central reservation service. Whilst these distribution options are also available to smaller scale operations, there is usually a need to rely upon third parties. This practice reduces the level of control that can be exercised. The use of third parties does, however, allow market reach to be extended and may provide access to specific markets such as airline travellers. In such cases an accommodation establishment may obtain preferred referral status from an airline by satisfying certain criteria such as offering a minimum allocation of rooms at a discounted room rate. Smaller operators find it more difficult to satisfy this criterion. Target markets respond differently to alternative distribution mechanisms. Visitation by sales representatives tends to be an effective means of distribution for targeting corporate clients and retail travel agencies. Leisure travellers respond better to Internet and advertising-based distribution strategies. Regardless of the size of budget, a mixed portfolio of distribution channels is generally preferred by accommodation establishments to maximize market reach.

In the case of YWCA Australia the challenge facing the organization was two-fold. First, there was a need to distribute products to both existing and new markets in a cost-effective manner. Secondly, expansion within Australia and overseas was needed through an expanded product range involving packaging the overseas YWCA and YMCA properties under a single banner – Travel Ys International. In order to overcome the barriers traditionally associated with the adoption of a so-called global approach, an Internet-based solution was sought.

The case study outlined in this chapter exemplifies the challenges confronting many nationally based organizations. In attempting to capitalize on their international affiliations they are often unsure about how to develop the relation-ships between the various levels of the organization, with particular reference to the sharing of costs and rewards associated with relatively high-risk investments. Before examining the case study in more detail it is appropriate to examine the literature focused on distribution in the accommodation sector generally. This provides a context for the case study and for the selection of an Internet-based distribution strategy in particular.

THE DISTRIBUTION OF ACCOMMODATION

The advent of mass tourism and the industry associated with it prompted the accommodation sector to acknowledge the need for a strategic approach to distribution. Thomas Cook provided his clients with hotel vouchers in the 1840s, linking hotels with tour wholesalers and travel agents and enabling access to an expanded market located distant from the destination (Swinglehurst, 1982). Accommodation establishments today are typically confronted with several distribution challenges. There is a significant penalty for failing to attract sufficient business since accommodation development typically involves large-scale capital investment. There is also a strong incentive to ensure that room capacity is occupied, even when marginal prices lead to a marginal contribution. Since a purchase of overnight accommodation invariably involves travel, a property must either approach the relevant markets directly, or deploy third parties to represent them in source markets. The hoteliers who collaborated with Thomas Cook exemplified the practice of collaboration. Kotler *et al.* (1998) highlight the continued relevance of maintaining the support of the travel agent network in a recent case study on Hilton Hotels.

In the twentieth century, the expansion of private transport led some sections of the accommodation sector to become complacent about distribution. Motels were established adjacent to highways with a view to capturing passing traffic. As motels proliferated, they increasingly relied on neon roadside signs to beckon the weary traveller. The payment of significant commissions to travel agents seemed to be an expendable luxury. It has become increasingly evident that waiting for passing trade is too reactive and susceptible to the adoption of a more strategic approach to distribution by competitors. The growing market share accounted for by groupings of motels, which undertake collaborative marketing activity and pay travel agent commissions, signals increased recognition of the need for a more strategic approach to distribution. Marketing consortia and motel chains have expanded, thereby securing the benefits of bulk purchasing, brand loyalty and cross-marketing. Flag Choice's 'Super Sally' reservations system, for example, has generated additional business for members of the group by facilitating the booking of accommodation at other member properties, particularly by motorists undertaking independent touring.

In a crowded and competitive marketplace, intra-sectoral competition is growing. Hotels are competing with serviced apartments, bed and breakfast establishments, resorts, spas and health resorts, farm stays, backpacker hostels, cruise ships and even camp-sites and caravan parks. Participation in computerized reservation and distribution systems has become an essential activity for hotel establishments (Beaver, 1995; Main, 1999). As is the case with tourism industry principals such as transport operations and attractions, the accommodation sector depends on a distribution network of travel agents, tour operators and a range of brokers/consolidators. Soon after the pioneering efforts of the airlines, major hotel groups such as Holiday Inns developed computerized reservation systems, in this case the HOLIDEX system. The interface of such reservation systems with the emerging Global Distribution Systems (GDS) was an acknowledgement of the need for distribution through the travel industry and particularly through travel agents. Major hotel groups such as Accor, Starwood and Shangri-La are active participants in GDSs. Meanwhile smaller non-aligned hotel properties struggle to secure access to such easy booking facilities and hence the market share that travel agencies are able to deliver.

Hotel distribution strategies have featured in the hospitality marketing literature (Buttle, 1986; Wearne, 1993). The selection of travel industry distribution networks by hotels has also been examined in a number of general tourism texts (Middleton, 1994; Holloway, 1998). The particular distribution challenges confronting the accommodation sector have been evaluated in the works of Chaspoul (1995) and Seaton and Bennett (1996). The role played by innovation, research and development in the development of accommodation distribution strategies has also been analysed by Viceriat (1988). These are particularly important components in the present case study. Giving examples from major tourism groups such as Accor, Pierre et Vacancies and Club Med, Viceriat stressed that innovation should involve generating new ideas and making improvements in all operational areas as well as introducing new technologies. Poon (1993) has also emphasized the importance of adopting innovative approaches to distribution, which extend beyond the adoption of new technology. She outlines the increasing prevalence of what she calls 'diagonal integration' and highlights the vulnerability of the accommodation sector as it increases its dependence on the travel trade for distribution and market intelligence and thus becomes detached from marketplace sentiment. From a consumer perspective, research by Williams and Dossa (1998) has examined the choice of distribution channel by the users of ski resorts. The study involved an investigation of accommodation users and their choice of distribution channels, with a comparison of the use of direct and indirect channels.

THE INTERNET – AS A NEW DISTRIBUTION CHANNEL FOR ACCOMMODATION

The importance of new information distribution technologies, particularly the Internet in the promotion and distribution of tourism products, was recently highlighted in a report prepared for the World Tourism Organization (WTO) (Richer and Carter, 1999). It was concluded that technology is providing smaller tourism organizations with a cost-effective channel through which to reach across the globe without the high distribution costs of conventional media. It was observed that information technology is not only changing the strategies of industry but also the habits of consumers. According to the WTO report: 'if you are not online then you are not on-sale'. Small and medium sized tourism enterprises (SMEs) have much to gain from the effective deployment of Internet-based technology. Despite the potential gains, Main (1998) has observed that while larger organizations have been optimizing their use of information technology, SMEs are still failing to act, thereby risking marginalization in the electronic marketplace. SMEs are relevant to the present chapter since Travel Ys International, as a division of YWCA Australia, may be classed as an SME, albeit in the context of a large-scale network.

Until recently, relatively few academic studies have examined the role played by technology generally and by the Internet in particular to the internationalization of SMEs (Poon and Jevons, 1997; Buhalis, 1998). It is, however, increasingly clear that the World Wide Web offers SMEs the opportunity to compete with larger businesses on a global scale (Quelch and Klein, 1996). Quelch and Klein identified Internet advertising as a means of counteracting the diseconomies of scale experienced by SMEs, by lowering the cost of international advertising, lessening barriers to entry, and by offering a critical mass of customers to small companies involved with niche markets and products. They concluded that the low costs associated with communications via the Internet might allow firms with limited capital to become global marketers very quickly (Buhalis and Main, 1998).

The significance of online technologies in the distribution of tourism products is particularly relevant in Australia, given its physical distance from the world's major tourism markets. The top four tourism spending countries: the USA, Germany, Japan and the UK account for 79 per cent of the world's current Internet population (Richer and Carter, 1999). Approximately 90 per cent of Australian tourism businesses may be classed as SMEs and one of the key principles for the development of the Australian Government's On-Line Tourism Strategy has been to encourage participation by SMEs (CRC Tourism, 1999). The challenge is significant since it is estimated that only one-quarter of tourism SMEs have an independent website. Most of these SMEs are in the accommodation sector including backpacker hostels, small hotels and bed and breakfast establishments.

Burger (1997) and Jung and Baker (1998) have shown that the Internet is a useful platform for the tourism industry to distribute information about products to customers throughout the world. In particular they draw attention to the hyper-text feature. Hyper-text is a special type of database system in which objects such as text, pictures and music are interlinked enabling movement between objects in different forms and locations and is regarded as particularly well suited to the needs of the tourism industry. Dorren and Frew (1996) have also noted that developments in electronic communication are significant for tourism service providers given the perishable, intangible, heterogeneous and high-risk nature of the product that they are selling. Since customers are often buying something that they have not previously experienced, they are likely to welcome the volume, accessibility and quality of information provided on the Internet in the form of videos, pictures and text.

Walle's (1996) observation that the Internet permits and encourages marketing efforts which bypass some intermediaries for tourism-related purchases is of particular interest. A number of authors have identified positive links between the Internet and the tourism industry. Hawkins *et al.* (1996) have outlined the view that the Internet will lead to a level playing field upon which small and large companies compete on equal terms at a global level. Some authors have expressed scepticism about the emergence of the new technology. Richer (1996), for example, has observed that traditional marketing and distribution tools have a number of advantages over online marketing. He concludes, however, that the lower transaction costs of online marketing do provide a financial rationale for embracing the new technology. According to Richer a fully functional Internet marketing and distribution system, providing real-time links to inhouse reservations systems is a modest investment relative to more expensive and established marketing and advertising medium, particularly television.

To date, product promotion and product information have been the dominant online functions adopted by tourism businesses. The functions of most of the SME websites are confined to the dissemination of information and few sites provide e-mail booking forms. The implementation of electronic commerce facilities using online booking and account settlement has been largely confined to larger international organizations such as airlines (CRC Tourism, 1999). Just as there has been some reluctance among organizations to fully utilize the Internet, consumers are also reluctant to fully embrace Internet services. There has been a tendency on the part of travellers to use the Internet primarily as a source of information and not for booking (Access Research, 1996). One reason for the reluctance of travellers to book online is security. It may take time before consumers become sufficiently confident to use their credit cards for Internet purchases (Weber and Roehl, 1999). Other potential limitations of the Internet include the ease with which consumers can compare the propositions of competitors, the ease with which websites can be changed or corrupted, and the over-estimation of consumers who have access to the web. Surveys estimating Internet usage indicate people mostly access the Internet from shared computers in the workplace, questioning people's ability to make personal purchases online.

THE YWCA IN CONTEXT

The case study of Travel Ys International exemplifies how YWCA Australia has embraced technology as a component of its distribution strategy. YWCA has been providing accommodation services since the late 1880s and operates over 220 travel accommodation properties in 44 countries. Though the YWCA is a recognized brand name, and offers an extensive number of locations and property styles ranging from basic to four-star hotels, it operates differently from other hotel chains that have chosen to expand internationally. The YWCA has been constrained by the absence of adequate capital for investment in appropriate structures and systems, by the high degree of autonomy exercised by individual YWCAs, and by the fact that hotel property development and hotel marketing lie outside the scope of YWCA's core activity of community service. The provision of accommodation by the YWCA in Australia had its own origins as a form of community service, and coincided with a shortage of safe housing for women migrant workers and female students. At the end of World War Two, there were 30 YWCA hostels in Australia offering full-board and overnight accommodation for travellers. Subsequently the demand for YWCA hostel accommodation has declined and competition for travellers has increased with the proliferation of specific tourist accommodation. By 1985 the number of hostels had declined to fewer than ten (Dunn, 1991).

In Australia the hostels which have performed best in financial terms have been those in major cities catering to the domestic tourism market. Despite the fact that boosting accommodation services became a priority in the late 1980s, the number of YWCA tourist properties had dropped to five by 1994. With the exception of one property which was undergoing refurbishment, the rest were ageing, insufficiently marketing-focused and generally uncompetitive. To ensure its survival the YWCA needed to take its tourist accommodation services seriously or seek alternative sources of income from outside tourism.

From a structural point of view, individual YWCAs are affiliates of the relevant national body corporate which is in turn an affiliate of the World YWCA. The relationship between the hotels, the YWCA of Australia, the World YWCA and Travel Ys International is set out in Figure 12.1. This structure is not dissimilar to other accommodation chains where members share a common brand name but are owned and operated independently. Examples include Flag Choice, Best Western and the Youth Hostels Association. However, YWCA differed from other chains which develop a brand name first and then seek members, since it had to craft a structure for an existing group of accommodation properties. In the early 1990s an urgent need was evident to group the five remaining properties and to introduce a structure conducive to market development.

Travel Ys International (previously known as YWCA Travel Accommodation) was established as a business unit of the YWCA of Australia in 1995. The development of a strong tourism marketing focus was a priority. Consistent with this approach, the unit has set out to become recognized as the leader inter-nationally in the marketing of YWCA travel accommodation services. Early initiatives included the establishment of national operational standards and

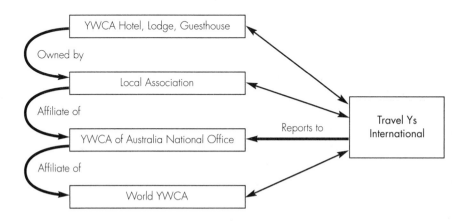

Figure 12.1 Relationship between the hotels, the YWCA of Australia, the World YWCA and Travel Ys International

procedures, the development of a national marketing strategy and the formation of a central reservations toll-free booking service for the group of five Australian properties. Over the period 1996–9, YWCA properties won a series of tourism industry awards for excellence at both state and national levels. Such awards have helped to demonstrate to other tourism industry operators that Travel Ys International is a serious industry player and to reassure the YWCA that its commitment to tourism is gaining recognition.

Through marketing agreements with independently owned accommodation outlets that offered similar standards and facilities, the YWCA chain has expanded into other capital cities with a view to providing economies of scale for the group. The addition of four such properties to the network brought the total number of properties to nine in 1998, thereby increasing capacity from 225 to 413 rooms. This expansionary approach was one response to consumer demand for YWCA-style accommodation in a range of locations, increasing the number of properties using Travel Ys International to distribute their product. Although there are only three YMCA tourist properties in Australia, their locations complement the existing YWCA network. The YMCA also plans to construct additional three-star properties over the next few years. The sustainability of the strategy of expansion relies on a public perception that the YWCA and YMCA are the same entity (when in fact they are separate organizations) and a shared corporate philosophy. One repercussion of the closer alignment between YWCA and YMCA has been that the marketing agreements struck with the independently owned properties have been phased out.

Direct channels have been the main methods of distribution used by the YWCA, a function of small marketing budgets and the YWCA's origins as a membership-based organization. Traditionally YWCA and YMCA properties were gender specific and for the exclusive use of members. Although these restrictions have been removed since the 1970s, considered as no longer relevant and as an impediment to competitiveness, the public perception has not kept up to date. This misapprehension may have been perpetuated by the continued use of direct marketing approaches to members and accommodation users.

The diversification of distribution channels was identified as a key to achieving the YWCA's objectives of increasing brand awareness, room sales and profitability. In recognition of the potential role for travel intermediaries, commissions were first paid to travel agents in the mid-1990s. Commission levels were capped at 10 per cent, consistent with the YWCA's policy of low room rates and affordable accommodation. This approach limited the ability of the properties to deal with domestic and international wholesalers (which demand up to 30 per cent commission). Compounding this limitation, the nature of the Travel Ys product does not lend itself to wholesale packaging because of the diversity of room configurations and the lack of provision for tour groups. Most guests tend to book through direct distribution channels, such as the property, the YWCA's central reservation service or the local YWCA or YMCA office. Anecdotal evidence also indicates that many travel agents refer guests who express a preference for Travel Ys accommodation directly to the central reservation service since the small commission they would earn is not considered to be worth the effort.

The use of the Internet medium did not occur immediately and emerged as a component of an established and multi-faceted distribution strategy. In 1995, YWCA Australia published what is believed to be the first detailed *YWCA International Travel Accommodation Directory*, as a form of collateral to alert the potential consumers to the network. Prior to the development of the directory, travellers who wished to obtain information or to make bookings were required to contact each YWCA directly by phone, fax or mail. Delays, inconvenience and expensive international telecommunication charges may have discouraged such travellers from proceeding to make forward bookings prior to leaving their point of origin. Building on its experience with the development of the accommodation directory, YWCA identified electronic distribution as a potential opportunity to reduce the cost of international communication and improve efficiency. The nature of the YWCA made the Internet a suitable medium.

DISTRIBUTION IN THE MARKETING CONTEXT

As a part of a non-profit community service organization, Travel Ys International has limited funds to market the group overseas. The search for a distribution channel offering low-cost global access is consistent with this desire to achieve a return on investment. Nonetheless, any significant investment should be contingent on the conduct of appropriate research. This dilemma is faced by equivalent organizations elsewhere, though it appears that YWCA has devoted an exceptional level of effort to enhancing its distribution capacity. To date YWCA Australia has relied on a narrow range of distribution channels, such as direct mail-outs and internal promotions to guests and staff. Advertising has been confined to a few consumer travel publications and overall awareness of the activities of YWCA's travel accommodation remains low. Though the YWCA brand is known inter-nationally, its 100-year plus history and welfare focus may have led to a community perception that it is an old-fashioned organization whose commercial focus is questionable. Earlier attempts to communicate the benefits of the YWCA's international network to previous guests were unsuccessful because of an over-reliance on mail communication and the absence of an up-to-date database of accommodation services including room rates.

The YWCA *International Travel Accommodation Directory* was an important precursor to the move into Internet distribution because it presented YWCA travel services to travellers in a convenient form. It provided a low-cost promotional medium which enabled individual YWCAs to assist one another in a cost-effective manner and gave travellers access to basic information. Given that YWCA accommodation is perceived to be inexpensive, travellers may accept this inconvenience though they would undoubtedly welcome the type of convenient and reliable service offered by the Internet. The participation cost for YWCA and YMCA hotels was determined following an assessment of other reservation services. The investigation concluded that the two most common methods of generating income were through advertising and commissions earned on sales. In the YWCA case, the fee would need to remain low, given the nature of the organization, its travel products and importance of ensuring participation, but high enough to achieve viability for Travel Ys International.

A flat commission fee was adopted by Travel Ys, since it offered the best prospect of achieving the objectives noted above. As a performance-based cost, the commission option provided a low risk for the hotels compared to advertising fees, since it offered entry at 'no cost'. This was the first time that many YWCAs and YMCAs had participated in a central reservation service, so minimizing the perceived risk would enhance the prospect of their participation. The administration was made simple by setting the commission fee as equivalent to the deposit required by consumers as a confirmation of booking. Deposits are paid directly to Travel Ys International and the balance is paid directly to the property when the guests arrive. This approach achieved an initial participation of 60 hotels covering every major continent and allowed Travel Ys International to offer a comprehensive accommodation listing to consumers when the website was launched. Once the site was operational and bookings were generated, it was anticipated that more hotels would choose to join.

DISTRIBUTION CHANNELS AND THE INTERNET: TRAVEL Ys INTERNATIONAL'S STRATEGY

In developing its Internet distribution strategy, Travel Ys International aimed to develop a custom-designed information and booking system to enhance its sales capacity internationally. A situation audit was undertaken and included an assessment of Internet deployment for distribution purposes by other accommodation providers. The situation audit established that the Internet offered significant possibilities for the fulfilment of the YWCA's objectives:

- to increase awareness among new and existing markets, particularly international markets;
- to increase room sales by providing easier booking access;
- to improve profitability by expanding the number of properties under the one banner.

The YWCA was quick to embrace the Internet, starting with the e-mail capability which was adopted as a way of speeding up and broadening communication within

Australia and overseas. Despite pressure to achieve immediate results, the conduct of appropriate research and product testing was also considered to be essential to ensure a strategic approach. Though large companies dominate the field, it was determined that the YWCA had the capacity to develop an online booking facility. Given that the financial and technical expertise required for a comprehensive e-commerce system was complex and costly, a compromise was arrived at whereby clients would be given a 24-hour response time with a choice of e-mail, fax or phone. It was anticipated that clients would not expect a real-time response provided that they were presented with an offer commensurate with the price being charged and the expectations associated with this.

Initial research provided an understanding of the Internet and its potential application, as well as its capability to achieve the strategic objectives of the group. It was quickly concluded that an information-only site would be insufficient and that the development of an online booking function and payment method was critical. Focus groups undertaken with existing YWCA customers indicated that the provision of up-to-date information on room rates, an online booking function with payment facilities and relative speed to down-load, was more important than spectacular graphic presentation and real-time interaction. A response turnaround of 24 hours was considered to be acceptable. YWCA soon discovered that potential applications of the Internet are not confined to accessing global markets. The opportunity to gather and monitor data through the Internet had not been predicted in the original YWCA strategy. It was discovered that consumer profiles could be extracted from information included in booking forms. Off-the-shelf software products were also available to record and analyse information about visitors to the website. This included the number of visitors to the site, the duration of any inquiries, pages visited, the type of information available by country of origin and the search engine deployed. Such data has helped to provide an assessment of the effectiveness of the site, identified potential improvements and provided a comprehensive profile of consumers interested in Travel Ys properties.

The Internet is of course only a single channel within an overall distribution strategy and does not eliminate the need for other mediums. Website addresses need to be promoted just as products need exposure. If a website receives inadequate exposure, it is unlikely to achieve its potential. The key to a successful site appears to be maintaining a mix of distribution channels within a compre-hensive strategy. The Internet simply provides the supplier with an additional means of accessing consumers and increasing product exposure and the consumer with an opportunity to choose their preferred channel. As previously mentioned, a consumer may confine their use of the Internet to gathering information and may prefer to e-mail, telephone, fax or even visit the supplier to make a purchase. The next phase of the research involved gaining an understanding of set-up and operational costs, human resource requirements and any organizational risk. These challenges were significant given the limited knowledge base of the participants and the small budget. It quickly became evident that the use of the Internet as a distribution channel should be consistent with overall strategy, and not an end in itself.

Funding has been a major challenge encountered by YWCA in embracing new distribution technology. It is critical to keep abreast of technological developments, particularly those associated with the Internet, but any investment must take immediate funding constraints into account as well as likely future returns. Although the Internet offers a lower cost distribution tool, a financial commitment by management is essential to bring about effective implementation. Skilled labour resources are required to research, update and monitor a website. Simply replicating a brochure in electronic form is unlikely to satisfy the customer expectation of interactivity. Computer equipment also needs to be reassessed and upgraded regularly. A two-stage approach was adopted to establish the Travel Ys International brand name as referring to any property listed on the website. Stage one involved assessing the feasibility of developing an Australian YWCA website that would highlight the participating hotels and associated traveller information. Stage two would use the Australian site to showcase the YWCA's capability to design and manage an international accommodation site combining YWCA and YMCA hotels worldwide. When the site was finally launched in mid-1999, 65 YWCA and YMCA hotels elected to participate.

PERFORMANCE ASSESSMENT

Three measures can be used to assess the effectiveness of the strategy over the period 1995–9, namely the business performance of the YWCA hotels, the performance of the YWCA's new central reservation service and the performance of the Internet site. As illustrated in Figure 12.2, the performance of the five hotels improved over the four-year period in terms of room nights sold, room occupancies and average room rates. A dip was experienced in 1998 as a result of the Asian financial crisis and the partial closure of the largest hotel for renovations. The 1999 results show an encouraging upward trend, particularly when compared with the Australian average for hotels, motels and guesthouses as shown in Table 12.1.

YWCA's development of its own central reservation service, based on a toll-free telephone number was the first step in creating a profile and underpinned the other marketing activities undertaken by the group. It also created a single point of entry for travellers inquiring about YWCA accommodation. The decision to employ full-time staff to handle the telephone service in 1998 encountered resistance within the organization and was considered to be excessively risky by many. There was concern that the costs would outweigh the benefits in the short term, and that the organization would be unable to provide adequate financial support for the concept on a medium- to long-term basis. To address such concerns

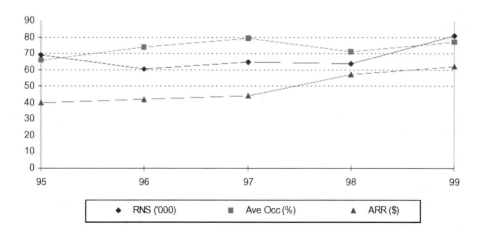

Note: RNS: Room Nights Sold; Ave Occ: Average Occupancy; ARR: Average Room Rate

Figure 12.2   YWCA hotel performance 1995–9

Table 12.1   Average room occupancy of YWCA compared to Australia, 1999.
Source: YWCA and Australian Bureau of Statistics, Survey of Tourist
Accommodation 1998 and 1999

	YWCA	**Australia**
1999	77%	59%
1998	71%	57%
Annual growth	6%	2%

Note: Figures based on national average room occupancy for Hotels, Motels and
Guesthouses, Australia

a cost–benefit analysis was prepared. It was shown that the potential increase in
room nights sold and the associated revenue would more than compensate for the
increase in staff and associated service costs. Since its establishment in mid-1996
the central reservation service has grown beyond expectations and by the end of
1999 had increased by 200 per cent a year, as measured by room nights sold and
room revenue. The conservative nature of the organization is reflected in its
approach to business development. New services are only introduced or expanded
upon when financial resources allow. The same approach was applied in the case
of introducing Internet-based services. The progressive application of Internet
features may be considered slow by commercial standards but has followed a
clearly defined implementation plan based on available funds. To date the

cost–benefit analysis of the Internet service has indicated a break-even perform-ance, though it is expected that the returns will be positive by the end of 2000. Given that the initial business plan did not expect a net positive return to be achieved until the end of a five-year period (2001), the actual achievement should occur a year ahead of schedule.

The performance of the website can be assessed in terms of online transactions, and visitors to the site measured by 'hits' (the number of webpages visited). Alternatively other web metrics can be applied in order to measure visitor activity, notably page impressions which count the number of times a page is viewed by a visitor. As previously mentioned, an important feature of the Australian website was the provision of an online booking inquiry form as an extension of the toll-free central reservations service. Following the introduction of the website in 1998, e-mail requests and bookings have increased steadily. It took four months to make the first room sale via the Internet but by the end of the first twelve months of operation, Internet-generated inquiries accounted for 16 per cent of total room sales. Now into its second year, the website has been expanded to include international properties. The Internet has grown faster than the central reservation service and now represents 28 per cent of room sales as at June 2000. Most (60 per cent) Internet-based inquiries originated outside Australia, supportive of the view that the Internet is capable of accessing travellers that the YWCA was previously unlikely to reach.

The first international YWCA web bookings were received in February 1999 for Kenya and India. This was a considerable breakthrough given that the inter-national site was still under development and was not officially launched until mid-1999. Visitation to the international website has grown rapidly. In the first six months following the launch, the site received an average of only 9000 page impressions per month. In the following six months the average number of monthly page impressions doubled, and for the month of August 2000 (thirteen months after the launch) 40,000 page impressions were recorded. During August 2000, 190,000 'hits' were recorded. This level of activity had the potential to attract advertisers, particularly those who target independent budget travellers. The importance of a multimedia promotion strategy was evident in the early success of the site at attracting visitors. The high recognition of the YWCA and YMCA brands was also a contributing factor, as was the absence of any other comprehensive YWCA or YMCA travel website. As a result the site received numerous referrals from YWCA and YMCA offices globally.

Since the site has been the only major marketing initiative by the group over the period, the results reported here suggest that the Internet is making a contribution to increased awareness. Approximately 60 per cent of the Internet inquiries received in 1999 originated from outside Australia, mainly from Internet users located in North America, Singapore and Japan who appear to have an interest in an Australian product. At this stage locations outside Australia account for less than 10 per cent of room sales. As more YWCA and YMCA hotels join Travel Ys International a more comprehensive site will increase the revenue generated through commissions, and further increase the prospect of attracting online advertisers. In addition an Intranet has been developed with a view to improving efficiency and reducing operational costs. At this stage it is too early to judge whether the objective of sharing costs and benefits has been achieved.

CONCLUSIONS AND RECOMMENDATIONS FOR FURTHER RESEARCH

The case study documented in this chapter has demonstrated the part that Internet-based solutions can play within the context of distribution channel strategies for the accommodation sector. It has shown how many SMEs in the accommodation sector were previously reluctant to distribute through travel agents, believing that commission rates were unnecessary and excessive. Ironically the Internet can provide such organizations with a direct marketing opportunity that was previously becoming difficult because of reliance on retail distribution. This opportunity has been embraced by many accommodation SMEs as evidenced by the figures for Australia where the accommodation sector has led the way in the adoption of Internet-based solutions. This chapter has documented the experience of the accommodation component of a not-for-profit organization confronting the challenge of how to embrace the Internet as an element of overall distribution strategy. The global channel strategy that has been adopted has helped to transform a modest division of YWCA Australia into a genuinely international travel organization. The application of Internet-based solutions has contributed to achieving the organization's tourism marketing and distribution objectives, and has provided additional benefits not originally anticipated such as database management and customer profiling.

As government funding for community service organizations has fallen, such organizations have been compelled to commercialize certain activities such as the one outlined in this chapter. In most cases development entails the highest revenue generating components which are often non-core activities with potential. This can lead to internal conflicts between community and commercially focused activities as they compete for limited resources. To minimize potential conflict, a commitment to long-term strategic objectives is crucial. Travel Ys International has pursued a clear marketing strategy and has embraced the importance of appropriate distribution channels. The commercialization of its travel accommodation provides additional benefits to the overall organization, including improved public awareness of the community aspects of the organization and the potential to increase membership numbers and attract donations and sponsorships.

A number of issues emerging from this chapter merit further investigation. To what extent can the deployment of Internet-based solutions generate short- and long-term financial returns for accommodation groups and what level of research and development is needed to ensure their sustainability? What is the likelihood of independent SME tourism sites attracting advertising revenue compared to the emerging so-called 'search engine portals' which are independent of the websites of particular suppliers? To what extent can the Internet be used by SMEs to address their consumer research needs?

It has been observed that hospitality SMEs have taken the lead in adopting Internet-based distribution. The accommodation experience should be instructive for other sectors of the tourism industry, which are showing greater reluctance over using the Internet. A further issue of critical interest to both the YWCA and YMCA is the extent to which the global strategies of the respective organizations embrace Internet-based booking systems. Finally it is hoped that the experience of different accommodation organizations such as the YWCA can assist in the development of conceptual frameworks to explain the relationship between distribution channel management and Internet-based solutions.

REFERENCES

Access Research (1996) *Emergence of Travel Distribution On-Line*. Australian Federation of Travel Agents, Sydney.

Australian Bureau of Statistics (1998 and 1999) *Survey of Tourist Accommodation*. Australian Bureau of Statistics, Canberra.

Beaver, A. (1995) 'Lack of CRS accessibility may be strangling small hoteliers, the lifeblood of European tourism'. *Tourism Economics*, **1**(4), 341–55.

Buhalis, D. (1998) 'Strategic use of information technologies in the tourism industry'. *Tourism Management*, **19**(3), 409–23.

Buhalis, D. and Main, H. C. (1998) 'Information technology in small to medium hospitality enterprises'. *International Journal of Contemporary Hospitality Management*, **10**(5), 198–202.

Burger, F. (1997) 'TIS@WEB – database supported tourist information on the web'. In A. M. Tjoa (ed.) *Information and Communication Technology in Tourism, 1997, Proceedings of the International Conference*. Springer-Wien, New York, pp. 39–46.

Buttle, F. (1986) *Hotel and Food Service Marketing: A Managerial Approach*. Holt, Rinehart & Winston, London.

Chaspoul, C. (1995) *Distribution of Tourism Products*. Cahiers d'Espaces, Paris. No. 44.

CRC Tourism (1999) *Meeting the Challenge: National Online Tourism Scoping Study*. Department of Industry Science and Resources, Canberra.

Dorren, C. and Frew, A. J. (1996) 'Intelligent agents and the UK hotel sector'. *Proceedings of the Hospitality Information Technology Association World-Wide Conference*. HITA, Edinburgh.

Dunn, M. (1991) *The Dauntless Bunch: the story of the YWCA in Australia*. Young Women's Christian Association of Australia, Melbourne.

Hawkins, D. E., Leventhal, M. and Oden, W. L. (1996) 'The virtual tourism environment: utilisation of information technology to enhance strategic travel marketing'. *Progress in Tourism and Hospitality Research*, **2**(3/4), 223–38.

Holloway, J. C. (1998) 'The hospitality sector: accommodation and catering services'. In *The Business of Tourism* (5th edn). Addison. Wesley, Longman, Harlow, pp. 142–58.

Jung, H. and Baker, M. G. (1998) 'Assessing the market effectiveness of the world-wide web'. In National Tourism Offices, *ENTER98: Information and Communications Technology in Tourism*. IFITT, Istanbul.

Kotler, P., Bowen, J. and Makens, J. (1998) *Marketing for Hospitality and Tourism* (2nd edn). Prentice Hall, New Jersey.

Main, H. C. (1998) 'Conference report: IT developments in the hospitality industry'. *Progress in Tourism and Hospitality Research*, **4**(1), 89–93.

Main, H. C. (1999) 'A preliminary study of data utilization by SMEs'. *International Journal of Contemporary Hospitality Management*, **9**(2–3).

Middleton, V. T. C. (1994) *Marketing in Travel and Tourism* (2nd edn). Heinemann, London.

Poon, A. (1993) *Tourism, Technology and Competitive Strategies*. CABI, Wallingford.

Poon, S. and Jevons, C. (1997) 'Internet-enabled international marketing: a small business network perspective'. *Journal of Marketing Management*, **13**, 29–41.

Quelch, J. A. and Klein, L. R. (1996) 'The Internet and international marketing'. *Sloan Management Review*, Spring, 60–75.

Richer, P. (1996) 'Should travel companies be selling online?' *Journal of Vacation Marketing*, **2**(3), 277–85.

Richer, P. and Carter, R. (1999) *Marketing Tourism Destinations Online: Strategies for the Information Age*. World Tourism Organization, Madrid.

Seaton, A. V. and Bennett, M. M. (1996) *Marketing Tourism Products: Concepts, Issues, Cases*. Thomson Business Press, London.

Swinglehurst, E. (1982) *Cook's Tours: the study of popular travel*. Blandford Press, Poole.

Viceriat, P. (1998) Dossier: *Tourist Accommodation of the Future: Forecasting, it's not Science Fiction!* Espaces, Paris. No. 150.

Walle, A. H. (1996) 'Tourism and the Internet: opportunities for direct marketing'. *Journal of Travel Research*, **35**(1), 72–7.

Wearne, N. (1993) *Hospitality Marketing*. Hospitality Press, Melbourne.

Weber, K. and Roehl, W. S. (1999) 'Internet commerce of travel products: profiles, practices and problems'. *Delighting the Senses. Ninth Australian Tourism and Hospitality Research Conference*. Bureau of Tourism Research, Canberra.

Williams, P. and Dossa, K. B. (1998) 'Ski channel users: a discriminating perspective'. *Journal of Travel and Tourism Marketing*, **7**(2), 1–3.

CHAPTER 13

Transforming relationships between airlines and travel agencies: challenges for distribution and the regulatory framework

Jaco Appelman and Frank Go

INTRODUCTION

This chapter describes the start of a transformation of a global distribution system (GDS). This system consists of two distinct units. One is concerned with cargo; the other with travel agencies and airlines engaged in international travel. The passenger distribution system is called IATA Distribution Services (IDS) and the cargo unit is called the Cargo Account Settlement Systems (CASS). Together they are known as IATA Settlement Systems (ISS) and this system is part of the International Air Transport Association (IATA). Agencies as well as airlines regard the passenger distribution system as the cornerstone facilitating scheduled international air travel. Domestic travel is therefore not considered in this chapter. The distribution system for international travel constitutes a global network connecting, approximately, 100,000 travel agents and 270 airlines. The only country not participating is the USA which has its own distribution system, the Airline Reporting Corporation and governance mechanism in the form of IATAN. The network itself and processing the distribution of tickets and revenues the network generates are its three main reasons for existence.

The chapter starts with a description of the history of this particular GDS and the way the relationship between agencies and airlines is organizationally embedded. This exposition provides the background that is essential to understanding the evolution of the relationship between airlines and their main distribution partners, the travel agencies. Drivers in the business environment such as deregulation, information technology and e-commerce, and concentration/ globalization increasingly exert their influence on the GDS, with both sectors complicating and driving the transformation process.

The chapter continues with a description of the causes that have led to a tense and conflict-ridden relationship between agencies and airlines. The reason for this is simple; if the relationship is filled with tension, a lot of energy is expended on conflicts and issues, negating the benefits and efficiencies a good working relationship brings. In the next section, a description is given of the two dominant ways in which a firm can enhance its performance in an information economy. The last section draws tentative conclusions on how the main airline GDS is likely to evolve and the effects this might have on:

- the relationship between airlines and agencies;
- the organization responsible for the operation and transformation of the GDS.

THE AIRLINE INDUSTRY AND DISTRIBUTION: CHANGE AND CONTINUITY

The main aim of IATA is to represent and serve the airline industry. IATA does so in a multitude of ways. For instance, it maintains contacts with suppliers (aircraft builders) and regulators (governmental bodies), sets worldwide standards in conjunction with relevant stakeholders, develops courses for the airline industry and accredited travel agencies and has several units that concern themselves with research and development on behalf of all airlines. Due to the wide array of tasks IATA must perform, it has a complex organizational structure and is largely structured as a professional bureaucracy. The modern-day IATA was founded in Havana, Cuba, in April 1945. The post-1945 IATA had to handle worldwide responsibilities. This was reflected in the 1945 Articles of Association:

- To promote safe, regular and economical air transport for the benefit of the peoples of the world, to foster air commerce, and to study the problems connected therewith.
- To provide means for collaboration among the air transport enterprises engaged directly or indirectly in international air transport service.
- To co-operate with the newly created International Civil Aviation Organization (ICAO – the specialized United Nations agency for civil aviation) and other international organizations.

The principle of regulated competition was the net result of these Articles of Association. The airline industry was granted anti-trust immunity, which means that airlines are allowed to collaborate on areas that are normally forbidden in the face of anti-trust laws such as the setting of fares and prices on a worldwide basis. Without anti-trust immunity airlines could be sued for collusion on a number of issues.

The airlines have integrated distribution into their value chain by locking their main partners in a principal–agent relationship. Control over the relationship is exercised through a political governance mechanism called the Passenger Agency Conference (PAConf). In the principal–agent relationship between agencies and airlines, it is the airlines that determine what the content of the resolutions will be. All airlines that are a member of IATA have a right to veto any proposal that runs counter to its interest. Inertia and slow reactions to exogenous change are the rule rather than the exception. The rules, coming forth from this PAConf, to which both parties have to adhere, are laid down in the Passenger Sales Agency Agreement (PSAA) in the form of resolutions. The PSAA is part of the Agency Programme (AP), which is a largely legislative framework stipulating minimum requirements that agents and airlines must perform vis-à-vis one another. The minimum requirements are laid down in resolutions and cover administrative, economic and other formal aspects of the airline–agency relationship. Adjustments to local or regional idiosyncrasies are laid down in the Sales Agency Rules. Consider the PSAA the constitution of the 'airline-nation'. Resolutions are thus treated as federal laws.

Just after 1945 the primary function of the distribution system was to be a clearinghouse. Its main goals were the efficient distribution and control of ticket numbers and the reporting and financial settlement of travel transactions. Development of the Clearing House was followed by the introduction of the Standard Agency Agreement in 1952. Under this Agreement, sales agencies are given the opportunity to prove their professional status under an accreditation process. Once accredited they can book any ticket from any IATA-affiliated airline. Accredited agencies enjoy a competitive advantage by gaining access to a worldwide distribution system because they get access to relevant information from all IATA airlines and are part of the largest expanding distribution network in the international air transport sector. Training is extensive and is developed in close co-operation with the United Federation of Travel Agent Associations (UFTAA), an organization that aims to represent all the travel agencies from around the world (IATA, 1999).

IATA Distribution Services (IDS) operates the BSPs (Billing and Settlement Plans) and CASSes (Cargo Account Settlement Systems), collectively known as IATA Settlement Systems (ISS), on behalf of the industry. As the focus of this book is on tourism and not transport, we will focus on the passenger-related services the IDS offers. The BSPs have been operational since 1971 and are a by-product of the accreditation system. BSPs simplify the selling, reporting and remitting procedures because, just as with a franchising agreement, all agencies that join the distribution system, in a specific region or country, must use the same procedures. Airlines and agencies that use BSPs are enabled to save on administrative overheads and traffic document inventory costs. They became the operational backbone of the AP and the distribution system because of these qualities. The year 1979 can be considered a watershed year for IATA and the airline industry. At that time deregulation started to gain momentum in the USA. Deregulation makes it impossible for the airline industry to co-operate on a range of issues, because anti-trust immunity is increasingly being lifted. Two of the most important, interrelated, effects are that:

- IATA cannot perform the policing function toward agencies, within the context of the principal–agency relationship, on behalf of all airlines which undermines the basis for a principal–agent relationship; and
- the funding of IATA is shifting from contributions paid for products and services rendered to the marketing of its products and services to member airlines, other airlines and other players in the travel, transport and tourism industry.

In other words, all parts of IATA threatened in their operations by deregulation need to become market-responsive business units. One of the most prominent business units that is transforming itself is the passenger and cargo distribution system. Although BSPs and CASSes are successful concerning growth, the management of the distribution system has initiated a restructuring process. The reasons for doing so are that they nowadays operate within a fragmented, decentralized and high-cost structure. Moreover, out-sourced service contracts are not co-ordinated and 45 separate data processing suppliers and 65 banks exist. The current distribution system is big, complex and fragmented and an organizational transformation has the potential to yield a more functional system that provides considerable scope to reduce overall costs and enhance the value for the customers of the distribution network.

The transformation plans initiated by IDS management have been approved and laid down in a resolution by PAConf. The process started in 1998 and has to be completed in 2003. IATA has a two-pronged approach with regard to the restructuring of the distribution system. On the one hand, the focus is on cost-reduction. Improvement of efficiency through a further standardization and automation of the transaction process is an example of this focus. On the other hand, value-adding activities are stimulated and developed. The IDS, for example, starts to offer a more diversified supply of services. Besides the processing of tickets it is currently possible to book a car or hotel through the distribution system. This increases the volume of transactions that need to be processed and enhances the value for its users and consumers. To be able to do so IDS needs to perform well in the following areas:

1. accreditation and training of travel agencies in conjunction with the Universal Federation of Travel Agents' Associations (UFTAA)
2. assignment, distribution and control of ticket numbers
3. reporting and financial settlement of travel transactions
4. development and support of new distribution technology
5. provision of other related travel and industry services.

Above all, IDS needs to maintain workable relationships with its suppliers (the airlines) and their sales force (travel agencies) in order to keep the network of BSPs growing. If the quality of the inter-organizational relationship of a distribution system or network deteriorates, suppliers as well as agencies will increasingly start to look for alternatives. The direct relationship between agencies and airlines is also of importance, because most agencies equate IATA with airlines. So if an agency has had a conflict with, for instance, British Airways and feels less committed and trusting, the agency will also feel this towards the distribution system. This is by no means an easy task because a number of causes systemically induce a lot of tension in the agency–airline relationship. Therefore we try to give an answer in the next section to the following question: 'How did this tension in the relationship come about and will it endanger the transformation?'

THE EVOLUTION OF TENSION IN THE RELATIONSHIP BETWEEN AIRLINES AND AGENCIES

The foundation for a working relationship is the existence of trust and commitment between partners. Trust lies at the root of any sustainable form of co-operation. Trusting your exchange partner implies that you believe the other is benevolent and honest (Morgan and Hunt, 1994, Geyskens and Steenkamp, 1995). Once trust between persons has been established and been apparent for some time, there is a great likelihood that trust (or other indicators of a good relationship) become institutionalized and a property of the inter-organizational relationship (Zaheer *et al.*, 1998). If this happens the performance of both parties could improve (Powell and Smith-Doerr, 1994; Uzzi, 1996; Gulati, 1998).

A group of agency and airline representatives called The New Millennium Task Force was installed in 1999 to investigate and review the airline–travel agent relationship. It was a joint endeavour of both parties. Currently, owing to a number of causes, the relationship between airlines and agencies is very tense. The tension is partly structural and therefore hard to change. The first structural cause of tension is the institutionalized power imbalance; the principal–agent relationship is an a-symmetrical relationship in terms of power. Airlines, in the form of PAConf, determine the rules. They are business partners but not on an equal footing. Such a-symmetrical relationships do have a tendency to generate frictions, if the expectations of both parties do not match. Secondly, both parties are bound to each other because both parties derive their main income from the selling of tickets. The resource, a ticket, is important to both parties. Airlines derive roughly 80 to 85 per cent of their income via travel agencies and travel agencies are, on average, 60 per cent dependent on the sale of tickets. They cannot exit the relationship because they would seriously damage their business in the process of doing so. The third cause is the perception by both parties that there is no real alternative to the current distribution system: agencies and airlines are linked whether they like it or not. Looking for an alternative distributor is still virtually impossible if you want to sell tickets. Formally, you have to be IATA-accredited to sell tickets. A fourth structural reason is the fact that the AP and PSAA set global standards. An optimal fit between local conditions and rules is thus hard to establish (Ross *et al.*, 1997).

Besides these structural reasons the situation is aggravated when interlining agreements caused an open market with high price sensitivity. Airlines know each other's prices almost instantaneously. The transparency of ticket prices or tariffs forced airlines to use Revenue Management Systems and yield management, resulting in complex fare structures. In the same time period the privatization of airlines forced them to shift their attention from satisfying their stakeholders to satisfying their shareholders. Taken together these reasons led to a cost-cutting focus in which control over the value creating process is imperative in order to give shareholders more dividends. The result was the development of a short-term view and a sole focus on profitability measured in financial terms. Airlines have accordingly developed a management style characterized by a pragmatic attitude and a focus on short-term gains (Hinthorne, 1996).

During the past two decades environmental variables in the form of a further development of IT and deregulation increased in importance. They started to exert their influence worldwide. Deregulation stimulated competition, which in turn prompted commission cuts, an action by the airlines that brought their distribution costs down but did serious damage to the quality of the relationship. Airlines have seized the opportunity to bring down part of their distribution costs and signalled at the same time to their travel agencies that the competitive environment is changing drastically. But deregulation did not dismantle or change the rules of the PSAA that the agencies had to abide by and that are prescribed by the airlines, the principal. Agencies thus have to compete in a new competitive environment, the information economy, with rules that are outdated and not in their favour. This fact also added substantially to the tension.

Additionally the progress in IT provides both parties an alternative distribution channel in the form of the Internet. The opportunity to engage in direct marketing, for the first time in their relational history, makes agents and airlines competitors in a multi-channel environment. Agencies have to learn to adapt to the fact that airlines are now increasingly allowed, because of deregulation, to individually determine the compensation agents get for the services they render to airlines. It is the strategy of airlines to stimulate the agencies in adopting a business model in which they charge the consumer fees for the services they provide to them (Go and Williams, 1993). Up until very recently all these costs were compensated through commissions. It also shows that both parties need to co-operate and communicate about how the relationship changes because they have also become competitors. The tension in the relationship is also fuelled by these factors. As we said before, the IDS is one of the main actors who will benefit directly from a less tense relationship between its two main customers. Improvement of the relationships between all parties concerned is something IDS strives to bring about. Why are good working relationships in an information economy that is largely based on services for value-creation so important?

THE INFORMATION ECONOMY AND COMPETITIVE ADVANTAGES

Competitive advantages to be derived from the Information Revolution, as opposed to the Industrial Revolution, reside in the way a firm enhances and facilitates the organizational interfacing of firms, nations, business-units and local governments. Dyer and Singh (1998) suggest that competitive advantages for the modern-day firm can be created through:

1. the access, control and co-ordination of information;
2. the stimulation of creativity in the organization, hopefully leading to innovations; and
3. strategic collaboration with other firms.

The increasing use of IT is one of the main drivers behind the creation of a 'global village'. Firms in such a 'village' are far more open to public scrutiny and feel therefore the need to legitimize their actions and guard their image and reputation. Customers and (potential) partners have to trust a firm or financial performance will be seriously affected. Who wants to buy from or work with an unreliable partner? In other words, firms become more and more a part of their environment because stakeholders are better informed. Firms need to become more responsible and accountable to the outside world. The most obvious way to do that is to become more open and establish relationships with stakeholders that matter and have a significant direct or indirect impact on the profitability of a firm. That is why relationship management increases in importance in an information economy.

Poon (1993) asserts that the key vehicle in influencing the value-creation process of the travel and tourist industry will become diagonal integration. As the industry is increasingly driven by information and consumers (demand), firms should diagonally integrate to control the more lucrative areas of value-creation. In other words firms should establish relationships with firms in other sectors that contribute one way or the other to their performance. For instance, close collaboration with caterers could deliver a number of advantages like a more diversified and demand-driven menu on flights or using the market power of an airline to obtain lower prices from suppliers (Table 13.1). The financial benefits can then be shared. The objective of diagonal integration is to produce a range of services and sell them to a target group of consumers. An airline could for instance co-operate with travel agencies and the accommodation sector when they open a new destination. A joint promotional campaign of the destination and the promise that the guests will receive the highest service levels will contribute to the satisfaction levels of the guests and attract, it is hoped, more bookings. The key attraction in diagonally integrating is the lower costs of production often associated with it. This is made possible through the *synergies* firms reap when they integrate that way, ultimately leading to systems gains and scope economies. The joint promotional campaign is a case in point. Opportunities for travel and tourism players to move into other industries can also be created; co-operation with the information sector is a prominent example. A lot of value-creating activities in the tourism industry (such as purchase of airline tickets) are information-driven. Or as Sheldon asserts: 'the tourism industry is highly information intensive and information is its lifeblood' (Sheldon, 1997, p. 7).

Table 13.1 Diagonal integration and product characteristics. *Source*: Adapted from Poon, 1993

Characteristics	Diagonal integration
Production focus	Many tightly related services
Objectives of integration	Get close to the consumer/Lower costs of production
Integration mechanism	Information partnerships/Strategic alliances/Strategic acquisitions
Operationalization	Synergistic production/Shared networks
Orientation of production	Consumer-oriented
Production concept	Economies of scale/Economies of scope/Synergies/Systems gains
Examples	American Express/Midland Bank

Airlines, in their attempt to reduce distribution costs, try to keep control over the information flow necessary to make transactions. Owing to the factors mentioned in previous sections, tourism will change the value chain in two areas. First, firms in control of the manipulation and distribution of the industry's information will increase their share of the industry's value. Airlines already have a head start in this area because of the ownership of some of the GDSs. Just as they initiated the development of Central Reservation Systems, they are now developing virtual ticket selling agencies in order to capitalize on the opportunities the Internet offers from direct marketing.

Secondly, firms closest to the consumer will also gain. Travel agencies and suppliers on site are therefore expected to increase their importance in the industry. If travel agencies can respond to the opportunities that allow them to increase their role, their prospects for increased wealth-creation will be enormous. Being close to the consumer means that you can gather valuable information about the preferences and desires a consumer has. If you can fulfil those desires or sell the information about consumers to interested parties, your performance as a firm will improve. In order to be able to fulfil those desires it pays to be diagonally integrated. A travel agent specializing in diving trips could, for instance, work together with a diving equipment rental service in order to accommodate those people who want specific diving gear. But agencies need to learn how to work with service fees or value-adding services in order to compensate for the reduced income in earnings from commissions. Value-adding services start well before actual transactions are made. One must enter the consumers' mind before being able to deliver the right services and products in order to stay competitive and create customer loyalty. This last point is also of increasing relevance for the IDS as they have their own strategy of becoming more consumer- or demand-oriented.

IMPROVING THE RELATIONSHIP: THE ROLE OF IATA

The transformation of the GDS will be eminently successful if the quality of the relationship between airlines and agencies improves to a level that both parties will want to work together instead of the current feeling that they need or ought to work together. In this last section the focus is on the implications of changes for the distribution system but we have also seen that the quality of the agency–airline relationship is of importance to the distribution system. The main customer bodies of the distribution system are agencies and airlines. Loyal customers create more value and will generate more revenues in the long run. Loyal customers are more committed and trusting as they feel that they derive (substantial) benefits from the relationship and their intention to stay will increase.

But what are the constraints and opportunities IATA and IDS in particular have in pursuing a strategy of becoming more customer-oriented and improving the quality of the relationships with is main customers? The model proposed (Figure 13.1) provides insight into the factors that determine the quality of the relationship. This model is based on the description of the causes of tension in the relationships. It is assumed that an improvement of some of these factors will deliver a better relationship between the IDS, the agency and airline communities.

To begin with the factor resource dependence and resource importance, these explain why agencies and airlines are inextricably linked to each other. They depend on each other because approximately 60 to 90 per cent of the revenue generated on either side is procured by selling the airlines' product. The fact that there is no real alternative to the current distribution system explains why agencies focus so much on trying to extend their influence in that direction and why the airlines zealously protect their current position. To be able to control the flow of distribution information is a competitive advantage in itself.

Trust and commitment levels in the system are low at the moment. Agencies feel that IATA is neither honest nor benevolent because IATA, because of its history, must represent the interest of their other main customer. This is an understandable position but it is detrimental to the strategy IDS has embarked upon. As was indicated above, abolishing the political structure governing the AP would greatly

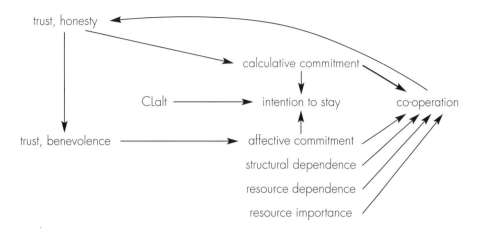

Figure 13.1 Factors inhibiting co-operation

enhance the current transformation and the chances of future success. A strategy abolishing the PAConf as a political governance-mechanism seems therefore logical. A board of directors supervising the IDS should be an appropriate control mechanism. Such a governance-mechanism will give IDS the room and flexibility it needs to complete the transformation process successfully and on time. In this way the inertia present in the system will have been circumvented.

If IATA succeeds in enhancing its image with agencies with regard to honesty and benevolence it is to be expected that commitment will increase, furthering the intention to stay and increasing the chances for co-operation that should lead to relational rents, increasing profitability and competitiveness for all parties concerned. Unfortunately the airlines have aggravated the situation through their current policy of cutting commissions. Agencies will focus on detailed contracts specifying mutual obligations, rules and procedures, because they perceive the commission cuts as opportunistic behaviour. Tension and trust levels have deteriorated as a result of these actions. If these demands are not met to a certain extent agencies will use every opportunity to make them less dependent on the current distribution system. Given these facts, the only major threat for the IDS seems the alliance formation within the airline industry. Some of the alliances strive to have a global coverage of destinations. If they succeed they will have the same advantages the industry as a whole now enjoys from IATA-IDS and they could develop and operate their own distribution system. This could, owing to information technological progress (the Internet), be more effective, efficient and interactive and they could become serious competitors. This is something the IDS needs to prevent as the value of the distribution network will decrease and they could lose valuable customers. The main contextual factors inhibiting co-operation to improve the relationship is the structural mutual dependence and power imbalance. This does not mean that total equality should be the aim. However, equal representation on areas that could lead to mutual benefits should be stimulated and implemented. An example of this would be working together to fight fraud with credit cards.

IDS should also include a clear customer voice, as they need to become demand-driven. As agencies and other service suppliers (car-rental companies, hotels, etc.) will eventually become the customers of the distribution system it is important for the IDS to understand their needs better and develop a sincere dialogue. Employing agency employees as managers and front-line staff who need to deal with agencies would help in improving the relationship and further the transformation. The first steps in transforming the distribution system have been taken. IDS-management has begun to create more opportunities to create value for the global network of agencies and airlines. This will hopefully lead to a distribution system that is capable of serving the travel industry for the future.

REFERENCES

Dyer, J. and Singh, H. (1998) 'The relational view: co-operative strategy and sources of interorganizational competitive advantage'. *Academy of Management Review*, **23**(4), 660–79.

Geyskens, I. and Steenkamp, J. B. E. M. (1995) 'Generalizations about trust in marketing channel relationships using meta-analysis'. Working Paper: Catholic University of Leuven, Department of Applied Economics.

Go, F. M. and Williams, A. P. (1993) 'Competing and co-operating in the changing tourism channel system'. *Journal of Travel and Tourism Marketing*, **2**(2/3), 119–48.

Gulati, R. (1998) 'Alliances and networks'. *Strategic Management Journal*, **19**, 293–317.

Hinthorne, T. (1996) 'Predatory capitalism, pragmatism and legal positivism in the airlines industry'. *Strategic Management Journal*, **17**, 251–70.

Morgan, R. M. and Hunt, S. D. (1994) 'The commitment and trust theory in relationship marketing'. *Journal of Marketing*, **58**, 20–38.

Poon, A. (1993) *Tourism, Technology and Competitive Strategies*. CAB International, Wallingford.

Powell, J. and Smith-Doerr, P. (1994) 'Networks and economic life'. In N. Smelser and S. Swedberg (eds) *The Handbook of Economic Sociology*. Princeton University Press, New York, pp. 368–403.

Ross, W. T. Jr., Anderson, E. and Weitz, B. (1997) 'Performance in Principal-Agent dyads: the causes and consequences of perceived asymmetry of commitment to the relationship'. *Management Science*, **43**(5), 680–704,.

Sheldon, P. J. (1997) *Tourism Information Technology*. CAB International, New York.

Uzzi, B. (1996) 'The sources and consequences of embeddedness for the economic performance of organizations: the network effect'. *American Sociological Review*, **61**, 674–98.

Zaheer, A., McEvily, B. and Perrone, V. (1998) 'Does trust matter? Exploring the effects of interorganisational and interpersonal trust on performance'. *Organisation Science*, **9**(2), 141–59.

CHAPTER 14

Airline distribution systems: the challenge and opportunity of the Internet

Bruce Prideaux

INTRODUCTION: AIRLINE DISTRIBUTION SYSTEMS AND THE INTERNET

The rapidity of change brought about by the growth of the 'new' information economy in the decade commencing in 1990, combined with the forces of deregulation and globalization, has forced scheduled airlines to totally re-evaluate their management systems and identify areas where costs can be reduced through enhanced efficiencies. One area that has been the focus of considerable attention in the late 1990s is airline distribution systems. In previous decades the targets of cost cutting included engineering, engine efficiency, air traffic control systems, administration, wage costs and improvements in the design of aircraft and related systems. Growth of Computer Reservation Systems (CRS) in the late 1970s and Global Distribution Systems (GDS) in the 1980s enabled airline managers to shift the emphasis from these previous areas of cost cutting to focus on distribution costs.

The emergence and rapid growth of the Internet in the 1990s has created new opportunities for reducing distribution costs. While new start dot.com companies including UK-based lastminute.com and Australian company travel.com.au have been quick to exploit the opportunities for direct access to customers via the Internet, airlines have been relatively slow to take advantage of Internet technology, although this situation is changing rapidly. The slow initial response to the possibilities of Internet commerce is surprising given the airlines' extensive experience of computer reservation systems and later, global reservation systems for bookings and as a source of management information. This chapter will examine the opportunities for airlines to redesign their distribution systems utilizing the Internet and electronic commerce while retaining their commitment to the travel agency system. To place the new opportunities for distribution in context the chapter will commence with a brief review of the changes that have influenced airline distribution systems in the past. The chapter will concentrate on the impact on scheduled airlines although it is recognized that the Internet has provided new opportunities for charter airlines.

Owing to the rapid rate of change, many of the sources used in this chapter to illustrate recent developments are sourced from the trade media. The academic literature is also responding to the growth of electronic commerce with the recent publication of a new journal, *Information Technology and Tourism*, an increasing number of papers in established journals, specialist conferences and a rapidly increasing number of monographs. As in any business enterprise the distribution system can be described as the infrastructure required to connect the manufacturer, or in this case airlines, with the client. Unlike physical goods such as consumer products, airline distribution systems do not rely on a logistics system comprising interlinked transport, warehousing and retailing. The sale of airline seats involves a mechanism that connects airlines to customers via a distribution system. Intermediaries such as tour operators, wholesale and retail travel agencies currently undertake a substantial percentage of airline distribution although airlines also operate their own retail offices and in recent years call centres. Retail travel agents have a significant advantage over airline retail offices because their geographic location generally places them in close proximity to their customers. In the future the ability of airlines to gain direct access to customers via the Internet may negate the retail travel agency system, substituting travel agent's geographic proximity with instantaneous 24-hour electronic access. These developments will create tensions in the relationship between travel agents and airlines that may force travel agencies to move to a fee for service pricing system for some airline products, particularly if airlines embark on a policy of reducing or eliminating the current commission structure.

THE COST OF DISTRIBUTION

In recent decades two types of airline structures have emerged, scheduled airlines and charter airlines. Scheduled airlines are common carriers and can be grouped into normal and no frills airlines. Traditional airlines offer a range of products including differentiated classes of seating, passenger lounges at airports and access to Frequent Flyer Programmes (FFP) while no frills airlines generally offer single class service with few of the more costly service enhancement benefits. Distribution costs are incurred by schedule operators including those offering no frills services because their product is either marketed directly to the public or via intermediaries. Charter airlines do not face these costs because their seats are purchased for on-sale by tour operators who emphasize low-cost travel versus the add-ons of the inflight entertainment, meals and wide pitch offered by scheduled airlines.

The modern aviation industry is a product of post-World War Two prosperity coupled with the growth of the retail and wholesale travel agency system in response to an increasing demand for travel, and the introduction of many new technologies including jet engines, new lightweight metals, radar and computers. Until the late 1970s airlines relied on the International Air Transport Association (IATA) to negotiate international fares on behalf of airlines and mediate between airlines and regulators on the determination of bilateral air service agreements and operation of the distribution system. Domestic fares were often subject to government regulation. Operating within the framework of fares determined by agreement between airlines and mediated by IATA, scheduled airlines engaged primarily in non-price competition with fellow airlines, utilizing strategies that included the payment of additional commissions (termed overrides) to agents and prizes for agents with high sales turnovers. With the introduction of airline deregulation in the USA in 1978 and the challenge to IATA's fare regime by non-IATA airlines in South East Asia (Singapore Airlines, Thai and MAS) the importance of IATA as a price regulator declined. These developments forced airlines to look at new areas for cost reductions, eventually focusing on distribution costs.

Until the introduction of deregulation and the parallel adoption of CRSs in the 1970s, airlines relied on travel agents to distribute their products in exchange for the payment of a commission ranging from 5 per cent on domestic travel to 10 per cent (or more) on international ticket sales. During this era distribution costs were regarded as a fixed cost and were usually included with promotions in company balance sheets. Doganis (1991) states that ticketing, which included the cost of commissions and promotional costs, generally averaged 18 per cent of the total operating cost of scheduled airlines. In the case of British Airlines, Doganis (1991) reported that in 1988/9 commission (net of commissions paid) represented 9.3 per cent of the airline's operating costs. Similarly, commissions represented 5.5 per cent of British Midlands total costs. Many authors, including Doganis (1991) and Pickrell (1991), writing in the period up to the early 1990s, generally regarded ticketing and promotional costs as fixed budgetary items and on the whole offered few comments on methods of achieving savings in connection with other components of airline costs.

Having exhausted many of the other avenues for internal cost savings, scheduled airlines are turning to distribution costs as the last remaining area where significant cost savings may be available. Some new start airlines have tried to bypass the agency system by either paying no commissions or encouraging customers to bypass the agency system by using direct Internet booking. In Australia for example, new entrant airline Impulse attempted to eliminate travel agency booking entirely by only accepting telephone or Internet bookings. This strategy was not entirely successful and the airline entered into undisclosed agreements with several national travel agency firms to market seats. In the USA a number of no frills airlines including Easyjet have energetically pursued Internet distribution in preference to retail agency sales. There is a danger for airlines in attempting to reduce distribution costs by arbitrarily reducing commissions paid to travel agents in that the travel agency system remains the single largest source of sales and independent advice to customers. If the agency system begins to break down through declining revenue and profitability airlines will be forced to reassess their distribution strategies.

Scheduled airlines also face considerable competition from charter airlines which, aside from having lower overheads because of the nature and standard of their service, have almost no distribution or promotional costs. For example, Doganis (1991) reported that compared to British Airways per head cost of £28.33 for ticketing, sales, commissions and promotion costs, charter airline Britannia had costs of £ 0.14 per person and Monarch incurred costs of £0.18 per person. Because of the nature of their service the Internet will offer few avenues for cost savings by charter airlines because distribution costs for their seats are generally incurred by tour operators.

STAGES IN THE DEVELOPMENT OF SCHEDULED AIRLINE DISTRIBUTION SYSTEMS

The development of airline distribution systems closely follows the introduction of new communications technologies and can be divided into a number of historical stages, each characterized by the dominant telecommunications technology of the time. The first stage spanned the period from the commercialization of airline passenger services in the 1920s until the introduction of CRSs in the mid-1970s. The second stage of development ended with the rapid growth of the Internet in the late 1990s. The third stage of growth of airline distribution systems will parallel the penetration of the Internet into the private household. Development of Internet distribution systems is a global phenomenon although growth in less developed countries will lag behind the developed economies and will impact on airlines servicing these countries.

The Pre-1970s distribution system

In the period prior to the widespread introduction of computer reservation systems from the mid-1970s onward, airline distribution systems relied on the telex, telephone and postal services for selling and distribution of tickets both for airline-owned retail offices and travel agents. The system was labour intensive, relatively slow and costly to administer. However, there were no other options. Clients often faced a considerable delay in confirmation of seats because reservations systems relied on paper-based storage and retrieval systems. Prior to airline deregulation in the USA the majority of ticket sales were made through airline-owned retail outlets.

The introduction of Computer Reservation Systems – the second stage

Computing provided the technological advance that laid the foundation for the next stage of airline distribution. Falling telephony costs, consumer demand for a faster service and the development of new computer systems paved the way for the introduction of CRSs in the 1970s followed a decade later by GDSs. These developments revolutionized airline distribution systems, enabling travel agents to check prices, seat availability and airline schedules from their desktop. Clients were offered options allowing them to make confirmed bookings at the time of first inquiry. It is probable that the rapid growth of credit cards during this period contributed to the success of CRSs as clients, freed from the need for a trip to a financial institution to withdraw cash or apply for a personal loan, were able to exercise greater control over their travel decisions.

Until 1975 US travel agents accounted for approximately 40 per cent of all sales rising to 85 per cent a decade later. Airline deregulation and the introduction of CRSs facilitated a proliferation of airfares, making retail agents a better source for cheap airfares than the airline-owned retail offices that had previously dominated airline ticket sales. As a consequence, the retail travel sector grew rapidly in size. In addition, the rapid penetration of CRSs took away much of the time-consuming task of booking seats by post or telephone that was a feature of pre-CRS travel agency operations (Pickrell, 1991). Other factors contributing to the change in airline distribution administration included privatization championed by British Prime Minister Margaret Thatcher and the introduction of new marketing strategies such as FFPs.

Airline deregulation forced airlines to either become competitive or exit the industry. At the same time, the use of CRSs was rapidly increasing, commencing with the first CRS installed in a retail travel agency by United Airlines in 1975 (Williams, 1994). The introduction of CRSs had an almost revolutionary impact on the way airlines organized their distribution systems. According to Williams (1994), airline-owned CRSs allowed a small number of carriers to achieve positions of market dominance via the airline's ability to control the sale of their product through retail travel agencies they did not own as well as enabling them to access information on rival carriers who used their CRSs. One example of this practice was the use of 'display bias' where the flights of the owner airline are displayed first, although this practice has now been outlawed in the USA (O'Connor, 1999). CRSs enabled the instant confirmation of bookings by remote travel agencies and intermediaries as well as providing airlines with a powerful database that enabled new efficiencies in inventory control to be implemented. Management strategies such as yield management were introduced and new relationships between principles and suppliers emerged. Commenting on the role of CRSs, Buhalis (1998, p. 412) states that they became central to the distribution mix and strategies employed by airlines: '[CRSs] are widely regarded as the critical initiators of the electronic age, as they formulated a new travel marketing and distribution system'. US airlines responded to deregulation by intensifying their search for new markets and the identification of internal economies.

GDSs are the logical extension of CRSs and allow agents to access a range of non-airline travel services such as hotels, car-hire, coach tours and attractions. In a sense, a GDS provides the travel agent with a 'one-stop-shop' for most travel products and has become an essential component of the distribution system. Buhalis (1998) described the role of GDSs as horizontally integrating airlines and vertically integrating all other tourism suppliers in a system that can be described as the circulation system of the travel industry. By 1995 the coverage of GDSs had expanded to such an extent that they could be termed 'Global travel and tourism information and reservation systems' (O'Connor, 1999).

Although CRSs and later GDSs provided airline managers with a powerful tool to identify new market segments and maximize yields, the use of GDS companies added to overall distribution costs. GDS companies provided services for a fee that had to be paid by the airline taking the booking. Where the GDS distributing company was owned by the airline providing the service (for example, American Airlines owned Sabre and United owned Apollo) this fee could be absorbed but where the service was provided by another GDS company the airline could not afford to refuse to pay the booking fee unless the company was prepared to forego potential revenue through lost bookings (Pickrell, 1991).

One of the major long-term impacts of the development of CRSs/GDSs has been the recognition by airlines that computer-driven systems offer airlines the ability to exercise greater control over the distribution of their products, reduce distribution costs and generate considerable product use information. The recent development of the Internet has provided airlines with the opportunity to circumvent payment of fees to GDSs, reducing the total cost of commissions paid to retailers, and to open direct channels to consumers.

Frequent Flyers Programmes (FFPs)

Airline deregulation in the USA also forced airline executives to pay more attention to the cost and effectiveness of marketing that previously had been regarded as a fixed budget item. Paralleling airline deregulation there was a rapid shift in political patronage away from national airlines, particularly after the Thatcher government in the UK commenced privatization of government-owned businesses including British Airways. With domestic deregulation spreading from the USA to many other countries and the weakening of the IATA tariff regime, airline managers became conscious of the need to find further areas for achieving efficiencies and turned their attention to marketing and ticketing budgets. Initially, efficiencies were achieved from the use of CRS and GRS systems. The significant cost of winning new customers as against retaining old customers pointed to the need to introduce schemes to retain existing customers. One response to this need was the development of frequent flyer

Programmes which aimed to use loyalty programmes to bond customers to a specific brand (Gilbert, 1996).

In the literature FFPs are often described as a form of Relationship Marketing (RM) where marketeers attempt to retain customer loyalty over a long period of time by club or loyalty programmes. In a wider sense RM can be described as marketing based on relationships, networks and interaction (Gummesson, 1999). Despite criticisms of RM (Chien and Mountinho, 2000) it has been widely adopted by airlines, commencing with the first loyalty schemes in the USA as early as the 1970s when Southwest Airlines introduced their 'sweetheart stamps' that allowed business travellers to take partners on a free flight. Later, other US airlines introduced a series of FFPs to retain patronage (Hanlon, 1996). American Airlines' AAdvantage programme, introduced in 1981, became the industry standard for FFPs and was adopted domestically and internationally. American Airlines capitalized on its FFP and Sabre CRS to identify new markets and develop new products to build a loyal customer base thus providing opportunities to maximize the benefits from expenditure on marketing. RM, particularly when combined with the benefits derived through FFPs, provides a valuable base that may enable airlines to circumvent traditional distribution systems and directly market to clients through the Internet. Figure 14.1 illustrates the differences between transaction marketing where the customer has no loyalty to the service provider and RM where the customer has a bond to the service provider through a loyalty programme.

The strength of FFPs is that they enable airlines to build a strong customer base thus reducing marketing costs and indirectly reducing distribution costs.

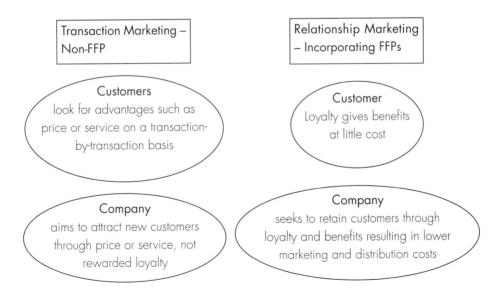

Figure 14.1   The advantage of FFPs as a form of relationship marketing (RM)

Programmes designed to strengthen loyalty may include additional or bonus points. In a sense, FFPs offer to the customer the benefits of loyalty that airlines previously attempted to build with travel agents through commission overrides and prizes for reaching sales targets, but at lower costs. The advantage of FFPs can be demonstrated by a study undertaken by the US General Accounting Office (1990) which indicated that 81 per cent of business travellers chose flights to increase their frequent flyer points. Membership lounges, often associated with FFPs, are another method of building customer loyalty.

THE INTERNET AS A DISTRIBUTION SYSTEM

The latest stage of distribution system growth occurred in the mid-1990s and parallels the rapid growth of the Internet and its widespread penetration into the household by the end of the decade. By 1999 the number of people with Internet access had risen to 43 per cent in Sweden and Canada, 41 per cent in the USA and 36 per cent in Australia (Taylor, 2000). The uptake of the Internet for booking travel has also been rapid with Internet travel sales forecast to increase from 0.5 per cent of all travel in 1999 to 2 per cent of all sales in Europe and 9 per cent of all sales in the USA by 2002 (Marcussen, 1999). This stage of airline distribution system development is currently in its infancy although airlines are beginning to exploit the new technology by establishing Internet travel distribution systems in much the same way as they established airline-owned CRSs in the late 1970s. In the future there is every possibility that new Internet-based, airline-owned distribution systems will reduce the proportion of sales made through intermediaries, displacing many retail travel agents in the process. While it is tempting to predict a return to the situation of the 1970s where travel agencies enjoyed lower commissions than those paid in recent decades and commanded a smaller percentage of total ticket sales, the future is more likely to be one where the role of travel agent changes as they compete for airline customers in areas other than price.

The impact of the Internet on airline distribution systems can be seen in three areas: the adoption of the Internet by airlines as a method to regain control of ticket sales from intermediaries; the development of new dot.com travel companies retailing online; and the response of intermediaries such as travel agents to these moves. The possible impacts of the Internet on airline distribution can be examined from four perspectives:

- The airlines.
- Intermediaries, principally retail travel agencies.
- The newly created dot.com online travel agencies.
- The customer.

Each of these groups view changes made possible via the Internet through the filter of their own needs. While travel agents may view the development of the Internet and possible loss of commissions with alarm and base their responses against this perspective, airlines appear to view the Internet as another method of reducing costs and part of an ongoing process that stretches back to the time when airlines first commenced airline operations. From the customers' perspective, the development of new methods of purchasing travel may be seen as another improvement to the business of shopping that in the past included the evolution of self-service shopping, credit cards and the obtaining of information through electronic advertising. If past trends in shopping and purchasing behaviour are a guide, the success of the Internet will depend on its ability to deliver to the customer benefits that can be measured in terms of reduced costs, improved quality, easier access, greater variety and new products.

Airline adoption of Internet technologies

Airlines have a number of options for Internet distribution including airline-owned websites, alliance sites, electronic intermediaries and other forms of sales including electronic auctioning of unsold seats. A major advantage of these types of services is the ability to offer 24-hour, 7-days-a-week service that in the near future will include bookings via cellular phones using Wireless Application Protocol (WAP) technology. Airlines initially lagged behind new start-up dot.com travel agencies in exploiting the potential of the Internet for direct ticket sales. This situation began changing rapidly from 1999 onward as airlines launched their own web ticketing operations as well as entering into joint ventures with other airlines to establish Internet sales agencies. In a survey of Internet distribution in Europe to the end of 1999 Marcussen (2000) found that both traditional and no frills airlines were experiencing rapid growth in Internet sales. British Airways was the clear leader in revenue but not in percentage of total sales with estimated Internet revenue of US$120m in 1999 based on 1 per cent of total sales. In comparison Easyjet achieved 63 per cent of total sales via the Internet to generate revenue of US$63m. The rapid growth in Internet sales by no frills airlines may pose a serious competitive challenge to traditional airlines in the next decade, forcing them to retreat from some markets or counter-attack by establishing their own no frills subsidiaries. This option has already been adopted by British Airways which operates Go and KLM which established Buzz.

In November 1999, United, Delta and American announced plans to launch a new travel portal to provide clients with online access to airline tickets, car rentals and other travel products. In early May 2000 an eleven-member European consortium announced the establishment of Basilica that will pool fares. British Airways, one of the consortium members, has publicly stated that the airline was aiming for 50 per cent of all bookings through the Internet as part of its strategy to achieve acceptable distribution costs (Lippiatt and McMahon, 2000). An interesting element of the establishment of Basilica is that its membership includes carriers that belong to rival Oneworld and Star Alliance alliances. Shortly after the announcement of Basilica, the Australian financial press reported that Qantas was co-operating with Singapore Airlines and Cathy Pacific to develop an online travel agency designed 'to cut intermediaries and other online travel retailers out of ticket sales' (Kitney and Sanderlands, 2000). Other Asian carriers were also reported to be potential members of the operation that will be established as a separate company with a separate board and initial working capital of US$100m. As was the case with Brasilica, airline partners in the venture include members of rival airline alliances Star and Oneworld. Each of the Internet portals will provide members with the ability to exploit their frequent flyers memberships by offering additional services. In the case of Qantas the membership of its FFP numbers 2.3 million, giving it a low-cost distribution system comprising customers who had a vested interest in maximizing frequent flyer points through incentive schemes. The success of these new airline initiatives in distribution will depend on a number of factors including the rate of penetration of the Internet into the domestic household, improvements to the speed of the Internet and design of the Internet portals that are consumer friendly.

The views of airline executives on the rate of acceptance of the Internet as the consumers' preferred booking option is not unanimous. For example, Geoff Dixon, Deputy Managing Director of Qantas, predicted that the percentage of bookings of Qantas flights over the Internet might reach 5 per cent by 2004 while BA is predicting that online bookings could reach 50 per cent later in this decade (McMahon, 2000). The benefits that may accrue from online ticket sales is illustrated by US carrier Southwest (Australian Aviation, 2000). By January 2000 online ticket sales accounted for 27 per cent of all revenue. Compared to January 1999 (percentages in parentheses) the composition of ticket sales was travel agents 30 per cent (37 per cent), reservations systems 43 per cent (49 per cent) and Internet 27 per cent (14 per cent). The airline reported that the cost of online sales was 10 per cent of that of a retail travel agent and 20 per cent of that of its regular reservation system.

The Internet has also enabled airlines to reduce the fees paid to CRS companies by substituting ticketless travel systems. In the USA low-cost ValuJet adopted the Open Skies computer management system which links the airline directly to its customers via the Internet thus eliminating many of the costs of handling tickets including commission and CRS fees. In Australia, however, Impulse airlines was not able to generate sufficient yield through the Internet-only booking system and was forced to enter into distribution agreements with several national travel agency chains. Under the Open Skies management system customers can book and pay for seats, amend departures and check flight status online. Other airlines have resorted to call centres where payments are made by credit card and the customer is given a booking number rather than a ticket.

Again, airlines using this system are able to achieve considerable costs in ticketing as well as eliminating commissions and at the same time receiving management information. While ticketless travel is suitable for commuting travel, it has yet to become widely used in more complex transactions that include hotel reservations and other services.

Airlines can also employ the Internet to strengthen existing relationships with travel retailers. Qantas Holidays has developed a website specifically for its preferred agents, enabling product advice, promotional fares, tickets, itineraries and credit card payments to be made online (*Travel Week Australia*, 2000). At the stage of development of airline-owned Internet booking systems evident in mid-2000 it is not possible to evaluate the degree of acceptance of this form of seat sales, particularly where sales involve complex products that include multi-sectors and a number of non-airline products. The evidence available from the experience of airlines like Southwest indicates that airlines can achieve considerable savings on Internet bookings of single-sector flights and on travel products where the client does not exercise options to modify the basic travel package. In the future it is highly probable that the percentage of tickets and other services purchased online will grow when travellers become confident in booking such transactions over the Internet.

Travel Agencies

The deregulation of airline fares in many countries combined with a reduction of IATA's influence over international fares and the growth of CRSs in the 1970s provided the foundation for the rapid increase in the number and importance of the travel agency sector as an intermediatory in the airline's distribution system. Faced with increased competition, airlines increased the size of commissions paid to travel agents as a competitive measure to gain customers. Between 1978 and 1993 commission payments as a percentage of fare revenue rose from an average of 4–5 per cent to 12 per cent (OECD, 1997). Evidence of the significance of travel agents in the airline distribution system is also demonstrated by the findings of the US General Accounting Office (1990) study which found that in the USA, 51 per cent of travel agents chose the airline at least half the time and about two-thirds of agents selected the airline on at least 25 per cent of the flights they booked. The OECD (1997), citing a Louis Harris survey, found that 51 per cent of agents selected a carrier on the basis of commission incentives at least some of the time.

Travel agencies appear to have the most to lose, with threats of reduced income from reduced commissions, reduced revenue as airlines increase sales of tickets online, and potentially the adverse reaction of customers to the introduction of fees that may be necessary to make up for revenue shortfalls. In the travel agencies' favour are a number of unique services that dot.com travel companies and airline Internet portals cannot offer. These include:

- The person-to-person nature of retail travel agency businesses
- The ability of agents to offer and explain complex fares options to clients
- Agents can design specifically tailored itineraries based on complex options that may not be able to be offered electronically
- Agents are able to discuss the advantages and disadvantages of destination selection
- Agents can also arrange visas, insurance and other travel documentation
- Clients have the option of developing long-term personal relationship with agents
- Agents can access brochures and present them in a more acceptable format than Internet information
- Agents can develop specialist knowledge of specific destinations
- Clients can obtain information on a number of competing products.

Additionally, intermediaries such as wholesalers can develop specialist tour products tailored for specific market segments that can then be sold through retail travel agencies. These products constitute a significant share of retail travel agency sales and the withholding of commissions on these products will be difficult because the non-airline components constitute a significant percentage of the value of such packages. Additionally, there is also the possibility that airlines may reintroduce or increase commissions to gain market share.

It is likely that airlines will only succeed in reducing commissions across the entire industry if they act in unison. Recent history suggests that this may not be possible except for a short period of time. In 1998, Ansett Airlines in Australia attempted to reduce the commission paid on domestic fares from 5 per cent to 4 per cent. Ansett's competitor Qantas did not match the cut and when travel agencies threatened to retaliate by referring all bookings to Qantas, Ansett backed down. In the event of a move to reduce commissions, the forces of competition are likely to prevail and airlines will regularly break ranks to pay increased commissions to increase market share. In previous years the competitive nature of the airline industry has resulted in agents being offered substantial override commissions as a means of increasing sales.

Given the ability of retail travel agencies to develop a personal relationship with customers that is not possible with computer sales, and the inability of computers to easily deal with complex travel questions, it appears unlikely that the retail travel sector will disappear, although the number of agents may decline. There is, however, a need for travel agencies to develop new strategies to cope with Internet travel booking operators, particularly airlines.

Travel intermediaries offer services and products that airlines do not offer, giving airlines limited scope to manoeuvre. Indeed, the relationship between airlines and intermediaries can be described as both conflicting and symbiotic in nature. Airlines rely on travel agents to sell their product, consisting mainly of seats, while intermediaries rely on airlines for commissions. While airlines may be able to reduce the level of commissions paid on seat sales, the sale of seats is only one portion of the bundle of travel services required by the consumer which includes accommodation, tours, meal options, activities, transfers and in some cases the services of guides. Unless airlines can offer alternatives to the current retail travel structure, they will continue to rely on intermediaries such as travel agents for ticket sales, particularly where the seat is part of a bundle of services offered as a package or where clients have specific requirements outside the standard package.

It is interesting to draw an analogy with the media in making these observations about the rate of acceptance of new technologies. The introduction of television was predicted by many to be the nemesis of the movie theatre. However, movie theatres responded by changing the format of their service delivery, a tactic they later repeated in response to the introduction of cable television and then the video. Today, the movie industry is vivacious and expanding, meeting each new challenge with adaptation and innovation. It is highly likely that the retail travel agency system will also adapt and innovate, offering new services and products, although those agencies that fail to change will exit the industry.

Dot.com travel agencies

Dot.com travel agencies eliminate the need for personal travel to a retail travel outlet but face the same dangers from increased airline Internet sales that are confronting shop-front travel agents.

Bjork and Guss (1999) suggest that there are four main barriers to wider adoption of the Internet by consumers:

- *Security.* The main concerns are lack of security of personal information and doubts over the ability of suppliers to guarantee security over financial transactions, particularly credit card numbers.
- *Scepticism.* Dimensions include questions over an airline's ability to deliver the services promised and bad experiences that may be exacerbated by concerns over the impact of computer viruses.
- *Perceived uncertainty.* The complexity of the system enhances users fear of making the wrong response and when attempting to master the skills necessary to use the Internet.
- *Loss of personal service.* The Internet precludes the option of face-to-face meetings where customers can ask for explanations, seek opinions and have options explained, compared and ranked.

In a recent paper Palmer and McCole (1999) argue that widespread adoption of the Internet may later lead to a re-intermediation of travel services where customers seek convenience and are willing to pay intermediaries to conduct their early search for information on travel products. Further, not all consumers prefer the move to self-service shopping such as Internet selling and may be willing to pay a premium for person-to-person contact. A development of this nature reflects current attitudes to service where there is demand for speed and economy paralleled by a willingness of the affluent to pay for higher levels of personalized service.

Discussion and conclusions

In the long run the ability of airlines to increase the percentage of seats sold through their own company-controlled distribution system will depend on the skill of customers in navigating Internet booking systems, the user-friendliness of Internet sales systems, price and competitive responses by travel agents. It is impractical to believe that all households will opt for connection to the Internet in the next few years although in the long term this is a distinct possibility. Many clients will continue to experience difficulty in mastering the skills required. Electronic sales systems must also develop strategies that can offer a personalized service and access to a range of competing products including airline fares. Suppliers, including airlines, will have to develop the capability of offering a selection of competing products to avoid the customer becoming suspicious that they are being exploited.

Travel intermediaries are unlikely to let the airlines go unchallenged on the question of commissions. They may respond by charging fees or rewarding airlines willing to pay higher commissions with preferential sales status. Travel agencies will also have the advantage of offering personalized service that can claim to give unbiased information on all travel products. Airline-owned distribution systems will find it difficult to mount a convincing case to the consumer that they will offer unbiased sales information, particularly when the manner in which airlines promoted their own products over their rivals on CRSs is considered.

Ultimately, the ability of airlines to reduce distribution costs via investment in Internet booking systems will be determined by the reaction of the customer. It is likely that some savings will be possible but it is unlikely that airlines will be able to regain the level of control over their distribution systems that existed prior to the introduction of CRSs and deregulation. Airlines have lost the monopoly powers they enjoyed when prices were controlled by IATA or government regulation and where the flow of information was limited to paper-based printed price schedules. The introduction of computers has worked for the airlines in that they can respond rapidly to changing demand by manipulating prices but, equally, computers have given the customer a far greater ability to make decisions based on competing prices and service standards.

REFERENCES

Australian Aviation (2000) 'Online ticket sales growth'. *Australian Aviation*, No. 161, May, p. 14.

Bjork, P. and Guss, T. (1999) 'The Internet as a marketspace – the perceptions of customers'. In D. Buhalis and W. Schertler (eds) *Information and Communications Technologies in Tourism*. Springer Computer Science, New York.

Buhalis, D. (1998) 'Strategic use of information technologies in the tourism industry'. *Tourism Management*, **19**(5), 409–21.

Chien, C. S. and Mountinho, L. (2000) 'The external contingency and internal characteristics of Relationship Marketing'. *Journal of Marketing Management*, **16**, 583–95.

Doganis, R. (1991) *Flying Off Course: the Economics of International Airlines*. Routledge, London.

Gilbert, D. C. (1996) 'Relationship marketing and airline locality schemes'. *Tourism Management*, **17**(8), 575–62.

Gummesson, E. (1999) *Total Relationship Marketing, Rethinking Marketing Management: From 4Ps to 30Rs*. Butterworth-Heinemann, Oxford.

Hanlon, P. (1996) *Global Airlines Competition in a Transnational Industry*. Butterworth-Heinemann, Oxford.

Kitney, D. and Sandilands, B. (2000) 'Qantas plans $173m ticket pact'. *The Australian Financial Review*, 17 May, pp. 1, 30.

Lippiatt, C. and McMahon, I. (2000) 'QF, CX, SQ web agency shock'. *Travel Week Australia*, No. 965, 24 May, p. 1.

Marcussen, C. H. (1999) 'The effects of Internet distribution on travel and tourism services in the marketing mix: No-frills, fair fares, and fare wars in the air'. *Information Technology and Tourism*, **2**, 197–213.

O'Connor, P. (1999) *Electronic Distribution Technology in the Tourism and Hospitality Industries*. CABI Publishing, New York.

OECD (1997) *The Future of International Air Transport Policy Responding to Global Change*. Organization for Economic Co-operation and Development, Paris.

Palmer, A. and McCole, P. (1999) 'The virtual re-intermediation of travel services: a conceptual framework and empirical investigation'. *Journal of Vacation Marketing*, **6**(1), 33–47.

Pickrell, D. (1991) 'The regulation and deregulation of US airlines'. In K. Burton (ed.) *Airline Deregulation International Experiences*. David Fulton Publisher, London.

Taylor, L. (2000) 'Talk about an old economy'. *The Australian Financial Review*, 27–28 May, p. 23.

Travel Week Australia (2000) 'QH uses e-commerce to help agents'. *Travel Week Australia*, 27 September, p. 26.

US General Accounting Office (1990) *Airline Marketing Practices: Travel agencies, Frequent-Flier Programs, and Computer Reservation Systems, Secretary's Task Force on competition in US domestic airline industry*. Washington, D.C.

Williams, G. (1994) *The Airline Industry and the Impact of Deregulation* (revised edn). Avebury Aviation, Aldershot.

227

PART 3

Destination and regional approaches to tourism

CHAPTER 15

Communication issues in NTO distribution strategies

Linda Osti and Harald Pechlaner

INTRODUCTION

Distribution channels are one of the most dynamic elements and competitive features in the tourism industry. This is due to the fast and rising development of information technology which has revolutionized the old way of communication and information channels between tourism service enterprises, tour operators, retailers and consumers (Buhalis, 2000a). National Tourism Organizations (NTOs) have also been affected by these changes: not only because of the recent development of information technology but also owing to the ongoing change in behaviour and desires of visitors and potential guests. 'Distribution or marketing channels are defined as sets of interdependent organizations involved in the process of making a product or service available for use or consumption. The ultimate objective of distribution channel can be summarized as: delivering the right quality and quantity of product, in the right place, at the right time, at the right cost, to the right customer' (Buhalis, 2000b). It is clear that NTOs, as the 'leader channel' of a (national) destination, have responsibility for developing competitive strategies for their own headquarter and subsidiary offices abroad and also giving clear guidelines to all the tourist organizations and operators in the country. The main aim of this chapter is to underline communicating issues that NTOs have to face both in marketing the destination to the new tourist of the third millennium and in organizing and managing a combine destination of products and local, provincial, regional resorts.

THE ROLE OF NTOs

NTOs were founded in each country under different constraints and issues and at different times. For example, the Italian State Tourism Board (Ente Nazionale Italiano per il Turismo) was founded in 1919; the British Tourist Authority with the Tourist Boards for England, Scotland and Wales were founded only in 1969 when the growth in the number of overseas visitors – over 5.8 million in 1969, spending £359 million – highlighted the potential of tourism as a creator of wealth and jobs (Lavery, 1989). In all the cases, NTOs' main responsibility lies in the overseas promotion of their own national tourism. They pursue this objective by adopting initiatives to raise awareness abroad of national and regional tourism resources (in particular their own country's natural, environmental, historical, cultural and artistic values), to lend assistance and offer technical services to the tourism enterprises on the territory and to enable them to penetrate foreign markets (ENIT, 1999). Therefore, given their responsibility for a general public interest, NTOs' core role consists of promotion and direct communication with possible consumers residing in foreign countries, and providing service to the national tourism enterprises. Table 15.1 illustrates the distribution role of NTOs.

Moreover, NTOs maintain, develop and oversee professional relations with national and foreign tourism demand enterprises in order to facilitate their commercial contacts. They also maintain, develop and oversee professional relations with the international press, opinion makers, and political, administrative and cultural representatives in the countries where the NTO offices operate, with the objective of fostering and developing encounters between international demand – whether organized or individual – and national supply. NTOs activities are therefore aimed basically at two categories of customers/users. First, collective/organized demand facilitated by national and foreign tour operators and travel agencies. Secondly, individual demand, consisting of all individuals that are current or potential users of tourism services.

THE ORGANIZATION OF NTOS AND NTAs

In some countries the National Tourism Administration (NTA) is the body responsible for the promotion and marketing of the (country) destination. Therefore it is not always possible to separate NTOs from NTAs (WTO, 1996). Taking as an example the Italian State Tourism Board (ENIT, 1999), the typical organizational structure consists of:

- A central office in the capital city of the country which normally includes a research and development/studies department; planning and marketing office; external relations; development, and events office; advertising and multimedia

Table 15.1 The distribution role of NTOs. *Source*: Hawes *et al.*, 1991; Adpated from ENIT, 1999

- studying international markets, and in particular the characteristics and trends in demand for individual and organized tourism;
- constantly monitoring the development of foreign tourism demand;
- planning operating strategies in agreement with the national tourism public and private operators;
- collaborating with other actors e.g. the Tourism Department at the Prime Minister's Office, Regions, central public administrations, boards, professional associations, and producers of tourism services: transport, hospitality, food service, public businesses, etc.;
- developing and planning objectives to be employed for each target market;
- identifying and employing the right combination of several marketing tools, such as:
  - multimedia communication
  - mass media advertising
  - print, multimedia, and audio-visual production
  - creating and managing data and image banks
  - traditional and electronic information distribution
  - material distribution
  - press relations in the country and overseas;
- analysing business strategies of main distributors;
- consulting services for regional and private operators;
- organizing marketing meetings between the national supply and foreign demand;
- arranging seminars for professional users;
- providing assistance to visits by national economic operators abroad, and by foreign economic operators to the country;
- facilitating meetings with main distributors and administrative authorities;
- organizing and taking part in fairs, expositions, exhibitions and large-scale events in the country and abroad;
- providing assistance and operative consulting services to national tourism enterprises,as to how to plan productive activities and promote the tourism services on foreign markets

---

systems office; computer and information management systems office; accounting office; personnel office; planning and methods office; administration, heritage, and general affairs office.

- In addition the foreign network which comprises a number of offices located in main international markets. ENIT, for example, has 21 offices: 13 in 11 European countries (Amsterdam, Berlin, Brussels, Copenhagen, Frankfurt,

London, Madrid, Munich, Moscow, Paris, Stockholm, Vienna and Zurich), and 8 in 5 countries outside Europe (Chicago, Buenos Aires, Los Angeles, Montreal, New York, Beijing, Sidney and Tokyo). Therefore, the ENIT network directly covers 16 markets accounting for more than 85 per cent of foreign tourism. This percentage has to be increased if we take into consideration all areas covered by the foreign network including the countries where, although lacking a permanent office, ENIT acts with its own resources. In fact, in some countries ENIT has no offices and its representatives are hosted by the Italian embassies and other governmental bodies abroad.

The typical role of NTOs is therefore to promote the destination to the most markets possible both to single visitors or potential visitors and to tourism business enterprises. This means that the same product is promoted to different target markets and to different subjects. Although this seems a fairly easy task, so far only few NTOs are able to organize in order to communicate different products to different markets and different information for different subjects. Nevertheless, the need to concentrate on special marketing strategies for tour operators and travel agencies has been faced fairly recently. Owing to the increasing competition from the Internet and new technologies, organizations have felt the need to develop business-to-business marketing (March, 2000). The process of communicating different things not only to different subjects but also to different markets and tourists is a recent development of the tourism market, and it is because of the ongoing change in behaviour of tourists and a consequent new dimension of resorts.

DESTINATIONS AS A TAILOR-MADE SERVICE/PRODUCT

To better understand the role of NTOs in the distribution channels, it is first necessary to define the tourism product. Recent studies have demonstrated that the destination is defined by the requirements and needs and in particular by the services that the potential guests intend to consume. The definition and delimitation of a destination changes in reference to the origin of the guest (the distance is the independent variable), and the knowledge and information that the guest has about it (Jäger and Pechlaner, 1999). This means that every visitor or potential visitor sees the destination as a combined package of products and services he/she decides to buy and consume in the geographic delimitation he/she decides.

The destination product includes a number of commercial tourist services, such as accommodation, catering, transport services, events and so on, as well as product components which sometimes represent an integral part of the destination, e.g. landscape, culture and heritage or destination's inhabitants (Inskeep, 1991; Bieger, 1998; Crouch, 1999). Moreover, the geographic area, chosen as holiday destination by the guest and 'experienced' during the stay, will depend on the travel motive, the offer and, of course, on his/her knowledge about the destination area (Buhalis, 2000b). At the same time, the sets of products which are expected by the guest are always different combinations depending on the respective guest.

Due to the growing development of the Internet, also the purchasing habits of the tourists are changing, indeed planning and preparing a holiday on the computer at home is getting easier and easier. The 1990s and the next decade of the year 2000 will belong to the individuals and the destination marketing, the development of new products and their distribution will have to be adapted to this new environment (Middleton, 1997; Jones, 1999). Therefore the destination management and NTOs need to offer a unique package made up of the composition of the different services as one brand. The destination needs to be shaped and packaged according to each of the different segments and types of tourists they want to attract. Tourists do not care about geographical boundaries set by the resorts nor about different companies working in the area. They are much more concerned about the ease of booking and buying the products and the services. Therefore destinations, in order to be competitive on the market, need to be organized in such a way that integration of services, products and geographical levels are the main strength and core competence.

THE NEW ROLE OF NTOs

Although it has been stated that 'the whole tourist marketing message from an NTO's point of view is to identify primary, secondary and opportunity markets for the tourist destination's product, build up a communications system with these markets and to maintain and increase the destination's market share' (Laws, 1995), our hypothesis led us to interview the directors of the different ENIT agencies in the world about their different methodologies used in the communication within their boundaries. The survey aimed to outline the way the NTO needs to become flexible and malleable – exactly as the destination itself – in communicating and distributing the destination product in the different markets of origin.

In connection with the change of customers' expectations, a nation should more than ever think about the reasons convincing a potential guest to visit the area, or certain destinations in the area. Political borders as regions, provinces, valleys and districts are losing their functions leaving space to the delimitation of adventure of guests with their own ideas of a destination (Gee and Fayos-Sola, 1997). This is very clearly shown by trends towards a greater number of shorter holiday stays as well as the individualization of holiday trips. A destination is the area of movement of the guest during their stay, often leading to co-operation among different tourist organizations and destinations. Co-operation is necessary to be able to offer the products being claimed by the different guests, and on the other hand to be able to guarantee the potential for a sensible appearance on the market. The direct consequence is that different levels of tourist organization (places and towns at the local level, geographic areas and valleys at the district level, regional and province level of states and lands, the national level and the international level across borders) can be interpreted as various levels of destinations. This is despite the fact that the guests' interpretation of a destination does not always correspond to the historically grown and politically influenced areas of a tourist organization.

Managing and marketing a destination as a product/market combination is the main focus at all levels of destinations. In fact destinations at the national level represent a set of destinations within the country. Therefore this set of products represent a big challenge concerning the establishment of priorities for the positioning of the destination and sets of destination on the markets. The work of the regional and provincial tourist organizations represents another challenge within the national organization, due to the distinctive product promotion done by the region itself, and to the resulting concentration of information and know-how on specific markets. The development of core competencies requires the national tourism organization to have the ability to make use of internal processes for the creation of core competencies and to be able to represent a co-ordinating authority for local and regional tourist organizations. This is particularly important as regards promotion and competition-oriented product development as for most NTOs this is the most important and difficult task. This last task can also be defined as the promotion of a combination of destinations. In this combination, the national tourist organization is the 'central office' for local and regional organizations: it has to formulate guidelines and criteria for destinations for the control of market appearance by means of market research, market promotion and communication and specific evaluation and use of past experiences.

Branding is a useful answer to the necessity of communicating a set or combination of destinations. Branding helps to increase the visibility of tourism regions and countries on the world. It is essential to attract clients from distant markets and from new sources in order to reduce dependencies. Branding is also a way of ensuring quality assurance for the products and services offered by the destination. It will be a further task of the tourist organizations and boards to decide to what extent they wish to develop quality control, and whether or not they would like to explore the opportunities that 'total quality management' might be able to offer to tourism. Branding improves, moreover, the return on investments in market communication, transforming casual business into repeat business (Keller, 1999). This is becoming particularly important owing to the emerging role of IT and the Internet. A country's destination management system has few chances to appear on the net among others, therefore branding becomes necessary for the loyalty not only of the destination (i.e. the country), but also the sub-destinations (i.e. regions, provinces and districts) which are under the same brand. One of the core responsibilities of the new NTO is therefore to communicate a co-ordinated brand which combine all tourism products and services at destinations. This task represents the co-ordination point of the local provincial and regional network and the integration of competencies and potentials.

In this instance, the co-operation of all destinations within one hierarchy requires real willingness to co-operate and a marked ability to combine products and services that traditionally compete. In the distribution of a destination, NTOs play a primary role in the communication with tour operators and airlines. While deciding to open the destination to new markets or to reinforce the old ones, both the NTO headquarters and the subsidiary offices are responsible for the co-ordination of packaging, distributing and marketing the destination/tourism product. New flights have to be encouraged by the NTO headquarters with the airlines flying between the destination and the source market. The subsidiary office is in charge of contacting the airlines of the source market and encouraging them to schedule new flights, and provide more seats. At the same time, subsidiary offices encourage tour operators based in the the source market to sell new packages to the destination and to fill the new air seats made available by the airlines. The task of the NTO is co-ordinated in co-operation with the subsidiary offices. Although commercial, industrial, partner stakeholders have a short-term perspective, NTOs have to undertake medium- to long-term planning. The new NTO needs also to assure the implementation of policies which can ensure a tri-dimensional (economy, culture and environment) sustainable development.

In the framework of a new overall role of NTOs, the national tourism organization in Switzerland is planning a totally new role. Along with the creation of an independent profile for a strong family brand Switzerland, new functions include direct information and co-operation with all destinations officially recognized as such. Bases are different service packages according to the scope of the respective brand: 'global brands' (destinations with more than 1 million overnight stays); 'international brands' (destinations with at least 600,000 overnight stays); and 'national brands' (destinations with at least 300,000 overnight stays). In addition, Swiss Tourism is also offering help with the development of products (supply function), as well as the development of new national brands (Bieger, 1998). In this way, Switzerland is one of the very few European NTOs breaking with the principle of vertical co-operation by means of a hierarchy based on the political definition of the areas. Several questions emerge on the strategic organization of an NTO, particularly with regard to the distribution of duties: Should they concentrate on central activities or extend their duties to include an active role in the industry? Should they centralize their function at their central office or should they seek stronger decentralization?

The best answer to the first question is that without doubt information and communication are tasks that also determine also the future work of NTOs concerning market as well as offer. New technologies are supporting the creation of knowledge-based management. Information systems within a destination, as well as new channels of distribution or electronic systems on the market, suggest that a much more proactive approach should be adopted. Information service for customers before and after their decision concerning a destination is one of the core activities of NTOs, closely connected to the strategy of market communication. Interfaces of information and communication are between the headquarters (NTO) and its subsidiary offices in other countries, and between potential customers and the subsidiary offices. New technologies, especially online services, have led to a better integration of interfaces (Gerdes, 1998).

Most NTOs in Europe still consider the establishment of reservation systems to be an additional task, mostly delegated to regional and local tourism organizations, even if the national tourism administrations are responsible for the creation of favourable basic conditions (Buhalis and Spada, 2000). The main scope of the tourism organizations is the promotion of a destination and market communication along with the provision of information to customers, before and after their decision concerning a travel objective. If the quality of the information distribution at the head office and in the branches is not sufficiently high, it can lead to considerable 'bad will' and, if it is not sufficiently targeted, it can be prohibitively expensive. Also in response to this question, the co-operation with both the higher and lower levels becomes a necessary condition. The higher level has, moreover, to consider whether or not to standardize their information and make the provision of information more professional (Keller, 1999).

Concerning the second question, one has to consider the current number of governments trying to increase the effects of decentralization of government authority. Political, cultural and economical aspects of the country are very important. In countries like Spain, for example, it is not so much a discussion of decentralization, but a matter of the division of political administration districts, provinces and regions that make a central degree of decentralization possible. On the other hand, a new investigation of regional and sub-regional tourism organizations in Italy has shown that a significant number of regional tourism organizations do not even consider the NTO as a superior authority, even if it is entitled to carry out certain measures of co-ordination between the regions' and provinces' tourism organizations (Pechlaner and Osti, 2000). Especially concerning destination marketing there is evidence of an overlap, a fact that has also been confirmed in other studies (WTO, 1996).

NTOs need to start a closer co-operation with the regional and local offices. A well-developed understanding of the respective target market's culture concerning knowledge, faith, art, morals, law, customs and traditions (Dülfer, 1999) is required for the management of NTO headquarters, and of course for the management of the subsidiary offices as well. This inter-cultural activity is the basis for a deeper understanding of potential customers, and results in the possibility of creating adequate strategies of destination marketing (Pizam and Jeong, 1996; Allison, 1999). In addition, destinations do not have geographical boundaries as the boundaries are defined subjectively by the prospective guests. This means that the NTO has to communicate the peculiarities of the country along with the main attractions, giving at the same time a general overview. In this effort, the co-operation of the subordinated levels is essential in several ways. NTOs must communicate on a regular basis with the subordinated regional and local tourism organizations in order to:

1. co-operate and keep up to date on eventual marketing promotions and to get marketing material delivered when requested;
2. be a communication centre or organizer among the subordinated organizations and the subsidiary offices around the world as regards the type of customers that are requiring information on the area and to pass on a database of addresses and names of those who have showed an interest in the destination;
3. carry out, in co-operation with the regional and local offices, market research on the source markets;
4. co-ordinate the different sub-destinations and their services and products in order to create a combination of potential destinations for each guest.

The NTO has also to communicate and co-operate with offices or bodies of a higher level. Intra-states bodies and offices for the promotion and marketing of areas are few but are growing in number. An example is the Alpine 'Mile', which aims to promote not only typical Alpine products, but also the Alps as a destination. So, NTOs are responsible for the co-ordination of 'sub'-destinations for the presentation and communication of the entire combination, but also for the co-operation with other NTOs or similar bodies in order to move the country to a higher position for the promotion of the area to (potential) guests who are distant from the destination or have a poor knowledge of it.

Taking the Italian case as an example, the results of the research show some of the common changes in the destination marketing mix that need to be undertaken in order to be competitive on the market. Although most of the ENIT offices declared they would co-operate with regional tourism organizations, no-one stated the desire to co-operate with some of the individual regions for specific oriented projects. The co-operation with the sub-destinations is evident, although both the offices and the regions do not take any advantage of each other's knowledge and core competences in specific markets. In addition the most important task to be declared in the co-operation between the offices and the regions has been the distribution of information material: market researches and special events have been far less important.

As regards the distribution of information, it has been noticed that there is a correlation based on the distance and knowledge of the market and the type of distribution channel. The more distance and the more unknown the market, the more importance is given to the connection with and distribution to tour operators and travel agents. As regards what in particular the ENIT offices are promoting, the answer has been all types of tourism and products available in Italy. In most cases there are no different marketing strategies nor activities employed in the different markets where the subsidiary offices are based. However, in some countries several niche products have been taken into consideration for a specific promotion. This is mainly in the new emerging markets for Italy such as distant markets and new developing markets.

CONCLUSIONS AND OUTLOOK

NTOs have to face several important challenges in order to stay in the market and promote a competitive product. The tourist product is the amalgam of all the different tourist (and non-tourist) services at the destination and is a combination of one or more sub-destinations. To meet the requirements of offering such a malleable product, IT provides the best solution. Nowadays, the Internet as a marketing tool provides the possibility not only of implementing the marketing mix quicker and with lower costs, but also transmitting to the potential guest emotions, which are not effective with other forms of marketing such as brochures or printed material. Three-dimensional images and virtual reality mixed with the possibility of choosing what to see and what to experience just with a click of the mouse, have an influence on the decision-making process before purchase and can help in customer loyalty towards a destination. Information technology, the development of destination management systems (DMS) and interactivity are making it easier to adapt the product to the potential guests with the creation of an ideal one-to-one marketing service (Go *et al.*, 1999; Buhalis, 2000b). With the offer of all the products and services in the destination and sub-destinations and the booking availability, potential guests can prepare their own tailor-made package (Dellaert, 1999). Keller (1999) has identified some of the main advantages of the implementation of a DMS (see Table 15.2).

Table 15.2 Benefits of destination management systems

1. the customer is able to obtain all the information he/she requires and even to book his/her holiday at little expense;
2. most of the authority over the destination returns to the NTO; formerly this was mainly in the hands of tour operators or the international tourism companies;
3. it is an excellent basis for database marketing;
4. interactive communication structures lead to a reduction in transaction costs and to economies of scale, both internally and externally.

The first websites were concentrated on the services and products offered, giving little importance to the graphic and marketing messages. More and more, IT will be able to assist in the creation of DMSs, which, along with an offer of integrated services and products, will be able to communicate marketing messages as well. The distribution through a DMS is possible only through the integration at the national level of databanks developed by local tourism offices and suppliers. DMSs are the basis for the distribution of information and the path to take for booking services and products in the future.

REFERENCES

Allison, R. (1999) 'Cross-cultural factors in global advertising'. In J. Bolten (ed.) *Cross-Culture – Interkulturelles Handeln in der Wirtschaft*. Verlag Wissenschaft und Praxis, Sternenfels, pp. 99–110.

Bieger, T. (1998) 'Reengineering destination marketing organizations – the case of Switzerland'. Discussion paper, TRC-Meeting held in Brijuni, Croatia, 15–18 May.

Buhalis, D. (2000a) 'Distribution channels in the changing travel industry'. The Dorchester, London, 9–10 December 1998. *International Journal of Tourism Research*, **2000**(2), 137–9.

Buhalis, D. (2000b) 'Marketing the competitive destination of the future'. *Tourism Management*, **21**(1), 97–116.

Buhalis, D. and Spada, A. (2000) 'Destination management systems: criteria for success'. *Information Technology & Tourism*, **3**(1), 41–58.

Crouch, G. I. (1999) 'Services research in destination marketing: a retrospective and prospective appraisal'. Paper presented at 1999 SERVSIG Service Research Conference.

Dalleart, B. G. C. (1999) 'The tourist as value creator on the Internet'. In D. Buhalis and W. Schertler (eds) *Information and Communication Technologies in Tourism 1999*. Proceedings of the ENTER International Conference in Innsbruck, Austria.

Dülfer, E. (1999) *International Management in Diverse Cultural Areas*. Oldenburg, Munich, Vienna.

ENIT (1999) 'L'attività promozionale dell'ENIT'. *Ottavo Rapporto sul Turismo Italiano*. Mercuy, Florence.

Gee, Ch. and Fayos-Sola, E. (1997) *International Tourism: a global perspective*. World Tourism Organization in co-operation with WTO Education Network, pp. 292–302.

Gerdes, H. (1998) 'A national destination management system (DMS) based on the examples of Germany and Swtizerland'. In D. Buhalis, A. M. Tjoa and J. Jafari (eds) *Information and Communication Technologies in Tourism 1998*. Proceedings of the ENTER International Conference in Istanbul, Turkey.

Go, F., Govers, R. and Heuvel, M. (1999) 'Towards interactive tourism: capitalising on virtual and physical value chains'. In D. Buhalis and W. Schertler (eds) *Information and Communication Technologies in Tourism 1999*. Proceedings of the ENTER International Conference in Innsbruck, Austria.

Hawes, D., Taylor, D. and Hampe, G. (1991) 'Destination marketing by states'. *Journal of Travel Research*, **30**(1), 11–17.

Inskeep, E. (1991) *Tourism Planning: An Integrated and Sustainable Development Approach*. VNR, New York.

Jäger, B. and Pechlaner, H. (1999) 'Kultur als destination?' In Harald Pechlaner (ed.) *Burgen und Schlösser – zwischen Tradition und Wirtschaftlichkeit*. Linde Verlag, Vienna.

Jones, C. (1999) *Applications of Database Marketing in the Tourism Industry*, [http://www.econres.cpm/PAPERS/dbase_mgt.html] (9 December 1999).

Keller, P. (1999) 'New trends in destination marketing: strategic issue'. In WTO, *The Future of National Tourism Offices*. World Tourism Organization, Madrid.

Lavery, P. (1989) *Travel and Tourism* (2nd edn). ELM Publications, Suffolk.

Laws, E. (1995) *Tourist Destination Management: issues, analysis and policies*. Routledge, New York.

March, R. (2000) 'Buyer decision-making behaviour in international tourism channels'. *International Journal of Hospitality & Tourism Administration*, **1**(1).

Middleton, V. C. T. (1997) 'Marketing issues in heritage tourism: an international perspective'. In *Tourism and Heritage Management*. Proceedings of the International Conference on Tourism and Heritage Management, Gadjah Mada University Press, Indonesia.

Pechlaner, H. and Osti, L. (2000) 'Nuove sfide per la destinazione turistica'. *La Rivista del Turismo*, **2**, 26–32.

Pechlaner, H. (1999) 'Management of tourism destination combines'. In J. Ruddy (ed.) *The 1999 European Conference of TTRA*. Dublin Institute of Technology, 29 September–2 October, Ireland.

Pizam, A. and Joeng, G. H. (1996) 'Cross-cultural tourist behaviour: perceptions of Korean tourguides'. *Tourism Management*, **17**(4), 277–86.

World Tourism Organization (WTO) (1996) *Towards New Forms of Public-Private Partnership: The changing role, structure and activities of National Tourism Administrations*. A special report for the WTO, Madrid, Spain.

CHAPTER 16

Tourism distribution channels in Canada

Atsuko Hashimoto and David J. Telfer

INTRODUCTION

Canada is currently ranked eighth in the world's top ten tourism destinations and ninth in the world's top ten tourism earners (CTC, 2000a). In 1999, there were just over 19.5 million tourists visiting Canada and just over 18.3 million Canadians going abroad (CTC, 2000a). Tourism in Canada is the country's twelfth largest industry in terms of GNP and it has a predicted growth rate of 2 per cent. The positive picture for tourism in the country is due in part to increased budgets, more aggressive marketing of Canada as a tourism destination and legislation such as the Open Skies agreement (CTC, 1998a). Recent statistics show that economic activities generated by tourism topped the CDN$50 billion mark and more than 500,000 workers are annually employed in 80 tourism-related occupations (Canadian Travel Press, 2000a). (See also Table 16.1.)

Table 16.1 Canadian tourism receipts and payments in 1999. *Source:* Canadian Travel Press, 200a

	Tourism receipts in Canada (CDN$ million)	Tourism payments outside Canada (CDN$ million)
USA	9,120	10,529
Other countries	5,749	6,234
Total	14,869	16,762
Growth rate over 1998	6.7%	5.0%

The purpose of this chapter is to outline the latest trends in the industry and highlight changes in tourism distribution channels in Canada. It begins by briefly outlining the key components in the Canadian industry. Current trends in Canadian distribution channels are highlighted for major suppliers and travel intermediaries. These trends indicate increased concentration of power in the tourism sub-sectors and the Canadian tourism industry's strong link to the globalization process. One of the significant components within the distribution system in Canada is the level of partnerships that exist between public and private organizations for inbound tourism. Strategic alliances and partnerships will be highlighted with examples from national, provincial and regional levels. The initiatives of the Canadian Tourism Commission (CTC) in facilitating product distribution are examined. The chapter concludes with future research needs. While information technology is rapidly becoming a major component within the distribution system in Canada and one cannot ignore the magnitude of its influence, this chapter will not explore information technology in any detail.

THE TRAVEL INDUSTRY IN CANADA

Summarized by the vision and mission statements of the CTC in Figure 16.1, the tourism industry in Canada has seen a growth in the diversity and number of new tourism products resulting in changes in distribution channels (Smith, 2000). The key components in the Canadian tourism industry are outlined in Figure 16.2 and include the public sector, private sector services, suppliers and intermediaries. The private sector includes financial and banking services, travel insurance companies, educational institutions, media such as the Canadian Travel Press, and organizations like the Association of Canadian Travel Agents (ACTA). Public sector involvement at the national level is led by the CTC followed by provincial/territorial tourism ministries, regional organizations and municipal tourism organizations. Each provincial government has extensive autonomy and works independently, while the CTC, which recently became a Crown Corporation, co-ordinates and facilitates tourism planning, research and development, packaging, marketing and promotion. At the provincial level in Ontario, for example, the tourism industry has gained increased recognition with the recent establishment of a stand-alone Ministry of Tourism, which previously was integrated within the larger Ministry of Economic Development, Trade and Tourism. Under the umbrella of each provincial tourism organization, there are a number of public, quasi-public and independent organizations, which work independently and in co-operation to create more attractive tourism products. Decreasing in scale in Ontario, for example, is the Southern Ontario Tourism Association (SOTA), the Niagara Economic Tourism Development Corporation (NETCOR) (Niagara Region based), the Niagara Parks Commission (park based) and the Niagara Falls Tourism (city based).

VISION

Canada will be the premier four-season destination to connect with nature and to experience diverse cultures and communities

MISSION

Canada's tourism industry will deliver world-class cultural and leisure experiences year round, while preserving and sharing Canada's clean, safe and natural environments. The industry will be guided by the values of respect, integrity and empathy.

Figure 16.1   Canadian tourism industry. *Source*: CTC, 1998b

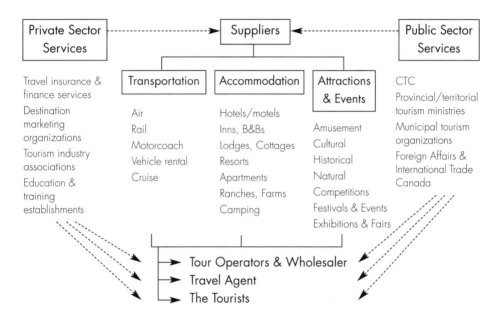

Figure 16.2   Key players in Canadian tourism. *Source*: Tourism Canada, 1994

As illustrated in Figure 16.2, the various sub-sectors must co-operate and work together to deliver better tourism products to potential customers. Although technological advancements and vertical marketing systems are gradually changing the face of distribution channels in Canada, tour operators, wholesalers and travel agents are still considered to play the most important roles in the distribution channels. According to the ACTA, 80 per cent of all airline tickets sold are still processed through travel agents (CTC, 2000b). Current trends for suppliers and intermediaries shown in Figure 16.2 will be highlighted in terms of implications for tourism product distribution channels in the following two sections. Many of these trends are a reflection of what is happening in the tourism industry worldwide and therefore are having similar impacts on distribution channels around the world. A detailed profile of travel agents and tour operators in Canada is presented as they are among the key players in the distribution process.

TRENDS IN TOURISM SUPPLIERS

It is important to understand emerging trends within the tourism supply system as they have a major impact on distribution channels and who controls the distribution channels. One of the major trends in the tourism industry around the world and in Canada has been the concentration of power in the various sub-sectors, which in turn, is concentrating distribution channels in the hands of a smaller number of companies. The process of concentration has primarily occurred through mergers, acquisitions and strategic alliances. Within the airline industry worldwide, there are 502 airline alliances with four groupings now dominating (World Tourism Organization, 1998). One of the dominant alliances, The Star Alliance, includes Air Canada, Air New Zealand, All Nippon Airways, Ansett Australia, Austrian Airlines, British Midland, Lauda Air, Lufthansa, Mexicana Airlines, SAS, Singapore Airlines, Thai, Tyrolean Airways, United and VARGIG. The number is still growing, giving the alliance a strong sphere of influence. In 1999 Air Canada took over Canadian Airlines, leaving one national airline in Canada. In the charter airline sector, the main players are Air Transat, Royal and Canada 3000. Transat A.T. Inc. bought one of the major networks of travel agencies. By this purchase, Transat A.T. now owns its own charter airline (Air Transat), tour operator (Air Transat Holidays) and an extensive network of travel agencies. Transat A.T. has now accomplished its goal of operating a vertical marketing system in its distribution channel.

Canada is a signatory to the Open Skies Policy, which has opened the borders and allowed foreign carriers greater access to Canadian customers and allowed customers greater choice. The Open Skies Policy agreement was introduced in February 1995 and took full effect in February 1998 with the result that airlines and not governments now decide which transborder routes they can fly. Over 90 new scheduled routes have been added by Canadian and American carriers since the signing of the agreement and 40 per cent have been added in Toronto alone. The rate of transborder traffic had increased from 13.6 million in 1994 to 17.9 million in 1997 (CTC, 1998a). Airline deregulation around the world has also led to the development of no frills, low-cost airlines, which are currently operating out of secondary airports. WestJet, for example, based in Calgary, Alberta, has expanded its operations and now flies out of Hamilton, Ontario. With the introduction of these still relatively small low-cost operators, major carriers internationally have taken notice and some of them have started to launch low-cost carriers. Elsewhere, privatization of national airlines continues as part of the globalization of airlines (World Tourism Organization, 1998).

A single carrier, VIA Rail Canada, also dominates the passenger rail industry. VIA Rail serves over 3.8 million passengers annually and of those, 3.2 million ride the train between Toronto and Québec City. The flagship of the industry is *The Canadian* which runs from Toronto to Vancouver, attracting over 150,000 passengers a year, most of them tourists (CTC, 1998a). VIA has recently received a major influx of funding (CDN$400m) from the Federal Government to upgrade existing facilities (TRDC, 2000). VIA claims to have been the world's first railway to provide interactive online access to timetables and fares followed by ticket reservation and payment. In 1998, the company had 23,500 Internet bookings which earned CDN$2m (Marcussen, 1999). The cruise industry has also showed improvements. In a study commissioned for the Northwest Cruise Ship Association for the 1999 season, results indicated that the direct economic impact of spending amounted to CDN$500m throughout Canada. The Vancouver Port Authority has reported a steady increase in passengers for 15 consecutive years to 1997 and is host to 24 vessels representing 11 cruise companies. Most of the volume originates from the world's third most popular cruise route from Vancouver to Alaska (CTC, 1998a).

The accommodation sector in Canada has been described as dynamic and characterized by fast-paced change (CTC, 1998a). Hotel ownership has shifted dramatically, resulting in the concentration of hotel assets in the hands of a few portfolio investors. Three real estate investment trusts including Legacy Hotels, Canadian Income Hotel Properties and Royal Hosts own more than 80 hotels with over 17,000 hotel rooms (CTC, 1998a). Similar to global trends, acquisitions are expected to continue across North America and branding has become increasingly important. In Canada, 76 per cent of hotel rooms located in hotels of 100 rooms or more are attached to a brand. The larger brand hotels operating in Canada include Best Western, Choice, CP Fairmont, Four Seasons, Hilton, Holiday Inn, Howard Johnson, Hyatt, Marriott, Melia, Radisson, Ramada, Sheraton and Westin. Choice Hotels in Canada represents seven different brands. Canada has also traditionally been affected by seasonality and has been known as a summer market for accommodation along with an emerging ski season. To combat this effect, hotel operators have begun to benefit recently from innovative programming and festival and creative packages by tour operators, which bring tourists in the off seasons (CTC, 1998a).

In the sub-sector of suppliers, use of information technology is worth mentioning here. With the rapid expansion of online booking engines, many suppliers are using their websites with exclusive 'agent only' pages. In the Choice Hotel website, for example, there is a special 'Travel Agents City' section and a valid IATA number must be entered to gain access. Once inside these pages, the travel agent can view Choice's special agent rates, book a room and collect commission. With travel agents representing 40 per cent of Choice Hotel bookings, the supplier could not afford to cut out the travel agent. This trend has also spread beyond the hotel industry as Toronto-based netfaresonline.com also offers an agent-only section. So far 17 Canadian air consolidators list their flights on netfaresonline.com including Fun Sun, Scanditours and Tourcan, and 850 agents have registered with the website. The website is also linked directly with the Sabre Reservation system and Galileo is expected to link in the near future. This trend saves agents from calling all of the air consolidators to get the best prices, which now can be obtained quickly over the Internet. Other suppliers prefer online booking engines as they offer the savings of automated booking while avoiding the Global Distribution System (GDS) fees. WestJet airlines, for example, announced higher commissions for bookings made over the Internet. WestJet flights, which are booked by telephone, earn 5 per cent commission while those made online will earn 9 per cent. The airline does not list any of its flights on any GDS (Lupton, 2000).

PROFILE OF TRAVEL AGENTS IN CANADA

As the majority of customers still prefer to arrange their tours through conventional intermediaries rather than through the Internet, this section now turns to look at the current profile of intermediaries in Canada. Statistics Canada conducts an annual survey of travel agencies and tour operators in Canada, which is prepared in association with the Canadian Tourism Commission, illustrating the commitment of the organization to partner with the tourism industry and produce information relevant to the needs of the industry (Canadian Travel Press, 2000c). In 1997, the number of travel agencies was 4760 establishments, and they employed an estimated 16,000 full-time and part-time employees. Of the 16,000 employees, 75 per cent have full-time status (Statistics Canada, 1997). The size of each travel agency ranged from 2 to 20 employees. As demonstrated in the map of Canada (Figure 16.3), the distribution of employment is concentrated in three provinces: Ontario (48.1 per cent), Québec (20.2 per cent) and British Columbia (16.4 per cent). This concentration is closely related to the concentration of revenue distribution: Ontario (41 per cent), Québec (22 per cent) and British Columbia (20 per cent). The travel agencies sector is characterized both by small operations and by recent business mergers and acquisitions, concentrating the industry in the hands of a few enterprises. In 1997, 94 per cent of travel agencies were incorporated, 63 per cent were affiliated with a chain, 43 per cent were affiliated with a franchise, and 55 per cent were members of a consortium (Statistics Canada, 1997).

The trend to merger and acquisition has also been recognized by the smaller agencies, which have taken advantage of strategic alliances and large national consortia enabling firms to increase buying power while sharing costs of technology (CTC, 1998a). Some of the major travel agency chains operating in Canada include Carlson Wagonlit Travel, Marlin Travel, Uniglobe, Algonquin, Thomas Cook, American Express and Goliger's Travel Plus. Another example of strengthening retail distribution by vertical integration is Transat A.T. Transat owns Air Transat Holidays, Voyages Nolitour, Regent Holidays and a 35 per cent share of World of Vacations. Transat has just bought out Consultour/Club Voyages, which is a network of travel agencies operating under three different name brands (Club Voyages, Voyages en Liberte and Inter Voyage). The company has 160 sales outlets in Eastern Canada and manages the Vacances Tourbec network under contract. Consultors also owns outright 15 Canadian retail travel agencies and 47 French retail agencies and also has an air ticket consolidator division. This purchase is part of the company's plan to bring all aspects of holiday travel together under one company (Canadian Travel Press, 2000b).

Two major sources of travel agency revenues in terms of customers are leisure travel and corporate/business travel. Fifty-one per cent of travel agency revenue is generated from the sales to household or individuals travelling for leisure purposes (Statistics Canada, 1997) which is a slight decline from 62 per cent in 1993 (Tourism Canada, 1994). Corporate travel stands at 39 per cent which is a 1 per cent decrease from 1993 and an 8 per cent increase from 1996. Repeat customers are also very important to Canadian travel agents. In leisure travel, 61 per cent are repeat

Figure 16.3   Provinces in Canada. *Source*: Brock University Map Library 1999

customers and in the business travel section 68 per cent are repeaters (Tourism Canada, 1994). Recent major revenue sources for travel agencies are transportation fares (53.3 per cent), tour packages (25.8 per cent), insurance products (5.2 per cent), cruise packages (5.1 per cent) and accommodation (4.0 per cent). Canadian travel agencies earn 63 per cent of their total revenue during Summer (32 per cent) and Winter (31 per cent), and 20 per cent of their total revenue in Spring (Statistics Canada, 1997). This seasonality phenomenon can be explained by Canadian travellers known as 'Snowbirds', who seek holidays in milder climates during the harsh winter months as well as by Canadian's love of winter sports.

Travel agencies are working in a highly competitive environment. On average, a travel agency represents four tour operators (Statistics Canada, 1999). In addition to acting on behalf of tour operators, the travel agency's services often include selling various transportation fares (e.g. air tickets), booking accommodation and transportation for clients, providing travel information, helping clients plan their trips and handling their problems and complaints. The recent commission cuts from suppliers and tour operators, and widespread sales over the Internet, have, however, forced travel agencies to diversify their companies or specialize their services. It has been suggested that with the restructuring in the industry, agents need to explore other avenues and offer more than just booking tickets. For example, some agencies are becoming specialized in niche markets such as eco-tours, adventure tours, senior holidays and rural tours. Some of the larger and many of the independent travel agencies provide a range of services such as 24-hour call centres, wiring money to stranded travellers or booking rooms late at night in foreign cities (CTC, 1998a). In addition, with this reduction in revenue, a trend is developing where agents are charging fees to customers for their services rather than charging the airlines. In terms of distribution, travel agents will be searching out the lowest price ticket or package (CTC, 1998a).

PROFILE OF TOUR OPERATORS IN CANADA

Tour operators and wholesalers buy a range of tourist products in bulk and package them for sale to travel agents or to individual customers. There were 957 establishments in 1997, 96 per cent of which are incorporated, and 79 per cent are affiliated with transportation companies. Some of the larger tour operators include Conquest Tours, Signature Vacations, Sunquest/Alba and their parent company Airtours, Air Transat Holidays, Canada 3000 Holidays and World of Vacations. There were 83 Canadian tour operators commissionable to travel agents in 1998 (CTC, 1998c) including a number of smaller speciality operators in the areas of eco/adventure travel. Similar to the travel agency industry, the tour operators/wholesalers are concentrated in Ontario, Quebec and British Columbia. In terms of employment, Ontario (44.9 per cent), Quebec (22.9 per cent) and British

Columbia (19.4 per cent) account for 87.7 per cent of the full- and part-time employment in the tour operator/wholesaler industry in Canada. Within these three provinces, part-time employment rates in the tour operator/wholesaler industry are 19 per cent for Ontario, 20 per cent for Quebec and 15 per cent for British Columbia.

The revenue distributions are highest in Ontario (49.1 per cent), followed by Quebec (22.9 per cent) and British Columbia (21.7 per cent). Tour operators/ wholesalers receive a large proportion of revenue from household clients (69.3 per cent), followed by foreign visitors (22.4 per cent) and corporate tour purchase account for 8.1 per cent. Their percentage distribution of revenue shows that travel to foreign destinations (excluding the USA) brings 57.2 per cent of the total revenue, and approximately the same proportions of the revenue from Canadian destinations (21.8 per cent) and the US destinations (21.0 per cent) (Statistics Canada, 1997). The role of tour operators and tour wholesalers have also been deeply affected by industry consolidation, airline deregulation and the growth in the number of packaged holidays to international destinations. These changes are forcing these organizations to develop differentiated products which are competitive in terms of pricing, margins or are branded (CTC, 1998a). Non-traditional sources of holiday packages are developing such as theme parks, cruise lines, resort and unique destinations, which are putting increased competitive pressures on wholesalers and operators. With airline deregulation there has been an increase in cross-ownership and marketing alliances between airline, wholesalers and tour operators. In turn, non-airline-owned operators have been seeking preferred supplier status with specific airlines as well as developing relationships with foreign travel suppliers to create additional inbound and outbound business (CTC, 1998a).

TOURISM INTERMEDIARIES AND THE INTERNET CHALLENGE

In charting a national research agenda for Canada, Smith (2000) highlighted that the number of new tourism products in Canada continues to grow and along with that, Smith suggested distribution strategies and channels might be growing even faster. In addition, other companies offering intermediary services allow users to have access to search multiple suppliers and they have direct access to reservation systems including WorldRes, Preview Travel or American On Line (AOL) (Smith, 2000). Among the many travel technology suppliers with offices in Canada are Amadeus Canada, Sabre, Softvoyage and Galileo Canada. Ticketless booking is another newly emerging distribution channel, and while it did not develop as rapidly in Canada as abroad, it is now becoming more common in the Canadian airline industry (Smith, 2000).

The facilitation of booking tourism products through electronic technology is leading many suppliers to increase direct sales, thereby bypassing the travel agent or other intermediaries. A quote by Mowat (2000, p. 11) illustrates the changing nature of the tourism product distribution system: 'Let's be perfectly clear: it will soon be commonplace for consumers to buy their travel products from a variety of sources.' He goes on to state that the bottom line is that the travel agent community will no longer have exclusive jurisdiction over the distribution of a supplier's products. As the shift continues on to the Internet, some travel agencies are keeping pace by opening virtual travel agencies. Vacation.com combines traditional brick-and-mortar agencies along with a virtual agency and it sees the Internet as a growing part of their business (Mowat, 2000). The traditional distribution roles of operator and agent are becoming blurred and some suppliers are now complaining that agents are stepping around traditional suppliers and acquiring wholesale airfares which are sold directly to their customers (Mowat, 2000). In 1999, Canada's Internet usage accounted for only 6 per cent of the world Internet usage compared to 50 per cent in the USA (Marcussen, 1999). While Internet use is growing, conventional distribution channels are still very important in Canada. As shown in Figure 16.4, the structure and interaction of tourism players in Canada has been changing. The tourism product distribution channel can no longer be discussed in a simple diagram of two or three levels of distribution channels (suppliers → tour operators → travel agents → customers). The major change is the placement of the Internet and Partnership Organizations in the distribution channel. The details of ideas and functions of partnership organizations will be discussed in the following section.

STRATEGIC ALLIANCES, PARTNERSHIPS AND THE CANADIAN TOURISM COMMISSION

High-profile strategic alliances outlined above with the airline industry, travel agents, accommodation and information technology highlight the growing trend of collaboration (Go and Williams, 1993). Within the tourism sector, Tribe (1997) suggests that alliances can help to market a product on a much wider scale while reducing competitive pressures as old rivals work together. Defined as 'voluntary arrangements between firms involving exchange, sharing, or co-development of products, technologies or services' (Gulati, 1998, p. 293), strategic alliances can occur as a result of a wide range of motives and goals and take on a variety of forms, while occurring across vertical and horizontal boundaries. Referred to as co-operative strategies, strategic networking, joint venturing and strategic partnering, strategic alliances all have some form of collaborative arrangement and the enterprises involved agree to share managerial control to some degree (Starke and Sexty, 1998). The alliances are strategically designed to build on core competencies, strengthen research and technology capabilities, address asymmetries in skill endowment of firms, reduce cost of entry into new markets, accelerate new product development and lead to higher capacity utilization and economies of scale (Rao

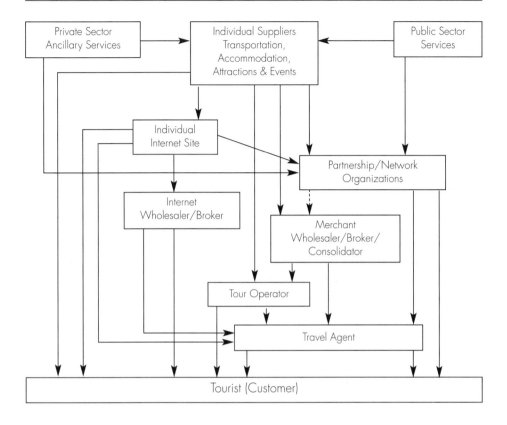

Figure 16.4 Structure of Canadian tourism

and Reddy, 1995). Vertical alliances between producers and their suppliers or distributors is focused more on maintaining flexibility and adding value while horizontal alliances are focused on protecting core competencies (Magun, 1996). As seen in the example of Transat A.T., tourism product distribution channels are becoming increasingly integrated as the main operators continue to integrate both vertically and horizontally. The benefits of joining a tourism strategic alliance have been explored within the Niagara Region (Telfer, 2000, 2001) in the context of Tastes of Niagara (alliance of producers, processors, distributors, restaurants, chefs and wineries) and the Niagara Wine Route, which now has over 50 wineries. Both organizations link partners to promote regional food and wine in the tourism industry.

The partnership organizations are closely linked with Public Sector Services such as the CTC and the Provincial Ministries of Tourism. Various suppliers and the private sector services are creating travel products, co-operating with selected travel agencies and directly selling to the potential consumers. The CTC is a working partnership between tourism industry businesses and associations, the provincial and territorial governments and the federal government of Canada (Goeldner *et al.*,

2000). The CTC has undergone a tremendous amount of change over the last twenty years and it recently has become a Crown Corporation, allowing it to respond more quickly to changes in the marketplace. The mandate of the CTC clearly indicates its role in the inbound tourism distribution process. The CTC has the authority to plan, manage, direct and implement programmes that promote tourism in Canada. The Commission Board is made up of industry representatives and as well as promoting Canada, the CTC provides information on the tourism industry and assistance in decision-making. The CTC co-ordinates the activities of key players in the industry, including hoteliers, attractions, tour operators, airlines, local and provincial associations and government agencies.

The CTC develops partnership programmes in marketing, research and industry and product development. There is co-operation between the CTC and each of the provincial tourism organizations. The focus of product and industry development programmes is to ensure that there is a match between customer requirements and Canada's tourism products. In addition the CTC provides support services in the partnership process as well as representing the interests of the Canadian tourism industry to the government and the private sector so that tourism will be included in development programmes (Goeldner et al., 2000). The CTC, for example, launched the Product Clubs as a way for helping small and medium-sized businesses across the country get connected with the CTC and developing new product initiatives. The concept behind the Product Clubs is to link small and medium-sized businesses with similar products together under joint marketing campaigns and promote product development. These alliances create greater integration between the components in the inbound distribution process. In the development of the programme, the CTC looked abroad and while some countries carry out marketing based on individual regions, and others build marketing around a specific product, the Product Clubs in Canada incorporate both a regional and a product focus (CTC, 1999). Total CTC partner funds for Product Clubs in the round of applications for 1999/2000 is CDN$1 million which is to be used in the formation of regional product groupings. In approving funds, the CTC looks for unique projects where the Product Club will contribute partner funding over the life of the agreement and will become self-sustaining by the end of the third year. The CTC has helped small and medium-sized businesses develop a variety of initiatives such as the Canadian Golf Tourism Alliance in British Columbia and the Bay of Fundy Product Club in Nova Scotia. Table 16.2 illustrates a partial list of the Product Clubs. Some of the Clubs listed demonstrate horizontal linkages while others involve suppliers and intermediaries creating vertical linkages. The Product Clubs generate new direct sell methods that are effecting conventional distribution channels providing more choice to consumers. The creation of the Product Clubs allows small firms to band together to sell their products in new ways with the power of increased market share.

Table 16.2 Canadian Tourism Commission Product Clubs. *Source*: CTC, 1999

Product Club	Province
Aboriginal Waterways Product Club	Saskatchewan
Adventure Product Club	Québec
Atlantic Economuseum Network Product Club	New Brunswick
Bay of Fundy Product Club	Nova Scotia
Canadian Golf Tourism Alliance	British Columbia
Conservation Lands Product Club	Ontario
Cross-Country Ski Product Club	Québec
Festival Network Product Club	Ontario
Greektown	Ontario
Heritage Product Club	Alberta
Independent Innkeepers Cultural Ecotourism	Ontario
Northern Wilderness Product Club	Yukon
Ontario East-Adventure	Ontario
Product Club for Tourists with Special Needs	Québec
Le Québec Maritime	Québec
Saskatchewan River Basin Product Club	Saskatchewan
Ski and Snowboard Industry Product Club	Ontario
Urban Cultural Tourism Product Club	British Columbia

CONCLUSION

Global trends are having major impacts on the tourism industry in Canada. Recent news in the travel industry is filled with mergers, acquisitions, airline deregulation, commission caps, strategic alliances, blurring of traditional distribution roles, far-reaching implications of new technology, branding, consumers becoming more demanding and having access to computers, and the consolidation of power. With these global trends, the various sub-sectors in the Canadian tourism industry face more intense competition, more demanding inquiries from more experienced customers and ever-changing information technology. Many suppliers and companies are implementing protective measures for conventional intermediaries such as travel-agent-only webpages. As an extreme example, WestJet does not list its products on a GDS, but prefers to use the Internet with preferential commissions for travel agents.

Another way to deal with the global trend of information technology and consequent intense competition is through mergers and takeovers, promoting vertical integration and consolidation. While the trends of horizontal and vertical integration continue, many tourism companies have also begun utilizing diagonal integration where they are establishing products/services in areas of private ancillary services to the tourism product such as in insurance or currency services (World Tourism Organization, 1998). As major tourism companies expand in terms of product base and geographic coverage, they have the ability to dictate market trends in terms of economies of scope and scale.

One unique feature of the Canadian tourism industry used to combat global competition is the forming of partnerships or alliances. Under the lead of the CTC at the federal level, provincial-level governments and quasi-government organizations are forming close links with suppliers and intermediaries. Product Clubs or partnership networks have been formed, promoting vertical and horizontal integration of the various components of the distribution channel. As this alliance is formed by Destination Management Organizations at various levels, suppliers and intermediaries within the alliance can offer the product directly to the customers while maintaining control of the distribution process. The main difference between corporate vertical integration and the Product Clubs is the ownership of the product and the distribution channel. There is no single dominant ownership of the products and process in the Product Club. This type of alliance and partnership is particularly beneficial to small and medium-scale businesses in terms of joint marketing and promotion.

Although the fundamental structure of the tourism product distribution channels in Canada is still intact, and perhaps will remain so for the foreseeable future, there are obvious changes in the levels of distribution channel. Direct distribution is gaining more and more popularity not only because of the emergence of the Internet, but also because of consolidation, alliance and partnerships. Conventional intermediaries are an integrated part of the vertical or diagonal system in the channel but the distinction between tour operators and travel agencies is gradually blurring. In this era of globalization, additional research is needed as traditional roles in the distribution system continue to change. In developing a national research agenda for Canada with respect to product and information distribution, Smith (2000, p. 304) suggested that the evolution of various forms of tourism product development, strategic partnerships and packaging need to be evaluated so that both 'best practices' and 'problem cases' could be identified. Investigations into strategic partnerships such as the Product Clubs in Canada need to be examined as they may serve as a model for other countries to follow.

REFERENCES

Brock University Map Library. Canada [JPG]. Software Edition. St Catharine, ON: Brock University Map Library, 1999.

Canadian Tourism Commission (CTC) (1998a) 'Landscape of the tourism industry'. Communiqué December 1998, **2**(12), 6–20.

Canadian Tourism Commission (CTC) (1998b) 'Tourism vision– special report'. Communiqué November 1998, **2**(11), 3.

Canadian Tourism Commission (CTC) (1998c) 'Canadian tour operators commissionable to travel agents 1998'. Communiqué June 1998, **2**(6), 10.

Canadian Tourism Commission (CTC) (1999) 'Small business boosted through product club program'. Communiqué January/February 1999, **3**(1), 5.

Canadian Tourism Commission (CTC) (2000a) 'Research section'. Communiqué March 2000, **4**(2), 18–19.

Canadian Tourism Commission (CTC) (2000b) 'ACTA to promote value of travel agencies'. Communiqué May 2000, **4**(4), 12.

Canadian Travel Press (2000a) 'Tourism spending on the rise in Canada' (ctp@baxter.net). posted on Canadian Tourism Exchange (CTX) [http://www.canadatourism.com/en/ctc/ctx]. (Site posted on 3 April 2000.)

Canadian Travel Press (2000b) 'Transat A.T. to buy 100 per cent share of Consultour/Club Voyages'. (ctp@baxter.net) posted on Canadian Tourism Exchange (CTX) [http://www.canadatourism.com/en/ctc/ctx]. (Site posted on 23 March 2000.)

Canadian Travel Press (2000c) 'CTC will soon be operating at the speed of business'. (ctp@baxter.net) posted on Canadian Tourism Exchange (CTX) [http:// www. canadatourism.com/en/ctc/ctx]. (Site posted on 12 April 2000.)

Go, F. M. and Williams, A. P. (1993) 'Competing and cooperating in the changing tourism channel system'. *Journal of Travel & Tourism Marketing*, **2**(2/3), 229–48.

Goeldner, C. R, Ritchie, J. R. and McIntosh, R. W. (2000) *Tourism Principles, Practices, Philosophies* (8th edn). John Wiley & Sons, New York.

Gulati, R. (1998) 'Alliances and networks'. *Strategic Management Journal*, **19**, 293–317.

Lupton, A (2000) 'More and more web sites are including travel agents'. Posted on Canadian Tourism Exchange (CTX) [http:// www.canadatourism.com/en/ctc/ctx]. (Site posted on 26 April 2000.)

Magun, S. (1996) 'The development of strategic alliances in Canadian industries: a micro analysis'. Working Paper No. 13, Industry Canada, Ottawa.

Marcussen, C. H. (1999) *Internet Distribution of European Travel and Tourism Services: the market, transportation, accommodation and package tours*. Research Centre of Bornholm, Nexø, Denmark.

Mowat, B. (2000) 'The gloves are off as industry becomes multi-channel'. *Communiqué*, March 2000, **4**(3), 11.

Rao, B. P. and Reddy, S. K. (1995) 'A dynamic approach to the analysis of strategic alliances'. *International Business Review*, **4**(4), 499–518.

Smith, S. L. J. (2000) 'Measurement of tourism's economic impacts'. *Annals of Tourism Research*, **27**(2), 530–1.

Starke, F. A. and Sexty. R. W. (1998) *Contemporary Management in Canada* (3rd edn). Prentice Hall, Scarborough, Canada.

Statistics Canada (1997) *Annual Survey of Travel Agencies and Tour Operators 1997*. Statistics Canada, Ottawa.

Statistics Canada (1999) *Tourism Statistical Digest 1999*. Statistics Canada, Ottawa.

Telfer, D. J. (2000) 'Tastes of Niagara: building strategic alliances between tourism and agriculture'. In J. Crotts, D. Buhalis and R. March (eds) *Global Alliances in Tourism and Hospitality Management*. The Haworth Hospitality Press, London, pp. 71–88.

Telfer, D. J. (2001) 'Strategic alliances along the Niagara wine route'. *Tourism Management*, **22**(1), 21–30.

Tourism Canada (1994) *Product Distribution in the Tourism Industry: a profile of tour operators and travel agencies in Canada*. Industry Canada, Ottawa.

TRDC (2000) 'Tourism Highlights 21–28 April 2000', posted on Canadian Tourism Exchange (CTX) [http://www.canadatourism.com/en/ctc/ctx]. (Site posted on 01 May 2000.)

Tribe, J. (1997) *Corporate Strategy for Tourism*. International Thompson Press, London.

World Tourism Organization (1998) *Tourism 2020 Vision Executive Summary Updated*. WTO, Madrid.

CHAPTER 17

Distribution strategies for regional and national tourism organizations: an Australian case study

John Jenkins

INTRODUCTION

Australian tourism organizations involved in channels of tourism distribution are great in number and varied in their structures, functions, operations and networks. This chapter provides insights into the structures, functions, operations and networks of a selection of tourism organizations operating at national, state and regional levels. The chapter is divided into four main parts. The first part briefly describes both the economic significance of tourism in Australia and the complexity of Australia's system of government with specific reference to tourism. This part serves to highlight the implications for tourism distribution channels of the constitutional, legislative and structural legacies embedded in Australia's system of government. The second part explains the structures, roles and functions of Australia's national tourism organizations (NTOs), particularly the Australian Tourist Commission (ATC). The third part presents an overview of Tourism New South Wales, an NSW (state) government statutory authority. The fourth and final part examines regional tourism organizations (RTOs) in New South Wales (NSW), identifying important issues in their operations and barriers to their survival. This latter part also demonstrates the vexed position of RTOs in Australia's channels of tourism distribution, wedged, as they are, between diverse state and local interests and aims.

THE SIGNIFICANCE OF TOURISM IN AUSTRALIA

In Australia, tourism organizations at every level of government (federal, state/territory and local) have embraced tourism as a means of expanding economic activity and employment opportunities in their jurisdictions. This was particularly the case amid the extensive and well-documented restructuring of the Australian economy in the 1990s. At the federal level, three key agencies are charged with well-defined roles. At the state and territory level, tourism statutory authorities/corporations have been established, with their primary aims geared to tourism marketing and promotion on behalf of their respective jurisdictions. In order to enhance the marketing and promotion power of local and regional areas, state governments have established and substantially supported RTOs, enveloping a collection of local government areas (LGAs) (see Figure 17.1).

Government interest in tourism in Australia is not unexpected. Tourism is one of Australia's fastest growing industries (see Tables 17.1 and 17.2 for international visitor arrivals, and current major markets respectively), is a major source of foreign exchange, offers substantial employment opportunities, and is a widely utilized mechanism for regional economic development and promotion. In 1988–9, Australia received 2.2 million international visitors, who generated $5.9 billion in expenditure. In that same period, tourism generated employment of about 448,000 people and contributed an estimated 1.5 per cent to Australia's Gross Domestic Product (GDP). At the present time, international visitor numbers are expected to increase from an estimated 4.2 million in 1998 to about 8.4 million in 2008, with 7.3 per cent average annual growth for this period. In 1996–7, tourism contributed about 5.8 per cent to Australia's GDP and was directly responsible for employment of more than 670,000 persons or about 8 per cent of the Australian workforce. In 1998–9, total domestic tourism expenditure was approximately $44.8 billion, accounting for just over 75 per cent of total tourism expenditures. Tourism is one of Australia's biggest foreign exchange earners, generating approximately $17.8 billion, or 14.9 per cent of total export earnings, in 1999 (Department of Industry, Science and Resources, 2000).

Table 17.1 International tourism arrivals in Australia. *Source*: Australian Bureau of Statistics (ABS), Catalogue 3401.0

Year	Visitor arrivals (millions)
1988	2.20
1993	3.00
1994	3.36
1995	3.73
1996	4.16
1997	4.32
1998	4.17
1999	4.46

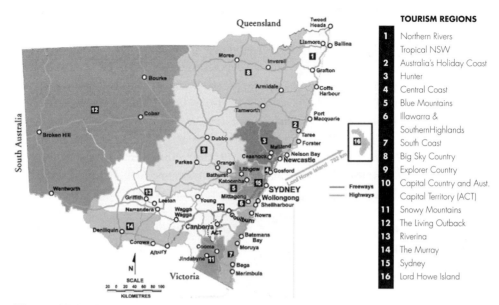

Figure 17.1 The tourism regions of New South Wales, Australia. *Source*: Tourism New South Wales (http://www.tourism.NewSouthWales.gov.au/tNewSouthWales/regions/index_regions.html)

Table 17.2 Overseas visitor arrivals by country/region, 1999. *Source*: Australian Bureau of Statistics (ABS), Catalogue 3401.0

Country	Year
Japan	707,500
China	92,600
Hong Kong	139,600
Korea	108,600
Taiwan	147,500
Indonesia	91,000
Malaysia	139,800
Singapore	267,000
Thailand	61,900
Other Asia	110,200
New Zealand	728,800
United Kingdom	528,400
Germany	144,500
Other Europe	399,400
USA	417,100
Rest of World	375,600
Total	4,459,500

Exceptional growth in some traditional international tourist markets (especially the USA and Europe) in 1998 and 1999, was generated, in part, by promotional campaigns by the ATC during the Asian economic crisis. However, the Asian markets and indeed Asian travel to Australia are recovering. Particularly strong growth is occurring in the Korean, Chinese, Malaysian and Thailand markets. The exceptions are Japan and Taiwan, where small reductions in visitor numbers have been experienced in the last year (Department of Industry, Science and Resources, 2000).

Tourism in Australia is very business-oriented with international visitor forecasts showing no signs of abating. But, the willingness of governments to intervene in tourism matters raises many problems, which have yet to be satisfactorily resolved and, in many respects, remain to be critically analysed. The following section presents an overview of Australia's government structures and reflects on broader economic and socio-political developments influencing government's means of intervention and channels of tourism distribution.

Australian Government structures and influences

Australia is a Commonwealth (Federation) comprising six States and two Territories. The basic legal document of Federation is the Australian Constitution, which was a British Act of Parliament passed in 1900. The Commonwealth of Australia has a hybrid form of government, combining parliamentary government, derived from British political institutions, with a federal system, derived from the USA (Summers, 1985). The establishment of the federal system of government in Australia in 1901 divided political powers and functions between the six States and the Commonwealth (Lansbury and Gilmour, 1977). Since federation, a three-tier system of government has also evolved (Commonwealth, state and local). The federal division of responsibilities has led to problems of policy co-ordination in such areas as transport, communications, resources development, resources marketing, energy policy, urban affairs, Aboriginal affairs and taxation.

Tourism has been no exception. Tourism is not explicitly mentioned in the Australian Constitution. As a result, the responsibilities of various levels of government for tourism have developed disjointedly under the divisions of powers that directly and indirectly affect tourism. The lack of specific powers to deal with tourism under the Constitution has resulted in the duplication of government responsibilities and, therefore, disagreement between the States and the States and the Commonwealth (Hall, 1991). For instance, the Northern Territory Government argued in a submission to the Senate Standing Committee on Environment, Recreation and the Arts (1992, p. 248), that it 'does not see a significant role or need for the co-ordination of foreign tourist development between the States, including the Northern Territory, by the Commonwealth Government'. Local government is not recognized in the Australian Constitution. Each Australian State has its own system of local government. Local governments derive their functions from Local Government Acts operating in each State. Those Acts give local governments many legal powers, including the power to deal with development generally and tourism development in particular, and to control health standards and rating structures according to State government frameworks (Jenkins and Hall, 1997). The roles and responsibilities of local government in tourism are not clear or well co-ordinated, with friction between the States and local authorities often arising with respect to the extent and nature of tourism development and marketing (e.g. see Craik, 1991a).

The role of local government in tourism is poorly defined and misunderstood despite the fact that the formal division of responsibilities for tourism between the Commonwealth and State Governments was established in the Statement of Government Objectives and Responsibilities in Tourism set out in the Tourism Minister's Council Agreement of 1976. Under the Agreement, the Commonwealth has primary responsibility for international tourism and in the formulation and implementation of policies which operate at a national level. The States and Territories have the responsibility for promoting and marketing state attractions and for the regulation of tourist development. In practice, there is no clear divide between the roles and responsibilities of the Commonwealth and State Governments. State, as well as regional and local, tourism organizations undertake overseas marketing and promotion, and do not always agree or comply with Commonwealth decisions and actions. Further, the Tourism Minister's Council Agreement (as with the Australian Constitution) does not detail the substantial responsibilities of local government in tourism development (Hall, 1991).

The search for comprehensive tourism policy integration (e.g. in marketing and promotion) in Australia has met with little success despite the release of the National Tourism Strategy by the federal Labor Government in July 1992, and its 'successor' (a markedly different document), under a new Coalition government, in 1996. The continuing fragmentation of responsibility for industry planning, development, marketing and promotion, for instance, ensures the status quo of overlapping policy goals and instruments. But, an initiative that has gone some way to alleviating the problems of overlap in state and Commonwealth marketing and promotion is the Partnership Australia programme, launched by the federal government in 1994. Partners include the ATC, state and territory marketing organizations/authorities, and private industry. Partnership Australia was devised to overcome co-ordination problems with the way the Australian tourism product is developed and marketed overseas. The principal objectives of Partnership Australia have been to:

- co-ordinate Australia's international tourism marketing and promotional efforts to improve efficiency and effectiveness (thereby eliminating costly duplication and fragmentation in marketing);
- develop a wider range of tourism product for international markets;
- provide information to overseas consumers and industry to generate more sales and extend product distribution; and

- motivate and train the overseas trade to sell Australia better (ATC, 1993, p. 1; also see ATC, 1995; Pearce *et al.*, 1998, p. 230).

The Partnership Australia programme had some initial problems, with members disagreeing about the constitution of the ATC board and the direction of marketing activities and proportional representation of States in such programmes. However, the programme has met with some success and much recognition, leading to the establishment of Aussie Helplines in Europe, North America, Asia, Japan and New Zealand. Travel counsellors, who staffed the phone lines in 1994/5, answered some 398,000 trade and consumer inquiries about Australian tourism, while partners spent approximately $26.7 million on short-term advertising campaigns overseas.

Effective co-ordination of tourism policies and programmes at the national, state and regional levels is moving forward steadily in the areas of marketing and promotion, but agreement and compliance will never be universal in a highly competitive market, where government intervention spans three levels of government in the way it does in Australia. Co-ordination is a very difficult task, in part because issues concerning tourism (including the structures, roles and functions of agencies centrally involved in tourism distribution channels) are often highly political and laced with administrative and historical legacies. The above discussion has briefly described some important issues in Australia's federal system of government and has highlighted the lack of clarity and co-ordination as well as the extensive problems of overlap in government roles and responsibilities with respect to tourism. These matters aside, recent rethinking on the role of the state in modern capitalist society has led to interesting developments in the ways in which governments set up tourism administrations to, among other things, market and promote destinations. The influences on channels of tourism distribution in Australia have been quite striking.

The role of the Australian state and tourism administration

In Australia, policies of deregulation, privatization, the elimination of tax incentives, and a move away from discretionary forms of macro-economic intervention, have been the hallmarks of a push towards 'smaller' government at state and federal levels. Such changes in political philosophy have significant implications for tourism policy-making, planning and development. Calls for smaller government in Western society have increased the demands from conservative national governments and economic rationalists for greater self-sufficiency in many industries, including tourism. Public sector involvement in tourism marketing and promotion has been characterized by the privatization or corporatization of tourism agencies or boards (Jeffries, 1988, in Jenkins and Hall, 1997). On occasions, governments have decided to withdraw industry support by abolishing entire tourism departments and corporations (e.g. the Swedish Tourist Board in 1992) or by reducing or terminating their funds (e.g. the United States Travel and Tourism Administration in 1995). In Australia, whereas we have witnessed the corporatization of state and Territory public sector tourism departments writ large, the resources provided by government for marketing and promoting tourism through these organizations have been remarkably resistant to cutbacks.

Despite the dramatic macro- and micro-economic restructuring of the Australian economy, federal, state and RTOs (see below) at present command significant resources as governments seek ostensibly to market and promote their respective tourism industries, domestically and internationally. As Pearce (1992, p. 187) pointed out, more widely increased expenditure on marketing and promotion is seen as the way to achieve or maintain growth, particularly in the face of increasing competition or depressed market conditions. Spending on an activity which is seen to contribute directly to growth thus has more appeal to politicians controlling the public purse strings and to private sector members than other related functions such as planning and research whose role in increasing arrivals is often perceived to be less direct and essential.

AUSTRALIA'S NTOs

The Commonwealth, through the responsible Minister, discharges its direct responsibilities for tourism through three main areas of government: the Sport and Tourism portfolio within the Department of Industry, Science and Resources; the ATC; and the Bureau of Tourism Research (BTR). Each of these bodies has a clearly defined role. The Sport and Tourism portfolio is responsible for co-ordination, regulation and planning. The BTR undertakes research on matters concerning tourism. The ATC markets and promotes tourism (Jenkins, 1995; Hall, 1998; Pearce *et al.*, 1998, Weaver and Oppermann, 2000). The ATC was established as a department by the Commonwealth government in 1967. It is now a statutory authority, established under the Australian Tourist Commission Act, 1987. Its prime task is to market Australia overseas as a tourist destination. The ATC is governed by a Board of Directors from private industry and is directly responsible to the Minister for Tourism. The Board comprises ten members appointed by the Minister. After the Australian Government Inquiry into Tourism (widely referred to as the Kennedy Inquiry) in 1986, the ATC's charter was revised to specify the following mission: 'to market Australia overseas for the economic benefit of all Australians in a way that enhances the quality of the visitor experience and preserves Australia's natural and social environment' (ATC, 1992). That mission was recently revised to: 'We promote Australia internationally to become the chosen destination for overseas visitors for the economic and social benefit of all Australians' (ATC, 1999). The ATC's principal objectives are:

- to increase the number of visitors to Australia;
- to maximize the benefits to Australia from overseas visitors; and

- to ensure Australia is protected from adverse environmental and social impacts.

The ATC promotes Australia in more than 40 countries from its Sydney Head Office and offices in Los Angeles, Hong Kong, Singapore, Taipei, Shanghai, Seoul, Tokyo, London, Frankfurt and Auckland. The ATC's marketing activities focus on consumer advertising on television and in print, the Internet, consumer promotions, public relations (e.g. a visiting journalists' scheme), information programmes and customer servicing, and the co-ordination of Australian industry participation in international trade events. It plays a role in trade marketing development and retail travel agent education programmes, and provides input into government and industry policies that affect tourism. Most recently, the organization has focused much on maximizing tourism opportunities related to the Sydney 2000 Olympic Games, by way of media programmes and alliances with global marketing partners (ATC, 1999). Table 17.3 highlights the objectives, strategies and outcomes concerning ATC activities for 1998/9. For many years, concerns have been raised about the ATC's activities and outcomes. Indeed, government support for the ATC was challenged during the 1989 Industries Assistance Commission (IAC) Inquiry.

In its draft report, the IAC suggested that government funding be withdrawn and that the tourist industry assume responsibility for promoting Australia internationally. The former Australian Tourist Industry Association responded with the claims that should government funding be withdrawn from the ATC, there would be substantial under-promotion of Australia as a tourist destination. Moreover, the problem of lack of contributions from industry cannot be overcome by imposing levies as in the case of wool, coal and other products. In addition to the practical difficulty of identifying 'tourism producers', industry levies are only feasible where the products are single, identifiable products. In contrast, the tourist industry provides thousands of different services for purchase by tourists (Grey *et al*, 1991, p. 62). Dwyer and Forsyth (1992) supported such claims. They declared that their analysis of the ATC: although highly tentative given uncertainty regarding impacts of promotion expenditure on tourism flows and tourism expenditure, suggests that additional promotion expenditure by the Australian Government would produce net benefits to the economy. Further research is appropriate both to develop theoretical analysis and to determine specific costs and benefits of inbound tourism promotion by Australia (pp. 24–5).

These earlier reports, coupled with the ATC's more rigorous accounting procedures and reporting of its objectives, strategies and outcomes, lend considerable justification to government funding of the ATC. In 1998, the federal government announced an increase of $50 million in additional funding to the ATC for the period 1998/9–2001/2, taking the total investment in that period to $359 million. This funding allowed the ATC to explore and forge its way into new markets, to undertake additional activities in existing markets and to increase its

Table 17.3 The ATC's objectives, strategies and outcomes, 1998/9. *Source*: ATC, 1999, pp. 5–6

Statutory objectives	Outcome indicators	Strategies	Outcomes
To increase the number of visitors to Australia from overseas	Change in number of visitor arrivals Change in Australia's market share in all countries where the ATC is actively marketing	Reinforce and expand the positioning of Australia through the development of Brand Australia, integrated public relations, promotional activities and tactical campaigns Convert interest in Australia into actual travel through a range of conversion programmes including referrals, tactical programmes and publications	Visitor arrivals increased by 1.6 per cent to 4.3 million in 1998/9 Australia gained market share in 17 of 25 countries/regions where the ATC is actively marketing
To maximize the benefits to Australia from overseas visitors	Change in total visitor expenditure in Australia by overseas visitors Change in average visitor expenditure in Australia by overseas visitors Change in total visitor nights in Australia by overseas visitors Change in geographic dispersal of overseas visitors	Utilize Partnership Australia as a vehicle for segment and market development and a mechanism for achieving dispersal and yield objectives Incorporate new destinations and new products that match market needs into tactical and other activities Access and target new or changing market segments which produce greater yield and/or dispersal of tourists throughout Australia Inform, encourage and assist identified decision-makers in the Meetings, Incentives, Conventions and Exhibitions (MICE) segment to promote Australia as a desired MICE destination	Total visitor expenditure by overseas visitors rose by 7.3 per cent since 1997 to more than $16 billion An increase of 10.5 per cent in average visitor expenditure by overseas visitors over 1997 Over 100 million visitor nights in Australia by overseas visitors, representing an annual increase of 9.3 per cent Decrease in geographic dispersal (travel beyond the top eight tourist regions) of overseas visitors by 0.4 per cent between 1997 and 1998
To ensure that Australia is protected from adverse environmental and social impacts of international tourism	Level of awareness by overseas visitors of the need to care for Australia's natural environment Level of acceptance by the Australian community of international tourist arrivals Change in Australians' attitudes to tourism as measured by ongoing quantitative research	Responsible strategic marketing that gives consideration to the impact of the tourism marketing strategy on the natural and social environment Contribution, in partnership with industry and government, to the development of a national approach to the management of the relationship between tourism and the environment in Australia Education and raising awareness on tourism and the environment Worked with a range of government agencies and industry partners to raise the level of awareness by overseas visitors of the need to care for Australia's natural environment	The number of environment-related pages accessed on the ATC's Internet site (australia.com) increased by 521 per cent between 1997/8 and 1998/9 A 93 per cent level of acceptance by the Australian community of the desirability of international tourists visiting Australia A 94 per cent level of recognition of the net benefits of inbound tourism as measured by ongoing quantitative research With industry partners, produced tour operator, travel agency and tour wholesaler environment manuals, *Being Green Keeps you out of the Red* and *Being Green is Your Business*

Table 17.4   New and intensified activities of the ATC, 1998/9. *Source*: Adapted from ATC, 1999, p. 56

- Cemented working relationships to gain benefits from Australia's hosting of the 2000 Olympic Games. Alliances generated additional publicity for Australia, estimated to be worth more than $60 million.

- Launched new $150 million Brand Australia promotional campaign, in order to build depth and dimension in the way the world sees Australia. The television campaign associated with this branding will be seen by an estimated 300 million people in 11 countries over 3 years. Qantas Airlines, Ansett Airlines, Singapore Airlines, various sectors of the tourism industry and state tourism authorities have joined with the ATC as partners in the campaign. In addition, the ATC and state partners are working together towards cohesive co-branding strategies to ensure that all global communications reflect the shared vision.

- Australia became the first Western nation to be granted Approved Destination Status by China. An ATC office was opened in Shanghai.

- Further development of marketing activities in India and Latin America.

- Identified IT (information technology) as central to the future of tourism promotion. After extensive research and planning, the ATC developed a significant and technologically advanced presence on the Internet and is integrating the online environment with all traditional marketing. The ATC appointed its first Chief Information Officer to help in developing and using innovative technology to promote Australia. In 1999, use of the ATC's consumer Internet site increased by 161 per cent from 1998. Almost 9 million pages of information were delivered to users in 212 countries, up from 144 countries in 1998/9. The ATC site is attracting audiences by integrating the website address (http://www.australia.com) into TV, print and cinema advertising, publications and collateral distributed around the world.

- Appointed a manager to oversee the ATC's worldwide promotion and development of indigenous tourism.

- Established Team Alliance, an alliance between the ATC and 13 of Australia's convention and visitors bureaus to better promote Australia as a destination for meetings, incentives, conferences and exhibitions.

- ATC's visiting journalists programme generated an estimated $1 billion of coverage in leading newspapers, magazines, radio and television programmes. The number of media sponsored under the programme increased by 36 per cent to 1453 in 1998/9.

- The Australian Tourism Exchange (ATE), a specialist travel trade workshop, is at the forefront of Australian marketing activities, both in Australia and in principal markets overseas. The main aim of this marketing forum is to familiarize international buyers with a vast array of Australian inbound tourism products and to provide the opportunities for existing and new products to be included in overseas tour programmes. More than 550 Australian tourism product organizations will be represented at the 2001 ATE. The Australian delegation will be selected to represent a balanced and wide cross-section of organizations with products suitable for the international tourist market. It is expected that approximately 750 international buyers plus overseas representatives of tourism authorities and domestic and international airlines will attend. Fifty leading travel writers representing all market areas will attend ATE and undertake product familiarizations.

- Traveller's Guides are the ATC's primary consumer publication for trade shows and presentations that highlight the diverse range of holiday opportunities throughout Australia. The Guides are used to satisfy responses to the ATC's television, website, radio and press advertising. They are also distributed through travel agents, airline offices, Australian Embassies, High Commissions and Consulates in each market region. More than 1 million copies a year are distributed, in six separate editions, covering 13 languages.

- Trade direct marketing and advertising – the ATC has developed extensive networks of travel agents and wholesalers in all regions with a particular interest in Australia and Australian product. These contacts are available to operators wishing to mail their material directly. Periodic mailings to these lists are also made by the ATC so operators not wanting to do their own mailing have the opportunity to have their brochures included in exclusive ATC brochure collections.

- The 'Tourism Source' is a comprehensive and easy-to-use resource. It is a publication that reaches the key markets of the USA, Europe, the UK, Asia, China, India, South Africa, the South Pacific and the Middle East. It allows Agents to access and provide up-to-date information, and design complete itineraries for clients. It provides a constant, reliable reference for agents, and gives Australian operators ongoing exposure to major industry players around the globe.

alliance with Olympics-related strategies. In 1998/9, the ATC received $89 million, and this was complemented by other sources of funding including $38.3 million in direct investment and $41.2 million from other alliances. Table 17.4 provides a list of some of the new and intensified activities of the ATC in 1998/9.

AUSTRALIAN STATE AND REGIONAL TOURISM ORGANIZATIONS: STRUCTURES, FUNCTIONS AND RELATIONSHIPS

State and regional tourism organizations are key marketing and promotional institutions in the tourism distribution channels of Australia (see Figure 17.2 for an overview of the Tourism New South Wales industry framework). They are agencies utilizing, by and large, familiar marketing tools – IT (e.g. Internet and worldwide web), brochures and other printed materials, advertising, public relations and sales promotion to attract tourists. The histories of state and regional tourism organizations in New South Wales and Queensland have been critically analysed elsewhere (Craik, 1991b; McMillen, 1991; Jenkins, 1995, 2000; Hall, 1998; Richardson, 1999). In NSW, there have been periodic and extensive shifts in the priorities of State Governments with respect to tourism policy, planning and marketing. Some of the most recent and significant shifts occurred in the early and mid-1990s. Tourism New South Wales is a statutory corporation, whose role is to promote and develop NSW as a tourist destination. In 1994, Tourism New South Wales launched both the *New South Wales Tourism Master Plan* and the *Regional Tourism Strategy*, which have served as the basis for subsequent organizational strategies, actions and reviews. Prior to July 1999, Tourism New South Wales' mission was 'To lead, organise and provide strategic direction to increase the efficiency and effectiveness of the tourism industry in New South Wales and market New South Wales as the destination of choice for Australian and international visitors, in order to generate economic, environmental, social and cultural benefits to the State'. That mission was revised and since July 1999, the mission of Tourism New South Wales has been 'To Advance New South Wales as Australia's premier tourist destination' (Tourism New South Wales, 1999a,b).

Under the Strategic Plan for 1999/2002, Tourism New South Wales' objectives are to:

1. Increase awareness, positive perceptions and intention to travel to NSW for a leisure holiday.
2. Convert awareness, positive perceptions and intention to travel to NSW into increased sales of NSW leisure holidays.
3. Grow business-related tourism in NSW.
4. Develop quality products and experiences that best motivate and meet customer demand.

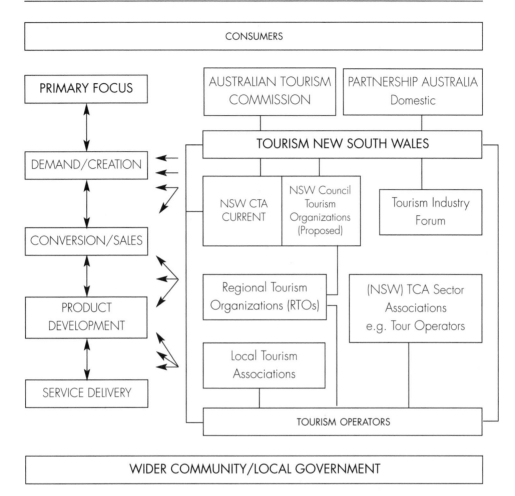

Figure 17.2 The Tourism New South Wales industry framework. *Source*: Tourism New South Wales, 2000a

5. Enhance the long-term sustainability of the NSW tourism industry.
6. Facilitate effective networks that develop the industry.
7. Deliver quality corporate services to key internal and external stakeholders (Tourism New South Wales, 1999b).

Examples of the major distributional activities of Tourism New South Wales are presented in Table 17.5. The aim of the 1994 Regional Tourism Strategy was 'to provide a long term and integrated framework for the development of tourism in New South Wales' (Tourism New South Wales, 1994, A11). A fundamental plank of that strategy was 'to add value to the drive of the private sector by creating a more effective structural base for the marketing and development of tourism and to facilitate initiatives such as product development, promotion and distribution

Table 17.5 Key distribution activities of Tourism New South Wales. *Source*:
Adapted from Tourism New South Wales, 1999a

Australian Cooperative programmes
- 'Experience it' campaigns – $8.1 million advertising campaign designed to reach consumers early in their decision-making process and to set NSW apart from other destinations. Sydney was promoted as the perfect winter destination; the 18–35-year-old market was targeted through radio, cinema and press advertising in Melbourne and Brisbane; several regional campaign partners launched associated print and retail advertising; a SkiNSW campaign was launched in association with Perisher and Thredbo resorts, targeting Brisbane and NSW first-timers, and Sydney and Brisbane more generally, via television, newspapers and radio. Experienced skiers in Victoria were targeted through transit media; ethnic communities (Chinese, Japanese, Spanish, Italian, Greek and Arabic) were targeted in an attempt to encourage them to travel *in* NSW.

Destination promotion
- Generated news leads, distributed news updates and placed editorial
- Hosted media visits of travel writers
- Provided production support for radio and television
- Capitalized on international publicity opportunities via brand and strategic communication agencies in London, Munich, New York, Hong Kong and Singapore.

New South Wales Holidays
- The New South Wales Holidays programme is a land-based wholesale programme, incorporating a print-run of 610,000 brochures, distributed to 4000 travel agents Australia-wide
- Travel agents' support base
- Incorporated into travel.com.au, Australia's largest internet travel agency, which now hosts the New South Wales Holidays database. Weekly e-mails are distributed to over 30,000 potential holiday purchasers, and the product database is also featured on Big Pond, Traveland, Harvey World Travel and 'ninemsn' Internet sites.

Regional marketing
- Invested $1.2 million in 109 regional marketing projects in 1998/9, and more than $4 million in support for co-operative and regional branding marketing
- Established the Pacific Coast Tourism Route, which was packaged in conjunction with international wholesalers, agent familiarization tours. This Route incorporates more than 200 participating properties and several transport operators
- Developed and distributed Bed and Breakfast guide.

Indigenous tourism
- Supported indigenous tourism operators to attend ATE
- Assisted tourism businesses employing indigenous people
- Conducted tourism awareness workshops.

Sydney marketing
- Developed an alliance with the Darling Harbour Authority and Sydney Harbour Foreshore Authority to boost Sydney's promotion as a tourism destination, initially in a way of a joint marketing plan, leading to consumer promotion, tourism trade marketing and provision of effective visitor information in Sydney.

International marketing
- Participates in Partnership Australia (see above)
- Conducted trade programmes such as ATE; hosted international market briefing with operators; attended the Travel Australia Business Show, where more than 700 delegates from Asia attend; undertook sales missions in New Zealand, India, Berlin, Europe, the United States and Japan; circulated international travel planner (10,000 copies) to US, Europe, New Zealand, and North and South-East Asia; published regular newsletters and communication updates in all major markets.

Other activities
- Much attention was given to events marketing and wider general consumer marketing activities domestically and overseas, using television, printed media (e.g. national magazines), the Internet. Some major events were utilized to enhance NSW's profile – golf, rugby union, the Australian Masters Games, and the NFL American Bowl.

opportunities for regional New South Wales' (Tourism New South Wales, 1997: 9). The strategy identified two key goals. First, to 'Foster and develop an integration of the tourism industry within regional New South Wales'. Secondly, to 'Promote an increase in the level of tourism visitation to regional New South Wales' (Tourism New South Wales, 1997: 5).

As part of the *Regional Tourism Strategy*, a network of seventeen regional tourism organizations was created (see Figure 17.1 for the location of RTOs in NSW) to develop regional product and competitive marketing. Tourism New South Wales identified 'a clear need to organize the State's fragmented tourism industry', and the establishment of regional zones was 'a basis upon which to develop strong regional tourism bodies' (Tourism New South Wales, 1994, p. 7). The promises of the State Government, however, would not be easily fulfilled. Indeed, as explained in the next section, developing an integrated tourism industry within regional New South Wales has proved difficult, sparking an extensive review of the 1997 regional tourism strategy from late 1999 to early 2000. After that review, Tourism New South Wales released the *Regional Tourism Action Plan 2000–2003*, the objectives of which are to:

1. Grow regional tourism in NSW.
2. Enhance the long-term sustainability of tourism in NSW.
3. Facilitate effective networks that develop the NSW regional tourism industry (Tourism New South Wales 2000b).

With respect to marketing and promotion, the main strategies of the *Action Plan* are to:

- Create an agreed marketing direction for each region.
- Develop clearer regional/destinational market positions that are integrated with Tourism New South Wales' definition of holiday types.
- Establish co-operative marketing agreements integrated with state-level programmes.
- Undertake co-operative tactical promotional campaigns with NSW regions and major tourism operators, focused on the major holiday types.
- Further develop the 'Visit New South Wales' website, establishing an e-commerce facility to both respond to inquiries and convert them to sales (Tourism New South Wales, 2000b).

According to Tourism New South Wales, the *Regional Tourism Action Plan 2000–2003* will take the relationship between Tourism New South Wales and the regions to another level, by introducing a strong planning focus. 'This planning focus will better enable targeted destination marketing and sustainable development' (Tourism New South Wales, 2000b). Such claims have merit. However, many RTOs have been faced with a host of operational issues, which have a lengthy history of proving difficult to resolve.

AUSTRALIAN RTOs: OPERATIONAL ISSUES

The functions of RTOs were defined by Tourism New South Wales as:

- to focus on *product development* opportunities for the broader region;
- to *develop marketing synergies* within the region to improve its product's exposure to the marketplace;
- to co-ordinate activities among all levels of government and industry within the region to ensure the *efficient, sustainable development and promotion of tourism*;
- to provide a local focus on tourism needs and operations; and
- to *maintain communications* on activities with their local communities and Tourism New South Wales (Tourism New South Wales, 1994).

RTOs undertake a range of distributional activities. Figure 17.3 demonstrates the distributional activities undertaken in 1998–9 by the Hunter Regional Tourism Organization.

All RTOs have been encouraged by Tourism New South Wales to develop a membership base, to become truly representative of their area, and to become financially independent. With all the good intentions of Tourism New South Wales, RTOs have not led easy lives. A number of RTOs are based on explicit geographical features/landforms like the coast (e.g. 'Australia's Holiday Coast') and the mountains ('Blue Mountains'; 'Snowy Mountains'). Other RTOs encompass very varied attractions and local government areas. For example, the Hunter region encompasses coastal areas (Port Stephens), developing wine areas (Cessnock and Singleton), and the nature-based recreation opportunities of the Barrington Tops, across a large geographical area. These regional disparities notwithstanding, RTOs do have some common purposes: building consumer brand awareness of the region to increase demand and visitation; developing co-operative opportunities through regional participation in marketing and promotion; developing and sustaining regional sponsorship; and planning, developing and marketing tourism (see The National Centre for Regional Tourism (NCRT), 1999). RTOs are also well placed to be actively involved in co-ordinating and disseminating tourism research, industry accreditation schemes and education initiatives and developing inventories of regional infrastructure. These latter activities seem to have eluded many RTOs, who focus mainly on the income streams and outcomes that stem from membership, and marketing and promotion respectively. Although RTOs have been around for many years, some are still struggling to attract local support, membership and funding. A recent survey of eleven New South Wales RTOs revealed that:

- only five have full financial support of their local government bodies through membership, with the remaining six regions having partial support for sponsoring some of the activities of RTOs;

- eight out of eleven organizations have in place a communication strategy with tourism operators, mainly in the form of a newsletter;
- four out of eleven organizations have a business improvement programme in place for tourism operators in the form of workshops and seminars;
- only four RTOs survey their membership to gauge their satisfaction with the organization;
- members feel the organization shows a lack of contact and general communication with its members;
- there is lack of knowledge about the benefits of working with the RTO;
- members feel direct relevance and benefits have to be apparent for them to continue membership;
- members want to see tangible evidence through increased business; and
- members feel small operators are not catered for (NCRT, c. 1999, pp. 5–6).

These problems are symptomatic of the narrow focus of many RTOs. Strategic or innovative approaches have been stifled as a result of the ever-present struggle to establish local support and ongoing funding, principally to drive marketing programmes. Moreover, there has been far too little consideration given by Tourism New South Wales, and RTOs themselves, to the internal and external operating environments of RTOs, and in particular the diverse stakeholders and goals which RTOs are expected to represent. RTOs are not private sector, profit-driven organizations; nor are they public sector agencies. The benefits they can afford in co-ordinating industry activity, especially in marketing and industry leadership and vision, are often intangible, and are principally designed to address what governments and Tourism New South Wales see as an important industry limitation – industry co-ordination. So RTOs are somewhat unusual, if not 'mixed' or 'informal', organizations, which, among other things:

- acquire contributions from public and private interests/stakeholders (see Table 17.6);
- are the conduit via which local operators must submit applications to Tourism New South Wales for marketing and special project funds (i.e. local operators must seek endorsement of their application from their RTO before Tourism New South Wales will even look at their application);
- are less sensitive to direct political influence than a public sector department, but are significantly influenced nonetheless by the decisions and actions of State Treasury and Tourism New South Wales, who provide grants and various support funds (indeed, many RTOs could not survive without such funds);
- are placed, for the most part, in the hands of local public and/or private sector officials, from whom they seek financial support;

- are agencies that have to meet public and private concerns simultaneously – working in private enterprise (e.g. marketing the region), constrained somewhat by the bureaucratic and political decisions mentioned above; and
- have developed a public image of being closely associated with Tourism New South Wales, an agency which has been seen in some rural areas to be closely linked with big business, and to be largely Sydney-oriented (Jenkins, 1999).

- advertised in the very widespread publications of motoring associations in NSW, Queensland and Victoria;
- undertook co-operative print and Internet campaigns with local tourist associations and Tourism New South Wales;
- produced and distributed the 'Hunter Discovery' brochure, which was used as a reference tool by Aussie Helplines, Travel Agents and Tourism New South Wales;
- mailed the 'Hunter Discovery' brochure to 2981 prospective tourists through a free dial (1800 call number) and coupon call-to-actions programme;
- participated in a domestic 'Short Breaks' wholesale programme with 13 local operators;
- conducted extensive familiarization programmes;
- generated extensive editorial coverage through media releases, briefings, and domestic and international familiarizations;
- participated in domestic trade events such as 'Talkabout' (Travel Agents), 'AIME 99' (conference and incentive buyers event), and 'Sydney on Sale' (conference and incentive buyers);
- participated in international trade events and missions, including Australia Tourism Exchange, Oz Talk Europe, and New Zealand and North America Sales Missions;
- distributed media kits in conjunction with the Australian Tourist Commission;
- undertook a New Zealand campaign in partnership with a local television company (prime television);
- used the official Hunter website in all television and print advertising. That website averaged 86,000 hits per month, with a peak of 112,656 hits in June 1999; and
- e-mailed regular 'Hotlines' to Hunter operators to inform them of marketing initiatives and advertising opportunities.

Figure 17.3 Distributional activities undertaken by the Hunter Regional Tourism Organization

Table 17.6   Key stakeholders

Stakeholders

Private operators	Accommodation establishments.
	Transport – bus, car-hire, rail, air, sea.
	Restaurants.
	Private education institutions.
	MICE industry.
	Attractions and destinations.
	Retailers.
	Tourism information providers.
	Consultants and planners.
Industry associations	Tourism Council Australia.
	Council of Tourist Associations.
	Incorporated Local Tourism Associations
	Australian Hoteliers' Association.
	Local Tourism Associations.
Government, public sector and quasi-autonomous government organizations (QANGOs)	*federal* (eg., Office of National Tourism; Department of Education, Training and Youth Affairs).
	State (e.g. Tourism New South Wales).
	Local (Local Government, e.g. councillors, planners and tourism managers; Local Tourism Associations).
Other	e.g. Incorporated Local Tourism Associations; other RTOs; Telstra.

Clearly, RTOs do not follow the classical or any other form of traditional organization, and do not possess a highly skilled or technical core (they are small organizations in their day-to-day operations). It is difficult for them to claim precise outcomes and therefore they will always be 'damned if they do' and 'damned if they don't' do something. RTOs might be a fundamental plank of the State's regional strategies, but they are in no hierarchical position of power. They cannot demand the commitment of state and local resources they need to survive, and for many, widespread stakeholder support has been inconsistent and/or lacking (see Jenkins, 1995; NCRT, 1999, c. 1999). There are significant challenges to formulating and implementing strategic directions in several regions in New South Wales, especially those where there is inherent physical and structural diversity in their tourism industry. The Hunter Regional Tourism Organization is a case in point, where tourism product diversity can be a strength, but is also a major hurdle to regional co-operation and developing cohesive, widely accepted regional images (Jenkins,

1999). The situation may be made even more complex because tourism development in some regions is in a state of flux, with evolving local destination images and varying stages of development among local operators, some of whom are experiencing and forecasting much stronger growth than others. Balancing these diverse, sometimes competing, interests has not and will not be easy. In this regard, RTOs should, at the very least, regularly monitor and evaluate stakeholder aspirations and perceptions, or risk alienating the stakeholders they were explicitly designed to help. Yet, as noted above, too few bother to do so.

NSW State Governments have not provided a stable platform for the development of tourism strategies (regional or otherwise), promulgating several major policy and programme backflips in less than a decade, amid intermittent calls for RTOs to become self-funding or conversely to become more integrated with state marketing and development objectives. One might generously label this discontinuity as a part of 'policy learning'! One might more critically view it in light of 'politics' and the clashes of values and interests more generally. In any case, Tourism New South Wales should critically examine its current regional structure and look for a more flexible approach to achieving tourism growth in New South Wales. So much of its focus is on marketing and promotion, and this focus flows down to RTOs in the way they operate and in the resources and other forms of support they seek. Avenues for industry facilitation may also occur within and outside the existing regional structure and across different industry sectors. Fostering regional leadership and initiatives beyond marketing and promotion are fundamental to regional development strategies. Regional marketing and promotion is of little value without industry leadership and direction, appropriate skills and well-developed product and infrastructure.

CONCLUSIONS

Governments are key agents in the channels of tourism distribution in modern capitalist societies, and Australia is a case in point. Australian Governments are overtly geared to developing, marketing and promoting tourism for economic gain. Tourism organizations at all levels of Australian government and at the regional level have been developed with an emphasis on hierarchy and centralization, but with insufficient co-ordination, and certainly without long-term, much less medium-term, stability. What we find at the Commonwealth level is something verging on policy evolution, especially in the marketing and promotion arena of the ATC, which has led to a relatively 'charmed' existence compared to state and regional tourism organizations. It has had considerable stability and, particularly for the latter part of its life, increasing levels of public and private sector support, notwithstanding some threats posed by recent reviews mentioned earlier. Developments at the federal level at least indicate that a clearer definition of roles and co-ordination with other levels of government, namely State Government, are paramount, and are being enacted.

At the state and regional levels things are not progressing smoothly throughout the State of NSW and elsewhere. State Governments have significant involvement in the activities of RTOs, which were established rather arbitrarily and without widespread community consultation. The relationships of tourist products within regions are not at all clear, and regional boundaries have often stifled co-ordination among suppliers in different regions when, logically, their products may be complementary and supportive. There is no consensus about the success or failure of regional approaches to tourism marketing and promotion. Regional approaches have been disjointed, subject to major changes in support and direction and the source of much speculation with respect to their merits. The problems facing regional approaches to tourism marketing and promotion in Australia, and as demonstrated in NSW, are complex and diverse, and are unlikely to be resolved in the short term.

REFERENCES

Australian Tourist Commission (ATC) (1992) *Annual Report 1991/92*. ATC, Sydney.

Australian Tourist Commission (ATC) (1993) *Australia*. ATC, Sydney.

Australian Tourist Commission (ATC) (1995) *Partnership Australia: Information for Australian Tourism Operators*. ATC, Sydney.

Australian Tourist Commission (ATC) (1999) *Annual Report, 1998/99*. ATC, Sydney.

Craik, J. (1991a) *Resorting to Tourism: Cultural Policies for Tourist Development in Australia*. Allen & Unwin, St. Leonards.

Craik, J. (1991b) 'Government Promotion of Tourism: the role of the Queensland Tourist and Travel Corporation'. Research Paper No. 20. The Centre for Australian Public Sector Management, Griffith University, Brisbane.

Department of Industry, Science and Resources (2000) *Impact: A Monthly Fact Sheet on the Economic Impact of Tourism and the Latest Visitor Arrival Trends*. June, Department of Industry Science and Resources, Canberra.

Dwyer, L. and Forsyth, P. (1992) 'The Case for Tourism Promotion: an economic analysis'. Discussion Paper No. 265. Centre for Economic Policy Research, The Australian National University, Canberra.

Grey, P., Edelman, K. and Dwyer, L. (1991) *Tourism in Australia: Challenges and Opportunities*. Longman Cheshire, Melbourne.

Hall, C. M. (1991) *Introduction to Tourism in Australia: Development, Dimensions and Issues*. Longman, Melbourne.

Hall, C. M. (1998) *Introduction to Tourism in Australia: Development, Dimensions and Issues* (3rd edn). Longman, Melbourne.

Jenkins, J. M. (1995) 'A comparative study of tourism organizations in Australia and Canada'. *Australian-Canadian Studies*, **13**(1), 73–108.

Jenkins, J. M. (1999) 'The Hunter Regional Tourism Organization: stakeholder perceptions'. Unpublished report to the Hunter Regional Tourism Organization, Newcastle.

Jenkins, J. M. (2000 – forthcoming) 'The dynamics of regional tourism organizations in New South Wales, Australia: history, structures and operations'. *Current Issues in Tourism*, **3**(3).

Jenkins, J. M. and Hall, C. M. (1997) 'Tourism policy and legislation in Australia'. In C. M. Hall, J. M. Jenkins and G. Kearsley (eds) *Tourism Planning and Policy in Australia and New Zealand: cases, issues and practice*. Irwin, Sydney.

Lansbury, R. D. and Gilmour, P. (1977) *Organizations: An Australian Perspective*. Longman Cheshire, Melbourne.

McMillen, J. (1991) 'The politics of Queensland tourism'. In P. Carroll, K. Donohue, M. McGovern and J. McMillen (eds) *Tourism in Australia*. Harcourt Brace Jovanovich, Sydney.

Pearce, D. G. (1992) *Tourist Organizations*. Longman, Harlow.

Pearce, P. L., Morrison, A. M. and Rutledge, J. L. (1998) *Tourism: Bridges Across Continents*. McGraw-Hill, Sydney.

Richardson, J. I. (1999) *A History of Australian Travel and Tourism*. Hospitality Press, Melbourne.

Senate Standing Committee on Environment, Recreation and the Arts (1992) *The Australian Environment and Tourism Report*. Senate Standing Committee on Environment, Recreation and the Arts, The Parliament of the Commonwealth of Australia. AGPS, Canberra.

Summers, J. (1985) 'Parliament and responsible government in Australia'. In D. Woodward, A. Parkin and J. Summers (eds) *Government, Politics and Power in Australia*. Longman Cheshire, Melbourne, pp. 7–27.

The National Centre for Regional Tourism (NCRT) (1999) *Regional Tourism Organisation's Best Practice Manual*. NCRT, Nowra.

The National Centre for Regional Tourism (NCRT) (c. 1999) *Regional Tourism Organisation's Best Practice Systems Project*. NCRT, Nowra.

Tourism New South Wales (1994) *Regional Tourism Strategy*. Tourism New South Wales, Sydney.

Tourism New South Wales (1997) *Regional Tourism Strategy 1997/8–1999/2000*. Tourism New South Wales, Sydney.

Tourism New South Wales (1999a) *Annual Report 1998/99*. Tourism New South Wales, Sydney.

Tourism New South Wales (1999b) *Strategic Plan 1999–2002*. Tourism New South Wales, Sydney.

Tourism New South Wales (2000a) [http://www.tourism.NewSouthWales.gov.au/tnsw/regions/index_regions.html] (as at 17 January 2000).

Tourism New South Wales (2000b) *Regional Tourism: Action Plan 2000–2003*. Tourism New South Wales, Sydney.

Weaver, D. and Oppermann, M. (2000) *Tourism Management*. John Wiley & Sons, Brisbane.

CHAPTER 18

Attracting Chinese outbound tourists: *Guanxi* and the Australian preferred destination perspective

Grace Wen Pan and Eric Laws

INTRODUCTION

On 22 April 1999 Australia became the first Western country granted Approved Destination Status (ADS) by the Chinese Government for Chinese travelling overseas for leisure (Farr, 1999; Southgate, 1999). As a result, Chinese citizens applying for tourist visas are now able to make leisure visits to Australia using ordinary passports whereas previously travel was restricted to official and business groups. Under the ADS Protocol the Mainland Chinese Government authorized 22 travel agencies based in Beijing, Shanghai and Guangzhou to deal with about 35 Australian nominated inbound tour operators in Australia to organize inbound tourism to Australia (ATC, 1998; Tourism Queensland (TQ), 1999). Mainland China is now acknowledged as an important emerging market by the Australian inbound tourism industry. Chinese visitors accounted for only 1 per cent of all international tourists visiting Australia in 1995 (Bureau of Tourism Research, 1996), but this is forecast to rise to 21 per cent of arrivals over the next decade (Tourism Forecasting Council, 1999). As the increasingly prosperous population takes advantage of international travel opportunities, mainland China is expected to join the five principal sources of tourists for Australia: Europe, the USA, Japan, Southeast Asia and New Zealand (Farr, 1999).

The introduction of ADS is particularly likely to increase the proportion of leisure tourists visiting Australia or those visiting friends and relatives (VFRs) (Tourism Forecasting Council, 1999). Therefore, an understanding of the special characteristics of the Chinese tourism market is important for Australian tourism suppliers, marketing practitioners and academics. However, little research has been conducted in regard to the Chinese outbound tourism market to Australia.

This chapter briefly discusses Chinese travel patterns and factors affecting Chinese visitor arrivals in Australia, before considering the business networks which underlie the sector. A comparative case study methodology was adopted to investigate how Australian tourism suppliers are responding to the new opportunities arising from inbound Chinese travel. Case study research is recommended where accepted principles and constructs have not been established or are clearly inadequate (Perry, 1998). The chapter concludes with some recommendations for further development of this market.

HOW ARE AUSTRALIAN TOURISM PRODUCT SUPPLIERS DEVELOPING THEIR STRATEGIES FOR THE CHINESE OUTBOUND TOURISM MARKET?

According to the Marketing Brief of Tourism Queensland (1998), there were only fifteen inbound tour operators dealing with the Chinese outbound tourism market when the researcher arranged the interviews. Interviews were conducted with six inbound agency senior managers and lasted about one hour. The interview schedule consisted of a series of semi-structured questions addressing five aspects, summarized in Table 18.1. Data from in-depth interviews with key senior managers was analysed to identify common themes and specific aspects of the characteristics of the Chinese tourism market to Australia. Inbound tour company managers responding to this study were discussing their experience of Chinese arrivals prior

Table 18.1 Major variables researched in describing the Chinese inbound tourists to Australia

Key aspects studied	Contents
Business	Background information on company
Chinese travel patterns	Manager's understanding of the characteristics of Chinese travel preferences
Chinese tourists	The factors Chinese tourists visiting Australia comment on, and management perceptions of cultural differences
Australian tourism product suppliers	The quality of services provided, suppliers marketing strategies, the role of relationship networks with Chinese outbound agencies
General questions	Supplementary part of interview to establish what managers consider important in organizing Chinese inbound travel

to the granting of ADS status to Australia. This is significant because pre-ADS, visitors were mainly members of official, trade or scientific groups, and an element of leisure activities was provided in addition to their main programmes. ADS and the easing of visa restrictions are likely to result in the arrival of Chinese visitors whose primary travel motivations are leisure or VFR. Their satisfaction with the leisure content of itineraries which they will be paying for from personal funds is therefore likely to become more critical.

CHINESE TRAVEL PATTERNS

The most common form of travel for Chinese tourists visiting Australia is the all-inclusive package tour (Table 18.2). A typical package includes international travel, private chartered coach within Australia, sightseeing excursions, local guides, accommodation and meals (mainly Chinese food with some Australian-style meals, such as a barbecue or an American breakfast). This form of tour arrangement can be compared with typical Western inclusive holiday packages (Laws, 1997), providing Chinese clients with similar advantages, particularly the benefit of knowing beforehand what to budget for their holiday, and relieving them of any concerns about difficulties of making their own arrangements in a foreign country.

CHINESE OUTBOUND TOURISM DEVELOPMENT

The Chinese Government until 1983 placed tight restrictions on outbound tourism. Then, the slightly liberalized policy first eased Chinese leisure travel to Hong Kong and Macau, because of ethnic, cultural and political connections (Cai et al., 1999). At that time, 'outbound travel' was defined as VFR. Thus the trip was sponsored financially by overseas relatives and friends so there was no drain on China's foreign exchange reserves.

With the development of Chinese travel to Hong Kong and Macau, more and more people expressed a desire to visit their relatives in other regions. Under this situation, in 1990, with the approval of the State Council, the China National Tourism Administration (CNTA), the Foreign Ministry, the Public Security Ministry and the Overseas Chinese Affairs Office declared 'the Provisional Regulations on Management of Organising Chinese Citizens to Travel to Three Countries in Southeast Asia'. This regulation enabled Chinese citizens to visit friends and relatives in Thailand, Singapore and Malaysia if sponsored by their overseas relatives and friends. The Philippines was added in 1992. Cross-border tours were also permitted. The flows include Northeast China to Russia, North Korea and Mongolia; Southwest China to Vietnam, Cambodia, Laos and Myanmar (Burma); and from Northwest China to Russia and other former Soviet Union countries (Dou and Dou, 1999).

Table 18.2 Features of Chinese package tours to Australia

Feature	Type	Main details
Form of travel	Group travel, business and leisure	Most business travellers are from Beijing and Shanghai
	Fully independent tours	Most leisure travellers are from Guangdong Province
		Very limited at present
Itinerary	General tour	7 nights 9 days or 8 nights 10 days Sydney-Canberra-Melbourne-the Gold Coast (at least two theme parks including Movie World and Sea World)-Brisbane
Levels of accommodation	The most impressive places	The trend is going to see the Great Barrier Reef, Sydney, the Gold Coast
	Budget	Most leisure travellers use budget accomodation (three-star hotels)
	Standard or deluxe	Business travellers use four-star hotels and government delegates use five-star hotels
Travel to other destinations	New Zealand	Some visit, but have difficulty getting tourist visas
	Hong Kong	Most visitors from Guangdong Province also go to Hong Kong

With the development of travel services, trips evolved from VFR to holiday leisure travel. In 1991, Singapore, Malaysia, and Thailand witnessed the rush of the first tour groups from Mainland China when the country began to permit its residents to travel to selected Southeast Asian countries for personal and leisure purposes. Subsequently, other Southeast Asian countries were awarded ADS by the Chinese Government. Australia and New Zealand were granted ADS in 1998. The total number of Chinese outbound tourists grew rapidly between 1994 and 1997 (Figure 18.1). Of the total outbound tourists from China, 54.3 per cent were for business purposes and 45.7 per cent for private purposes, including leisure and VFR (China National Tourism Administration, 1997). The World Tourism Organization (WTO) (1998) stated that the number of Chinese outbound tourists in organized tour groups increased by nearly 130 per cent to 1,640,000 between 1993 and 1996 (in Cai *et al.*, 1999).

Three main categories of destinations were identified by the National Tourism Administration of the People's Republic of China (Table 18.3). These are Chinese

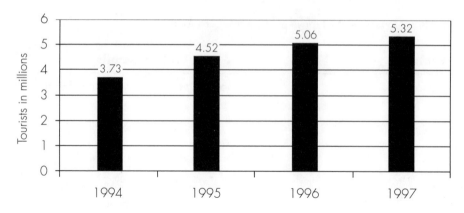

Figure 18.1 Chinese outbound tourists. *Source*: China Statistical Year Book, 1998

outbound tours, cross-border tours, and tours to Hong Kong and Macau. It should be noted that only cross-border tours do not need a visa. Although Hong Kong and Macau have now become Special Administration Regions (SARs) of China, Chinese tourists still have to apply for a visa to visit them. In 1997, the major destinations of Chinese outbound tourists organized by travel agencies were: Hong Kong, Macau, Myanmar, Thailand, Vietnam, Russia, Singapore, Malaysia, North Korea and the Philippines (CNTA, 1997). Hong Kong and Macau, Thailand, Singapore, Malaysia and Philippines currently account for 75 per cent of China's outbound tourism (Wang and Sheldon, 1995).

Table 18.3 Major destinations of Chinese outbound tourists. *Source*: CNTA, 1997

Destinations	Outbound (thousands) 1997	Change (%) over 1996
Thailand	220.7	−2.6
Singapore	86.3	3.0
Malaysia	81.7	0.5
Philippines	13.8	50.0
Myanmar	234.7	−50.3
Vietnam	212.9	44.9
Russia	75.1	14.5
North Korea	52.6	124.8
Hong Kong	465.7	10.9
Macau	333.4	−14.4

On 1 July 1997 the 'Provisional Regulations on the Management of Outbound Travel by Chinese Citizens at Their Own Expense' were issued jointly by the CNTA and

the Ministry of Public Security after approval by the State Council, establishing a new management system for outbound travel to meet the growing demand of Chinese citizens to travel outside of China (CNTA, 1997). Under the regulations, outbound tours by Chinese citizens must be conducted in a planned, organized and controlled manner. Only approved travel agencies can take the responsibilities of managing outbound travel by Chinese citizens. Category A agencies are authorized to operate international travel business. Category B agencies are allowed to receive and entertain international tourists to China while Category C agencies are only allowed to operate domestic travel business. China has 360 Category A travel agencies. In addition to seeking their own clients directly, some of the authorized outbound Category A travel agencies receive passengers from Categories B and C travel agencies. Therefore, Category A agencies can be regarded as wholesalers as well. Out of 360 Category A travel agencies 67 are authorized to handle Chinese outbound travel services because of the demand for international services. Twenty-two of the 67 Chinese travel agencies were authorized to handle the Chinese tourism market to Australia. These 22 travel agencies are located in Beijing, Shanghai and Guangzhou. The Ministry of Public Security is responsible for the management of passports for outbound travel, and its procedures are based on the Chinese exit and entry laws and regulations. These regulations determine that the major pattern of the Chinese outbound leisure travel is package tours, not fully independent tours (FITs). Compared to other markets, the Chinese Government is still very careful with outbound tourism, especially the outbound tourism market to Australia, mainly because it was the first non-Asiatic destination granted ADS status.

When Australia was granted ADS by the Chinese Government, ATC and the CNTA set unified prices on package tours for Chinese tourists visiting Australia. For example, a nine-day tour departing from Beijing or Shanghai is priced at RMB18,000 (approximately AU$3371), and departure from Guangdong Province is RMB14,000 (=AU$2622). These unified prices are a condition of visa approval for Chinese tourists visiting Australia. In contrast with the literature suggesting that Chinese people are highly price sensitive (Zhou *et al.*, 1997), unified pricing implies that Chinese tourists do not have any bargaining power if wishing to visit Australia as a leisure destination. Furthermore, most of the package tours available to Chinese tourists are very similar, offering trips to Sydney, Canberra, Melbourne, the Gold Coast and Brisbane, and itineraries which include at least two of the three theme parks on the Gold Coast, Movie World, Sea World or Dream World. The lack of variety in the products available to the Chinese outbound tourism market could ultimately detract from Chinese tourists' interest in visiting Australia.

In contrast, the Chinese outbound travel agencies are highly price sensitive. Chinese travel agencies try to reduce the price of land services provided by Australian inbound tour operators to obtain a higher profit margin from the fixed sales price. Price competition also results in a poor quality of services provided to Chinese tourists, and there was evidence in this study of dissatisfaction among

Chinese tourists with the standards of accommodation provided on package tours to Australia. Differentiating and developing products with unique Australian characteristics appears to be the best strategy to minimize price competition between them for the inbound tour operators in Australia.

THE CHINESE TOURISM MARKET TO AUSTRALIA

Little research has yet been conducted regarding the determinants of Chinese tourism demand for visits to Australia. Similarly Prideaux (1998) has stated that the development of Korean inbound tourism to Australia during 1988–95 was characterized by a lack of understanding of the unique features of the Korean tourism market compared to other Asian markets, and noted that the lack of appropriate preparation for the rapid growth of inbound Korean tourism to Australia has brought a lot of problems which have impacted both on the Australian tourism market and on business itself. This suggests that there is a need for research to identify the special characteristics of the Chinese market in order for Australian inbound tour operators to maximize their opportunities.

Table 18.4 Critical factors affecting the decision of Chinese tourists to travel to Australia

Visa	Consistent with other research on the factors affecting Chinese tourists visiting Hong Kong and Singapore, Malaysia and Thailand (SMT) (Qu & Lam, 1997; Qu & Li, 1997; Cai *et al.*, 1999), visa requirements to enter Australia are one of the major obstacles to expanding the outbound travel market from China. This barrier has been eased by the granting of ADS status.
Language	Although most Chinese tourists cannot speak English, language problems are not a significant problem because Chinese groups are always accompanied by tour guides. However, it might be a problem if a Chinese FIT market to Australia develops.
Cultural differences	Cultural differences are not likely to deter Chinese tourists from visiting Australia. On the contrary, experiencing Western culture is a big priority for Chinese tourists to choose Australia instead of other ADS countries as a destination. At the time of writing (September 2000), only two Western countries, Australia and New Zealand, have been granted ADS status. All the other countries approved as ADS for Chinese tourists are Asian countries, i.e. Singapore, Thailand, Malaysia, Philippines and South Korea.

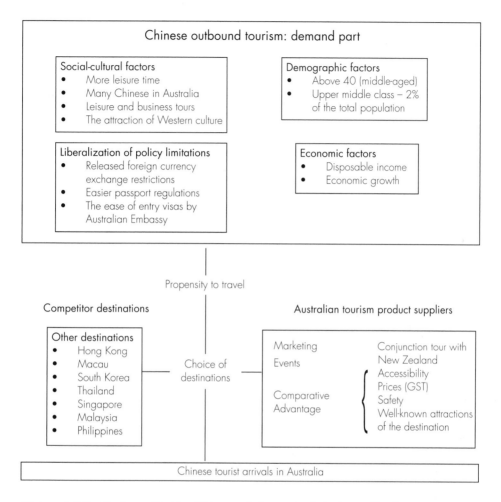

Figure 18.2 Factors affecting Chinese visitor arrivals in Australia. *Source*: Adapted from Faulkner, 1996, p. 235

The literature on travel decisions by Asiatic travellers indicates that there are significant differences between Asiatic countries. This is exemplified in previous studies on the four Asian dragons: Singapore, Hong Kong, South Korea and Taiwan (Chai and Skene, 1996; March, 1997; Oppermann, 1997; Prideaux, 1998). This stream of research has found that they have different cultures and histories, and consequently their people have different values, perceptions and desires compared to the other major outbound market, Japanese residents. Consequently as Oppermann (1997) suggests, catering to tourists from different markets requires different approaches. An extensive range of tourism literature shows that international visitor arrivals to Australia are largely determined by income levels per capita in the generating markets, relative prices (including exchange rates), population growth and destination marketing. Disposable income is the most important factor influencing visitors' decisions whether to travel or not (Poon, 1993; Karwacki *et al.*, 1997; Qu & Lam, 1997; Tourism Forecast Council, 1998). Faulkner (1996) discussed the factors affecting international visitor arrivals in Australia. However, his study predates the arrival of Chinese visitors (Figure 18.2). The findings of the current study identified three key factors which directly impact on Chinese tourists' decision to travel to Australia, as illustrated in Table 18.4.

THE BUSINESS NETWORKS UNDERPINNING INBOUND CHINESE TOURISM

The establishment and operation of business networks has become an important topic of business research (Halinen *et al.*, 1999). Social networks, as a sub-network within the business network, have been acknowledged as important when establishing new relationships in an international context (Björkman and Kock, 1995; Holmlund and Kock, 1998). Due to the extensive range of relevant parties in relationship marketing, Kotler (1998, p. 12) suggested building a unique company asset called a marketing network. A marketing network consists of the company and all of its supporting stakeholders: customers, employees, suppliers, distributors, retailers, ad agencies, university scientists and others with whom it has built mutually profitable business relationships.

A common theme in the literature is that key elements of relationship marketing are trust and commitment (Rust *et al.*, 1995; Tax *et al.*, 1998). Although relationship marketing has been a major topic in marketing literature, limited research has been conducted to conceptualize the relationship and its interactions in either the tourism (Laws, 1997) or Chinese contexts (Wong and Tam, 2000). Most studies of relationships in business networks have their roots in American and European cultures; although China has opened its gates to the West for more than twenty years, its Confucian culture still plays a dominant role. For example, Chinese people have distinct social orientations and commitments, which are different from Western culture. Chinese people are extremely cautious and reluctant to get involved in fields or relationships that they are not familiar with (Kim *et al.*, 1998; Lowe and Corkindale, 1998). Thus, familiarity with the partner is critical in the process of setting up relationships in China. As a result, Western business theories and practices are not directly applicable to the Chinese context, and success requires an understanding of the similarities and differences in the process of relationship-building (Wong, 1998).

It has been suggested that Western and Asiatic cultures can be distinguished along a continuum of high to low contact. Hall (1976) defined Western, low-context cultures as fragmented, in which people are highly individualized and somewhat alienated, with relatively little involvement with others. High-context cultures such as the Chinese are those in which people are deeply involved with each other. Kim *et al.* (1998) further discussed that as a result of intimate relationships among people in high-context cultures, a structure of social hierarchy exists, individual inner feelings are kept under strong self-control, and information is widely shared through simple messages with deep meaning. China is noted for its high-context culture and it is a country where business depends more on connections and relationships than in Western countries such as Australia with its low-context culture.

Guanxi is the term used in Chinese to describe the Chinese system of business networks. *Guanxi*, roughly translated as a personal relationship or connection, is a specific term for Chinese relationships combining cultural characteristics in terms of social networks with the deliberate process of building up a Chinese business network. *Guanxi*, a deep-rooted social-cultural phenomenon, has been defined as 'friendship with implications of a continual exchange of favours' (Chen, 1995, p. 53). In a typical Chinese context, guanxi operates by 'creativity and flexibility through a network of personal relationships' (Wong and Tam, 2000).

The general perception amongst Chinese people is that if you manage to develop a good personal relationship with the central decision-maker you have a good chance of getting business deals controlled by this person. One of the Australian managers interviewed related how he firstly set up a personal relationship (*Guanxi*) with a Chinese agency, then was able to do business smoothly. It is important to have Chinese staff to tap into the Chinese tourism market. During their development of the relationship with their clients, the Australian counterparts tried to develop as much as possible in the first contact and do business in the Chinese (or Asian) way. For example, a lot of business is not done in the office but in some other places like Karaoke. Loyalty can make a business relationship personal. The Australian managers maintained their relationships with Chinese travel agencies by sending them birthday cards and seasonal greetings if they do not celebrate Christmas.

Guanxi, face and *renqing* are the three keys for understanding Chinese social behavioural patterns and their business dynamics (Yang, 1986; Chen, 1995; Davies *et al.*, 1995; Wong, 1998; Wong and Tam, 2000). An individual's 'face', defined as one's dignity, self-respect and prestige, is a key component in the dynamics of *Guanxi*, while *renqing*, defined as one of the commonly accepted social concepts regulating Chinese interpersonal relationships based on the Confucian concept of reciprocity, plays an important role in the cultivation and development of *Guanxi* (Chen, 1995). The basic rule is 'a favour for a favour, an attack for an attack'. This is different from the Western culture in which the business is obliged to follow rules of equity; the Chinese culture favours dominant roles as evident in the 'need' rule (Chen, 1995; Wong, 1998). The essence of this is that 'if you do me a favour, I owe you a favour, so next time if you need any help, I will return the favour to you'.

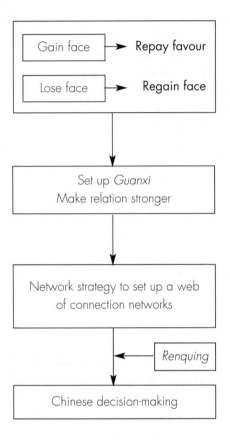

Figure 18.3 Chinese relationship marketing. *Source*: Based on: Huang (1989) in Chen (1995), p. 64; Wong (1998), pp. 25–42; and Chen (1995), pp. 52–68.

Guanxi and *renqing* are the major factors influencing Chinese decision-making (Chen, 1995; Wong, 1998). Chen (1995) pointed out that *renqing* and *Guanxi* can be interchangeable because *renqing* is intertwined with *Guanxi*. Huang (in Chen, 1995) identified the interactions between *Guanxi* and face in his dynamic chart for the first stages of setting up the relationships. Chen (1995) and Wong (1998) explain the dynamic of the *Guanxi* network building needed if the seller intends to establish long-term relationships with buyers from China, as is illustrated in Figure 18.3.

BUSINESS NETWORKS AND CULTURAL DIFFERENCES

The findings of the current study emphasize the importance of setting up a long-term relationship between Chinese travel agencies and inbound tour operators in

Australia. However, there is no previous research on marketing networks between Australian tourism product suppliers and Chinese travel agencies. Trust, loyalty and commitment are the key issues in setting up and maintaining the relationship. In addition, face-saving and *Guanxi* are critical in the relationship between inbound tour operators in Australia and Chinese travel agencies.

It is important for inbound tour operators in Australia to conduct their business with Chinese travel agencies in the Chinese way. The Chinese Government has authorized 22 travel agencies to handle Chinese outbound tourism to Australia. Four out of six inbound tour operators have already done so, while the other two have not yet established a business relationship. The most successful Australian inbound tour operators are those who have been able to establish relations with Chinese travel agents. There is little evidence of any other Australian inbound tour operators dealing with inbound Chinese groups.

Most of the inbound tour operators in Australia for inbound Chinese tourists are themselves overseas Chinese or at least Asiatic, so they do not experience significant cultural differences. Furthermore, they know which areas of China to target, namely Beijing, Shanghai and Guangzhou. Nevertheless, cultural differences could be a problem for the non-Asiatic inbound tour operators in Australia interested in tapping into the Chinese tourism market. The best solution to this problem is to have qualified Chinese staff who understand the cultural differences between China and Australia, and know how to do business in China. Understanding Chinese culture not only helps understand Chinese tourists' behaviour, but also more importantly assists Australian tourism product suppliers marketing in China.

RECOMMENDATIONS

Based on the findings of this study, it is clear that all-inclusive package tours are the most appropriate travel patterns for Chinese tourists at this stage of market development. Thus, it is important to improve the composition of Chinese package tours, and provide marketing strategies into the Chinese tourism market by improved networking. Some specific recommendations emerging from the current research are as follows:

Develop Australian tourism products: With regard to the similarity of the composition of Chinese package tours, it is more important for inbound tour operators in Australia to develop Australian tourism products catering for Chinese tourists than to compete on price. Differentiated package tours could provide Chinese tourists with a greater variety of options, and help them get to know the diverse range of Australian tourism products; and additionally, it will be more difficult for Chinese travel agencies to make simple comparisons of Australian inbound packages or to bargain based solely on price.

Develop multi-destinations in Australia: As Chinese tourists can only visit Australia once in their trip at present, it is necessary to make Australia more appealing by developing more tourism places catering for Chinese tourists. Many Chinese are interested in visiting more than one major city, and experiencing the theme parks of the Gold Coast or viewing some of Australia's natural resources such as the Great Barrier Reef.

Australian brand: It is also necessary to make the Australian tourism product meet the needs of this particular market segment. Creating an 'Australian Brand' could provide the impetus for Chinese tourists to visit Australia. Similarly, a study of Korean tourists visiting Australia revealed that there were complaints about the lack of unique Australian-made souvenirs and goods available for sale (Prideaux, 1998). Chinese tourists who can afford to visit Australia will be relatively well off, and an aspect of their culture is to return from long journeys with gifts for family, friends and colleagues. This implies opportunities to develop Australian products for the Chinese tourism market. Some sectors which have great potential for development include natural therapy cosmetics, opal-related products, and woollen clothing.

The role of Australian Government organizations: Australian government organizations play an important role in assisting inbound tour operators to set up a relationship with Chinese travel agencies. As a government tourism organization, the ATC, and all the state tourism organizations, mainly Tourism Queensland, Tourism NSW and Tourism Victoria, have the ability to organize sales calls and trade shows in China to create opportunities for the inbound tour operators to establish contact with the 22 approved travel agencies. In addition, seminars regarding Chinese inbound tourism to Australia should be held to help inbound tour operators in Australian better understand the special features of this market.

Education programme: An education programme could be very beneficial in the process of setting up a business network between Australian tourism product suppliers and Chinese travel agencies. In this programme, government tourism organizations should take the initiative in setting up an educational bridge between the Chinese outbound tourism market and Australian inbound tour operators (Figure 18.4). Universities and other training providers could develop specific course content. The education programme includes not only educating Chinese travel agencies and Chinese tourists about the Australian pricing system, cultural differences and tourism products, but also educating inbound tour operators in Australia about cultural differences and the way to do business in China, as well as providing basic training in spoken Mandarin.

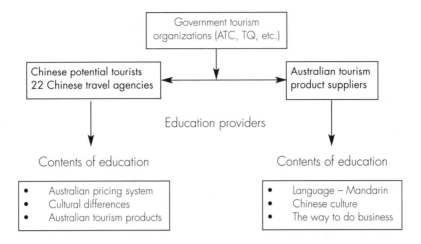

Figure 18.4 Training programmes to develop the Chinese tourism market to Australia

LIMITATIONS AND FURTHER RESEARCH

The first limitation to note is that although Australia was the first Western country granted ADS to China, few leisure tourists from Mainland China had arrived when the interviews were conducted. Therefore, the characteristics of leisure tourists from Mainland China still need further research. Secondly, in order for Australia to expand its market share in the Chinese outbound tourism market, it is necessary to understand the particularities of this market and its distribution system, and to analyse the responses to Australia as ADS. The perspectives of inbound tour operators have been identified, but the response of Chinese travel agencies regarding Australia as ADS will be the subject of a further stage of this study.

CONCLUSIONS

The principles of Chinese business practice summarized in the phrase *Guanxi* discussed above suggest that Australia's status as the first Western country granted ADS is a precious step towards a profitable long-term business partnership. With the well-documented growth of prosperity in China (Davies *et al.*, 1995; CNTA, 1997; Farr, 1999; and the Tourism Forecasting Council, 1999), and the long pent-up interest among the Chinese for international travel, Australia with its relative geographic proximity to China appears to be uniquely placed to develop as a major destination for leisure travellers. However, success depends on whether inbound operators are able to create effective distribution and marketing links with their Chinese outbound business partners.

REFERENCES

Australian Tourism Commission (ATC) (1998) *Market Profile: Your Guide to Marketing in North Asia-China, Hong Kong, Korea, Philippines and Taiwan.* ATC, Sydney.

Björkman, I. and Kock, S. (1995) 'Social relationships and business networks: the case of western companies in China'. *International Business,* **4**(4), 519–35.

Bureau of Tourism Research (BTR) (1996) *China's Economy and Tourism to Australia.* BTR Conference Paper 96.9.

Cai, L., Boger, C. and O'Leary, J. (1999) 'The Chinese travellers to Singapore, Malaysia, and Thailand: a unique Chinese outbound market'. *Asia Pacific Journal of Tourism Research,* **3**(2), 2–13.

Chai, P. and Skene, J. (1996) *Diversity of Visitors from Asia.* The Asia Pacific Tourism Association '96 Conference, BTR Conference Paper 96.10. BTR, Australia.

Chai, P. (1996) *China's Economy and Tourism to Australia.* BTR Conference Paper. BTR, Australia.

Chen, M. (1995) *Asian Management Systems: Chinese, Japanese and Korean Styles of Business.* Routledge, London and New York, pp. 52–68.

China National Tourism Administration (CNTA) (1997) *China Tourism Annual Report.* National Tourism Administration of the People's Republic of China, Beijing.

Davies, H., Leung, T., Luk, S. and Wong, Y. (1995) 'The benefits of "Guanxi": the value of relationships in developing the Chinese market'. *Industrial Marketing Management,* **24**, 207–14.

Dou, Q. and Dou, J. (1999) 'A study of the Chinese Mainland outbound tourist markets'. *Tourism 2000: Asia Pacific's Role in the New Millennium, Conference Proceedings.* Asia Pacific Tourism Association Fifth Annual Conference, Hong Kong, Vol. II, pp. 751–8.

Eisenhardt, K. (1989) 'Building theories from case study research'. *Academy of Management Review,* **14**(4), 532–50.

Farr, M. (1999) 'Chinese tourism invasion'. *Daily Telegraph,* 22 April, p. 3.

Faulkner, H. (1996) 'Towards a strategic approach to tourism development: the Australian experience'. In W. Theobald (ed.) *Global Tourism: the next decade.* Butterworth-Heinemann, Oxford, pp. 231–46.

Halinen, A., Salmi, A. and Havila, V. (1999) 'From dyadic change to changing business networks: an analytical framework'. *Journal of Management Studies,* **36**(6), 779–94.

Hall, E. T. (1976) *Beyond Culture.* Anchor Books/Doubleday, New York.

Hedges, A. (1985) 'Group interviewing'. In R. Walker (ed.) *Applied Qualitative Research.* Gower, Aldershot.

Holmlund, M. and Kock, S. (1998) 'Relationships and the internationalism of Finnish small and medium-sized companies'. *International Small Business Journal,* **16**(4), 46–63.

Hsieh, S. and O'Leary, J. (1994) 'A travel decision model for Japanese pleasure travel'. *Travel and Tourism Research Association Annual Conference,* pp. 94–104.

Karwacki, J., Deng, S. and Chapdelaine, C. (1997) 'The tourism markets of the four dragons – a Canadian perspective'. *Tourism Management,* **18**(6), 373–83.

Kim, D., Pan, Y. and Park, H. (1998) 'High- versus low-context culture: a comparison of Chinese, Korean, and American cultures'. *Psychology & Marketing,* **15**(6), 507–21.

Kotler, P. (1998) *Marketing* (4th edn). Prentice Hall International Editions, New York and Sydney.

Laws, E. (1997) *Managing Packaged Tourism: relationships, responsibilities and service quality in the inclusive holiday industry.* International Thomson Publishing Company, London.

Lowe, A. and Corkindale, D. (1998) 'Differences in "cultural values" and their effects on responses to marketing stimuli a cross-cultural study between Australians and Chinese from the People's Republic of China'. *European Journal of Marketing*, **32**(9/10), 843–67.

March, R. (1997) 'Diversity in Asian outbound travel industries: a comparison between Indonesia, Thailand, Taiwan, South Korea and Japan'. *International Journal of Hospitality Management*, **16**(2), 231–8.

Oppermann, M. (1997) 'The outbound tourism cycle and the Asian Tourism tigers'. In M. Oppermann (ed.) *Pacific Rim Tourism*. CAB International, New York, pp. 60–75.

Perry, C. (1998) 'Processes of a case study methodology for postgraduate research in marketing'. *European Journal of Marketing*, **32**(9/10), 785–802.

Poon, A. (1993) *Tourism, Technology and Competitive Strategies*. CAB International, Wallingford.

Prideaux, B. (1998) 'Korean outbound tourism: Australia's response'. *Journal of Travel and Tourism Marketing*, **7**(1), 93–102.

Qu, H. and Lam, S. (1997) 'A travel demand model for Mainland Chinese tourists to Hong Kong'. *Tourism Management*, **18**(8), 593–7.

Qu, H. and Li, I. (1997) 'The characteristics and satisfaction of Mainland Chinese visitors to Hong Kong'. *Journal of Travel Research*, Spring, 37–41.

Rust, R., Zahorik, A. and Keiningham, T. (1995) *Service Marketing*. HarperCollins, New York, pp. 374–99.

Southgate, L. (1999) 'Tourists will create 2 million more jobs'. *Australian*, 30 April.

Tax, S., Brown, S. and Chandrashekaran, M. (1998) 'Customer evaluations of service complaint experiences: implications for relationship marketing'. *Journal of Marketing*, April, pp. 60–73.

Tourism Forecasting Council (TFC) (1998) 'Inbound update'. *The 7th Report of the TFC*, March, pp. 4–8.

Tourism Forecasting Council (TFC) (1999) 'Inbound tourism on the mend'. *The 9th Report of the TFC*, August, pp. 4–14.

Tourism Queensland (TQ) (1998) *The Queensland Tourist and Travel Corporation 1997/98 Annual Report*. Tourism Queensland (formerly called the Queensland Tourist and Travel Corporation).

Tourism Queensland (TQ) (1999) *International Marketing Briefs 1999*. Tourism Queensland.

Wang, Y. and Sheldon, P. (1995) 'The sleeping dragon awakes: the outbound Chinese travel market'. *Journal of Travel and Tourism Marketing*, **4**(4), 41–54.

Wong, Y. (1998) 'The dynamics of Guanxi in China'. *Singapore Management Review*, pp. 25–42.

Wong, Y. and Tam, J. (2000) 'Mapping relationships in China: *guanxi* dynamic approach'. *Journal of Business & Industrial Marketing*, **15**(1), 57–70.

World Tourism Organization (WTO) (1998) *Tourism Market Trends: East Asia and the Pacific 1997–1998*. WTO Commission for East Asia and the Pacific, Thirty-Second Meeting. WTO, Madrid.

Yang, M. (1986) *The Art of Social Relationships and Exchange in China*. University of California, Berkeley, CA.

Yin, R. (1989) *Case Study Research: Design and Methods*. Sage, Newbury Park, CA.

Yin, R. K. (1994) *Case Study Research – Design and Methods*. Applied Social Research Methods Series Vol. 5, rev. edn. Sage Publications, Newbury Park.

Zhou, L., King, B. and Turner, L. (1997) 'The China outbound market: An evaluation of key constraints and opportunities'. *Journal of Vacation Marketing*, **4**(2), 109–19.

CHAPTER 19

Use of tourism destination channels for destination marketing: a model and case study

Noel Scott and Eric Laws

INTRODUCTION

Tourism systems are dynamic. They involve the continual interaction of differentiated groups of market actors. Each set of actors has distinct and potentially conflicting objectives. Visitors are subject to personal and societal trends, which affect their motivation to travel and their perceptions of novel, interesting and satisfying destinations that meet their needs. Travel distribution channel members (wholesalers and retailers) require profit and hence balance revenue and costs through promotion and marketing of travel alternatives; transportation operators match capacity and demand for their services. Destinations themselves are a mix of organizations, notably accommodation and attractions, that both compete and collaborate. State Tourism Offices (STOs) intervene in this dynamic environment by providing co-ordination and collaborative management. To perform these roles effectively, they require a clear understanding of the whole tourism system and of critical areas where they can add most value. This chapter provides two related case studies of how Tourism Queensland deals with this complexity, and a model of the dynamic tourism system in which it operates.

STAKEHOLDERS AND THE ROLES OF STOs

Tourism distribution channels traditionally have been thought of as means for distributing information and obtaining bookings for particular holiday packages featuring the destination and products available within the destination such as hotels, resorts, transportation and activities (Getz, 1986; Go, 1993). The national or state organizations typically play a central role in promoting the destination, co-ordinating alliances with the key industry representative bodies and large tourism entities such as hotels. Dyer and Singh (1998) have argued that a firm's critical resources may span its boundaries and be embedded in inter-firm processes, therefore the network of external relationships may be an important unit of analysis. The foregoing suggests that there are a number of stakeholders involved in and affected by destination management policies. Sautter and Leisen (1999, p. 313) have reviewed the growing literature on stakeholder involvement and note that:

> Stakeholder theory, pioneered by Freeman (1984) suggests that an organisation is characterised by its relationships with various groups and individuals including employees, customers, suppliers, governments and members of communities (with) a legitimate interest in aspects of the organisation's activities . . . and has either the power to affect the firm's performance and/or has a stake in the firm's performance.

Selin (1993) has looked at alliances using collaboration theory and noted that for collaboration to persist over time there is a need to manage stakeholder interactions in an increasingly systematic manner. Structuring refers to the process of institutionalizing the shared meanings that emerge as tourism develops. Opinions differ as to the identity of tourist destination stakeholders. Laws (1995) discusses a quartet of destination management destination concerns – its society, economy, environment and ecology – and speculates that policy towards these and tourism is determined by a plurality of interest groups, residents, investors and employees. Buhalis (2000, p. 98) lists indigenous people, businesses and investors, tourists, tour operators and intermediaries, and interest groups. He notes that the resulting relationships are dynamic, and that destination organization 'strategies and actions should take into account the wishes of all stakeholders' but also cautions that many businesses follow their own marketing strategies. This requires the development of 'shared meanings' that all stakeholders ascribe to.

INDUSTRY STRUCTURE

On another level of abstraction, the unpredictable, chaotic nature of much of the tourism industry has received increasing analytical attention recently through approaches grounded in systems, complexity and chaos (Faulkner and Russell, 1997; Klomp and Green, 1997; Faulkner, 2000). McKercher (1999) criticizes early models of tourism because they 'recognise the complex nature of the tourism system but fail to appreciate the chaotic nature of tourism systems'. He notes that systems models argue that tourism

1. can be controlled
2. disparate tourism players function in a formally, co-ordinated manner to form a whole
3. is organized and that the organization can be controlled by a top-down management approach
4. individual businesses function to achieve a set of common, mutually agreed goals
5. is the sum of its constituent parts
6. by understanding how each part works, an understanding of how it works as a whole will emerge.

Commenting on tourism in Australia, McKercher (1999, p. 428) notes the complexity resulting from the situation in which: 'one Commonwealth government, six States, two Territories and over 700 local authorities are involved in tourism at some level. Each works first for its best commercial or political interest.' Because the relationships are open and so complex and because this complexity engenders an innate level of instability, it is extremely difficult to predict accurately the future movement of the system.

THE TOURISM DESTINATION SYSTEM

This chapter presents an integrative framework describing the tourism destination 'system' along the lines of previous work by Mill and Morrison (1985). Figure 19.1 presents a systems model conceptualizing the network of relationships within which destination organizations operate to perform key functions. The model consists of five main elements (or sub-systems) with the Destination sub-system as the hub around which distribution channels, promotion, research and transportation move. All these revolve within the broader environmental contexts of the external environment and particularly general policy and planning agendas set by the government for the area's administrative bodies, of which the Destination Management Organization is one. Each sub-system is subject to dynamic 'push' and 'pull' factors in the form of operator objective, capacity, competition and resources, while changing consumer demands, technological advances and so on are simultaneously changing demand. At the same time operators work both co-operatively and collaboratively to achieve the diverse outcomes for the stakeholders who comprise the destination community.

The framework is developed from the viewpoint of the visitor and consists of several interacting, but separate elements. Each element contains a set of stakeholders and customers with different and competing aims and objectives. Stakeholders within the distribution element compete for customers and select combinations of destinations and transportation that meet their needs. Customers

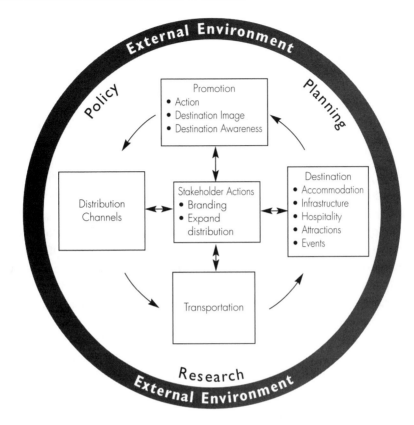

Figure 19.1 The tourism destination system framework

choose amongst these competing distribution stakeholders to meet their holiday needs. Thus supply and demand interact both within and between elements of the tourism system. Stakeholder collaboration across and within these dynamic elements may be attempted through co-operative marketing programmes, branding and other initiatives. These may be introduced by an STO. Such a framework has a number of uses. It can help define the role of an STO and develop an understanding of critical functions required in a dynamic market. It can help characterize a tourism destination by providing a standard set of important parameters that can be profiled and compared. It can also help focus attention on the interrelatedness of distribution activities that occur in spatially or temporally diverse locations. It can also help provide a 'shared meaning' across the stakeholders in each sub-system and make explicit the extent of collaboration and co-operation that currently and potentially exists. As the title of this chapter indicates, most emphasis will be given to a discussion of the distribution aspects of the model. However, it is based on an understanding of the way in which consumers choose a destination to visit, and a brief overview of this topic now follows.

CONSUMER CHOICE

A distribution channel provides the means by which an STO can deliver tangible or intangible material to a potential traveller. In order to understand the best way of doing this a model is useful, showing the various points that a traveller goes through in choosing a destination, and what is required to influence them positively at each stage. Figure 19.2 includes means for communicating destination image as well as information on tangible aspects of a destination (both commercial and non-commercial). Finally it involves the mechanisms for booking a holiday. The underlying consumer communication theory on which the process of influencing customers is based is derived from a 'hierarchy of effects' theory (Rossiter and Percy, 1996).

From a customer perspective, a destination can be viewed like any other 'product'. Product branding is the concept of creating customer identification with products based on their attributes and benefits. The hierarchy of effects model (Figure 19.2) provides an understanding of how a destination brand can influence the travel decision process. This travel process involves a series of steps (need arousal, information search, purchase and usage). Brand marketing can be targeted to influence each of these steps. However, the actual tools used may differ. For example, influencing need arousal in favour of a specific destination involves marketing of the particular tourism characteristics of that type of destination and linking that type to the specific in the consumer's mind. Alternatively a travel agent familiarization tour may be used to demonstrate the tourism brand through direct experience and hence influence a travel agent in selling that destination. The ultimate aim for development of a brand is a high brand awareness and favourable brand attitude across the consumer/trade channels.

Rossiter and Percy (1996) provide recommendations about how to implement this brand influence process for a variety of different types of product. Holiday

Figure 19.2 Buyer behaviour and branding effects. *Source*: Adopted from Rossiter and Percy, 1996

travel in this theory is a high involvement transformational product where the motive for purchase is positive and the customer is highly involved in the purchase. The implementation of a branding approach for destination marketing requires identification of specific target audiences for whom the material is designed and emotional authenticity and integration of information in all aspects of the marketing mix (product, price, distribution channels and promotion) (Kotler *et al.*,1993). Additionally it involves co-ordination and collaboration of a variety of stakeholders for effective implementation. The two case studies that follow provide illustrations of the use of such an approach by Tourism Queensland in marketing a variety of destinations within Queensland, Australia.

TOURISM QUEENSLAND

Tourism is an important part of the State economy for Queensland Australia, with an overall contribution of tourism to Gross State Product (GSP) of around 10 per cent in 1997. The STO is Tourism Queensland (TQ, previously the Queensland Tourist and Travel Corporation (QTTC)), a Queensland Government-owned enterprise. Its role is defined by an Act of Parliament as 'promotion of Queensland as a Tourist Destination'. As a result of TQ's marketing activity (along with that of tourism operators), Queensland has very strong, positive perceptions in the domestic (Australian) market as a destination offering sun, fun, warmth, activity and friendliness, and has also become a major holiday destination for international holiday visitors. Tourism Queensland uses a variety of tools and techniques to attract potential travellers. These include destination (brand) image, co-operative advertising, PR, consumer promotion (travel shows, shopping centre promotions) and trade promotion (i.e. familiarization tours, etc.). Most recently, an Internet site has been developed. Table 19.1 shows the diversity of visitor origins and their regional dispersion around Queensland. The mix of visitors, their absolute numbers and their activities vary significantly between destinations. These characteristics and others have been used by Tourism Queensland to classify the destinations, as will be discussed later.

TQ makes use of a combination of push-and-pull strategies to maximize its distribution channel investments, all based around the concept of branding. Woodward (2000, p. 119) notes that the choice of push-and-pull strategies, or a combination of both, has implications for supply and demand and the organization's approaches to branding. Sheldon (1993) discusses the three traditional forms of destination information distribution common to National Tourism Offices (NTOs), brochures and guide books mailed to intending visitors, usually in response to queries or advertisements, through their network of visitor information centres (VICs) in key domestic origin markets, and through offices in the country's major foreign markets. (STOs follow similar patterns of information distribution.) But travel agents play a crucial role in the tourism distribution channel, and are a predominant intermediary between travellers

Table 19.1 National Visitor Survey and International Visitor Survey 1998 for Tourism Queensland

	Gold Coast	Tropical North Qld	Sunshine Coast	Hervey Bay	Bundaberg	Outback
Visitors by origin:						
Domestic ('000)	3,150	1,164	2,400	1,066	549	737
Interstate (%)	69	58	48	28	24	25
Intrastate (%)	31	42	52	72	76	75
Activities (% of visitors)						
Go to the beach	56	37	63	34	20	4
Eat out/restaurants	35	23	31	15	18	19
Visit friends and relatives	33	30	35	42	35	17
Go shopping (pleasure)	30	18	21	13	11	5
Walk around/sightseeing	26	27	24	18	20	18
Visit amusements/theme parks	22	1	6	1	1	—
Visit casinos	17	6	—	—	—	—
Pubs/clubs/discos	16	12	12	11	8	8
Visit natural parks, walking	9	26	18	16	11	6
Go fishing	4	18	12	21	14	8
Attend performance arts	3	1	—	2	—	2
International Visitors (000's)	855.9	704.2	180.2	158	37	34

and travel suppliers, like airlines and hotels and destination authorities (Snepenger *et al.*, 1990). The travel agent, as the main intermediary, is the final link between customers and suppliers of various tourism goods and services. One of the important roles travel agencies play is that they are also counsellors who try to promote the efficiency and the quality of the various travel products (Gee and Fayos-Sola, 1997). Travel agents' own advertising is one of the determinants in consumers' decision-making (Raaij, 1986). In effect, they push customers through the distribution channel, complementing and leveraging the pull of the destination's own promotional efforts. Dann (1977, p. 168) following a different usage of the phrase, explains that push factors are those that provide the impetus for individuals to travel, raising the question of where to go. 'Pull factors are the destination specific attributes which tend to determine whether the traveller will go to A or to B.'

DISTRIBUTION – QUEENSLAND TRAVEL CENTRES AND SUNLOVER

TQ is unusual in Australia in that it also operates several retail travel outlets (Queensland Travel Centres) and owns a large wholesale operation (Sunlover

Holidays). Sunlover Holidays is the self-funding wholesale arm of TQ and the largest land-based (accommodation/tours only) wholesaler of Queensland holiday product in Australia. The Sunlover range includes more than 3800 Queensland tourism products from more than 800 operators. These products are distributed through a network of ten Queensland Government Travel Centres around Australia, providing information and booking services to the public, as well as by over 5000 travel agencies in Australia and New Zealand. Both Sunlover and the Queensland Travel Centres can be thought of as tools, each having a particular function. The company provides a wider variety of Queensland product on the brochure racks of Australian travel agents. Additionally, it provides a means of ensuring the distinctive Queensland brands are communicated both to retail agents and the end consumer through a variety of marketing media. Sunlover has achieved a substantial share of the wholesale market for Queensland tourism product within Australia. It has in the process developed the well-known trade brand 'Sunlover Holidays' synonymous with Queensland and its destinations. It operates by developing packaged holidays and distributing this product through retail travel agents. In order to facilitate these sales, the wholesale department operates an online computer-based reservation system and supports this with an Agents Reservation Centre that provides telephone support and electronic distribution of product. Woodward (2000, p. 126) notes that Sunlover 'had the highest brand equity score amongst travel agents but only 53% of end consumers were aware of this brand consequently, this brand needs the middle person in the chain to maintain its sales'.

In the late 1990s the evolution of the New Zealand market and the development of regional destinations within Queensland such as Tropical North Queensland (TNQ) provided the impetus for TQ to re-examine the methods of distribution of tourism product in that country. While previously the product was distributed through wholesale operators, thereafter the product was available to travel agents direct through access to the computer reservation system described above. A strategic analysis of the needs of destination marketing led to the adjustment of the distribution channels in a manner that was of significant benefit to the many destinations within Queensland. Sunlover expanded its distribution into New Zealand in order to expand the range of travel product available to the New Zealand retail distribution system and in the process provided brochure material focused on 'new' destinations within Queensland, especially Tropical North Queensland. In these terms, then, the sales and distribution channels for travel become channels for the STO to achieve destination objectives.

TOURISM DESTINATION SYSTEM FRAMEWORK USES

The tourism destination system framework presented in Figure 19.1 provides a conceptual framework for examining the whole process involved in influencing potential travellers. By recognizing that tourism involves a series of interconnected elements it is possible to 'granulate' the role of an STO into functions that concentrate on influential steps of the consumer decision process. It also allows the stakeholders in each relevant sub-system to be identified and opportunities for collaboration to be found. By understanding each step it is possible to identify priority areas along the distribution chain and determine the functions and resources necessary to achieve objectives. In grouping STO activities by elements and assessing expenditure amounts for each as indicated in Table 19.2, STOs are also better able to measure the effectiveness of each of the activities engaged in and then review the contributions of these activities on overall outcomes. Table 19.2 provides a pro forma for comparing expenditure on various activities with overall tourism system expenditures, determining the contribution made to each activity and element in the overall tourism. The higher the proportion an STO contributes, the more that activity would be expected to be a critical function of an STO and overall tourism system. Such an analysis will not only facilitate STOs in identifying their most important roles, but could also reveal possible needs for expenditure re-allocation to other activities as critical points change over time. Use of a tourism system analysis pro forma as shown in Table 19.2 provides a framework for benchmarking and comparison between similar systems. While each tourism system is expected to contain the elements indicated in Figure 19.1, the actual activities undertaken may vary.

Table 19.2 Pro forma, tourism system financial contribution analysis

Element	Function	State Tourism Office $s	Tourism System $s	STO Contribution %
Promotion	Familiarization tours	e.g. 23m	e.g. 68m	e.g. 33%
	Press advertorials			
	Co-operative marketing programme development			
	Destination image development			
Distribution	Product development			
	Retail activities			
	Wholesale activities			
Transportation	Airline proposals			
Destination	Planning & development			
	Hospitality programmes			
Stakeholders	Co-operative marketing activities			
	Government co-ordination			
Planning, Policy and Research	Development of tourism development plans/strategies			

DEVELOPED AND EMERGING TOURIST DESTINATIONS IN QUEENSLAND

Queensland is unique in Australia in that it has five developed tourist destinations as well as a number of emerging destinations (Table 19.3). This is evidenced by a very high proportion of tourism visitation in Queensland taking place in non-capital city areas compared to other States. TQ categorizes regional destinations into two types, developed and emerging, based on the characteristics of their tourism features. Table 19.4 shows, for each of the tourism destination system elements, the differences between developed and emerging regions. An audit of a destination system can readily identify distinct differences between destinations for each element. Destinations within Queensland such as the Gold Coast or Tropical North Queensland are widely recognized as 'sun and sand' destinations. They are well represented domestically in wholesale brochures and on travel agents' shelves. A high proportion of domestic visitors travel exclusively to the Gold Coast on their trip, and repeat visitation is high. Internationally, a growing number of wholesalers feature the Gold Coast in their programmes.

The Gold Coast has extensive international and domestic air linkages and access by road and rail. There is a wide range of accommodation and a number of large man-made theme parks as well as the beach and hinterland natural attractions. The Gold Coast is also host to a number of large events such as Indy Car races. Surveys show that visitor perception of the standard of service in the destination is high. There is significant public infrastructure for tourist usage, from parks and gardens to visitor information centres, patrolled beaches, public malls, etc. In comparison, emerging regions have little recognition and less well-developed images. Few travel agents or wholesalers stock their tourism product. Transport links are less extensive and these areas, mainly in the Outback, offer

Table 19.3 Developed and developing destinations in Queensland

Developed destinations	Emerging
Gold Coast	Townsville
Sunshine Coast	Toowoomba and the Golden West
Tropical North Queensland	Southern Downs
The Whitsundays	Gladstone
Brisbane	Capricorn
	The Outback
	Fraser Coast-South Burnett
	Bundaberg
	Mackay

Table 19.4 Developed and developing tourism system elements contrasted

Tourism System element	Developed destination	Emerging
Destination awareness	International – moderate Interstate – moderate-high Local – high	International – low Interstate – low Local – moderate
Destination image (of those aware)	Attractive as a tourist destination	Not attractive as a tourist destination
Intention to travel	Moderate-high	Low
Purchase facilitation		
• Retail	Developed	Low
• Wholesale	Developed	Low
Transportation links	High capacity High variety Often mono-destination trip	Low capacity Low variety Often part of multi-destination trip
Destination		
• Accommodation	High capacity and variety	Low capacity and variety
• Attractions	Competitive range	Few small attractions
• Events	Numerous	Few small events
• Hospitality	High standards	Low standards
• Infrastructure	Complex	Simple

limited accommodation and few developed attractions. In general, the focus for a developed destination is promotion while in a developing destination the focus is on product development. The appropriate strategy is based on both a sound knowledge of consumer motivations (pull factors) and industry resources (push factors). Queensland's developed destinations have undergone a branding process to improve the consistency of communication messages. Similarly, comprehensive plans have been prepared for each of the emerging regions of Queensland to facilitate the development of their tourism infrastructure.

USING THE TOURISM SYSTEMS FRAMEWORK – A TROPICAL NORTH QUEENSLAND CASE STUDY

One distinguishing characteristic of the developed destinations listed above is that a large proportion of visitors are mono-destination travellers. In practical terms this means that travellers see the destination either as their only destination or as their most important destination (for touring travellers). The successful development of TNQ over the past fifteen years, especially the introduction of an international airport, has led to a destination with a number of five-star hotels and sophisticated tours based on natural attractions. The presence of these developed facilities indicates that TNQ has a number of geographically defined markets including interstate and international travellers. In addition, they act as pull factors in the distribution system by undertaking their own promotional activities. The existence of these facilities characterizes TNQ as a developed destination. However, Cairns is a three-hour flight from its main domestic source markets of Sydney and Melbourne and research shows that for many people in these markets it is still considered remote. The geographical distance and lack of familiarity of potential travellers with the destination reinforces the need for an attractive and easily communicated destination image.

TNQ has developed its image on proximity to the Great Barrier Reef and the World Heritage-listed Daintree rainforest. The process of image development involved identification of a target market, marketing objectives, destination position and development of a creative execution for the advertisement(s). Here the destination image has been chosen to increase its potential to attract visitors. The tangible marketing expression of this image includes television, newspaper and radio advertising, emphasis of specific destination features or operators in trade and media familiarization tours and development of creative linkages to individual operator advertising.

In developing this suite of marketing materials, the aim is to communicate to the potential visitor the destination image for TNQ and to reinforce this at many stages along the decision-making process. In developing the marketing programme and reviewing the target markets, it became apparent that the New Zealand consumer had similar characteristics and could be treated similarly to the Australian interstate market. They had approximately the same distance to travel, benefits sought from the holiday, awareness and image of TNQ, and also spoke English. However, it was also clear that the tourism distribution systems in New Zealand did not reflect this consumer perspective. Instead New Zealand distribution channels treated TNQ as a typical international destination, including only limited product in wholesaling programmes. This led in part to the decision to expand Sunlover distribution into New Zealand, described above.

CONCLUSION

This chapter has provided an overview of a tourism destination system. The use of this in practical terms has been illustrated by reference to TQ. The framework developed in this chapter provides a useful way of visualizing the process of distributing information and influencing the consumer in relation to the visitor travel process from origin-based information collection to post-trip evaluation.

A number of topics for further research present themselves. These include the relationship between specific operator marketing and choice of distribution channels and the impact of new distribution techniques such as the Internet on the tourism distribution system.

This chapter has taken a strategic perspective on the issue of tourism distribution channels. It has described the travel distribution system in terms of its usefulness to an STO. Tourism distribution systems look different and have different uses, depending on the viewer and their particular perspective and objectives. From the viewpoint of an STO, travel distribution channels are a means to an end, not an end in themselves. They are a way of communicating destination image and information and as a result making bookings to the STO's destination.

REFERENCES

Dann, G. M. S. (1977) 'Anomie, ego-enhancement and tourism'. *Annals of Tourism Research*, **4**, 184–94.

Dyer, J. and Singh, H. (1998) 'The relational view: co-operative strategy and sources of interorganizational competitive advantage'. *Academy of Management Review*, **23**(4), 660–79.

Faulkner, B. (2000) *'The Future Ain't What It Used To Be': Coping with change, turbulence and disasters in tourism research and destination management*. Griffith University, Gold Coast.

Faulkner, B. and Russell, R. (1997) 'Chaos and complexity in tourism: in search of a new perspective'. *Pacific Tourism Review*, **1**, 93–102.

Freeman, R. (1984) *Strategic Management: A stakeholder perspective*. Pitman, Boston.

Gee, C. and Fayos-Sola, E. (1997) 'Travel distribution systems'. In *International Tourism: A Global Perspective*. World Tourism Organization, Madrid, pp. 95–116.

Getz, D. (1986) 'Models in tourism planning: towards integration of theory and practice'. *Tourism Management*, **7**(1), 21–32.

Go, F. M. and Williams, A. P. (1993) 'Competing and co-operating in the changing Tourism Channel System'. *Journal of Travel and Tourism Marketing*, **2**(2/3), 229–48.

Klomp, N. and Green, D. (1997) *Complexity and Connectivity in Ecosystems*. Paper presented at the Third Australian National Conference on Complex Systems, Albury (cited in McKercher, 1999).

Kotler, P., Haider, D. H. and Rein, I. (1993) *Marketing Places*. Free Press, New York.

Laws, E. (1995) *Tourist Destination Management: Issues, Analysis and Policies*. Routledge, London.

McKercher, B. (1999) 'A chaos approach to tourism'. *Tourism Management*, **20**, 425–34.

Mill, R. C. and Morrison, A. M. (1985) *The Tourism System: An introductory text.* Prentice Hall International, Englewood Cliffs, New Jersey.

Rossiter, J. R. and Percy, L. (1996) *Advertising Communication and Promotion Management.* McGraw-Hill, Sydney.

Sautter, E. T. and Leisen, B. (1999) 'Managing stakeholders: a tourism planning model approach'. *Annals of Tourism Research*, **26** (July), 312–28.

Selin, S. W. (1993) 'Collaborative alliances: new interorganizational forms in tourism'. *Journal of Travel and Tourism Marketing*, **2**(2/3), 217–27.

Sheldon, P. (1993) 'Destination information systems'. *Annals of Tourism Research*, **20**(4), 633–49.

Sheldon, P. (1997) *Tourism Information Technology.* CAB International, Wallingford.

Snepenger, D., Meged, K., Snelling, M. and Worrall, K. (1990) 'Information search strategies by destination-naïve tourists'. *Journal of Travel Research*, **29**(2), 13–16.

Van Raaij, W. F. (1986) 'Consumer research on tourism mental and behavioural constructs'. *Annals of Tourism Research*, **13**, 1–9.

Woodward, T. (2000) 'The comparative measurement of the brands of tourism destinations'. Tourism Queensland, Brisbane (unpublished report).

PART 4

Transformation in tourism distribution

CHAPTER 20

Transformation and trends in the tourism industry: implications for distribution channels

Chris Cooper and Jan Lewis

INTRODUCTION: DISTRIBUTION CHANNELS AND THE TOURISM SECTOR

Once the Cinderella of the marketing mix – unglamorous but essential – distribution is now seen as central to many economic sectors. As Kotler *et al.* observe, 'competition, a global marketplace, electronic distribution techniques and a perishable product have increased the importance of distribution' (1999, p. 451). They go on to define a distribution channel as

> a set of independent organisations involved in the process of making a product or service available to the consumer or business user. Development of a distribution system starts with the selection of channel members. Once members have been selected, the focus shifts to managing the channel. Distribution networks in the hospitality industry consist of contractual agreements and loosely organised alliances between independent organisations.

Distribution channels are complex behavioural systems in which people and companies interact to accomplish goals. Rosenbloom (1999) adds to this definition by stating that distribution channels are in turn comprised of negotiations between channel participants (including consumers) who form the distribution channel itself.

In tourism, distribution is a fundamental process serving both the consumer and the disparate elements of the industry – accommodation, tour operators, transport operators, etc. By bringing together these hybrid elements of tourism supply to create products and then marketing those products to the consumer, distribution 'makes markets' (Wanhill, 1998). As distribution is central to the marketing function in tourism it is much more than simply a support to the other elements of the marketing mix. The growing importance of distribution is a result of:

- the need to gain competitive advantage;
- the growing power of intermediaries in the channel;
- the need for suppliers and operators to reduce the costs of distribution; and
- the role of the Internet and technology (Rosenbloom, 1999).

As a result, the tourism sector is seeing new channels emerge and power structures shift. For example, in tourism, in the past, intermediaries were the norm rather than the exception, partly because of the disparate nature of the product, but also because of the physical distance between the consumer and the product. Intermediation comes about through tour operators or wholesalers assembling the components of the tourist trip into a package and retailing the latter through travel agents, who deal directly with the public (Wanhill, 1998). In this way, intermediaries can bring significant benefits to producers, consumers and the tourism destination itself. These benefits may include:

- the transfer of risk from the producer to the intermediary;
- reduction of promotion costs for suppliers and destinations;
- consumers' avoidance of lengthy searches for products; and
- consumers gain from the reduced prices obtained by intermediaries purchasing elements of supply in bulk.

By establishing this link between the demand for and the supply of tourism, distribution channels have to be as efficient and responsive as possible. They are thus vulnerable to both demand-side and supply-side transformations in both the tourism market and beyond. Indeed, throughout the world tourism is undergoing a period of rapid change, partly driven by the processes of globalization, but also galvanized by changing consumer behaviours, and technological innovation such as transportation and computer reservation systems (Cooper and Buhalis, 1998). Underlying these changes is a maturing tourism industry as population growth and demand slows in the countries that have traditionally been the leading generators of tourism. All of these factors mean that the environment for distribution is transforming into one that is ever more complex. This chapter draws together these transformations and trends, and examines their impact upon tourism distribution channels.

TOURISM TRANSFORMATION TRENDS AND THEIR IMPLICATIONS FOR DISTRIBUTION CHANNELS

There is a variety of converging transformations impacting upon those who make decisions about distribution strategy and tactics in tourism. These decision-makers include those responsible for marketing in all sectors of the tourism industry as well as those managing tour operators, travel agencies and reservation systems. For this group, an awareness of the changing environment is an essential part of management. Macro-environmental transformations (demographic, economic, technological, political, legal, social and cultural) as well as micro-environmental transformations (customers, competitors, distribution channels, suppliers) that may impact upon a channel need to be monitored as both potential threats and opportunities. Yet, 'travel information managers find it difficult to stay abreast of the rapid growth in the travel industry and the changing needs and conveyances of information for the travelling public' (McGann, 1999). Technological changes have been so rapid that many managers who are accomplished at 'environmental scanning and strategic visioning skills are hard-pressed to make sense of the complex world that their organisations now inhabit' (Kauffman, 1999). For example, the emergence of the Internet as an electronic channel has forced many managers to rethink their distribution strategy as business-to-business (B2B) transactions emerge. For the purposes of this chapter we have classified the key environmental transformations into demand side and supply side.

DEMAND-SIDE TRANSFORMATIONS

Distribution strategy closely reflects the needs of the target market, which includes market geography such as demographics and spatial distribution. The changing nature of the tourism market, and in particular changing patterns of consumer behaviour, are strongly influencing distribution channels in the leading tourism-generating markets. There are a number of general transformations in society here that impact upon tourism markets and their geography:

- Increasing racial and cultural diversity impacts upon the distribution of tourism products through the desire for these market segments to have their own services and distribution channels, which in turn can pass on large discounts to ethnic communities.
- Increasing cultural awareness and recognition of cultural diversity has spurred some travellers to move off the beaten path in search of authentic experiences, often in remote areas and has resulted in the emergence of a new type of tourist who seeks a more adventurous, interactive and unique travel experience.
- Changing family structures and lifestyles, including larger numbers of single-person households, larger numbers of single-parent families and the changing role of women, each affect purchasing behaviour. Changing lifestyles may boost the use of alternative, home-based channels such as the Internet, TV and home shopping. The increased use of technology in homes has both positive and negative implications for travel distribution channels and is discussed in greater detail later in this chapter.

- Increased penetration of technology in the home means that the use of the personal computer has moved from its original primary function of allowing work from home for parents, to use by the whole family as a leisure interest. Connection to the Internet has allowed families to access topical information at the click of a mouse.
- The populations of most of the leading tourism-generating countries are ageing but are less technologically able than their children and, being more conservative, will thus have less of an impact on distribution channels.
- In many countries – such as the USA and Australia – there is evidence of a population movement to the sunbelt, from rural to urban locations and from the cities to the suburbs. Clearly these population shifts have significant implications for the location of retail outlets and distribution points of sale.

Woven through these transformations are also shifts in values and culture underpinning many consumer behaviour decisions. In tourism in particular we have seen a transformation in consumer behaviour in the last quarter of the twentieth century leading to what Poon (1993) has termed the *new tourist* (see also Buhalis, 2000). Figure 20.1 illustrates the characteristics of the new tourist's consumer behaviour. One implication of this transformation of consumer behaviour is the need for tourism marketers to have a very clear view of their target market. The following are examples of key markets and their implications for distribution:

The leisure market

- **The seniors/mature market** (born before 1946)   Almost half of the discretionary income in the USA ($600 billion) belongs to those in the over 55 year age group (Kotler *et al.*, 1999, p. 188). Most of this group is fit and healthy with many of the same needs and wants as younger people. They have worked hard at their jobs and are now active, energetic, happy and hopeful senior citizens. Even those with special needs are happy to travel providing that their needs can be met. As noted above, their use of distribution channels is traditional but increasingly they will seek points of sale that offer personalized services and a social connection.
- **The baby boomers** (born 1946–1964)   This group has enormous implications for tourist providers and they comprise over 4 million people in the USA alone. It is seen as the most self-absorbed generation with relatively high levels of education and income that implies emphasis on quality and value (Sheth *et al.*, 1999). Increased leisure time coupled with high disposable incomes are a feature of this group who will consume more leisure services than any other demographic group in history. The older members of the baby boomers are entering the empty nest stage of the family life-cycle. Consequently, they will have more free time and money to spend on themselves. The baby boomers

- They demand better service.
- They are better educated and may seek products that have an element of education and information – sometimes known as *edutainment*.
- They are more environmentally aware and may seek out 'green' tour operators, accommodation and destinations.
- They have greater mobility.
- Women have control of more disposable income.
- They are prepared to spend more of their disposable income on travel.
- They are more critical and more likely to express their dissatisfaction.
- They engage in more comparison shopping when price is an issue.
- They take shorter vacations with a shorter planning horizon.
- They demand products that are more activity-based than passive.
- They want individualized tourism packages, resulting in a more segmented market.
- They seek value for money including the time spent in planning and travelling.
- Thus, they may fall into more than one pre-defined market segment.

Figure 20.1 Characteristics of the new tourist's consumer behaviour

are also *adventure travellers* (Beresford *et al.*, 1995, p. 2) who are increasingly using outdoor active recreation facilities in the USA. For example, the American Recreational Vehicle Industry Association predicts a large increase in the purchase of recreational vehicles and use of camping grounds for baby boomers, who like to camp in comfort. Distribution of tourism products to this group will tend to be through more conventional outlets rather than through the use of new technologies. Personal service may be more important to baby boomers than information obtained from an impersonal source.

- **Generation X** (born 1965–1976) Generation Xers vary from students to young executives. They have been described as 'more multicultural, media-savvy, tech-oriented, and cynical about their future than baby boomers' (Assael, 1998, p. 392). While their individual buying power is small, as a group they have large amounts to spend and they spend it all. Saving for the future is not their goal (Sheth *et al.* 1999). This is the first technological generation that has been brought up with computers. They are the most likely group to use the Internet to make reservations and purchases and to drive through changes in distribution patterns from a consumer point of view. This group, when of university age, form the growing backpacker market and make use of some organized tours, especially in Europe where the aim may be to see as many countries as possible in the shortest period of time.
- **Generation Y** (born after 1978) This group are the children of the baby boomers and they are influential in family vacation decisions. They have grown up with the use of both the Internet and multimedia entertainment and have

become the most sophisticated generation – possibly more knowledgeable, materialistic and self-confident than their parents. They have been termed the *dot com generation* and will be the group that reinforces the changes in consumer use of distribution channels, begun by their parents.

The business market

In 1997, in the largest segment of American hotels, the business traveller, reservations were personally made by over 60 per cent of business people – 'Toll free numbers are very important to business travellers' (Kotler *et al.*, 1999, p. 257). Whilst corporate business travel departments may view the Internet as a means of cutting out intermediaries, the time spent obtaining fares and information by the corporate traveller may be more costly than using an intermediary. Vellas and Bécherel (1999, p. 114) quote Charles Schwab's estimate of $55 to $60 of company time spent planning and booking a business trip with an inhouse travel agent. In comparison, use of the Internet is expected to reduce the cost to around $18. This fails to take into account the time that travellers may spend seeking out information that may not be entirely relevant to the trip but was found as an interesting link from another site. Similarly, there are those in corporations who are not especially computer-literate and they will thus spend longer on the Internet to obtain the relevant information. Even then, they may still feel the need to seek advice from an associate or a travel agent before making the purchase.

SUPPLY-SIDE TRANSFORMATIONS

A variety of supply-side transformations affect distribution decisions in tourism. These include:

* the legal and political environment,
* destinations, small to medium-sized enterprises (SMEs) and sustainability and
* technology.

The legal and political environment

Globalization is reinforcing the contradictory trends of borderless trade, whilst restrictive trade blocs are being established (for example the EU, NAFTA and ASEAN) (Wahab and Cooper, 2000). Generally, however, both within and between these mega-markets, barriers to entry are being reduced. For distribution channels this allows organizations to acquire channels internationally, or more problematically to establish their own channels overseas. This can be difficult because trade practices and consumer behaviour vary nationally and a tour operator who has been successful in say, a British environment, may find operation in another European country difficult.

In the past too, the tourism industry was highly regulated, with governments determining price levels and in the case of the transport industry in particular, routes and timetables. This acted as a major constraint upon distribution channels as the geographical scope of distribution was constrained. With the political trend towards deregulation these constraints have been removed. However, as products become more complex, so the need for consumer legislation increases. The nature of the tourism product, and the risks involved in intermediation, have meant that tourism has attracted considerable consumer legislation (such as the European Union's Package Travel Directive that applies to intermediaries (Cooper *et al.*, 1998, p. 261)). The legal environment within which channels operate is continually evolving and increasingly applies to participants in the channel – examination in the UK, for example, of monopoly situations between tour operator and travel agencies is a case in point here.

Destinations, SMEs and sustainability

In most destinations, the 'primary' tourism suppliers who are seeking to distribute their products to the market – such as accommodation, food and beverage outlets and transport firms – are small to medium enterprises (SMEs) ranging from one-person operations up to medium-sized companies. Here there is a real issue for destinations in terms of co-operative distribution where destinations encourage not 'competition' between operators but 'co-opetiton' (Buhalis and Cooper, 1998). Effectively this means that all those in the destination's value chain should work together for the destination in a business-to-business approach rather than setting up competing channels (see, for example, Cooper and Wahab, 2000). This also allows for all those in the value chain to respond to demands for environmental accountability at the level of the destination as intermediaries begin to realize the importance of investing in destinations rather than simply exploiting them (see, for example, the initiatives of the Centre for Environmentally Responsible Tourism, 2000).

However, whilst it is increasingly accepted that destinations will transform from an adversarial type of competition in the distribution channel to this more cooperative model (Crotts and Wilson, 1995), they do have to compete with global players. Indeed, destinations criticize the strength of the economic buying power of large tour operators, allowing them to purchase beds at prices below those that would occur in markets where competition prevails. These large tour operators have the specialist knowledge that allows them to influence consumer behaviour and switch sales to destinations that are more profitable to the company. One option for local operators to compete with global players is to produce tailor-made packages and market directly to clients using the Internet. However, regional operators who work together to market tourism often do not have the Internet facilities available to make direct bookings through their website, nor often do they have the knowledge or expertise to utilize the

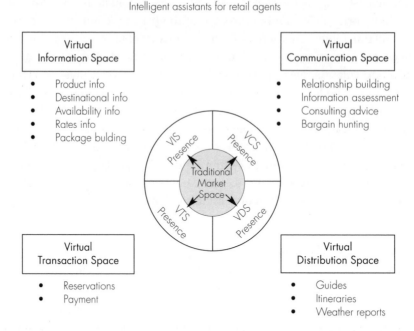

Figure 20.2 Classification of market space into four further spaces. *Source*: Angehrn, 1997

emerging technology. Additionally, they are isolated from the transport arrangements needed by travellers to reach the destination area. Hence we will see regional destinations forming co-operative agreements with conventional travel agents, virtual travel agents or directly with transport suppliers. This will give their destination a position on global electronic distribution systems and open up the destination to many more potential tourists.

Technology

Technology is radically transforming the way that organizations engage with their customers (Lovelock and Wright, 1999). Indeed, Judge (1998) classifies consumer behaviour according to ability and willingness to use technology – a technographic approach to segmentation. In any discussion of the impact of environmental transformations upon distribution strategy it is impossible to ignore the role of technology, and in particular the use of the Internet and its successors as electronic marketing channels. Rosenbloom (1999, p. 451) neatly sums up the concept of electronic distribution as: 'the use of the Internet to make products and services available so that the target market with access to computers or other enabling technologies can shop and complete the transaction for purchase via interactive electronic means'. In effect we are seeing the adoption of a concept of *market space* rather than *marketplace*, providing consumers with more choice as to how they deal with an organization (Lovelock and Wright, 1999).

As Figure 20.2 shows, Angehrn (1997) classifies this *market space* into four further spaces, namely:

- information
- communication
- distribution
- transaction.

This *ICDT* model is useful as it opens up the debate as to whether electronic intermediaries can replace the traditional competencies of travel agents and tour operators in each of the four spaces. In other words, will electronic distribution channels become more efficient than conventional channels? Whilst some argue that the Internet cannot be efficient in each of the four *ICDT* spaces, there is much to commend the Internet as an efficient channel. As illustrated in Figure 20.3, the Internet provides several advantages and disadvantages.

The general points raised in Figure 20.3 are supported by tourism data – in a survey undertaken by Weber and Roehl (1999, p. 299), problems associated with use of the Internet for purchases included:

Credit card security	77.8%
No assessment of product quality	76.0%
Privacy issues	57.7%
Prefer to make local purchases	41.3%
Unfamiliar vendors	37.5%

However, even given these issues, there is no doubt that the Internet can link suppliers directly with consumers. Some argue that this means intermediaries are redundant in the channel, leading to a process of *disintermediation*. This is particularly an issue for tourism where the flow in the channel is of information rather than tangible products. 'Information that was previously available only to travel agents is now open to everyone, and business and vacation travellers can now do much more to take charge of their own travel' (Schley, 1997). 'Booking travel accommodation is a good fit for the Internet because travel is an information-based product – and the Internet is an information medium' (Connolly *et al.*, 1998).

Growth in the usage of the Internet has been accompanied with growth in e-commerce, with travel being one of the fastest growing areas. However, it should be remembered that 80 per cent of Internet traffic ends up at only 0.5 per cent (around 15,000) of all URLs (Tchong, 2000). The estimated size of the Internet economy in 1999 was $507 billion and is expected to rise to $1.2 trillion by 2003 (the Internet economy includes computer hardware and software, online retailers and brokers and other Web-related business and has been termed *the seventh continent*).

Advantages of the Internet	Disadvantages of the Internet
• Gives global scope and reach • Can be used anytime and anywhere • Facilitates tangibility of the tourism product through transmission of colour images • Allows arm's-length transactions • Allows suppliers to control the contact with the consumer • Provides convenient and rapid transactions • Has information processing efficiency and flexibility • Allows database management and relationship capabilities and • Has lower distribution costs	• Web clutter and confusion – information is unstructured, badly organized and takes time and energy to access • It can be slow and awkward • It ignores personal motivations and • It requires security when purchasing

Figure 20.3 Advantages and disadvantages of the Internet as a distribution mechanism. *Source*: Rosenbloom, 1999

In terms of users, Internet travel purchasers are usually between 26 and 55 years of age (Weber and Roehl, 1999), have high incomes, are employed in managerial, professional or computer-related occupations and are experienced online users. However, it should be noted that there is no gender gap in either travel information search or purchase. In the USA an increasing number of frequent travellers book online. However, for the less experienced traveller the trend is to use the Internet to research their travel needs and then to purchase offline, supporting the notion of the need for *re-intermediation* (TIAA, 2000). These consumers are seeking more information concerning travel options and destination information and the virtual travel agent must satisfy this need either through massive data warehouses or through links to other sites. The latter option is risky for the travel agent, as once a consumer leaves the agent's site they may not come back and, consequently, a sale may be lost. Additionally, an information overload may deter consumers from revisiting a site.

There is no doubt that tourism enterprises that do not have a presence on the Web will face difficult times in the twenty-first century and risk reduced profitability and acquisition by larger firms seeking new databases. Here, co-operative partnerships with other established online firms in the channel help to deliver increased efficiency, reduced costs and new markets, as discussed later in this chapter (Tweeney, 1997). For example, the introduction of new technologies has enabled travel agents to be more time efficient and gain faster access to information such as current room rates and accessibility (Connolly *et al.*, 1998). Global Distribution Systems (GDSs) will continue to focus on supplying information technology services to airlines but are increasingly transforming their databases to include descriptions and images of destinations for all leisure segments, especially tours and cruises.

Of course the Internet is not the first technological innovation to transform distribution in tourism. Computerized Reservations Systems (CRSs) and Global Distribution Channels (GDSs) such as ABACUS, Galileo and SABRE were partly responsible for 'drawing the travel industry into the age of automation and IT' (TravelAsia, 1999, p. 1). The application of multimedia format and 'virtual reality' to tourism websites has placed these sites at the forefront of technological development. Usage of the World Wide Web by tourism operators is transforming the tourism distribution system, with information and communication technology driving these changes. Rosenbloom (1999) suggests that at the end of the day it will be efficiency in the distribution channel that will decide the future. In fact we may begin to see the re-emergence of intermediaries to support the electronic channel through a process of *re-intermediation* as consumers despair of the ability of the Internet to deliver structured, quality and reliable information.

This raises the question as to the response of the intermediaries to the new opportunities created by technology. Returning to Angehrn's (1997) *ICDT* model of market space, O'Brien (1999) argues that travel agents must reposition themselves if they are to survive in the twenty-first century. Whilst electronic distribution may be able to replace the three market spaces of information, distribution and transaction, agents can reposition their role to capitalize on the communication element of market space. Here, O'Brien sees the agent as an information broker, making sense of web clutter, and acting as a consultant to the new tourist. In other words, the agent must build relationships with their customers, add value and recognize the transforming nature of the distribution process. In tourism, whoever controls information in the channel, controls the channel.

THE RESPONSE OF TRADITIONAL
TOURISM DISTRIBUTION CHANNELS

Traditional tourism distribution channels were loosely arranged collections of organizations and individuals. These channels and their participants have responded in three important ways to the transformational pressures identified in this chapter. These responses are:

- mergers and the formation of strategic alliances;

- channel re-organization; and
- the changing role of distribution in the marketing mix.

Alliances and partnerships

One of the consequences of globalization for tourism distribution is the opportunity to work with other channel members to gain competitive advantage. Dyer and Singh (1988) provide a useful checklist of the determinants of competitiveness for such alliances and partnerships:

- relation-specific assets – matching specific assets between organizations to gain competitive advantage;
- knowledge-sharing routines and inter-organization communication;
- complementary resources and capabilities. The integration strategies of tourism companies are clearly evident here in the restructuring of global distribution channels; and
- effective governance – a final critical area in terms of the management of the relationship and the value chain, and one where tourism is lagging behind other sectors.

Here, the concept of the value chain is pivotal. Traditionally the value chain has been seen as one in which each organization maximizes its own success. In this traditional model, information, strategies and resources are not shared and the chain is inefficient (Ashkenas *et al.*, 1995). However, in a globalized society the value chain represents the process by which organizations and enterprises are linked together to create products and services that have more value *combined* than *separate* (Ashkenas *et al.*, 1995). In other words, organizations look outside their own boundaries and aim to strengthen the whole web, not simply their own part of it. This concept has triggered a new way of thinking in the tourism distribution channel as individual tourism businesses, intermediaries and tourists cease to be adversarial in the channel and move to a more co-operative model where, for example, intermediaries will invest in destinations (Crotts and Wilson, 1995). This is a logical strategy given that intermediaries ultimately depend upon destinations for their product creation – in other words the recognized strategic focus should be in the value-creating system where all those involved work to co-produce value (Normann and Ramirez, 1993). The forging of alliances and partnerships demands that organizations go through a particular process of strategy development, partner search, negotiation and alliance operation (Pekar and Allio, 1994; Crotts and Wilson, 1995).

Channel re-organization

Inevitably as new channels develop in response to the forces identified in this chapter, channel competition will develop and companies need strategies to deal with this. *Intertype channel competition* occurs when a new form of channel overtakes a traditional form of channel. An example here is the emergence of the *virtual travel agent* to compete with the retail agent. In the USA these virtual travel agents include *Travelocity, Expedia, Preview Travel* and *ITN*. Some sites are used to promote last-minute discount purchases, backfill fares and ticket auctions (such as *lastminute.com* and *travel.com.au*). Others offer a complete travel package including airfares, car rentals, accommodation and ground tours together with destination information. The virtual travel agents are linked to GDS or CRS to access systems containing global information on a 'worldwide-product-set as well as the necessary reliable functionality' (Werthner and Klein, 1999, p. 260). These new entrants into tourism often come from other areas of business such as the media and information, as well as communication technology fields. In contrast, unco-ordinated channels may experience *vertical competition* where members of the channel at different levels compete for business – for example, retail agents find their market share eroded by principals deciding to seek new distribution outlets. Responses to these challenges are as follows:

- **Vertically organized channels** A common response has been to create vertically organized or integrated channels. These are characterized by producers, wholesalers and retailers acting together with a shared goal, and dominated by one channel member who provides leadership to achieve their overall goals and reduce channel conflict (Rosenbloom, 1999). In such a channel each member is at a different level but the integration allows channel members to:
  - gain economies of scale through the linking of complementary activities, investing in new technologies and improved management expertise;
  - manage conflict;
  - share goals;
  - eliminate duplication; and
  - lever bargaining power.

There are a number of ways that these vertically organized channels operate and develop. For example, as Wanhill (1998) notes, the purchase of a travel agent by an airline brings the airline closer to the market and can be seen as forward integration towards the market. In contrast, tour operators may purchase accommodation units as an example of backward integration towards the supplier. Of course, vertically organized channels may achieve integration through ownership, contracting, franchising or developing partners and alliances. One of the main reasons to opt for a *franchising* arrangement is for the increased distribution cover it provides as the service is often delivered through national or global chains (Lovelock and Wright, 1999). In contrast, *alliances* allow access to new markets (exemplified by airline alliances) or diversified locations for sales (travel agents selling ski clothing, for example).

- **Horizontal marketing systems** A contrasting strategy is the development of horizontal marketing systems. Here two or more companies at the same level in the channel pool their capital, production capacity or marketing to gain more than if they were working alone. This was a very common response in the UK intermediaries' market in the 1980s and 1990s, as companies jostled for market share – spatial coverage is a very important driver of this behaviour. Also for intermediaries, horizontal integration strengthens buying power and gives the economies of scale necessary to begin to develop a corporate identity to raise awareness of the company and build loyalty in the channel. Independent intermediaries have responded to these trends by forming loose consortia – in effect their own horizontal marketing system.

In either vertical or horizontal systems, selection of channel members as partners is critical. Choice of partners demands a number of considerations: can they pay their way in terms of the business they bring and are they appropriate to the company's goals and marketing position? (Crotts and Wilson, 1995). Other considerations include the way that partners deal with each other in terms of ethics and social responsibility (Kotler *et al.*, 1999) and increasingly we are seeing broad guidelines for behaviour being developed at the corporate level. This behaviour can be monitored by an auditing procedure.

The changing role of distribution in the marketing mix

Distribution has played something of a *Cinderella* role in the marketing mix. This is no longer the case, however, as the transformational trends, particularly on the demand side, have increased the status of distribution. In terms of gaining competitive edge, distribution channels offer three advantages:

- they require structures,
- they require a long-term commitment and
- they deal with people and relationships.

Distribution is a key element of the marketing mix and thus must conform to the overall market objectives of an organization and the particular positioning of the product in order to attract appropriate targeted market segments. Distribution channels have therefore become much more integrated into the other elements of the marketing mix. For example, price and competition pressure has worked to improve productivity and efficiency in the channel. Integration of distribution with service quality has demanded that distribution becomes much more customer-driven (Lovelock and Wright, 1999), but of course increasing the level of service provided involves intermediaries in a cost that they may recoup through a *fee-for-service* charge. For tourism, distribution channels help to tangibilize the product and the physical and personal setting of the service delivery (such as a travel agent) is important, given also the high level of customer involvement in a tourism purchase. Increasingly distribution is used as a competitive tool, for example by protecting a company's market position by guaranteeing retail outlets and securing supplies in a particular geographical area or market. Distribution strategies are closely linked to the stage of development of either the tourism product or the destination. With maturity, distribution channels become more complex and relationships develop to boost the efficiency of the channel.

Market geography and characteristics are an important consideration for distribution strategy (Rosenbloom, 1999). For example with the increased complexity of target market segmentation, companies use more than one channel to access their market segments – this multi-channel approach also allows a company or destination to spread risk. In tourism, the distance between the market and the product means that intermediaries are commonly used, as noted above. The larger the market the more common the use of intermediaries, whereas for geographically and culturally remote destinations, sales representatives are a more effective distribution channel than travel agents. The smaller the market, or the denser the market, the less intermediaries are needed because the market is easier to reach. Where consumers buy in small quantities it is common to develop long channels with many stages – as in some tourism markets. Where consumer behaviour is a family-driven decision – as in tourism – traditional retail points of sale can influence the purchase decision.

CONCLUSIONS

This chapter has identified a number of key transformational forces that are impacting upon tourism distribution channels in the early years of the twenty-first century. The key forces identified are consumer behaviour and supply-side forces such as technology and the nature of the destination. What is clear is that these forces have transformed the role of distribution from a somewhat unglamorous support to the other elements of the marketing mix into a key competitive tool. In part, this has come about because of the role of technology that allows consumers to interact directly with suppliers and is dramatically transforming ways that business is transacted. We have identified a number of responses to these forces and it remains to be seen just how significant these developments will be in transforming the landscape of intermediaries. What is not in doubt is that the larger the firm, the more power it has and more flexibility in choosing channels. Technology, however, is levelling the playing field allowing small companies and destinations to have global reach and impact in their distribution through the Internet. As distribution channels develop from disorganized, loosely knit collections of organizations into highly efficient integrated channels we will see distribution come of age to meet the challenge of a rapidly maturing tourism sector.

CHRIS COOPER AND JAN LEWIS

REFERENCES

Angehrn, A. (1997) *The Strategic Implications of the Internet*. Proceedings of the 1997 European Conference on Information Systems, University College, Cork, Ireland.
Ashkenas, R., Ulrich, D., Jick, T. and Kerr, S. (1995) *The Boundaryless Organization*. Josey Bass, San Francisco.
Assael, H. (1998) *Consumer Behaviour And Marketing Action* (6th edn). South Western College Publishing, Cincinnati.
Beresford, L., Chun, J., Page, H. and Phillips, D. (1995) 'Looking at the top trends of today and tomorrow'. *Entrepreneur Magazine*, December, pp. 1–14.
Buhalis, D. (2000) 'Globalisation and the new tourist'. In S. Wahab and C. Cooper (eds) *Tourism in the Age of Globalisation*. Routledge, London.
Buhalis, D. and Cooper, C. (1998) 'Competition or co-operation: small and medium sized tourism enterprises at the destination'. In E. Laws, B. Faulkner and G. Moscardo (eds) *Embracing and Managing Change in Tourism*. Routledge, London, pp. 324–46.
Centre for Environmentally Responsible Tourism (2000) http://www.c-e-r-t.org/. Visited 17/03/00.
Connolly, D. J., Olsen, M. D. and Moore, R. G. (1998) 'The Internet as a distribution channel'. *Cornell Hotel & Restaurant Administration Quarterly*, **39**(4), 42–55.
Cooper, C. and Buhalis, D. (1998) 'The future of tourism'. In C. P. Cooper *et al.* (eds) *Tourism Principles And Practice*. Longman, Harlow, pp. 447–63.
Cooper, C. and Wahab, S. (2000) 'Tourism in the age of globalisation'. In S. Wahab and C. Cooper *Tourism in the Age of Globalisation*. Routledge, London.
Cooper, C., Fletcher, J., Gilbert, D., Shepherd, R. and Wanhill, S. (eds) (1998) *Tourism Principles and Practice*. Longman, Harlow.
Crotts, J. C. and Wilson, D. T. (1995) 'An integrated model of buyer–seller relationships in the international travel trade'. *Progress in Tourism and Hospitality Research*, **1**(2), 125–40.
Dyer, J. H. and Singh, H. (1988) 'The relational view: co-operative strategy and sources of inter-organizational competitive advantage'. *Academy of Management Review*, **23**(4), 660–79.
Judge, P. C. (1998) 'Are tech buyers different?'. *Business Week*, 26 January, pp. 64–8.
Kauffman, R. J. (1999) 'Book reviews'. *Electronic Markets*, **9**(4), 284–91.
Kotler, P., Bowen, J. and Makens, J. (1999) *Marketing for Hospitality and Tourism* (2nd edn). Prentice Hall, Englewood Cliffs, New Jersey.
Lovelock, C. and Wright, L. (1999) *Principles of Service Marketing and Management*. Prentice Hall, Englewood Cliffs, New Jersey.
McGann, R. (1999) 'Public-access interactive computers at state welcome centers in the United States: 1991 and 1995 studies'. *Journal of Travel Research*, **37**(3), 249–56.
Normann, R. and Ramirez, R. (1993) 'From value chain to value constellation: designing interactive strategy'. *Harvard Business Review*, July, August, pp. 65–6.
O'Brien, P. F. (1999) 'Intelligent assistants for retail travel agents'. *Information Technology and Tourism*, **2**(3/4), 213–28.
Pekar, P. and Allio, R. (1994) 'Making alliances work – guidelines for success'. *Long Range Planning*, **27**(4), 54–65.
Poon, A. (1993) *Tourism, Technology and Competitive Strategies*. CAB, Wallingford.
Rosenbloom, R. (1999) *Marketing Channels: A Management View* (6th edn). The Dryden Press, Fort Worth.
Schley, R. (1997) 'Travel planning online'. *Futurist*, **31**(6), 12.
Sheth, J. N., Mittal, B. and Newman, B. I. (1999) *Customer Behavior: Consumer Behavior and Beyond*. The Dryden Press, Fort Worth.

330

Tchong, M. (2000) *'Anniversary'* Http://Www.Iconocast.Com/Issue/20000224.Html. Visited 3/03/00.

Travel Industry Association of America (TIAA) (2000) *'Internet Usage by Travelers Continues to Soar'*. http://www.Tia.Org/Press/020800int.Stm. Visited 17/03/00.

TravelAsia. (1999) *'Changing CRS Needs'*, http://www.Travel-Asia.Com/Database/Abacus/ Abacus_Change.Htm. Visited 8/02/00.

Tweeney, D. (1997) 'Making money on the web: what is really working?'. *Infoworld*, **19**(36), 63–8.

Vellas, F. and Bécherel, L. (1999) *The International Marketing of Travel and Tourism: A Strategic Approach*. Macmillan Press, London.

Wahab, S. and Cooper, C. (eds) (2000) *Tourism in the Age of Globalisation*. Routledge, London.

Wanhill, S. R. C. (1998) 'Intermediaries'. In C. P. Cooper *et al.* (eds) *Tourism Principles and Practice*. Longman, Harlow, pp. 247–69.

Weber, K. and Roehl, W. S. (1999) 'Profiling people searching for and purchasing travel products on the World Wide Web'. *Journal of Travel Research*, **37**(3), 291–9.

Werthner, H. and Klein, S. (1999) 'ICT and the changing landscape of global tourism distribution'. *Electronic Markets*, **9**(4), 256–62.

CHAPTER 21

The transformation of tourism distribution channels through information technology

Peter O'Connor, Dimitrios Buhalis and Andrew J. Frew

Technology can act as 'a creator, protector, enhancer, focal point and/or destroyer of the tourism experience' (Stipanuk, 1993). However, technology's greatest impact on tourism is its ability to improve the sale and delivery of goods and services. Distribution, the manner in which companies bring their products to the marketplace, is a cornerstone of any competitive strategy (WTO, 1997). However, understanding the roles that technology plays in tourism distribution can be troublesome. Technology itself is rapidly evolving, and has been identified as one of the top five most volatile factors affecting the sector (Olsen *et al.*, 1995). This chapter examines the effect of these changes on tourism distribution channels and highlights key areas of concern for tourism suppliers.

INFORMATION IN TOURISM DISTRIBUTION

Middleton (1994) proposes that a 'distribution channel is any organised and serviced system, created or utilized to provide convenient points of sale and/or access to consumers, away from the location of production and consumption, and paid for out of marketing budgets'. However, this definition ignores the promotional and market research activities undertaken by channel members while also underestimating the information provision function (Buhalis, 2000). Information is acknowledged to be the 'lifeblood' of tourism, as without the effective distribution of information, the potential customer's incentive and ability to book is severely limited (Wagner, 1991). In few other economic activities are the generation, gathering, processing, application and communication of information as important for day-to-day operations due to the intangibility of the product and the distance between vendors and customers.

Travellers need information before going on a trip to help them plan and choose between options. They also increasingly need information during the trip as the trend towards more independent travel increases. The greater the degree of perceived risk in a pre-purchase context, the greater the consumer propensity to seek information about the product (Buhalis, 1997 and 1998). Particularly with leisure travel, the annual holiday or even the weekend break is increasingly associated with financial and emotional risk as the entire family is involved and it is one of the few times in the year when essential compromises need to be made. In Western society, time has become a scarce commodity, and, particularly for couples, shared time is even more elusive (Muqbil, 1998). Therefore, for many consumers their annual holiday represents a major emotional investment that cannot easily be replaced if something goes wrong (Pollock, 1995). To try to reduce their risk, consumers always choose carefully and seek out as much information as possible in order to make an informed decision and minimize the gap between their expectations and their experience. The growth of the tourism industry and long haul travel has increased the need for further information about places and products. Since they cannot pre-test the product or get their money back easily if the trip does not meet their expectations, access to accurate, timely and relevant information is therefore essential to help people make an appropriate choice.

This need for information is heightened by certain characteristics of the tourism product. Foremost among these is its intangibility: unlike manufactured goods, it cannot be inspected prior to purchase and therefore is almost completely dependent on representations and descriptions to help consumers make a purchase decision (Go and Pine, 1995). It is also fixed geographically, and thus the customer cannot pre-test the product and must travel – and thus in effect consume the product – in order to experience what they are buying (Bennett, 1993). Consumers then are highly dependent upon representations to help them differentiate among competing products, and to help gain an indirect sense of their intangible qualities (Poon, 1994). Two other characteristics are its complexity and its interdependence. Tourism products are diverse, and in many cases it is this heterogeneity that makes them attractive in the first place. They are rarely consumed in isolation, and the endless combinations and permutations of alternative travel routes, transportation modes, time and lodging accommodation make travel decisions difficult even for the initiated consumer (Kaven, 1994). Suppliers, on the other hand, face a challenge, which Kaven has described as trying 'to gain identity with untold millions of potential customers covering the whole spectrum of incomes, interests, knowledge, sophistication and needs'. Tourism products therefore meet the definition proposed an 'information intensive product' (Porter and Millar, 1985) and as a result, fast, efficient exchange of information is critical for effective distribution, sales and customer service (O'Brien, 1999).

Suppliers traditionally provided information to both end-consumers and intermediaries in the form of print-based media, such as brochures or flyers, and through listings published in local or regional guides. However, developing and distributing such promotional material is costly, time-consuming and labour-intensive. Limitations of space mean that difficult choices must be made as to images and copy, and the publication designed to appeal to the widest possible audience (Pollock, 1995). Information included in printed media is, by definition, static, while much of the data needed to make a booking, such as availability and rates, changes frequently, particularly as the reservation date approaches. As a result, consumers usually had to contact suppliers directly to ensure that the product was available and to confirm the rate at which it would be sold (Bennett, 1996). The tourism product is volatile in that if it is not sold on a given night, it represents lost revenue. Therefore, as its 'use-by-date' approaches, information about it tends to change frequently as suppliers adjust prices in an attempt to manipulate demand to ensure that all are sold. Accurate and timely information about availability and rates must therefore be made available instantly over distribution channels to both intermediaries and direct buyers at the right stage in their purchasing process (Strategic Advisory Group, 1997).

INFORMATION IS NOT ENOUGH

Customers or their agents often use traditional channels in combination. To effectively distribute the product requires both an advertising medium (for example, brochures or guidebooks are used to disseminate information to a broad audience), and then an interactive medium (such as, for example, a salesperson or a telesales agent) are needed to process transactions (Kling, 1994). As a result, actually distributing the product takes at least three time-consuming steps, i.e. searching, contacting and finally booking, which is unsatisfactory from everyone's point of view. Suppliers have to maintain large clerical centres to sort mail, type letters, answer telephones and perform other administrative tasks. Even when the shortage of skilled labour is ignored, this results in high costs, and customers experience considerable delays between requesting a reservation and receiving confirmation.

Simply making information available about the product is not sufficient – a mechanism must also be provided that allows the customer to purchase the product (Castleberry et al., 1998). This usually involves both the negotiation of the terms and conditions of the transaction, and settlement, thus resulting in a contract between the two parties (Schmid, 1994). Information therefore also has to be able to flow in the opposite direction, as in order to make a booking, the customer's contact, payment details and preferences have to be sent to the supplier, and thus an effective and efficient method of communication is needed (Frew and Pringle, 1995). The convenience of this phase, i.e. the ease with which the consumer can complete the transaction, is critical, especially when the sale is facilitated through an intermediary, who has an interest in handling the most easily sold products and may well direct clients to competing operators if their product is more easily accessible (Bennett, 1993). In addition, travel products are increasingly being viewed as commodities and consumers are becoming less loyal, and thus the supplier that succeeds in simplifying the reservations process can expect to be rewarded with the highest levels of bookings (Olsen, 1998).

THE ROLE OF INFORMATION TECHNOLOGY

To respond effectively to the dynamic character of the tourism industry, information must be able to flow among the client, intermediaries and each of the suppliers involved in servicing the client's needs. As a result, information technology (IT) – the convergence of computing, communications and electronics – has become an almost universal distribution platform of the tourism industry. IT reduces the cost of each transaction, minimizes print and distribution costs, allows for short notice changes, supports one-to-one interaction with the customer and enables organizations to reach a broad audience (Poon, 1993). The power of IT allows information to be managed more effectively, and transported worldwide almost instantly (Frew and Pringle, 1995). In contrast to static media such as print, an IT-based system can incorporate such dynamic data as room inventory, has no capacity limitations and has a low marginal cost. In addition, it provides infinitely more reach, which is becoming increasingly important given the global nature of the marketplace. Customers are becoming more sophisticated in how they shop with the aid of new technologies. They want instant access to price and product comparison information about any product or service that they wish to purchase and routinely expect such information to be available electronically (Vaughan *et al.*, 1999). The Internet also allows travellers to undertake reservations in a fraction of the time, cost and inconvenience inherent in traditional methods (Buhalis, 1998). As a result, IT is helping to change the way in which customers look for information and how they purchase travel goods and services (Connell and Reynolds, 1999).

Information technology has not affected all sectors equally. Certain sectors, such as the airlines, have been keen adopters of technology, using it to help manage and streamline their operations and to gain strategic advantage (McGuffie, 1994). Others, in particular the hotel sector, have been less enthusiastic, and have only recently begun to take advantage of many of the benefits which technology can bring (Connolly and Olsen, 1999). Many traditional travel agencies are still lagging behind in technological adaptation and it is increasingly evident that experienced consumers are often better informed than professional advisers. However, given the way in which information technology is reshaping the basic structure of both commerce and society in general, its importance to the success of all types of tourism companies can only grow in the future (Davis and Davidson, 1991; WTO, 1991). As a result, tourism companies have to change the way in which they conduct their business, and are under pressure to invest in new technology in order to maintain their competitiveness (Buhalis, 1997).

ELECTRONIC DISTRIBUTION: THE EVOLUTION
OF AIRLINE CRSs TO GDSs

Electronic distribution systems in tourism have their origins in the inventory systems that were installed by airlines at the end of the 1950s and during the 1960s. Originally developed as internal control systems, their scope was expanded to inter-organizational systems in the mid-1970s by installing terminals in travel agencies and travel departments of large firms (Kärcher, 1995). This gave travel agents instant access to real-time availability and pricing information, as well as the ability to make instant bookings, thus helping them to greatly improve the quality of service to their customers. The airlines also benefited from this arrangement, as it was less expensive to distribute the equipment needed to permit direct access than to hire additional staff to cope with the increasing levels of business. In addition, it quickly became apparent that travel agents were more likely to make bookings with airlines that supplied them with reservations equipment, a phenomenon that became known as the 'halo effect' (Burns, 1995). This helped increase market share and aircraft load, as well as attracting incremental passenger revenues, and therefore changed the economies of operating such systems from one of simple cost reduction to one of more strategic importance (Copeland, 1991).

Deregulation of the airline sector in the USA in the late 1970s gave great impetus to the growth in the adoption of computerized reservation systems (CRSs). In essence, deregulation triggered both the introduction of new airlines and also allowed more airlines to compete on the same routes. This combination of factors resulted in an absolute increase in the number of flights and the number of fare options, while at the same time producing significant difficulties for travel agents through increased competition and reductions in airfares. As a result, the use of a CRS became practically essential to try to cost-effectively untangle the complex web of information (Hitchins, 1991). CRSs introduced three major financial benefits for vendor airlines: a wide distribution network and CRS services; revenues generated from services to third parties; and incremental benefits through directional selling to the parent carrier (Sloane, 1990; Wheatcroft and Lipman, 1990; Copeland, 1991; Truitt et al., 1991; Sheldon, 1997; Inkpen, 1998).

However, developing and operating such systems was expensive, and there were simply not enough airline bookings being processed to provide sufficient return on investment. To counteract this, most operators of systems began cross-selling complementary travel products, such as hotel rooms or car hire, along with flights. Having grown comfortable with the process of booking air products online, agents wanted to be also able to source information about and make bookings for these other travel products on their computer terminals. These two factors prompted the reservations system operators to begin using spare capacity to distribute complementary travel products over their systems (Coyne, 1995). As a result, today's Global Distribution Systems (GDSs) service a much broader range of travel-related products and have effectively become travel supermarkets offering information and reservation capabilities for the entire range of travel products. These include scheduled and charter airline flights, hotels and other forms of accommodation, car rental, package holidays, ferry, rail and bus tickets, cruise packages, yachting, excursions, theatre tickets and even flowers and champagne. In effect, the GDSs provide a one-stop-shop for all the travel information and reservations needs of travel agents (WTO, 1994; IHA, 1995; Kärcher, 1996).

HOTELS AND GDSs : INTEGRATING SERVICE

One of the first complementary products distributed through GDSs was hotel accommodation. Initially hotel chains loaded their various room types, descriptions and price categories into spare capacity on the GDS database, thus making such information available to thousands of travel agents worldwide. Hotels benefited by having their product distributed to a wider audience, travel agents benefited by being able to book a wider range of products through their computer systems and the GDSs benefited as a result of increased booking volumes that helped to offset their operating costs (O'Connor, 1999 and 2000). It was mainly hotel chains, using standardized procedures and facilities, often located in city centres and targeting business travellers, that took advantage of GDSs. Smaller and independent properties in peripheral and resort areas had a much slower adoption rate (Buhalis and Main, 1998).

However, the GDSs were far from effective as a sales tool for hotel products. A variety of problems arose as a result of the data architecture of the GDSs because they were originally designed solely to distribute information about airline seats (Emmer et al., 1993). In contrast to hotel rooms, airline seats are relatively homogeneous. The GDS did not have the capacity to cope with the diversity of the hotel product. As a result, only a sub-group of the available room types and rates could be displayed on the system, and travel agents quickly realized that in many cases more favourable products could be found by contacting the property directly (McGuffie, 1994). The rigid database structure also limited the textual information that could be stored about the product itself, meaning that the detailed descriptions necessary to describe a property could not be incorporated in the system. In many cases, simplified, abbreviated and truncated descriptions had to be used, frequently to the point where product differentiation and even clarity had to be sacrificed (Burns, 1995). Hotels also experienced problems in maintaining the data in the system. Loading or modifying data was relatively technical, as each system used different protocols and syntax, and there was also a long lead-time between changing data and it appearing live on the system (Coyne and Burns, 1996).

These three problems – limited number of rates, inadequate descriptions and unacceptable lead-time – meant that travel agents were not completely confident about the hotel information provided by their systems. As a result, the effectiveness of the GDSs as a hotel distribution channel was questionable, and hotel companies began to doubt the value of loading their product on the GDSs. Most hotel chains subsequently developed their own reservation systems, with database structures more appropriate to the hotel product. These were then linked electronically to the GDS to permit access to the travel agent network. A transaction fee is paid to the GDS operator for each booking processed. This system overcomes the data architecture problem whilst giving hotels electronic access to the increasingly important travel agent market.

However, as each of the major GDS serviced different geographical markets, hotel chains needed to be represented on each of them in order to gain maximum benefit. This involved developing multiple interfaces, as each was different in terms of its technical requirements and methods of operation. Several of the leading players in the sector combined to develop the concept of a 'universal switch' such as THISCO and WIZCOM. Such switches act as a bi-directional translator, connecting the hotel CRS to the numerous GDS platforms that exist at a relatively low cost. The use of a switch means that only a single interface, between the hotel CRS and the switch, has to be created to give access to all of the major GDS systems (Archdale, 1993; Werthner and Klein, 1999; Ader *et al.*, 2000). In developing their own systems, hotel chains were able to benefit from the experience gained by the airline companies. Following the same implementation philosophy, the initial hotel reservation systems helped to manage inventory for the entire group, developed central telesales offices, company-wide yield management systems and corporate sales departments. As the capital cost of both developing and maintaining a CRS was substantial, over one-fifth of the major international hotel companies currently outsource some aspect of their reservations function to a third party (HEDNA, 1997). Different levels of reservation service are available. Where both voice and electronic distribution services are being contracted, cost to the hotel company is normally on a transaction basis, which allows the company to profit from the benefits of electronic distribution with a minimum of capital outlay. Such an approach is attractive to smaller hotel groups and independents, which in many cases join consortia as a means of gaining cost-effective access to electronic distribution channels (PriceWaterhouseCoopers, 2000).

DISTRIBUTING AND MANAGING THE DESTINATION AS AN ENTITY

Although information technologies have hitherto not been regarded as a critical instrument for the development and management of destinations, destination management organizations increasingly use technology in order to improve their organizational function and performance. Destination Management Systems (DMSs) support both the local suppliers as well as co-ordinate the management of the entire region. DMSs revolutionize destination marketing as they combine a radically improved and rapidly evolving technology in order to satisfy the growing needs of the tourism demand and supply. As these systems enable the dissemination of information and reservation functions for destinations, DMSs are emerging as a major promotion, distribution and operational tool for both destinations and small and medium-sized tourism enterprises. Moreover, their contribution to strategic management and marketing, which is demonstrated by their ability to integrate destinations as well as increase the intra-channel power of principals within the distribution channel, elevates them to strategic tools (Archdale *et al.*, 1992; Buhalis, 1993, 1994 and 1997).

DMSs are generally state sponsored and are more diverse in their product offering than GDS/CRS (Bender, 1999). They concentrate on distributing a wide variety of different tourism products and services primarily focused on the leisure customer, and they pay particular attention to distributing the offerings of smaller and independent tourism suppliers, but also include hotel groups (Vlitos-Rowe, 1992). Public tourist organizations are traditionally involved in destinations' information provision and marketing. DMSs facilitate this function by administrating a wide range of requests and by providing information to an ever-increasing tourism supply, in an efficient and appropriate way. Thus, information technologies provide a way to improve the accessibility of, and the quantity and quality of information on the destination's facilities while they present travellers with options in minimizing their search costs (Sheldon, 1993). Moreover, destinations take advantage of the database marketing techniques, in order to identify and target profitable market niches, by tailoring market-driven products for particular customers. Although it is estimated that 200 destination-oriented systems of various kinds emerged in the late 1990s, to date their impact has been minimal, and they have failed to evolve into full commercial systems except in a small number of European countries (Frew and O'Connor, 1999). However, most analysts agree that the importance of electronic distribution will continue to grow, particularly in light of the shake-up in the marketplace discussed in the next section.

INFORMATION TECHNOLOGIES IN
TOUR OPERATORS AND TRAVEL AGENCIES

In contrast with business and independent leisure travellers, a considerable number of consumers normally purchase 'tourist packages' arranged by tour operators and often use charter flights and small accommodation establishments for their annual holidays. Tour operators tend to distribute their products by displaying brochures of their packages in travel agencies (Wanhill, 1998). Hence, in Northern European countries, where tour operators dominate the leisure travel market, traditional airline and hotel CRSs and GDSs are used less frequently for arranging leisure travel. In the early 1980s, tour operators realized that they had to capitalize on information technologies and utilize more effective distribution methods, in order to enhance productivity, improve their holiday capacity management and provide a better service to both agencies and consumers. Gradually, all major tour operators developed or acquired databases and established electronic links with travel agencies, aiming to reduce their information handling costs and increase the speed of information transfer and retrieval. They also utilized available market intelligence data arising from the systems to adjust their supply to the demand fluctuations, as well as to monitor the booking progress and productivity of travel agencies (Kärcher, 1996; Inkpen, 1998).

Information technologies also provide a wide range of tools for travel agencies, by providing the mechanism for information exchange and tourism product distribution. They have enabled agencies to build complicated travel itineraries in minutes, while they provided up-to-date schedules, prices and availability data. The proliferation of CRSs and GDSs also provided an effective reservation mechanism which supports travel agencies to get information, make reservations and issue travel documents for the entire range of tourism products efficiently and at a fraction of the time required if these processes were made manually. Therefore travel agencies use information technologies to access tourism suppliers' databases, to verify availability and rates, and to confirm reservations. In addition, these technologies have introduced major improvements in the organization of travel agencies. By integrating their 'back office' (e.g. accounting, commission monitoring, personnel) and 'front office' (e.g. customers' history, itinerary construction, ticketing and communication with suppliers), travel agencies have achieved significant synergies, efficiencies and cost savings. Multiple travel agencies in particular experience more benefits through facilitating branch control by their headquarters. As transactions made in branches can automatically be reported back to the head office, a tighter financial control can be performed. In addition, transactions provide invaluable marketing research data, which can almost instantly report market movements and ameliorate tactical decisions. Hence, travel agencies increasingly rely on computerized systems not only to respond to travel inquiries but also for facilitating both their tactical and strategic management and marketing functions (Bennett, 1993; Sheldon, 1997; Inkpen, 1998).

THE INTERNET COMMERCE REVOLUTION

Until the 1990s, the electronic channels of distribution that serviced tourism were institutionalized and everyone co-operated, rather than competed with each other, to facilitate distribution (see Figure 21.1). Relationships were linear and each participant within the chain had a mutually beneficial role to play (Anderson

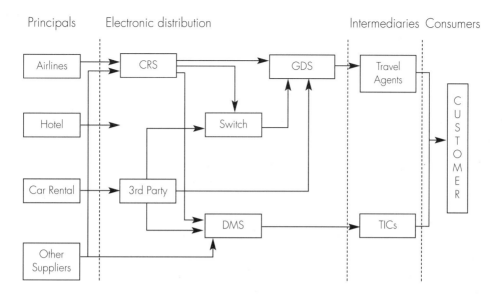

Principals   Electronic distribution   Intermediaries Consumers

Figure 21.1   The proprietary electronic distribution channels

Consulting, 1998). Mutually beneficial refers to win-win partnerships where each contributor adds value and benefits to the chain and to the system as a whole. The systems were in effect a closed user group, as the information they contained was distributed over proprietary networks and was not available to the general public (Wade, 1998). Use of these distribution channels was lucrative, but was also expensive and lacked flexibility. For example, between 1993 and 1997, hotel commissions and other reservation costs, measured on a per available rooms basis, grew from US$429 to US$930 – an increase of 117 per cent in four years (Waller, 1999). This increase in costs, together with the growth in the use of direct marketing, convinced many suppliers of the need to find alternative and cheaper ways to distribute their product, preferably to the customer directly (Dombey, 1998).

In 1994, the proliferation of the Internet and the arrival of the World Wide Web as a mainstream communications medium provided just such an opportunity (Smith and Jenner, 1998). Widely promoted as a medium for electronic commerce, opportunities on the Web have been quickly exploited by tourism actors, partly because of the existing high level of computerization in airlines and travel agencies (*Web-Week*, 1997). Suppliers can achieve a lower booking cost by selling over the Web, as the distribution cost of voice calls and commission levels are eliminated (ByLine Research, 1999). The Web facilitates direct access to customers with a high propensity to travel as it presents little or no barrier to entry, and it provides companies with substantial opportunities to communicate directly with their customers (Jeong and Lambert, 1999). The majority of the actors in tourism distribution have begun distributing over the medium (Pusateri and Manno, 1998) and it is having a profound effect on the way in which travel products are being marketed, distributed, sold and delivered (Williams and Palmer, 1999). Thus, the Internet provides the facility to transform the operation, distribution and structure of the tourism industry (Buhalis, 2000).

Individual suppliers are also taking advantage of the opportunities presented by the Web. For example, in a survey of the top 50 hotel companies carried out in 1999, over 90 per cent of the hotel chains examined had a chain website, with nearly 80 per cent of these providing reservation facilities to allow the customer to book directly (O'Connor and Horan, 1999). The advantages of setting up their own site are clear – lower distribution costs, increased sales as a result of specific promotions and increased customer loyalty (Wade, 1998). Hotel chain sites appear to be highly effective, with the vast majority of Internet bookings (over 80 per cent) flowing through these sites rather than through Web intermediaries (HSMAI, 1999). Furthermore, in addition to being represented on their chain sites, many individual hotels have developed their own pages (HEDNA, 1999). The attraction of Internet-based channels for hotels is easy to understand. If they select the service(s) carefully, hotels have few up-front costs and no initiation or periodic fees. That gives them a risk-free supplemental source of confirmed reservations, allowing them to take advantage of endless marketing opportunities (Chervenak, 1999). Thus they can avoid GDS fees and, in certain cases, travel agent commission, and more importantly they can reach the customer directly. For the 2000 to 2003 period, cumulative gross savings are estimated to reach US$1.3 billion in travel agent commissions and GDS fees, representing an annual saving equivalent to 1.7 per cent of total industry profits in 2000 declining to 0.8 per cent by 2003 (Ader et al., 2000). Furthermore, little or no capital investment is required, and thus these new systems make global distribution possible for many smaller establishments that could never have afforded to be included in the traditional GDS/CRS channel (Buhalis and Main, 1998; Dombey, 1998).

Distribution over the Web also has the potential to be far more effective. In addition to simply providing data and pricing, the Web allows images and short video clips to be delivered on demand. Today's more advanced websites allow customers to 'visit' hotel properties, take virtual tours and to develop their individualized package by collecting products in their basket (Cline and Rach, 1997). Thus the Web is far more effective as a sales tool than the text-based GDSs. Lastly, customers are becoming increasingly comfortable booking tourism products over the Web, with recent research demonstrating that customers are more willing to purchase hotel rooms online than any other product (Dryden, 1997). As a result of these advantages, suppliers would ideally like to direct all electronic distribution to the channels they control best. Moreover, most also seem to realize that a viable third party online distribution network will remain an integral part of the way in which travel gets sold for the foreseeable future. While less than 1 per cent of hotel bookings were made over the Internet in 1998, PhoCusWright estimate that over 5 per cent will be made over the medium in 2001, with the majority (51 per cent) being made through third party sites rather than direct to the supplier (Ader *et al.*, 1999).

The arrival of the Web has upset the distribution apple cart. Chervenak (1999) has described it as the 'prime agent for change in central reservations'. The Gartner Group claims that travel companies that fail to react appropriately to its potential have a 70 per cent probability of being driven out of business in the next five years (Gartner Group, 2000). Yet according to many industry analysts, many companies and particularly smaller players are barely at the threshold of using the tools made available by the Internet to communicate directly with their customers, cultivate loyalty and generate business (Ader *et al.*, 2000). Unless tourism suppliers address this deficiency, and take active control of their own distribution, there is a clear danger that they will lose their ability to dictate the terms of condition of the sale of their product, and will become mere suppliers of a commodity rather than the prime drivers of the sector.

CONFUSION IN THE MARKETPLACE

Perhaps the most significant effect is the shake-up in distribution mechanisms currently in progress. In addition to co-operating with each distribution channel member as they did in the past, most tourism actors have started, or are starting, to compete with each other by creating their own websites with information provision and booking facilities. The situation is described as 'little short of a technological stampede. Up and down the traditional distribution chain . . . providers are working feverishly to re-engineer their travel systems . . . to bypass both the GDS and the travel agent to create a direct link with the customer' (Dombey, 1998). Each is trying to circumnavigate intermediaries lower down in the distribution chain and transact business directly to the customer in order to minimize costs, interact with consumers and enhance their competitiveness (Jarvela *et al.*, 1999). As in the past, the airline sector seems to be leading the trend. Most airlines are encouraging their best customers to book online at their own websites (Stoltz, 1998). United, Northwest and Delta have all introduced incentives to book via this rather than any other route. Ryanair and Easyjet are widely reported to achieve two-thirds of their bookings through the Internet and they offer a significant discount to consumers who are doing that. This is placing pressure on many of the 'traditional' intermediaries, with a large proportion of travel agents forecasted to go out of business within the next few years. Similarly, as demonstrated in Figure 21.2, the Switch and GDS companies have created their own form of onward distribution, and are gradually transforming their operations from being behind the travel agency-initiated and -led transaction, to the sharp-end arena with direct customer contact over the Web. Tour operators, travel agents suppliers – all are busily engaged in setting up Web presences and attempting to distribute online (Reynolds, 1998).

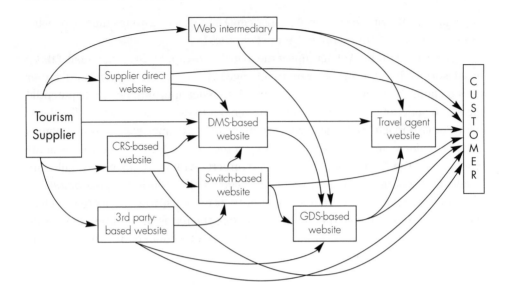

Figure 21.2   A new model of hotel electronic distribution channels

In essence, the level of mutual dependence between participants within the arena has decreased. Each supplier and intermediary now has the potential and frequently the facility to distribute directly to the end-consumer (HEDNA, 1997). Such disruption is only the beginning, with another boost to direct sales forecast from the potential widespread diffusion of technologies, such as Wireless Application Protocol (WAP), General Packet Radio Service (GPRS), Bluetooth and interactive television. These technologies revolutionize the interaction between consumers and organizations, as they will enable them to interact, from everywhere, at all times, using their mobile telephones, interactive television sets and remote devices.

COMPETE, CO-OPERATE, BUT MAINLY SERVE THE CUSTOMER

Paradoxically, in addition to there being more competition between the distribution players, there is also more co-operation. Most online travel agency sites offer multiple products (air, hotel, car, etc.) from multiple vendors. Their selling point with customers is that they are full-service and offer the ability to research and purchase an entire trip online (Ader *et al.*, 1999). To do this, they need detail content and access to reservation facilities that they can only get by co-operating with other distribution channels. For example, the GDSs, in addition to distributing directly to the consumer over the Web (e.g. Travelocity), are also servicing the reservation requirements of a variety of new players such as travel agency websites (e.g.

Expedia) and corporate booking sites (Dombey, 1998). Non-exclusive virtual alliances are also being formed, with companies combining to form new synergistic relationships. An example of such alliances is demonstrated by Pegasus Systems. In addition to distributing its hotel products directly to the consumer through its TravelWeb product (www.travelweb.com), Pegasus also provides the information and hotel booking engine behind other Web-based travel services such as Microsoft Expedia and Preview Travel – services that many see as the company's competitors. However, each partner benefits – Pegasus by leveraging its investment in developing and maintaining its hotel reservation system and its allies by having access to an efficient and effective service without having to develop one for themselves. The co-existence of competition and co-operation has given rise to 'coopetition' where competitors collaborate on win-win partnerships (Werthner and Klein, 1999)!

Like most of the e-commerce world, online travel distribution is still in its embryonic stage. Thousands of travel-related sites have emerged in the past few years, and more are being launched every day. Alternative business models and operating procedures are constantly being tested and refined (Ader *et al.*, 2000). Companies from outside what is normally regarded as the travel industry have also identified the potential of Internet-based distribution, have attacked and strongly positioned themselves in the distribution chain (Nealon, 1998). These include publishers such as Lonely Planet, software developers such as Microsoft and media owners such as CNN (HEDNA, 1997). In general, such companies have positioned themselves as general-purpose travel retailers, providing a wide variety of travel information and booking services (e.g. Expedia, Travelocity, Travel Web, ITN), usually in co-operation with existing intermediaries. Coming from outside the industry, most have no pre-existing relationships with other players which permits them to position themselves advantageously. For example, WorldRes, an Internet-based hotel-booking service, is primarily focused on providing Web reservations facilities to member hotels, but has been able to expand rapidly by forming alliances with destination management organizations, other Internet-based travel services and special interest/activity-focused intermediaries (Chervenak, 1999). Paradoxically, the very forces that are causing this growth in intermediaries may eventually cause their downfall. Since the tourism product is becoming fairly homogeneous, some experts believe that it will become increasingly commoditized. As such, it is anticipated that price competition will intensify and that intermediaries may eventually be eliminated (Ader *et al.*, 2000). Perhaps the recent growth in the use of auction sites, such as E-bay, NetMarketer, SkyAuctions.com and TravelBids, and bidding services such as Priceline.com is a reflection of this trend. According to Jupiter Communications, 'the auction concept is perfectly suited to the Web and is one that will become commonplace as the medium matures' (Jupiter Communications 1997). Travel and tourism products are acknowledged to be one of the most popular products available over this medium (Tjostheim and Eide, 1998). When distributing tourism products, these services emphasize price and location instead of service, reputation or amenities, thus driving the industry towards commoditization and reducing the significance of brand (Connolly and Olsen, 1999).

CONCLUSION AND THE FUTURE

In addition to the rapidly expanding number of channels available, most of the channels are becoming interconnected, with each system offering multiple routes to the customer. Probably, each channel will target different segments and will provide comprehensive and integrated service to niche markets (Buhalis, 1998). Multiple channels and strategies are likely to be required in the foreseeable future, as no one channel is likely to have enough distribution capability to place a product in front of all potential buyers (Ader *et al.*, 1999). Specialized service providers will develop market-specific niche products and will use individual suppliers to develop the value chain. Thus, suppliers will need to use not just a single distribution channel, but a distribution 'system' – a portfolio of distribution channels that operate in parallel with, in competition with and in co-operation with each other. And, it is likely that the pace of development seen in recent years will continue and perhaps even accelerate. As Go and Pine (1995) point out,

> competition is a constantly changing landscape in which new product, new ways of marketing, new production processes and new markets emerge. Today's dynamic competitive environment is characterised by change and innovation. As long as competitive innovations occur and entrepreneurs seek to implement them in search of survival, growth and profit, channels of distribution are subject to change.

Ultimately the Internet and the emerging technologies provide unprecedented tools for communication and interaction, bridging the gap between tourism suppliers and consumers on a global basis. As with any industrial revolution there will be several winners and several losers in the process and therefore non-competitive players will suffer the consequences of the evolution. Most importantly, for the first time ever suppliers have affordable tools and efficient mechanisms to serve their customers without having to rely on intermediaries. This will enable them to realign the power structure in the distribution channel and if they are competitive enough to develop and distribute innovative offerings. This will empower and enable them to strengthen their competitiveness and succeed in the global marketplace.

REFERENCES

Ader, J., Lafleur, R. and Falcone, M. (1999) *Internet Travel: Point, Click, Trip – An introduction to the on-line travel industry*. Bear, Stearns, New York.

Ader, J., Lafleur, R., Yurman, J. and McCoy, T. (2000) *Global Lodging Almanac – 2000 Edition*. Bear, Stearns, New York.

Anderson Consulting (1998) *The Future of Travel Distribution: Securing loyalty in an efficient travel market*. Anderson Consulting, New York.

Archdale, G. (1993) 'Computer reservation systems and public tourist offices'. *Tourism Management*, February, pp. 3–14.

Archdale, G., Stanton, R. and Jones, G. (1992) *Destination Databases: Issues and priorities*. Pacific Asia Travel Association, San Francisco.

Bender, D. (1999) 'The virtual metropolis. Marketing cities on the World Wide Web'. *HSMAI Marketing Review*, Spring/Summer, pp. 7–9.

Bennett, M. (1993) 'Information technology and the travel agency – a customer service perspective'. *Tourism Management*, August, pp. 259–66.

Bennett, M. (1996) 'Information technology and databases for tourism'. In A. Seaton and M. Bennett (eds) *The Marketing of Tourism Products: Concepts issues and cases*. Thomson International Business Press, London, pp. 423–50.

Buhalis, D. (1993) 'Regional integrated computer information reservation management systems as a strategic tool for the small and medium tourism enterprises'. *Tourism Management*, **14**(5), 366–78.

Buhalis, D. (1994) 'Information and telecommunications technologies as a strategic tool for small and medium tourism enterprises in the contemporary business environment'. In A. Seaton *et al.* (eds) *Tourism – The state of the art: the Strathclyde symposium*. Wiley & Sons, Chichester, pp. 254–75.

Buhalis, D. (1997) 'Information technologies as a strategic tool for economic, cultural and environmental benefits enhancement of tourism at destination regions'. *Progress in Tourism and Hospitality Research*, **3**(1), 71–93.

Buhalis, D. (1998) 'Strategic use of information technologies in the tourism industry'. *Tourism Management*, **19**(5), 409–21.

Buhalis, D. (2000) 'Tourism and information technologies: past, present and future'. *Tourism Recreation Research*, **25**(1), 41–58.

Buhalis, D. and Main, H. (1998) 'Information technology in small and medium hospitality enterprises: strategic analysis and critical factors'. *International Journal of Contemporary Hospitality Management*, **10**(5),198–202.

Burns, J. (1995) 'Electronic GDS distribution – what are your options?'. *Hospitality & Automation*, **3**(5), 1–11.

ByLine Research (1999) *Going Nowhere Fast: E-commerce in the travel industry*. ByLine Research, London.

Castleberry, J., Hempell, C. and Kaufinan, G. (1998) 'Electronic shelf space on the Global Distribution Network'. *Hospitality and Leisure Executive Report*, **5** (Spring), pp. 19–24.

Chervenak, L. (1999) 'CRS today and tomorrow'. *Lodging*, January, pp. 75–7.

Cline, R. and Rach, L. (1997) *Hospitality 2000: A view to the next millennium*. Arthur Anderson and New York University, New York.

Connell, J. and Reynolds, P. (1999) 'The implications of technological developments on Tourism Information Centres'. *Tourism Management*, **20**, 501–9.

Connolly, D. and Olsen, M. (1999) *Hospitality Technology in the New Millennium: Findings of the IH&RA Think-Tanks on Technology*. International Hotel & Restaurant Association, Paris.

Copeland, D. and McKenney, J. (1988) 'Airline reservation systems: lessons from history'. *MIS Quarterly*, **12**, 535–70.

Copeland, D. (1991) 'So you want to build the next SABRE system?' *Business Quarterly*, **55**(3), 56–60.

Coyne, R. (1995) 'The reservations revolution'. *Hotel & Motel Management*, 24 July, pp. 54–7.

Coyne, R. and Burns, J. (1996) 'Global connectivity'. *Hotel & Motel Management*, 22 April, p. 29.

Davis, S. and Davidson, B. (1991) *2020 Vision: Transform your business today to succeed in tomorrow's economy*. Simon & Schuster, New York.

Dombey, A. (1998) 'Separating the emotion from the fact – the effects of new intermediaries on electronic travel distribution'. In D. Buhalis *et al.* (eds) *Information Communication Technologies in Tourism*. ENTER Conference Proceedings, Springer, Vienna, pp. 129–38.

Dryden, P. (1997) 'Scarce sparks site revamp'. *Computerworld*, **31**(44), 43–4.

Emmer, R., Tauck, C., Wilkinson, S. and Moore, R. (1993) 'Marketing hotels using Global Distribution Systems'. *Cornell Hotel and Restaurant Administration Quarterly*, December, pp. 80–9.

Frew, A. and Pringle, S. (1995) *Multi-media Marketing Across ATM Broadband Networks – A hospitality and tourism perspective: Part One*. The Hospitality Information Technology Association Worldwide Conference. Hospitality Information Technology Association, New Orleans.

Frew, A. and O'Connor, P. (1999) 'Destination Marketing System strategies: refining and extending an assessment framework'. *Information Technology and Tourism*, **2**(1), 3–13.

Gartner Group (2000) *Online Travel Forecast*. Gartner Group, Stamford, Connecticut.

Go, F. and Pine, R. (1995) *Globalisation Strategy in the Hotel Industry*. Routledge, New York.

Go, F. and Williams, P. (1993) 'Competing and co-operating in the changing tourism channel system'. *Journal of Travel & Tourism Marketing*, **2**(2/3), 229–48.

HEDNA (1997) *Onward Distribution of Hotel Information via the Global Distribution Systems*. Partners in Marketing, London.

HEDNA (1998) *GDS Trends Survey 1997*. Hotel Electronic Distribution Network Association, London.

HEDNA (1999) Electronic Distribution Trends Survey – Executive Summary. Hotel Electronic Distribution Network Association, London.

Hitchins, F. (1991) 'The influence of technology on UK travel agents'. *EIU Travel and Tourism Analyst*, **3**, 88–105.

Hospitality Sales and Marketing Association (HSMAI) (1999) 'Interview with Phillip C. Wolf, President and CEO of PhoCusWright Ltd'. *HSMAI Gazette*, **13**.

IHA (1995) *The Communications Superhighway: From multimedia to personalised service*. International Hotel Association, Paris.

Inkpen, G. (1998) *Information Technology for Travel and Tourism* (2nd edn). Addison Wesley Longman, London.

Jarvela, P., Loikkanen, J., Tinnila, M. and Tuunainen, K. (1999) 'Business models for electronic commerce in the travel services'. *Information Technology and Tourism*, **2**(3/4), 185–96.

Jeong, M. and Lambert, C. (1999) 'Measuring the information quality of lodging web sites'. *International Journal of Hospitality Information Technology*, **1**(1), 63–75.

Jupiter Communications (1997) *Web Auctions*. www.jup.com/newsletter.

Kärcher, K. (1995) 'The emergence of electronic market systems in the European tour operator business'. *EM – Electronic Markets*, 13/14, 10–11.

Kärcher, K. (1996) 'The four Global Distribution Systems in the travel and tourism industry'. *Electronic Markets*, **6**(2), 20–4.

Kaven, W. (1994) 'Channels of distribution in the hotel industry'. In J. Rothmell (ed.) *Marketing in the Services Sector*. Winthrop Publications, Cambridge, Mass., pp. 114–21.

Kling, A. (1994) *The Economic Consequences of WWW*. Second International WWW Conference, Chicago.

Knowles, T. and Garland, M. (1994) 'The strategic importance of CRSs in the airline industry'. *EIU Travel & Tourism Analyst*, **4**, 4–6.

McGuffie, J. (1994) 'CRS development in the hotel sector'. *EIU Travel & Tourism Analyst*, **2**, 53–68.

Middleton, V. (1994) *Marketing in Travel and Tourism*. Butterworth-Heinemann, London.

Muqbil, I. (1998) *Ten Hospitality Trends for the Tourism and Hospitality Industry*. Travel Impact Newswire.

Nealon, T. (1998) 'New age travellers'. *Revolution*, pp. 42–4.

O'Brien, P. (1999) 'Intelligent agents for retail travel agents'. *Information Technology and Tourism*, **2**(3/4), 213–28.

O'Connor, P. (1999) *Electronic Information Distribution in Tourism and Hospitality*. CAB International, London.

O'Connor, P. (2000) *Using Computers in Hospitality* (2nd edn). Cassell, London.

O'Connor, P. and Horan, P. (1999) *Failing to Make the Connection? – An analysis of Web reservation facilities in the top 50 international hotel chains*. Hospitality Information Technology Association Worldwide Conference. Hospitality Information Technology Association, Edinburgh.

Olsen, M. (1998) *Visioning The Future*. International Hotel and Restaurant Association, EuroHotec, Nice.

Olsen, M., Murthy, B. and Inagaki, T. (1995) *Scanning the Business Environment: A strategic planning tool for the multinational hotel industry*. International Hotel Association, Paris.

Palmer, A. and McCole, P. (2000) 'The virtual re-introduction of travel services: a conceptual framework and empirical investigation'. *Journal of Vacation Marketing*, **6**(1), 33–47.

Pollock, A. (1995) 'The impact of information technology on destination marketing'. *EIU Travel & Tourism Analyst*, **3**, 66–83.

Poon, A. (1993) *Technology and Competitive Advantage*. CAB International, London.

Poon, A. (1994) 'The new tourism revolution'. *Tourism Management*, **15**(2), 91–9.

Porter, M. and Millar, V. (1985) 'How information gives you competitive advantage'. *Harvard Business Review*, July/August, pp. 149–60.

PriceWaterhouseCoopers, (2000) 'New forces are shaping the European Hotel Sector'. *Hospitality Directions – European Edition*, pp. 19–32.

Pusateri, M. and Manno, J. (1998) 'Travellers take to the "Net"'. *Lodging*, June, pp. 23–4.

Reynolds, I. (1998) *The Changing Face of the Travel Industry: Distribution Channels in the Changing Travel Industry*. Access Conferences International, London.

Schmid, B. (1994) 'Electronic markets in tourism'. *Revue de Tourisme*, **2**, 9–11.

Sheldon, P. (1993) Destination Information Systems'. *Annals of Tourism Research*, **20**(4), 633–49.

Sheldon, P. (1997) *Information technologies for Tourism*. CAB, Oxford.

Sloane, J. (1990) 'Latest developments in aviation CRSs'. *Travel and Tourism Analyst*, No. 4, 5–15.

Smith, C. and Jenner, P. (1998) 'Tourism and the Internet'. *Travel & Tourism Intelligence*, **1**, 62–81.

Stipanuk, D. (1993) 'Tourism and technology: interactions and implications'. *Tourism Management*, August, pp. 267–78.

Stoltz, C. (1998) 'The E-travel revolution is over'. *Washington Post*, E01.

Strategic Advisory Group (1997) *Information Society Technologies (IST) for Tourism*. 5th Framework Program on Information Society applications for transport and associated services, Brussels.

Tjostheim, I. and Eide, J.-O. (1998) 'A case study of an on-line auction for the World Wide Web'. In D. Buhalis *et al.* (eds) *Information Communication Technologies in Tourism.* ENTER Conference Proceedings, Springer, Vienna, pp. 149–61.

Truitt, L., Teye, V. and Farris, M. (1991) 'The role of Computer Reservation Systems: international implications for the tourism industry'. *Tourism Management,* **12**(1), 21–36.

Vaughan, D., Jolley, A. and Mehrer, P. (1999) 'Local authorities in England and Wales and the development of tourism Internet sites'. *Information Technology and Tourism,* **2**(2), 115–29.

Vlitos-Rowe, I. (1992) 'Destination databases and management systems'. *EIU Travel and Tourism Analyst,* **5**, 84 –109.

Wade, P. (1998) *L'impact des nouvelles technologies sur les systems d'information et de reservation.* Conseil Nationale de Tourisme, Paris.

Wagner, G. (1991) 'Lodging's lifeblood'. *Hospitality,* December, p. 105.

Waller, F. (1999) 'The distribution revolution'. *Hotels,* March, p. 103.

Wanhill, S. (1998) 'Intermediaries'. In C. Cooper, J. Fletcher, D. Gilbert, R. Shepherd and S. Wanhill (eds) *Tourism: Principles and Practice* (2nd edn). Longman Publishing, London, pp. 423–46.

Web-Week (1997) 'Travel industry embraces Web'. *Web-Week,* **3**(ii).

Werthner, H. and Klein, S. (1999) *Information Technology and Tourism: A challenging relationship.* Springer-Verlag, Vienna.

Wheatcroft, S. and Lipman, G. (1990) 'European liberalisation and world air transport: towards a transnational industry'. Special Report, No. 2015. Economist Intelligence Unit, London.

Williams, A. and Palmer, A. (1999) 'Tourism destination brands and electronic commerce: towards synergy?' *Journal of Vacation Marketing,* **5**(3), 263–75.

World Tourism Organization (WTO) (1991) *Tourism to the Year 2000.* World Tourism Organization, Madrid.

World Tourism Organization (WTO) (1994) *Global Distribution Systems in the Tourism Industry.* World Tourism Organization, Madrid.

World Tourism Organization (WTO) (1997) *Tourism – 2020 Vision.* World Tourism Organization, Madrid.

CHAPTER 22

A new paradigm for tourism and electronic commerce: experience marketing using the virtual tour

Yong-Hyun Cho and Daniel R. Fesenmaier

INTRODUCTION

The Internet is revolutionizing tourism marketing whereby it has evolved into a dynamic source for information as well as an effective marketing tool that is able to reach tourists efficiently (Hoffman and Novak, 1996; Werthner and Klein, 2000). Due to the increased use of personal computers and the decrease in prices of Internet services, the Internet has become a source for gathering timely information and converting information into profitable results at a faster rate for tourists. Online purchases have become the fastest-growing activity on the Internet, and even users who are not online buyers search the World Wide Web (WWW) for information (Donthu and Garcia, 1999). Socio-demographic changes such as active ageing population and childless couples have also led to substantial changes in travel and tourism demand (Hall and Weiler, 1992). An important consequence of these social changes is a greater variety in pleasure travel. Increasingly, new, experienced, sophisticated and demanding travellers are actively seeking information about more exotic destinations and authentic experiences in order to satisfy their specific needs and wishes. That is, tourists are increasingly seeking information which enables them to 'experience' the destination instead of simply obtaining facts about 'how the destination is'. These trends for tourism suggest that travel has become a means for finding personal fulfilment, identity enhancement and self-expression. And, perhaps even more important, travellers have become especially concerned not with just being 'there' but with participating, learning and 'experiencing the there' they visit (Stebbins, 1982; Pearce, 1988; Pine II and Gilmore, 1998).

Because of the intangible nature of tourism product, tourists make decisions about travel in a condition of substantial uncertainty (Roehl and Fesenmaier, 1992;

Reid and Crompton, 1993; Goossens, 1994; Vogt and Fesenmaier, 1998; Jeng, 1999). Therefore, prior to taking a trip tourists actively seek travel information to create a clear understanding of the benefits offered by the destination (Moutinho, 1987; Fodness and Murray, 1997; Mäser and Weiermair, 1998; Vogt and Fesenmaier; 1998). However, relatively little travel information is available before actual visitation to a destination because a large part of tourism information is 'experiential information' that only can be delivered through the onsite experience. With the development of the Internet, however, the quantity and quality of available information have increased substantially (Kiani, 1998; Donthu and Garcia, 1999; Werthner and Klein, 2000). Although the Internet cannot deliver the same amount of information as an actual experience, it offers the potential to provide an extremely rich perceptual and cognitive environment. Through the virtual experience, tourists are able to gain a considerate amount of experiential information before the actual travel and, therefore, they will be in a better position for decision-making.

The purpose of this chapter is to identify and discuss a new paradigm of experience marketing that is emerging for the Internet marketing environment. The present study will outline a conceptual framework and then offer a series of propositions for assessing the nature and impact of a WWW-based virtual tour. In addition, future studies related to the virtual tour will be suggested.

TOURISM AND ELECTRONIC COMMERCE

In the past few years there has been an explosion of online commercial activity enabled by the Internet and this is generally referred to as electronic commerce. The shift towards electronic commerce is revolutionary because it offers several powerful marketing opportunities. Researchers have found that marketing in electronic commerce is more 'flexible' than the traditional media; marketers can immediately add new items and update information based on the direct feedback received from consumers (Hagel and Lansing, 1994; O'Keefe, 1995). Updating information in electronic commerce costs much less than creating new traditional brochures or catalogues. 'Accessibility' is another powerful characteristic of the Internet. Through the Internet anyone on the earth can access the information 24 hours a day. Companies can increase their business hours and consumers can reach needed information or even purchase a product at anytime. Hammond *et al.* (1995, p. 28) suggests that 'one of the benefits of Internet advertising is that each time a user connects to a WWW site, the site provider has a record of the user's electronic address. Thus, companies can build list of customers who participated in the online comercial activity.' Although the database marketing is not new, low-cost and high-speed electronic management of communication is revolutionizing marketing (Blattberg and Deighton, 1991). Compared to traditional media, marketing in electronic commerce is a faster, less expensive, highly immediate communication (Ellsworth and Ellsworth, 1997). Communication shifts from 'one-way' to 'two-way' information flows between marketers and consumers (Blattberg *et al.*, 1994), and from 'one-to-many' to 'many-to-many' where consumers and marketers can individually interact within the medium (Hoffman and Novak, 1996). Many-to-many communication brings many changes in marketing environment. Importantly, it changes the orientation of information from 'supply side' to 'demand side'. Electronic commerce users want control over information search where they initiate their own contacts, control information flow and experience online. It also encourages them to want messages from other online customers for their own individual needs. Thus, communication is becoming more and more consumer-oriented (Rayport and Sviokla, 1995).

The WWW brings additional advantages to the electronic commerce over the traditional marketing in that it provides infrastructure for the inexpensive delivery of multimedia information (Hoffman and Novak, 1996). In addition, online consumers can easily gain access to graphics, sound and even movies. More importantly, the WWW offers access to virtual hypermedia environments, enabling real-time interactivity between humans and computers. This is the most compelling advantage the WWW has over other traditional streaming multimedia such as TV and video. Because the tourism product is basically an experience, true representations of tourism products (i.e. attractions or destinations) cannot be realistically displayed or inspected before purchasing. Thus, tourists depend upon visual and/or verbal representations of experiences of the destination as 'created' by the destination marketer. Vogt and Fesenmaier (1998) and others (e.g. Dann (1996)) have argued that tourism information seekers need rich sensory and emotional information for their hedonic and aesthetic choices. However, mass media-based information usually cannot satisfy visitor information needs because some types of information cannot be acquired without experience. Thus, the Internet enables tourists to 'explore and immerse' themselves within an interactive multimedia environment in order to gain needed 'experiential' information about a destination.

The unique and powerful characteristics of the Internet that enable tourists to experience virtually a destination is leading to a new paradigm in tourism marketing called 'experience marketing'. The Internet brings a new way for communicating with potential visitors. That is, traditional principles of mass media advertising generally assume a passive and captive customer. However, in the new communication environment customers can easily check and compare prices and promotions, obtain electronic brochures and 'visit' a destination. They can therefore become substantially more knowledgeable (i..e. experienced) about a destination prior to the trip (Aldridge *et al.*, 1997). Poon (1993) found that 'new' (i.e. Internet-enabled) tourists are more experienced, more educated, more destination-oriented, more independent, more flexible and more 'green'. This increase in consumer knowledge and sophistication, therefore, requires flexible, specialized, accessible and interactive products and communication. In this new marketing environment, marketers consider consumers individually, enabling them (the consumer) to customize their products and services online through dialogue and through a rich immersive informational environment.

DEFINING THE VIRTUAL TOUR

Although the term 'virtual tour' is already widely used on the WWW sites for tourism destinations, it appears never to be defined by researchers. A well-known concept of 'virtual reality' provides the basic framework for defining virtual tour. Virtual reality is usually considered a complex mechanic system for training or games. However, researchers have proposed a variety of definitions of virtual reality using the concept of 'telepresence'. The idea of telepresence first arose from anecdotal references to 'a sense of being' displaced from a local control room into a remote area when using a tele-operator. Following Akin *et al.* (1983), telepresence was defined as 'a mental state in which a user feels physically present within computer-mediated environment'. Steuer (1992) further defined virtual reality as 'the sense of being' in an environment by means of a communication medium. Sheridan (1992), on the other hand, defined telepresence as the phenomenon in which a media user loses awareness of the physical environment.

Csikszentmihalyi's (1975) concept of 'flow' explains the notion of telepresence well within the context of personal psychology. The flow experience is a state in which one concentrates so much on an activity that he/she becomes 'unconscious' of stimuli outside of the activity, including even awareness of self and the passage of time. Flow is a multi-dimensional construct that represents the user's perception of the medium as playful and exploratory. The theory of flow suggests that involvement in a playful, exploratory experience is self-motivating because it is pleasurable and encourages repetition. Flow and telepresence are similar in that the most singular characteristic of each is a high degree of involvement in a task or activity. In both the impact of concentration excludes distracting stimuli to the point of loss of awareness of self as separate from the task. Thus, the concept virtual tour can be defined as a tour through a virtual environment where one experiences 'flow'.

Telepresence is generally hypothesized to improve efficiency by reducing user workload. During a virtual tour, exploration and manipulation of the computer-mediated environment are often the goals without reference to completing a specific task. Therefore, telepresence itself may be an important criterion of virtual tour performance. A number of studies have indicated the level (i.e. 'quality') of the virtual experience is influenced by three categories of variables including: 1) technical factors; 2) contents factors; and 3) human factors. Technical factors influence mainly the quality of virtual display. Steuer

(1992) suggested that vividness and interactivity determine the level of telepresence. Vividness refers to the level of sensorial richness of mediated environment and includes sensory breadth (i.e. number of sensory dimensions simultaneously presented) and sensory depth (i.e. resolution of each perceptual channel). He defined interactivity as the degree to which users can participate in modifying the form and content of a mediated environment in real time. Three sub-factors that contribute to interactivity include speed (i.e. the rate at which input can be assimilated into the mediated environment), range (i.e. the number of possibilities for action at any given time) and mapping (i.e. the ability of a system to map its controls to changes in the mediated environment in a natural and predictable manner). Sheridan (1992) suggested three somewhat similar determinants of experience level; these are: the fidelity and richness of sensory information, the dexterity of sensor control and the ability to affect the remote environment. Slater and Usoh (1993) also indicated display quality, consistency of presentation across displays and the ability to interact with environment as internal determinants of the sense of telepresence. Figure 22.1 shows the determinants of the level of virtual experience.

Contents factors (referring to the congruency, realism and meaningfulness of the contents of virtual tour) are important in creating telepresence. Information received through all modalities should describe the same objective world; if information from one modality provides a message that differs from that

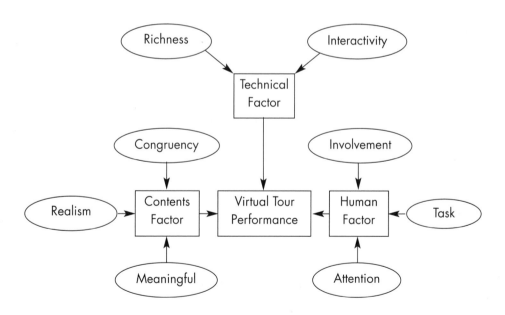

Figure 22.1 Components of virtual tour performance

experienced through a different modality, telepresence may be diminished. Telepresence level should increase as a function of virtual environment scene realism. Scene realism refers to the connectedness and continuity of the stimuli being experienced. The more consistent the information conveyed by a virtual environment is with that learned through real experience, the more telepresence should be experienced in that virtual environment (Held and Durlach, 1992). Meaningfulness is another important factor effecting teleprescence in that it should increase as the situation presented becomes more meaningful to the person. Meaningfulness is often related to many other factors such as motivation to learn or perform, task saliency, and previous experience. Individuals probably will experience a greater sense of presence in an environment if they are able to anticipate or predict what will happen next, whether or not it is under personal control.

Individual psychological factors such as task difficulty, involvement and attention allocation have also been found to play an important part in determining the level of experience. Slater and Usoh (1993) indicated personal information processing and involvement as the factors using the terms of representation system and perceptual position. Csikszentmihalyi and LeFerve (1989) found that people report flow occurs when they perceived task-related requirements were high but in balance with their perceived skills. Research by Draper *et al.*(1998) indicates that the attentional resource is related to task performance, interpreting telepresence as a state arising from commitment of attentional resources to the virtual environment. The importance of personal factors on the level of telepresence has been supported by the studies examining the effects of multimedia (Petty *et al.*, 1983; Smith and Buchholz, 1991). Although several studies have been conducted to examine the effect of multi-sensory media, divergent results have been found. Leigh (1991) suggested that procedural or contextual differences can explain the variation in findings; Smith and Buchholz (1991), on the other hand, found that the effects of multimedia vary based on the involvement level of people and the congruency between different types of sensory information. They both agree that a number of psychological factors influence the effects of multimedia. That is, richness of sensory information has potential to help users to be immersed to the virtual environment. However, this potential does not always result in individuals gaining telepresence; it partly depends on the psychological factors such as involvement or congruency between information.

DEFINING THE EXPERIENCE MARKETING PARADIGM

The experience marketing paradigm is based on the emergence of experience economy and the development of information technology. Pine II and Gilmore (1998) suggested that experience is the fourth economic offering and it is distinguished from services. They also proposed that experiences have emerged as the next step in the progression of economic value and indicated the examples of tourism destinations that offer authentic experience to the tourists. An experience becomes a commercial product when the experience is 'memorable' to the customers. Thus, marketers can increase the value of their product by 'adding' a memorable experience to the functional products. Theme parks are good examples in that they explicitly try to offer experiences as well as provide basic functional service products.

As the 'memorable experience' becomes more important in travel, the most important challenge in travel marketing is that of creating expectation of travel experience. When tourists are able to establish clear expectations, they will be in a better position to make decisions about a travel destination. Most tourists, however, have difficulty creating clear expectations because detailed 'experiential information' is generally not available. Experiential information can be defined as information that the customer wants and needs, but can be acquired only through actual use. Nelson (1974) examined the role of 'experiential information' in the decision-making process through the concept of 'search goods' and 'experience goods'. Search goods are defined as those dominated by product attributes for which full information can be acquired prior to purchase. Experience goods are dominated by attributes that cannot be known until the product is purchased and used. Zeithaml (1988) suggested similar concepts by the terms of 'extrinsic attributes' and 'intrinsic attributes'. Extrinsic attributes are those that are observable 'outside of the product' such as price and brand. Intrinsic attributes are often unobservable prior to purchase and include kindness, taste and texture. She also indicated that most service buyers, as like tourists, relied more on extrinsic attributes because of the high cost and evaluation barriers in assessing intrinsic attributes prior to product purchase.

Uncertainty in travel decision-making has been studied using the perceived risk theory (Moutinho, 1987; Roehl and Fesenmaier, 1992; Mitchell *et al.*, 1999) and has shown that tourism products have unique characteristics (i.e., intangibility and inseparability) that do not allow tourists to reduce easily uncertainty prior to an actual visit. Thus, in general, travellers tend to consider personal information sources more reliable and useful. Traditional mass media sources (i.e. television, newspaper, etc.), on the other hand, do not provide sufficient experiential information and therefore, are more effective in creating awareness than providing information useful for travel planning and decision-making. In addition, experiential information is often difficult to find, anecdotal, and highly subjective (Mitchell *et al.*, 1999).

The development of information technology changes the marketing environment (i.e. many-to-many communication) and tourists become able to confirm more experiential attributes of the destination prior to the trip. The uniqueness of the Internet (e.g. interactivity, flexibility, accessibility, and so on) brings more chances to access the experiential information through virtual communities. Tourists can actively request the newest information and collect experiential information from other members of the virtual community who have actually experienced a particular destination. In addition, tourists can create 'personal expectations' of travel through the active and interactive information search because they can 'virtually experience' a travel destination. The virtual experience could more closely resemble the direct onsite experience. Direct experience is considered to be the most important source for information that can reduce uncertainty in the choice process. Research examining the effects of product trial indicate that consumers are more likely to become convinced with the product after direct experience with the trial than after exposure to the advertisements (Smith and Swinyard, 1982, 1983, 1988). However, it is difficult to accumulate tourism experience of a destination because tourism products are not frequently purchased and are destinations that are often sought because they offer new experiences. Thus, the purpose of the virtual tour in experience marketing is to provide a rich informational environment that can reduce the uncertainty about a destination by converting experiential information into searchable information.

In order to create an effective and valid virtual tour, marketers need to figure out what fixed or controllable attributes of their tourism product are being considered to be the perceived risk by tourists. Researchers have found that perceived risk of a tourism product is context-specific and hard to generalize (Gemunden, 1985; Dowling, 1986; MacCrimmon and Wehrung, 1986; Roehl and Fesenmaier, 1992). For example, Mitchell *et al.* (1999) successfully investigated the relationship between perceived risk and the reduction strategy in the choice of package tour. But they limit the meaningfulness of their findings in package tour products. Thus, tourism marketers have to find the experiential information of the destination using a context-specific instrument. If they do not use a context-specific measure, they will lose the most meaningful and real perceived risk and there will be a lack of managerial specificity of the virtual tour.

The choice of appropriate techniques and media play an important role in the representation of virtual environment that shows the fixed or controllable experiential attributes of tourism products. The factors relating to the level of virtual tour performance (see Figure 22.1) should be considered in order to create an effective virtual tour. The World Wide Web (WWW) offers the potential to be a medium for the virtual tour because many applications are available on the WWW. Basically, the WWW helps tourists to find experiential information easily through the virtual communities. More importantly, the WWW provides the basis for tourists to obtain 'objective' experiential information. For example, the quality of hotel is one of the risky factors in the choice of package travel (Mitchell, 1999). When the hotel does not have brand loyalty, tourists mostly have relied on subjective imagery and the experiences of friends or relatives in order to be convinced with the hotel quality. However, with the emergence of the WWW and the virtual tour, tourists

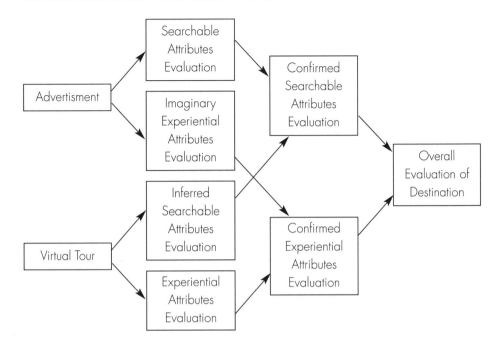

Figure 22.2 Positive interaction between advertisements and the virtual tour

become able to virtually visit the hotel and have experiential information and confirm how nice the hotel is through his/her own experience.

The interaction between advertisements and the virtual tour is an important factor that makes the virtual tour a valid information source for tourists. Although virtual tours offer rich perceptual virtual environment that includes important direct evidence of experiential information, they may not enable users to keep confidence in the product as strong as that gained from direct experience due to the differences between virtual experience and actual experience. Studies about ambiguous experience (Hoch and Ha, 1986; Deighton and Schindler, 1988) supported the suggestion that the advertisement and trial interact positively when the trial is not enough to make the customers convinced about the product. In this context, the virtual tour seems to be more useful when it is used with advertisements. Research by Wright and Lynch (1995) also supports the importance of positive interaction by finding that beliefs about search attributes can be influenced more effectively by advertisements than by trial. Tourists might make inferences about search attributes even though no real evidence is provided by experience (e.g. tourists might infer the price of hotel by the virtual experience). However, the price is usually confirmed by the advertisement.

Figure 22.2 presents a model describing the positive interaction between advertisements and the virtual tour. The information process could be different based on the order of the tourists' exposure. When tourists are exposed to advertisements, they will be more convinced with the search attributes and create the evaluation of experiential attributes based on the imagery evoked by the advertisement. Through the virtual tour, they will have confirmation about experiential attributes. However, they may not make much inference from virtual experience because they are already convinced by the search attributes. In comparison, when tourists are exposed to the virtual tour first, they are more likely to be convinced by experiential information and, therefore, will confirm the inference through the exposure to the advertisements.

THE VALUE OF EXPERIENCE MARKETING

As a new paradigm of tourism marketing for a new communication environment, experience marketing aims to provide more and better (i.e. experiential) information to potential tourists. By offering chances of 'unique and memorable virtual experiences', marketers can enable the tourists to evaluate and realize the 'value' of actual travel experience. In this section, the effects of virtual experience on the tourism-related perceptions and behaviours will be discussed. Destination image, intention to visit, satisfaction and information search are the factors that are studied frequently in relation to tourism marketing. Through the propositions about the effects of experience marketing on the four major factors in tourism marketing, the potential of experience marketing will be suggested.

Before the discussion about the effects of experience marketing, the potential effectiveness of virtual experience needs to be discussed because the impact of experience marketing/virtual tour will be influenced by a variety of factors related to the nature of the tourism product, holding all other aspects constant. That is, experience marketing could be effective for some destinations, but not for some others. First, brand loyalty of destination will influence the effectiveness of experience marketing because it itself reduces the uncertainty about destination. Well-known destinations with very famous attractions usually have less uncertainty than unknown destinations. Thus, it is expected that the effects of the virtual tour is greater in unknown destinations than in well-known destinations. Second, the amount of experiential information is also dependent on the heterogeneity of the destination attributes (Mitchell *et al.*, 1999). When the destination has many different types of attractions, tourists will need more experiential information than they need with a destination with limited attractions. Thus, experience marketing would be more effective when the destination has various attractions. Third, the type of the main attraction of destination may affect the effects. When tourists are seeking activity-oriented travel experience, they may need more experiential information than tourists whose purpose is relaxation. In the case of adventure travel, the virtual tour may provide the greater value of 'virtual experience'. With a lower level of sensory richness and interactivity, the superficial outlook of the destination could be delivered. However, it is often difficult for the tourists to experience the feeling of activities without a high level of telepresence. Thus, adventure travellers should realize greater benefits from a virtual experience than other 'lower risk' activities. This conceptual foundation provides the basis with which to develop a series of propositions that establish a framework for assessing the value of experience marketing using the WWW.

Effects on image formation

Destination image has been studied in many aspects because it is strongly related with decision-making in tourism (Echtner and Ritchie, 1991; Fakeye and Crompton, 1991; Dann, 1996). Experience marketing will influence the formation of destination image. The models about destination image suggest that destination image is formed based on all the information, knowledge, impressions, prejudices and emotional thoughts an individual has of a particular place. In addition, research indicates that personal characteristics such as value, socio-economic status and personal experience influence the formation of destination image. The created or changed destination image is composed of cognitive and affective components. The cognitive component is the sum of beliefs and attitudes of a place. Affective component refers to the feelings about the place (Gartner, 1993). Researchers agree that the affective component can be distinguished from the cognitive component, but it is formed based as a function of cognitive component (Russell and Pratt, 1980). This suggests that, in large part, destination image is formed based on the information that was personalized by the tourist. Thus, Gartner (1993) suggested the sources for information as the agents of image formation.

Figure 22.3 presents a simplified model of the destination image change process. Tourists use various types of sources for information before the actual trip to the destination. Then, destination image is changed when the tourists acquire new information about destination. Fakeye and Crompton (1991) conceptualized a model of a tourist's image change process based on Gunn's (1972) seven phases of a travel experience. According to the model, individuals have a certain image (naïve image) about a place even before one considers the place as a travel destination. They develop the image with gathered information about a destination through various channels in order to decide their destination. Prior to actual travel, tourists search information from advertising, word-of-mouth and other types of public information and from their expectation (informative image). Then, they obtain experiential information and new information by actual experience and compare the experience with the expectation (complex image). Fakeye and Crompton found that tourists, through experience, acquire some information that cannot be delivered by other sources for information and their destination image tends to be more realistic, complex and differentiated.

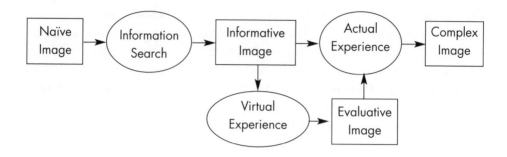

Figure 22.3 Simplified model of destination image formation

Virtual tour users will have more information than non-users about the destination because they have not only traditionally searchable information but also a certain amount of experiential information. With only traditionally searchable information, tourists could have a superficial image about the attractions of the destination. However, with the experiential information, tourists can evaluate 'how memorable the travel experience is' and create expectations about what they will experience at the destination. The powerful characteristics of the WWW such as sensory richness and interactivity enable the tourist to create his/her personal virtual experience. With the help of interactive media, each tourist can compose the virtual tour with their favourite attractions and enjoy the virtual experience. Thus, virtual experiences help tourists plan what they will do at the destination and they can then make a 'personal story' of their travel prior to actual trip. The personal story that the tourists experienced in the virtual tour should include a 'memorable experience' that enhances the value of the travel experience. The memory and recollection of the memorable experience leads the tourist to be convinced by the experiential information of the destination. Through this process, tourists can create a more detailed, clear expectation about their travel and they can develop a more vivid destination image. Thus, the virtual experience should enable tourists to better establish a context within which to create more personal and vivid evaluations (even stories) of the destination. (See Figure 22.4.) These findings lead to the following propostion:

Proposition 1: Virtual tour users will be able to create more vivid destination images than non-users

> P_{1a}: *Virtual tour users will have a lower level of perceived risks than non-users*

> P_{1b}: *Virtual tour users will have a more confident emotional response than non-users*

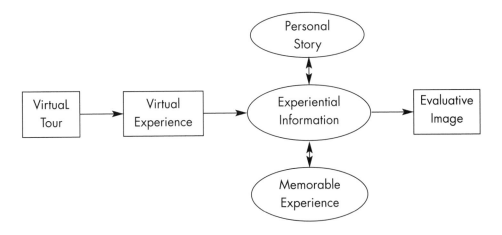

Figure 22.4 Effects of the virtual tour on the formation of destination image

Intention to visit

More vivid imagery will increase the tourist's intention to visit the destination. Many researches supported the view that destination image plays an important role in tourism decision-making and choice behaviour (Woodside and Lysonski, 1989; Um and Crompton, 1990, 1992). Virtual experience will reduce the level of perceived risks and help tourists have more confidence in their emotional responses. The practical usefulness of perceived risk theory, in consumer behaviour, is that it describes the relationship between perceived risk and purchase intention. Dowling (1986) examined nineteen correlation coefficients used to estimate the relationship between perceived risk and product preference and he found that 19.5 per cent of variance can be explained. Greenleaf and Lehmann (1995) also found that uncertainty is one of the major reasons for a delay in decision-making. Other studies about attitude–behaviour consistency (Smith and Swinyard, 1983, 1988; Berger and Mitchell, 1989) found that direct experience (e.g. product sampling) can lead consumers to create strong beliefs and attitudes and the purchasing behaviour is more predictable when customers are confident in their beliefs and attitudes. Thus, it is posited that experience marketing will promote the tourist's intention to visit. Virtual tour users can create stronger positive beliefs and attitudes because marketers will provide mainly positive experiential information. In addition, the virtual experience will bring a stronger attitude–behaviour consistency to the tourists. Therefore, the following proposition supports the notion that experience marketing using a virtual tour will increase the user's intention to visit and finally actual purchase:

Proposition 2: Virtual tour users will have a greater intention-to-visit consistency than a non-user

> P_{2a}: *Virtual tour users will have stronger beliefs and attitudes than a non-user*

> P_{2b}: *Virtual tour users will have more attitude–behaviour consistency than a non-user*

Satisfaction from reduced discrepancy

Tourists' satisfaction comes from a good match between what the tourists want and what the destination offers. One way to encourage such a match is to provide tourists with good information about the available options so that they can make the best choices about what they do and where they go. Mack and Thompson (1991) examined the value of information provision to assist visitors in the use of time during visits to Rocky Mountain National Park. The results of this study suggested that the new communication design could be successful in increasing activity participation by improving visitor knowledge of alternatives. Experience marketing using a virtual tour can provide potential tourists with more and better information about what experience is available for each tourist. Tourists become able to identify their favourite experience in advance and make more detailed plans concerning how they will spend their time at the destination. It helps tourists to reduce the gap between expectation and actual experience that can cause unpleasant surprises and dissatisfaction on the part of tourists. The well-informed tourist is also more convinced that they have made the best decision among those available. It leads them to be more satisfied with the actual experience regardless of the quality of the actual experience. Therefore, it is postulated that virtual tours and experience marketing will help potential visitors become more satisfied with the actual experience at a destination:

Proposition 3: Virtual tour users will be more satisfied with the actual travel experience than non-users

> P_{3a}: *Virtual tour users will have less discrepancy between the expectation and the actual experience than non-users*

> P_{3b}: *Virtual tour users will be more convinced about their decision-making than non-users*

Information search

The extent of information search depends on a trade-off between the perceived costs of additional search and the expected benefits of that search (Stigler, 1961). That is, consumers continue the information search only when the expected benefit is greater than the perceived cost. So far, tourists had to travel to the destination to have experiential information and it has been impossible because the travel experience itself is the tourism product. Thus, tourists have had to make destination decisions without important experiential information about destination. However, experience marketing using virtual tour can change tourists' information search behaviour. Through the virtual experience tourists can acquire greater benefit of experiential information at a much lower cost than before. The development of WWW-based technology reduces the cost for experiential information and removes other difficulties. In particular, the use of the virtual tour will influence the individual's direct and indirect (perceived) costs of experiential information search (Klein, 1998). That is, by allowing the tourists to experience a destination prior to an actual visit, tourists will be able to search information through experience. If experiential information were available via the information search process (i.e. a virtual tour) and the costs to obtain them were reduced via the WWW, we could expect there to be an increased reliance on those 'intrinsic' attributes. Tourists can be more convinced by the experiential information, and it appears that the virtual tour is a form of the media that can change the travel experience from experience goods to search goods in the tourism field. As tourists get used to confirming 'experiential attributes of destination' prior to their trip, they will no longer make decisions without 'searchable experiential information'. Tourists will seek virtual experience before their actual travel for better decision-making or anticipation of travel. Thus it is suggested that after getting used to virtual experience, tourists will have a higher level of needs for experiential information and will continuously seek information until they can reduce their uncertainty to a satisfactory level.

Proposition 4: Tourists will be more likely to seek experiential information prior to decision-making

DISCUSSION AND CONCLUSIONS

The Internet offers great advantages over traditional media as a marketing tool. It is accessible from worldwide, fast and flexible. Never before have so many people been exposed to and used a single information sharing system. The powerful characteristics of the Internet have generated a new marketing environment. A successful marketing programme requires that information should be communicated by an appropriate format and that the opportunities offered by the medium should be used effectively. The WWW provides the opportunities that have not been available in other traditional media. Thus, tourism marketers should use them correctly to achieve their objectives. They will need new marketing paradigms that can facilitate the benefits of the new marketing environment.

The purpose of experience marketing is to provide 'experiential information' to tourists. Although tourists, as people looking for an experience, need experiential information prior to purchase, most experiential information has not been available due to the intangible nature of tourism experience. However, in a new marketing environment, the WWW offers the potential to create a virtual environment in which tourists can acquire experiential information. The WWW has great diversity in terms of both sensory richness and interactivity in that it delivers a variety of data ranging from text to streaming multimedia; the level of interactivity is defined by the user. Thus, the WWW could be an impersonal mass media or a very personal medium enabling the tourist to have his/her own virtual experience. Tourists can acquire experiential information through the virtual experience on the WWW. Therefore, the virtual tour is emerging as a tool that can deliver more and better information to tourists than any other sources for information.

The present study has identified the factors influencing the effectiveness of experience marketing using the virtual tour that refers to the reduction of perceived risks and a confident emotional response. Besides the level of virtual destination, characteristics of the real destination, human factors and other information sources affect the level of the virtual tour performance. This research suggests guidelines for the development of a virtual tour within the context of experience marketing. The primary effects of the experience marketing are proposed as follows:

- Tourists can be more convinced with the experiential information. It enables tourists to reduce the risks, evaluate memorable experience more accurately, enhance the memory, and create a personal story of the destination. Thus, they form a more vivid and clear destination image.
- Tourists will be in a better position to choose a destination because the uncertainty from experiential information will be removed. It will increase tourists' intention to visit. Tourists will be more convinced with their decision and have higher attitudes–behaviour consistency.
- Reduced uncertainty helps tourists make detailed plans and reduces the discrepancy which can cause dissatisfaction.
- Information search behaviour will be changed because tourists can realize substantial benefits of experiential information at a lower cost. Tourists will get used to searching experiential information before decision-making. Thus, tourists' tolerable level of uncertainty will be lowered.

This research has focused on experience marketing using the web-based virtual tour because the WWW is now one of the most widespread media and it has unique potential of interactivity. Although the potential of the WWW as a medium for virtual tour is apparent, the limitation of bandwidth causes problems. High richness of sensory information requires huge amounts of data and it slows the speed of the WWW and degrades the level of interactivity. Another limitation of this research is that it does not mention the motivation of the tourists. Tourists' information needs are partially dependent on tourism motivation. Thus, motivation is expected to influence the effects of experience marketing. More studies about the relationship between travel motivation and the effects of the virtual tour will be needed.

There are many interesting topics for future studies. One of the most interesting contributions of the virtual tour for the tourism industry is its ability to affect the implementation of sustainable tourism. As proposed above, the virtual tour may support/facilitate destination marketing. Using the virtual tour, tourism marketers avoid unnecessary development of environmentally or culturally important resources. Sustainable tourism is a typical type of experience-oriented tourism and the destination usually provides very unique and exotic experiences; thus, it is especially difficult for tourists to form an accurate destination image. Virtual tours can help potential tourists to develop expectations about what they can experience at the destination. Importantly, tourists can learn about the uniqueness of a destination through the virtual tour in a natural way. In addition, tourists can learn how they are supposed to behave to minimize their negative impact on the destination. This education, in turn will facilitate implementation of a sustainable tourist programme.

REFERENCES

Alba, J., Lynch, J., Weitz, B., Janiszewski, C., Lutz, R., Sawyer, A. and Wood, S. (1997) 'Interactive home shopping: consumer, retailer, and manufacturer incentives to participate in electronic marketplace'. *Journal of Marketing*, **61** (July), 38–53.

Akin, D. L., Minsky, M. L., Thiel, E. D. and Kurtzman, C. R. (1983) 'Space applications, robotics, and machine intelligence system (ARAMIS) Phase II. V.5: Executive summary (Tech. Report NASA-CR-3736)'. Huntsville, Ala.:NASA, Marshall Space Flight Center.

Aldridge, A., Forcht, K. and Pierson, J. (1997) 'Get linked or get lost: marketing strategy for the Internet'. *Internet Research*, **7**(3), 161–9.

Berger, I. and Mitchell, A. (1989) 'The effect of advertising on attitude accessibility, attitude confidence, and the attitude-behavior relationship'. *Journal of Consumer Research*, **16** (December), 269–79.

Blattberg, R. C. and Deighton, J. (1991) 'Interactive marketing: exploiting the age of addressibility'. *Sloan Management Review*, pp. 5–14.

Blattberg, R. C., Glazer, R. and Little, J. D. C. (eds) (1994) *The Marketing Information Revolution*. Harvard Business School Press, Boston.

Csikszentmihalyi, M. and LeFevre, J. (1989) 'Optimal experience in work and leisure'. *Journal of Personality and Social Psychology*, **56**, 815–22.

Dann, G. M. S. (1996) 'Tourists' image of a destination – an alternative analysis'. *Journal of Travel and Tourism Marketing*, **5**(1/2), 41–55.

Deighton, J. and Schindler, R. M. (1988) 'Can advertising influence experience?' *Psychology and Marketing*, **5** (Summer), 103–15.

Donthu, N. and Garcia, A. (1999) 'The Internet shopper'. *Journal of Advertising Research*, **39** (May/June), 52–8.

Dowling, G. R. (1986) 'Perceived risk: the concept and its measurement'. *Psychology and Marketing*, **3**, 193–210.

Draper, J. V., Kaber, D. B. and Usher, J. M. (1998) 'Telepresence'. *Human Factors*, **40**(3), 354–75.

Echtner, C. M. and Ritchie, J. R. B. (1991) 'The meaning and measurement of destination image'. *The Journal of Tourism Studies*, **2**, 2–12.

Ellsworth, J. H. and Ellsworth, M. V. (1997) *Marketing on the Internet*. Wiley, New York.

Fakeye, P. C. and Crompton, J. L. (1991) 'Image difference between perspective, first-time and repeat visitors to the Lower Rio Grande Valley'. *Journal of Travel Research*, **2**, 10–16.

Fodness, D. and Murray, B. (1997) 'Tourist information search'. *Annals of Tourism Research*, **24**(3), 503–23.

Gartner, W. C. (1993) 'Image formation process'. *Journal of Travel and Tourism Marketing*, **2**(2/3), 191–215.

Gemunden, H. G. (1985) 'Perceived risk information search; a systematic meta-analysis of the empirical evidence'. *International Journal of Research in Marketing*, **2**(2), 79–100.

Goossens, C. F. (1994) 'External information search: effects of tour brochures with experiential information'. *Journal of Travel and Tourism Marketing*, **3**(3), 89–107.

Greenleaf, E. A. and Lehmann, D. R. (1995) 'Reasons for substantial delay in consumer decision making'. *Journal of Consumer Research*, **22** (September), 186–99.

Gunn, C. A. (1972) *Vacationscape: Designing tourist regions*. Bureau of Business Research, University of Texas, Austin.

Hagel, J. III and Lansing, W. J. (1994) 'Who owns the customer?' *The McKinsey Quarterly*, **4**, 63–75.

Hall, C. M. and Weiler, B. (1992) 'Introduction: What's special about special interest tourism?' In *Special Interest Tourism*. Belhaven Press, London.

Hammond, K., Pluim, D. and Eynde, K. V. (1995) 'Interactive mass media: a review of evidence and expert opinion from the USA and UK'. Working Paper No. 95–801. Center for Marketing, London Business School, November, p. 28.

Held. R. and Ourlach, N. (1992) 'Telepresence'. *Presence: Teleoperators and Virtual Environments*, **1**(1), 109–12.

Hoch, S. J. and Deighton, J. (1989) 'Managing what consumers learn from experience'. *Journal of Marketing*, **53** (April), 1–20.

Hoch, S. J. and Ha, Y. (1986) 'Consumer learning: advertising and the ambiguity of product experience'. *Journal of Consumer Research*, **13** (September), 221–33.

Hoffman, D. L. and Novak, T. P. (1996) 'Marketing in hypermedia computer-mediated environments: conceptual foundations'. *Journal of Marketing*, **60** (July), 50–68.

Jeng, J. (1999) 'Exploring the travel planning hierarchy: an interactive Web experiment'. Doctoral dissertation. University of Illinois, Champaign.

Kempf, D. S. and Smith, R. E. (1998) 'Consumer processing of product trial and the influence of prior advertising: a structural modeling approach'. *Journal of Marketing Research*, **35** (August), 325–38.

Kiani, G. R. (1998) 'Marketing opportunities in the digital world'. *Internet Research*, **8**(2), 185–94.

Klein, L. R. (1998) 'Evaluating the potential of interactive media through a new lens: search versus experience goods'. *Journal of Business Research*, **41**, 195–203.

Leigh, J. H. (1991) 'Information processing differences among broadcast media: review and suggestions for research'. *Journal of Advertising* (June), 71–5.

MacCrimmon, K. P. and Wehrung, D. A. (1986) *Taking Risk*. Free Press, New York, p. 100.

Mack, J. A. and Thompson, J. A. (1991) 'Visitor center planning: using visitor interests and available time'. In G. Moscardo and K. Hughes (eds) *Visitor Centers: Exploring new territory*. James Cook University, Australia, pp. 113–20.

Mäser, B. and Weiermair, K. (1998) 'Travel decision-making: from the vantage point of perceived risk and information preferences'. *Journal of Travel and Tourism Marketing*, **7**(4), 107–21.

Mitchell, V. W., Davies, F., Moutinho, L. and Vassos, V. (1999) 'Using neural networks to understand service risk in the holiday product'. *Journal of Business Research*, **46**, 167–80.

Moutinho, L. (1987) 'Consumer behavior in tourism'. *European Journal of Marketing*, **21**(10), 5–44.

Nelson, P. J. (1970) 'Information and consumer behavior'. *Journal of Political Economy*, **78**(2), 311–29.

Nelson, P. J. (1974) 'Advertising as Information'. *Journal of Political Economy*, **83** (July/August), 729–54.

O'Keefe, B. (1995) *Marketing and retail on the World Wide WWW: The new Gold Rush is hosted on the WWW.* URL:[http://www.rpi.edu/~okeefe/nikkei.html].

Pearce, P. L. (1988) *The Ulysses Factor: Evaluating visitors in tourist settings.* Springer-Verlag, New York.

Petty, R. E., Cacioppo, J. T. and Schumann, D. (1983) 'Central and peripheral routes to advertising effectiveness: the moderating role of involvement'. *Journal of Consumer Research*, **10**, 135–46.

Pine II, B. J. and Gilmore, J. H. (1998) 'Welcome to the experience economy'. *Harvard Business Review* (July–August), 97–105.

Poon, A. (1993) *Tourism, Technology and Competitive Strategies.* CAB International, Wallingford.

Rayport, J. F. and Svioka, J. J. (1995) 'Exploiting the virtual value chain'. *Harvard Business Review* (November–December), 75–85.

Reid, I. S. and Crompton, J. L. (1993) 'A taxonomy of leisure purchase decision paradigms based on level of involvement'. *Journal of Leisure Research*, **25**(2), 182–202.

Roehl, W. S. and Fesenmaier, D. R. (1992) 'Risk perceptions and pleasure travel: an exploratory analysis'. *Journal of Travel Research*, **30**(4), 17–25.

Russell, J. A. and Pratt, G. (1980) 'A description of affective quality attributed to environment'. *Journal of Personality and Social Psychology*, **2**, 311–22.

Sheridan, T. B. (1992) 'Musings on telepresence and virtual presence'. *Presence*, **1**, 120–6.

Slater, M. and Usoh, M. (1993) 'Representation systems, perceptual position, and presence in immersive virtual environments'. *Presence*, **2**, 221–33.

Smith, R. E. and Buchholz, L. M. (1991) 'Multiple resource theory and consumer processing of broadcast advertisements: an involvement perspective'. *Journal of Advertising* (September), 1–7.

Smith, R. E. and Swinyard, W. R. (1982) 'Information response models: an integrated approach'. *Journal of Marketing*, **46** (Winter), 81–93.

Smith, R. E. and Swinyard, W. R. (1983) 'Attitude–behavior consistency: the impact of product trial versus advertising'. *Journal of Marketing Research*, **20** (August), 257–67.

Smith, R. E. and Swinyard, W. R. (1988) 'Cognitive response to advertising and trial: belief strength, belief confidence and product curiosity'. *Journal of Advertising*, **17**(3), 3–14.

Stebbins, R. A. (1982) 'Serious leisure: a conceptual statement'. *Pacific Sociology Review*, pp. 251–72.

Steuer, J. (1992) 'Defining virtual reality: dimensions determining telepresence'. *Journal of Communications*, **42**, 73–93.

Stigler, G. J. (1961) 'The economics of information'. *Journal of Political Economics*, **19** (June), 213–25.

Strader, T. J. and Shaw, M. J. (1999) 'Consumer cost difference for traditional and Internet markets'. *Internet Research*, **9**(2), 82–92.

Um, S. and Crompton, J. (1990) 'Attitudes determinants in tourism destination choice'. *Annals of Tourism Research*, 432–48.

Um, S. and Crompton, J. (1992) 'The roles of perceived inhibitors and facilitators in pleasure travel destination decisions'. *Journal of Travel Research*, **30**(3), 18–25.

Vogt, C. A. and Fesenmaier, D. R. (1998) 'Expanding the functional information search model'. *Annals of Tourism Research*, **25**(3), 551–78.

Werthner, H. and Klein, S. (2000) *Information Technology and Tourism – A challenging relationship*. Springer Computer Science, Wien, New York.

Woodside, A. G. and Lysonski, S. (1989) 'A general model of traveller destination choice'. *Journal of Travel Research*, **4**, 8–14.

Wright, A. A. and Lynch, J. G. Jr. (1995) 'Communications effects of advertising versus direct experience when both search and experience attributes are present'. *Journal of Consumer Research*, **21** (March), 708–18.

Zeithaml, V. A. (1988) 'Consumer perception of price, quality, and value'. *Journal of Marketing*, **52** (July), 2–22.

CHAPTER 23

Tourism distribution channels: agendas for future research

Eric Laws and Dimitrios Buhalis

INTRODUCTION

It is hoped that this book will stimulate discussion on the tourism distribution channels and encourage more researchers to deal with this dynamic and complex issue in tourism. In describing and analysing current patterns of tourism distribution and the changes occurring in the sector, the contributors to this book have highlighted a number of topics, which deserve further attention in future academic research. The editors hope that readers will find inspiration both for research topics and appropriate methodologies in the preceding chapters, and in the research agendas mapped in outline in this chapter.

TOURISM DISTRIBUTION RESEARCH TOPICS

Structure in tourism distribution channels

A variety of distribution systems have been described. However, the lack of any consistency between places and industry sectors as well as the dynamic character of the industry clearly indicate that we still do not know enough about this research area. This book has contributed to the understanding although it will be unrealistic to expect a text of this scale to document all possible structures. There are many opportunities for future researchers to undertake case study work to add to our knowledge of tourism distribution by describing alternative structures and identifying the criteria by which to classify them.

Power structures in tourism distribution channels

It is increasingly evident that intra-channel power determines the competitiveness and profitability of participants at the micro level and the impacts of tourism at the macro level (Buhalis, 2000). Research into the power distribution and the tools available to strengthen the negotiation power of the weakest partners, which are actually the ones who own resources and have far more legitimate rights to gain a larger share of the benefit generated, should also be explored. This is particularly important for smaller principals in peripheral and insular destinations.

Tourism distribution system change and technology

Change is impacting on society, emanating from the adoption of new technologies and new patterns of work, leisure, family and consumption habits which together provide new opportunities and new challenges for managers. Electronic commerce changes radically the way we do business and the mobile revolution will enable us in future to have access to real-time location-dependent data. These changes, of course, extend far beyond distribution or tourism, and have been discussed by many of the contributors to this book. A number of research questions arise, including detailed monitoring of the way that tourism distribution actually does change in the coming years, identifying and accounting for discernable differences that may appear between the rate and way that sectors of tourism respond to new technology, and consideration of cultural, business or economic rationales for differences between adoption practices in various countries. A wide range of opportunities and threats emerge for all players in the distribution channel and the key success factors for the competitive organization of the future need to be identified and explored.

Efficiency of tourism distribution systems

The basic justification for a particular form of organization in a distribution channel is that it achieves greater efficiency than would result without it. However, different stakeholders have different efficiency criteria in mind. Each of the companies contributing to a tourism distribution channel endeavours to achieve individual objectives such as growth or profitability. This raises two important questions, first how the overall efficiency of the channel is to be evaluated, and secondly how the channel members share distribution functions, costs and profits.

Stakeholders in tourism distribution systems

Stakeholder interest groups provide a convenient framework to investigate the efficiency of particular distribution systems. Inevitably it is unlikely that all will benefit equally from a given system and the issues of power and negotiation need to be explored in order to identify methodologies for achieving equitable benefits. The discussion of research opportunities is relevant to several categories, particularly tourists/customers and destination communities. However, all players in the distribution channel need to be analysed in order to appreciate the complexity of the benefit trade-offs and networks.

Customer outcomes

The most important customer outcome, from the perspective of the long-term sustainability of the industry, is customer satisfaction with tourism services. Band (1991), arguing for the need to create more value for the customer, has advocated the systematic examination of all facets of a company's operation to identify their contribution (active and potential, positive and negative) to customer satisfaction. In the case of tourism, the appropriate level of analysis is the channel or network of tourism organizations from which the consumer obtains tourist services, and this reinforces the need to identify all relevant elements in a service system, and to model them systemically.

Destination communities

The foregoing suggests the need to develop appropriate ways of managing supplier quality in tourism. Much of tourism channel management is based on adversarial practices, for example switching, offering only short-term contracts, and inadequate specification of performance criteria. The benefits of collaborating with suppliers to create competitive market advantages through advanced supply chain management techniques including supplier performance development, process design involvement, certification, rewards and improvement targets should be a rich field for future research as the industry becomes more mature. It is critical to identify methodologies that will enable destination communities to control their destiny and to benefit most from their resources in a sustainable and enriching way.

TOURISM DISTRIBUTION RESEARCH METHODOLOGIES

Traditionally, researchers adopt either quantitative or qualitative approaches in social science research, although scientific (or quantitative) methods have dominated (Walle, 1997, p. 524). Increasingly, interest is turning to qualitative methods, or the joint use of both approaches towards triangulation of data (Bonoma, 1985; Yin, 1994). This is particularly useful for the tourism distribution channels as there is still a great need for exploratory research and understanding of the fundamental factors determining the partners' behaviour. Case studies as a research method have been championed by a number of researchers who argue that the method is particularly suitable for the investigation of contemporary phenomenon within its real-life context where the boundaries between the phenomenon and the context are not clearly evident (Yin, 1994, p. 13). Yin identifies four core components of case study research:

- investigation of a contemporary phenomenon within its real-life context; when
- boundaries between phenomenon and context are not clearly evident,
- multiple sources of evidence are used, and
- research should be part of a comprehensive research strategy, not just a data collection tactic or a design feature.

Case study approaches have been adopted by several contributors to this book, and serve well in informing readers about the variety and complexity of tourism distribution practices. These seem to differ according to the scale of the business, but also by the country involved and the type of tourism or market sector served. There is a basic need for more case studies to expand the documented knowledge of current practices at a time of fundamental change, but more importantly some way is needed to identify the key factors in each case leading to the particular distribution pattern adopted. Identification of these contingencies are important if researchers are to understand why there are different forms of distribution, particularly when, in future years, the ways in which various distribution systems have changed come to be researched. The outcomes for key stakeholders of each form of distribution also need to be studied on a comparative basis, and with greater emphasis placed on the point alluded to above, that different distribution systems appear to have varied consequences for destinations and their host communities.

The practical difficulty with case-based research is that of access. Many aspects of distribution management are quite sensitive, and it is difficult to persuade managers to give researchers access to detailed information. The variety of formulations and the fluidity of the distribution channel are also additional factors that prevent generalizations out of case studies.

Managers often perceive academic research to be slow to reach conclusions, and the direct significance of these to operational decisions is often unclear. Furthermore, the style of academic journal articles does not appeal to many managers, and there is therefore something of a confidence gap between the academic community and the industry community, despite their shared enthusiasm for tourism.

CONCEPTUAL ISSUES IN TOURISM DISTRIBUTION RESEARCH

Kuhn (1970) has explained the importance of the paradigm on which any research is based. A research paradigm is the framework of concepts and assumptions that underpin the researcher's thinking and importantly these are normally shared by most, if not all, people in a research community (those undertaking research into particular problems at one time). Much of the current thinking about tourism reflects themes in economic theory which exhibit a preference for mathematical analysis of a set of forces tending to stability and equilibrium, in contrast to the heterogeneous, dynamic forces tending to greater diversity and increasing complexity in tourism. These can be more realistically modelled through chaos theory (Gleick, 1987; Faulkner and Russell, 1997).

Transactions in tourism do not have the directness of results which characterizes modern mass-produced goods and the processes of their production. Equifinality is a key concept in systems theory, it recognizes that given inputs into complex processes may result in differing outcomes (Bertalanffy, 1968). The lack of relative certainty for tourism arises from human involvement in the service delivery processes, both as consumers and as producers, further compounded by the roles of individual expectations and perceptions in service quality judgements, making consensual evaluation of service quality problematic.

CONCLUSIONS

The emergence of information technology-based market solutions in the final decades of the twenty-first century is already challenging the ways in which the tourism industry has traditionally conducted its business. Several chapters in this book consider the advantages of IT-based distribution while others detail some of the responses being made by established players to these new ways of doing business. The pace of change in favour of IT business practices seems to be increasing, but it is too early, as the first year of the new millennium closes, to point with any certainty to an inevitable end to the distribution systems for tourism described in most chapters of this book. Whatever changes do transpire, this book presents a collection of informed chapters describing the current distribution systems and may act as a point of reference for future authors looking back on what will surely be one of the most interesting periods of change for the tourism industry.

The pace of tourism research continues to quicken, as evidenced by the increasing number of academic journals specializing in the field and the numbers of postgraduate courses and PhD work going on in universities around the world. Many major consulting groups and international development and regulatory agencies commission research into operational aspects of the tourism industry. In addition, tourism businesses and destination authorities regularly commission research into operational issues, but the data generated, and the findings that emerge, are often commercially sensitive and are regarded by managers as the property of the sponsoring organization. As a consequence, much remains inaccessible to academic researchers. However, many managers now reaching senior positions in the industry are themselves graduates of tourism courses, and it is to be hoped that they will be more supportive of the needs of research and the benefits that may flow in terms of enhanced understanding of operational matters, and greater awareness of the interdependent nature of this complex, rapidly changing industry which is likely to continue to be one of the main engines of economic and social development for many countries.

REFERENCES

Band, W. (1991) *Creating Value for Customers: Designing and implementing a total corporate strategy*. John Wiley & Sons/Coopers Lybrand, New York.

Bertalanffy, L. (1968) *General Systems Theory*. Brazillier, New York.

Bonoma, T. (1985) 'Case research in marketing opportunities, problems, and a process'. *Journal of Marketing Research*, **12**, 199–208.

Buhalis, D. (2000) 'Relationships in the distribution channel of tourism: conflicts between hoteliers and tour operators in the Mediterranean region'. *Journal of International Hospitality, Leisure and Tourism Administration*, **1**(1), 113–39.

Faulkner, H. W. and Russell, R. (1997) 'Chaos and complexity in tourism: in search of a new perspective'. *Pacific Tourism Review*, **1**(2), 93–102.

Gleick, J. (1987) *Chaos*. Sphere Books, London.

Kuhn, T. S. (1970) *The Structure of Scientific Revolutions*. University of Chicago Press, Chicago.

Walle, A. H. (1997) 'Quantitative verses qualitative tourism research'. *Annals of Tourism Research*, **24**(3), 524–36.

Yin, R. K. (1994) *Case Study Research*. Sage, Thousand Oaks.

INDEX